THE ROADS TO HILLBROW

POLIS: *Fordham Series in Urban Studies*
Edited by Daniel J. Monti, Saint Louis University

POLIS will address the questions of what makes a good community and how urban dwellers succeed and fail to live up to the idea that people from various backgrounds and levels of society can live together effectively, if not always congenially. The series is the province of no single discipline; we are searching for authors in fields as diverse as American studies, anthropology, history, political science, sociology, and urban studies who can write for both academic and informed lay audiences. Our objective is to celebrate and critically assess the customary ways in which urbanites make the world corrigible for themselves and the other kinds of people with whom they come into contact every day.

To this end, we will publish both book-length manuscripts and a series of "digital shorts" (e-books) focusing on case studies of groups, locales, and events that provide clues as to how urban people accomplish this delicate and exciting task. We expect to publish one or two books every year but a larger number of "digital shorts." The digital shorts will be 20,000 words or fewer and have a strong narrative voice.

The Roads to Hillbrow

MAKING LIFE IN SOUTH AFRICA'S COMMUNITY OF MIGRANTS

Ron Nerio and Jean Halley

FORDHAM UNIVERSITY PRESS   NEW YORK   2022

Fordham University Press has no responsibility for the persistence or accuracy of URLs for external or third-party Internet websites referred to in this publication and does not guarantee that any content on such websites is, or will remain, accurate or appropriate.

Fordham University Press also publishes its books in a variety of electronic formats. Some content that appears in print may not be available in electronic books.

Visit us online at www.fordhampress.com.

Library of Congress Cataloging-in-Publication Data available online at https://catalog.loc.gov.

Printed in the United States of America

24 23 22   5 4 3 2 1

First edition

To Beverley Ditsie, the memory of Simon Nkoli,
and the people of Hillbrow

Contents

List of Acronyms and Abbreviations   ix

Prologue 1: Return to Hillbrow   1

Prologue 2: Being White and the Politics of Not Seeing   9

1. South Africa: A History of Land Dispossession and Migration   13

2. Hillbrow and Apartheid   37

3. Uprising and Change, 1976–93   59

4. Hillbrow in a New Country, 1994–99   97

5. Hillbrow in the Twenty-First Century   125

6. A Web of Relationships   187

7. Hillbrow's Credoscapes — Spaces of Hope and Connection   213

Conclusion   225

Epilogue: The COVID-19 Crisis in Hillbrow   229

Acknowledgments   239

Notes   243

Index   269

Photographs follow page 132

Acronyms and Abbreviations

ANC	African National Congress
AWB	Afrikaner Weerstandsbeweging
CBD	Central Business District
DEIC	Dutch East India Company
DRC	Democratic Republic of the Congo
GALA	Gay and Lesbian Queer Archive
GALZ	Gays and Lesbians of Zimbabwe
GASA	Gay Association of South Africa
GLOW	Gay and Lesbian Organisation of the Witwatersrand
IFP	Inkatha Freedom Party
IMF	International Monetary Fund
IOM	International Organization for Migration
MSF	Doctors Without Borders (*Médecins Sans Frontières*)
PAC	Pan Africanist Congress
SABC	South African Broadcasting Corporation
SAPS	South African Police Service
SAR	South African Republic
US	United States
UK	United Kingdom
UNHCR	United Nations High Commissioner for Refugees
WNLA	Witwatersrand Native Labour Association
ZANU	Zimbabwe African National Union

THE ROADS TO HILLBROW

Prologue 1: Return to Hillbrow

Ron Nerio

For twenty-three years I longed to revisit South Africa. I wanted to see Hillbrow again. When I knew it in 1990, this one-mile strip of dense urban landscape was the most exciting neighborhood I had ever seen. It was one of South Africa's only "grey zones," a racially mixed neighborhood of streets lined with cafés, restaurants, bookstores, record shops, and nightclubs. Its sidewalks[1] bustled with the disparate populations that had made it their home: working-class whites, Black people recently arrived from townships, college students, elderly Jewish people, disaffected youth, petty thieves, sex workers, and drug dealers. Amid this hive of diversity, a burgeoning queer[2] community had also emerged and made itself visible in a handful of bars and restaurants. In a notoriously conservative and repressive country, the vibe in Hillbrow was cosmopolitan and bohemian, optimistic about the future and perhaps fatalistic at the same time.

The fatalism was warranted. Hillbrow had already grown rough around the edges by 1990, or so it would seem from news reports of widespread criminal activity dating from that era. I was twenty years old at the time and do not remember it that way. I recall walking along Pretoria and Kotze Streets, its main thoroughfares, day or night, alone or with friends, and not thinking for a moment about danger. Anna Hartford[3] notes that as early as 1980, the minister of community development had denounced Hillbrow as a "scandal and a slum." This only meant, she writes, that it was the place to go for excitement seekers "in a country otherwise so conservative television was banned until 1976."

The minister's description was a laughable exaggeration, but change was imminent and in terms of crime would prove overwhelming. "At the dawn of 1991," writes Phaswane Mpe in *Welcome to Our Hillbrow*, his haunting, elegiac tribute to the beauty and tragedy of the neighborhood, "Hillbrow was a menacing monster, so threatening to its neighbors like Berea and downtown Johannesburg, that big, forward-looking companies were beginning to desert the inner city."[4]

By the mid-1990s, Johannesburg was beset by an "incredible tsunami of crime," says Clifford Bestall in his documentary *Hillbrow: Between Heaven and Hell.*[5] Hillbrow was at the center of that tsunami. As apartheid ended, hundreds of thousands of people who had previously been prohibited by racial laws made their way to Johannesburg. They came from South Africa's crowded townships and the desolate rural areas. They left the war zones and politically troubled countries to the north and sought refuge in the most developed, most industrialized metropolis on the continent. It was not a city beset by crisis that they sought; it was safety, opportunity, and a chance to live a new and better life. But the city was unprepared and, with one-third of its people already unemployed, unable to offer work for many. Those with resources — especially the white population — fled from Hillbrow and its nearby inner-city environs, such as Yeoville, Joubert Park, and Doornfontein. Businesses closed, buildings were "hijacked," and people were left to fend for themselves. Hillbrow, Berea, and Yeoville acquired a reputation as a "no-go" zone.[6]

On that first trip, in 1990, I spent only five months in Hillbrow, a total of six and a half in South Africa. Back in the United States, by the end of that year, I found it difficult to follow developments in the neighborhood. That was before the days of the internet. Most news about Johannesburg that filtered its way to US media dwelt on its violent crime rate, which had risen to the highest in the world by the end of the 1990s, without much context. Having had many years of experience in Michigan cities that had at various times the highest crime rates in the US — Flint, Saginaw, Detroit — I knew that such statistics never tell the full story. I was determined to return, to see what elements of the former Hillbrow had survived and to see what life was like there now.

During the past decade,[7] a slew of articles, documentaries, novels, and photo blogs have focused on Hillbrow. Some of the documentaries have more than a tinge of racist nostalgia, such as *Epilogue to Hillbrow, RIP*[8] and *The Death of Johannesburg,*[9] which want only to recall the "good" old days of apartheid and seem almost to revel in the city's postapartheid troubles. Other videos, however, are more earnest, and together they provide a complex picture of the neighborhood's current condition. Their titles alone make an impression. There is *Hillbrow: Home of the Homeless,*[10] which focuses on five hundred heroin addicts living in Pullinger Kop Park. *Hillbrow: The Danger Zone Some Call Home*[11] is more hopeful than its title implies. It shows the work that eKhaya, a nonprofit neighborhood organization (discussed in chapter 6), has done to restore spaces around buildings that had severely deteriorated. *Receive Me Hillbrow*[12] is a Christian-themed documentary that shows how people, many of them recently arrived migrants, have sought refuge from Hillbrow's harsh streets through faith. It opens with a quote: "As legend has it, Hillbrow is one of the deepest circles of Dante's hell, a chaotic swirl of drug dealers and murderers that any visitor would be lucky to escape. A post-apocalyptic Wild West that leaves hardened police pale with fear." The point of *Receive Me Hillbrow* is to counter that "legend." The most extensive documentary treatment of Hillbrow is the aforementioned *Hillbrow: Between Heaven and Hell*,[13] which tells the stories of recent arrivals from the Democratic Republic of the Congo (DRC), the Republic of the Congo (Congo-Brazzaville), and Zimbabwe.

In 2013, I finally returned to Hillbrow. Wary of walking alone, I took my first foray into the neighborhood in twenty-three years with a tour guide named Jabu. A soft-spoken, slender man from Durban, he acknowledged the fear attached to the neighborhood while also showing me that he and I could amble down most blocks together without trepidation. We spent the day on foot, wandering through Alec Gorshel Park and past the Hillbrow Tower, stopping for sandwiches at a supermarket and for beer at a pub frequented by Nigerians. Around us were the same buildings and streets of my fondest memories. But the sidewalks were now more crowded and many of the structures in extreme states of disrepair. In some, the windows were shattered from the bottom floor to the top. I spotted the places where I used to stop for coffee, play chess, or order Chinese food. Those storefronts were vacant, with most of the commerce now taking place on the pavements or in small stalls lining the streets.

The following day, July 20, I met with a guide whose organization, Gay and Lesbian Archive (now called the GALA Queer Archive), offered queer history walking tours of Hillbrow. I was the only attendee present that morning as he pointed out the remnants of the queer spaces that had once peppered the area. The old signage was well preserved, but the businesses were long gone. That evening, Gustav, the owner of the offbeat downtown hotel where I was staying, asked me how I had spent my day. I told him about my interest in Hillbrow and he chortled with excitement. "I love adventure!" he proclaimed, "and I love danger, too! Tomorrow night, I will have my bodyguard Emmanuel take us to Hillbrow. You will be able to see it at night."

It may have been overkill, but Emmanuel, a broad-chested, good-humored man from the DRC, picked us up in a massive armored van. At Gustav's direction we visited some of Hillbrow's busiest clubs, along with Di's Bistro, the sole remaining queer space in the neighborhood.[14] Its seven patrons and the bartender chatted to us about how risky it was for them to socialize there. The bartender asked Emmanuel, not entirely in jest, if he would spend a few nights a week protecting his establishment.

That visit in 2013 offered just a taste of the new Hillbrow. I returned to the US more determined than ever to know Hillbrow systematically and intimately. I resolved to learn everything I could whether by digging into historical archives or by reading novels, reportage, and academic papers. During my subsequent ten visits to Johannesburg, I spoke with anyone who would talk to me about Hillbrow and the neighborhoods that surround it. I attended churches and synagogues and met their congregants. I visited social workers and teachers, drug recovery counselors, landlords, tenants, housing developers, and a theater director. I learned that almost every waitperson in Johannesburg restaurants, no matter how distant from the inner city, lives in Hillbrow, and many of them agreed to meet with me. Over coffee, they described their journeys from Harare or Bulawayo in Zimbabwe or Lusaka in Zambia to reach Hillbrow. I passed out food with a church group from the DRC and spoke to small business owners from Tanzania, Nigeria, and Malawi. I met with people who had lived in Hillbrow for more than four decades and some who had been there for scarcely four months. I learned, too, from those who had lived in Hillbrow during earlier eras and had left it behind.

This book explores what has led people to Hillbrow during its century and a quarter of existence and examines what these experiences reveal about the old and the new South Africa. Most early residents of the neighborhood were Jewish and traveled from Eastern Europe to escape oppression and anti-Semitic violence. As Marian Robertson and Mendel Kaplan[15] write, Johannesburg was the only city in the modern world where Jewish people played a pivotal role in city-building from the very beginning and did not feel as if they were outsiders in a community previously established by someone else. Though not immune from anti-Semitism, they were insiders in a racially stratified society where others bore the brunt of outsider status. After World War II, Hillbrow developed into a landscape of high-rise apartment buildings that, under apartheid, filled with members of Johannesburg's white middle class—both Jewish and otherwise. During the 1960s and 1970s, South Africa's white nationalist government attempted to bolster the size of the white population by luring new immigrants from Southern and Central Europe. The "continentals," as they were called by locals,[16] opened many of the cafés, restaurants, and shops that made Hillbrow the most popular destination in Johannesburg for entertainment and leisure.

The Soweto Uprising of 1976, during which as many as seven hundred people were massacred, changed South Africa's political landscape. The results were pronounced in Hillbrow. It was among the first neighborhoods in the country to experience extensive residential integration, as Indians and then Black Africans[17] defied apartheid and moved into what was still legally classified a whites-only zone. The prominent actor John Kani[18] told me that Hillbrow, during this era, was like a "postcard from South Africa's future," where racially mixed jazz clubs and hotel ballrooms gave the impression of a democratic, nonracial society that might one day be possible.

As Hillbrow became a more racially mixed "grey zone," investment halted. Landlords stopped maintaining their buildings and overcrowded them to extract as much rent as possible. South Africa entered a deep recession in the late 1970s and began the 1980s as a pariah state, with calls for boycotts growing louder around the world. More and more of the already strained national budget was diverted to combat internal mass resistance and to fund intervention in the civil wars roiling newly independent Angola and Mozambique. With the apartheid government reducing its already dismal budget for housing in Black, Coloured, and Indian townships, residents in those communities moved in ever larger numbers to Hillbrow and surrounding Berea, Doornfontein, and Yeoville. They sought better quarters and a life closer to the center city.

In the 1980s, Hillbrow was famous for its discos and dance contests, bookstores and record shops, and all-night pizza parlors. The writer and bookshop owner Matthew Krouse[19] recalled a burgeoning landscape of queer establishments that became ever more daring in flouting laws against "sexual immorality." But beneath the revelry was a society in turmoil. The Afrikaner folksinger Johannes Kerkorrel, whose songs were banned on state-controlled radio, moved to the neighborhood in the mid-1980s and recorded his best-known track, "Hillbrow." His song is a plea for empathy for the neighborhood's growing numbers of lonely misfits, "tramps," and "junkies."[20]

Waves of violence gripped Johannesburg in the 1980s. It came mostly in the form of state-sponsored repression in the townships, but also in the form of bombs detonated by both left-wing and right-wing groups. In Hillbrow, Umkhonto we Sizwe, the African National Congress's armed wing, set off an explosive device in Temple Israel in 1983[21] and in the popular Café Zurich in 1987.[22] The right-wing paramilitary organization, Afrikaner Weerstandsbeweging (AWB), staged a protest at the Hillbrow swimming pool in 1989 demanding the expulsion of all Black people from the facility—and from Hillbrow itself. In what was perhaps an unexpected turnaround, the leaders of the AWB demonstration were arrested for disorderly conduct and the pool remained open to all.[23]

Whites began to desert the neighborhood. But Hillbrow still beckoned for those previously denied a chance to live in so central a location. In the now-classic novel *Welcome to Our Hillbrow*, Mpe's main character, Refentše, moves from rural Tiragalong to study at the University of the Witwatersrand in 1991. He is overwhelmed on his first day by the roaring traffic and crowds of pedestrians rushing to work, and terrified on his first night when he hears gunshots and the screams of someone begging for help. Just when he considers returning home, he experiences the luxury of a hot shower and remembers how the water pumps in the village provide only one cold bath per week.[24]

Refentše was neither the first nor the last to trek from rural South Africa in search of Hillbrow's "greener pastures." People like him were joined by hundreds and then by thousands in the early 1990s from the Republic of Congo, the DRC, Mozambique, Nigeria, and Zimbabwe. They settled uneasily among their native-born neighbors. Black South Africans were ready to celebrate a new democracy that promised opportunities only whites had enjoyed for centuries. Their wariness of arrivals from other parts of the continent who might compete for the same prospects often led to xenophobic recriminations and sometimes to violence.

Like Refentše, our interviewees took their own paths to Hillbrow. Patricia moved from the United Kingdom (UK) during the 1970s and, she says, found a "paradise." Edith, a Xhosa woman from the Western Cape, became a chef at an Italian restaurant in Hillbrow in the late 1980s. She later moved to Yeoville and now describes Hillbrow as a neighborhood too dangerous to enter. Bongani moved with his family from the Eastern Cape in the early 2000s when he was a young boy and now operates a small studio producing recordings of neighborhood musicians. In the early 2000s, Thomas traveled by bus from Lubumbashi, DRC, through Zambia and Zimbabwe and ended up living in a two-bedroom flat with more than ten men from his home country. He is now a Christian minister who lives in a prosperous northern suburb and returns to Hillbrow once a month with his congregation to distribute food and offer pastoral counseling. Kevin moved from Port Harcourt, Nigeria. Having experienced arson and multiple burglaries in his hometown, he describes Hillbrow as the safest place he has ever lived.

In Sue Nyathi's 2018 novel *The Gold-Diggers*,[25] her characters take a crowded van from Bulawayo, Zimbabwe, in search of new lives in Johannesburg. At the South African border, they get out of the vehicle and wade across the crocodile-infested Limpopo River. One person is dragged away, screaming, by a crocodile and never heard from again. The survivors are accosted by robbers on the other side who take all their money and kidnap one of the teenage girls traveling with them, who is also never heard from again. Five hundred miles later, the same van disgorges them in Hillbrow, where they meet disparate fates, most of them shockingly tragic.

   As in *The Gold-Diggers*, the buildings in Hillbrow today are overcrowded and many are crumbling. While developers have restored thousands of units that provide safe, clean housing to those who can afford it, for most such flats are priced far beyond reach. Yet Hillbrow's nightclubs still hum into the morning hours. People travel from across Johannesburg for its Nigerian, Angolan, Congolese, and Zimbabwean grocery stores, and takeaway restaurants. Would-be tenants balance their fears of crime with the fact that, compared with any other neighborhood, Hillbrow offers quicker and less expensive transit routes to the job-rich northern suburbs. The neighborhood still offers hope and promise, just as it offers pain and despair.

Prologue 2: Being White and the Politics of Not Seeing

Jean Halley

Like Ron Nerio, I was initiated into political activism through the antiapartheid movement. Unlike Nerio, who grew up in an urban working-class Latinx community, I grew up with a wealthy white paternal grandfather who was a member of the Ku Klux Klan. It took me many years to say this definitively, and many years even though the KKK has sometimes been as normal, as American, as apple pie, perhaps more so. Many people dislike apple pie. In contrast, most white Americans in the first half of the twentieth century supported the KKK.[1]

It is funny that seeing something so obvious as my grandfather's racism took me time, circling back and reviewing scenes from the past, each time realizing a little more of what was clearly there all along. It did not take so long for me to call my grandfather a racist, although I was not brave. I waited for his death back in June 1993. And even then, I mostly only said it to myself.

I remember the moment when I recognized his racism. I was in college in Colorado Springs and my grandparents had driven from Wyoming to visit me. At college, I had become a radical feminist and active in the anti–nuclear weapons movement. I worked to raise awareness of US-supported dictatorships in Central America, and got involved with a group of students, several from the US and several from South Africa, who were working to push our college to divest from South Africa. We held protests, camped on our campus in tents, and took over administrative offices. In spite of this widespread movement to divest, the United States under and even after Ronald Reagan never passed a federal law mandating divestment. The US supported the white apartheid government until it finally fell. Years later a relative told me that my grandfather's business also remained invested there through all of the final years of apartheid.

In the US, many white people, like me and like my grandfather, were involved in South African and Central American politics. I took part in the divestment movement happening across the country on college campuses. My grandfather supported and benefited financially from the racist white apartheid government in South Africa. My grandfather did not go to war in other countries; instead he supported transnational racist white power through his investments. At home he played a more active role in advancing racism. In contrast, other racist whites, historian Kathleen Belew explains, worked as mercenary soldiers. Like my grandfather, these were active members of the US white power movement. Yet they "walked the walk" by going to South Africa and working as soldiers to preserve white rule in Rhodesia and South Africa as well as to overthrow leftist governments in Central America, much as they worked to maintain racist white power in the US.[2] This native component of US white power history entailed support for racism in the existing US government from the 1960s through the 1980s. As a white person, I was born, grew up, and spent my years in college surrounded by this racism. It was as natural as air.

The threads of white supremacy and racism are all produced and interconnected in the modern world system. Belew argues that the Vietnam War birthed a paramilitary white power movement at home through a narrative that pulled the movement together and "inspired its paramilitary culture and infrastructure." The right-wing white power veterans believed the government had put them in a brutal war against evil people — Vietnamese communists — and then "denied them permission to win by limiting their use of force" against people these racists believed to be a "beastly, subhuman enemy." When these self-understood-to-be-patriotic white warriors returned home, they felt the public "spat on" them and their sacrifice, calling them "baby-killers." A subset of these veterans like white power activist Louis Beam believed they needed to continue the battle, yet now the fight was at home in the US against all people of color, and all those understood to be communists. Belew believes these veterans did not merely come home racist, they went to war racist, hanging Confederate flags in their living spaces and harassing servicemen of color.[3]

I grew up in a white and rural community in the post-Vietnam era. And although not overtly racist, I went to college with the obliviousness-at-best of most US white people. During my years in college, and at the time of my grandparents' visit, I had only just begun to pull my own skin away from myself, to see who I was, where I came from, more clearly. My moment of realizing what I already knew about my grandfather, about his racism, happened while walking in a garden during that visit my grandparents made. When it happened, I was with my grandparents at their hotel, the historic Broadmoor that opened in 1918.

My Gram, my grandfather, whom we called Mac, and I were walking in the Broadmoor garden. I followed behind my grandparents as we slowly circled. An African American man in his Broadmoor uniform stood by the garden door ready to open it when we returned to the old hotel. As we looped slowly past him I heard my grandfather say something, seemingly to himself, but loud enough so that we all heard, about [n-words]. Stunned, I made eye contact with the man at the door; he faintly smiled and stood there, otherwise still, almost as though he had not heard my grandfather, even though I think we both knew we both had. I glanced at my grandmother, now just ahead of me, slowly turning a corner in the garden, walking with intentionality and grace. Her posture erect, she looped her arm through that of my grandfather. Gram had the expression she often had, a look of benign acceptance, reddish-pink lipsticked lips gently pressed together, eyes only slightly turned downward, the proper look for an Irish Catholic woman.

Dizzy and confused as the ground seemed to move ever so slightly beneath me, I did what white people so often do in the face of racism, and what, it seemed, my grandmother regularly did. I pretended that it had not happened. This pretending was not just pretending as a performance for others, for the man at the door, for my grandmother, herself well versed in this same pretending, and for my grandfather, the only one of the three of us white people who did not pretend. This pretending was perhaps most for myself. It happened internal to my own experience of those minutes spent walking in a beautiful garden with one old white woman, and one old racist and rich white man, and one working-class African American man perhaps in his thirties. This memory of my grandparents and me and the man at the door sat, for years, in that in-between place, a purgatory for memories neither fully forgotten nor remembered, those resting on the edge of my consciousness. Today, some thirty years later, I pull this moment into consciousness through the writing of it. Years before, I had forgotten other things: the time we found my grandfather's KKK costume, the time he took me as a small child to a KKK meeting.

My memory of their visit now remains only and completely stuck on this moment. I cannot remember anything else that was done, anything else that was said, on that weekend with my grandparents. At the time, I was proud that they came to visit me, proud that my grandmother loved me so much she would make a trip to see me. Yet today at fifty-two, both grandparents dead, and me living far away from Colorado Springs, I can remember nothing of our weekend except that moment and that word and my own shock as though my grandfather pushed me off the edge of something, had sent me falling through the air, with that one simple and enormous word.

Since that day in Colorado Springs with my white supremacist grandfather, I have spent decades researching and writing about racism, white privilege, patriarchy, and sexual violence. I explored my grandfather's sexual and other violence against me and others in my family and the ways in which his racist violence against people in our community mirrored his profound control over, violence against, and even hatred of, women in our family. I wrote a book on ways of thinking about touching children in the United States, *Boundaries of Touch: Parenting and Adult-Child Intimacy* (2007), and a memoir, *The Parallel Lives of Women and Cows: Meat Markets* (2012), about the violence in my childhood family and in my grandfather's cattle-ranching business that helped make him rich. (His investments in South African apartheid furthered that cause.) I coauthored a book introducing undergraduates to racism and white privilege, *Seeing White: An Introduction to White Privilege and Race* (2011), and another book about sexual and gender privilege, *Seeing Straight: An Introduction to Gender and Sexual Privilege* (2017). Most recently I studied, and wrote a book about, love, girls who love horses and the ways that their love of horses brings power to girls, *Horse Crazy: Girls and the Lives of Horses* (2019). When Nerio offered me the opportunity to work with him on a book about Hillbrow in South Africa, I jumped at the chance. This project about racism and the courage of so many to challenge it, about queer lives, about love and hope even in the face of profound violence, brings together so many strands of my scholarship and life. Ultimately it is an opportunity for me to see more clearly and make more visible, to face the history within which my own family played a brutal and oppressive role.

1
South Africa
A History of Land Dispossession and Migration

Migration is an expression of the human aspiration for dignity, safety and a better future. It is part of the social fabric, part of our very make-up as a human family.
— BAN KI-MOON, FORMER SECRETARY-GENERAL OF THE UNITED NATIONS[1]

South Africa has become a major "hub" for global migration.[2] In 2020, it was the world's fifteenth-most-frequent destination for international migrants and the most common destination in Africa. In the last decade alone, according to the International Organization for Migration (IOM), the number of international migrants within the country doubled from two million to four million.[3] Just over half of South Africa's new arrivals settle in Gauteng, the heavily urbanized province that is home to Johannesburg.[4]

Johannesburg also draws people from every province within South Africa. During most of the twentieth century, South Africa's former government reserved urban areas for the white minority and consigned the Black majority to the status of "temporary sojourners." As Letlhogonolo Gaborone candidly summarizes: "The history of South Africa is one of massive and well-orchestrated land dispossessions, from the colonial era until the demise of apartheid."[5] For decades, activists and organizations mobilized around the right of the majority to occupy and benefit from spaces they have been denied.[6] With the collapse of formal apartheid in the 1990s, most South Africans experienced the right to move freely for the first time.[7] So many migrated to Johannesburg during the end of the last century and the beginning of the new one that just over 40 percent of its inner-city residents in 2003 had been living in their homes for a year or less. Much of the city's population growth continues to be driven by, in Loren B. Landau's words, "newly urbanized South Africans."[8]

These two major trends — transnational and internal migration — intersect in Hillbrow, a one-mile strip of land in what is now Johannesburg's inner city. About 40 percent of Hillbrow's approximately ninety thousand residents have arrived from twenty-five other countries, including Zimbabwe, Nigeria, the Democratic Republic of Congo (DRC), Mozambique, and Malawi. Thousands of others have traveled from other parts of South Africa.[9] Tanja Winkler describes Hillbrow as one of Johannesburg's most significant "port-of-entry" neighborhoods. Such communities are urban landing spaces where new arrivals can readjust, develop a sense of a new city, and build new networks. Hillbrow, like all port-of-entry neighborhoods, is characterized by density, heterogeneity, and continuous change.[10] Because of its numerous high-rise apartment buildings, access to transportation, and proximity to job-rich suburbs,[11] Hillbrow makes a logical port of entry for people both from South Africa's other provinces and from countries to the north. It is often the first neighborhood that any new migrant arriving in Johannesburg by bus or passenger van will see.

But Winkler also refers to Hillbrow as Johannesburg's "most demonised and stressed inner city neighborhood."[12] For many, Hillbrow proves a challenging, sometimes dangerous, place to make a home. Most new arrivals find shelter in aging, often neglected and overcrowded buildings, while others "sleep rough" on sidewalks and under bridges. Many will not find the better economic opportunities they sought and must exist on survival wages or, as is the case for almost 19 percent of Hillbrow's residents, no income at all. At the same time, competition for living space pushes rents ever higher. Living in Hillbrow, therefore, requires continuous adaptation and innovation. Despite these adverse conditions, many of Hillbrow's residents develop a strong identification with the neighborhood and come to regard it as a "home away from home."[13]

In this chapter, we describe the historical circumstances surrounding Hillbrow's emergence as a neighborhood and the larger forces that shaped its evolution. One in every thirty people in the world is an international migrant, and Hillbrow offers a powerful lens for understanding the experiences of migration in one region. Such experiences in southern Africa must be viewed within the context of the centuries-long colonization of the continent and the development of land ownership and labor patterns that exclusively benefited white people. Those experiences must also be understood within the context of how various successive governments and institutions constructed ideas of racial difference to control access to resources: land, education, skills, jobs, and social and political power.

We interviewed over one hundred people who live in or have lived in Hillbrow or nearby neighborhoods such as Berea, Doornfontein, and Braamfontein. During its century and a quarter of existence, Hillbrow came to epitomize at different times an unusual mix of prosperity, modernity, rebellion, despair, violence, and poverty. It still represents these qualities, although the descriptions may shift depending on who is doing the describing. Most of our interviewees refer to Hillbrow today as a difficult place to live, and some — though certainly not all — have compared it to "hell." To understand why, we must look back to significant developments in colonial and apartheid history.

Hillbrow, Black Labor, and the "Instant City"

Hillbrow has always been a community of migrants. In this sense, Hillbrow is not unique. Humans have always moved. It is how the continents populated and cities came to be. The IOM's most comprehensive version of the term "migrant" includes any individuals or groups who move from one place to another.[14] Migrants may cross national borders or relocate within a country. Their reasons for moving range from the search for better opportunities to escaping situations that place them at extreme risk. Some migrants may intend to stay only briefly — a few months or a few years — in their new living space. They may be en route to other destinations, or they may travel frequently among several destinations for business or family reasons. Others intend to remain in a new place for the rest of their lives.

Reece Jones points out that during the nineteenth century poor Europeans migrated by the millions with few or no restrictions to Africa, Australia, and North and South America in search of better living conditions. In the world before passports and border guards, they left Europe for some of the same reasons that poor Africans leave their home countries today: overcrowded cities, major economic dislocations, state-sponsored violence, and population growth. As European countries grew rich from their colonies, their expatriates settled in those same colonies — or former colonies — with reasonable chances of finding economic prosperity. Some could arrive "penniless" and accumulate great wealth, as the diamond and gold magnate Barney Barnato did in Johannesburg.

But "today's poor countries do not have colonies to exploit," Jones writes, "and have to contend with wealthy countries that maintain control over most international institutions." Their citizens face numerous obstacles as they try to cross borders and, when they do so without authorization, they risk uncertain or precarious conditions as "undocumented" migrants. During the last two centuries, capitalism intertwined with colonialism to produce the enormous wealth gaps that exist among countries. For instance, Norway and Qatar today have the highest per capita incomes in the world, at US$97,000 per year, while the Democratic Republic of the Congo (DRC) has the lowest, at US$300. That means a typical worker in Norway earns in one day what an average worker in the DRC makes in one year.[15] Since the 1990s, tens of thousands of people from the DRC have headed to Johannesburg in search of better lives. Many went to Hillbrow.

The city of Johannesburg itself is the result of sudden and intense migration. Until the mid-1880s, little more than a series of white-owned farms stretched along the Witwatersrand, the thirty-five-mile-long escarpment (a steep slope of a plateau) that runs through what is now the city. Few people had settled nearby because the land surrounding the escarpment was poorly suited for agriculture.[16] Among them roamed prospectors who had been lured to the region from Europe, North America, and Australia from the 1870s, following the discovery of gold dust. In 1886, one of them, an Australian migrant named George Harrison, "stumbled" across a speckled bit of earth on a widow's farm.[17] This discovery of gold would fundamentally alter the politics, economy, and social order of southern Africa.

By the time Harrison entered into a prospector's agreement with the farm's owner, news of his find had traveled and set off a frenzied rush toward the Witwatersrand. Nearby farms, such as Doornfontein and Turffontein, filled up with dozens and then hundreds of gold-diggers within months.[18] Harrison may not have realized it, but he had found the reef containing the largest gold deposits in the world. He sold his claim for a pittance and moved on.[19]

Because there were no roads from the Witwatersrand to South Africa's ports, it took weeks for letters to reach investors in London and at least as long for mining equipment — which had to be delivered by oxcart from Kimberley, Durban, or Europe — to arrive in this part of South Africa's interior. Nonetheless, within a year, banks from Cape Town were opening local branches and investors had established a stock exchange. Despite several early boom and bust cycles, Johannesburg became an "instant city . . . whose sole *raison d'être* was an unbridled desire for material wealth."[20]

By the end of the nineteenth century, Johannesburg was producing over a quarter of the world's gold, and by the outbreak of World War I, that proportion had increased to 40 percent. As Charles van Onselen writes, this precious metal made Johannesburg a "giant" that "bestrode the economic world."[21] Mining proved such a source of wealth and fueled such economic growth that by the 1930s the industry accounted for 50 percent of South Africa's tax revenues and, through its ancillary industries, employed about half of the country's population.[22]

White people with power and white supremacist ideology determined who could access mining wealth. From the earliest days of the gold rush, the South African Republic (SAR), which had jurisdiction over the Witwatersrand gold mines, restricted all diggers' licenses to whites.[23] Amid the frenzy to prospect for precious metal, Black people were restricted to roles as laborers and prevented from staking claims of their own. The diggers of 1886 and 1887 had set up small claims and used basic tools, but it soon became apparent that most of the Witwatersrand's gold lay deep below the earth's surface. Extracting it would require expensive equipment and a vast supply of human labor. During boom times, investment flowed into the city, leading to the consolidation of mining companies and fueling the growth of secondary industries: retail stores, construction, taverns, and brothels. In these industries, too, Black people could be workers but not owners.

To ensure that gold would remain profitable, mine owners sought not only a reliable supply of workers but strategies to force their wages as low as possible. The Chamber of Mines, which formed as the mines consolidated under a few large owners, would demand that the provincial government institute "pass laws" to control where Black workers—who were initially and almost exclusively men—could live, work, or walk.

Hillbrow was established as a white suburb in 1895, the year before pass laws were adopted in Johannesburg. The pass laws were soon tightened to specify that no "natives" could be present on the Rand unless they were employed by a "master." In Hillbrow, which was always a residential neighborhood, that meant that Black occupants could only live legally in the suburb as domestic workers—although there were ways to evade the pass laws. Employed Black men were required to wear a metal plate or badge indicating so, until the plates and badges were replaced by printed passes.[24]

Johannesburg was, therefore, shaped from the beginning by white supremacy, class hierarchy, and the related national struggles that would leave indelible imprints on the city. The "colonial colour bar" afforded white workers a monopoly on high-skilled positions and the right to unionize; nonetheless, these same workers often clashed with mine owners during economic downturns, when employers tried to reduce white pay. As mining activity intensified, mine owners pursued elaborate and ruthless measures to recruit Black labor. From 1896, the Chamber of Mines began actively recruiting tens of thousands of Black men from "native reserves," rural territories that would, under apartheid, become known as "homelands."

During the early twentieth century the Chamber of Mines turned to Portuguese East Africa (now Mozambique) in its endless thirst for labor. By 1910, through a system of agreements with Portuguese colonial administrators, a majority of Black mineworkers on the Witwatersand (often called the Rand) were drawn from that colony. A quest for yet more workers led mine owners to colonies even farther afield, including in what are now the countries of Malawi, Botswana, Namibia, Zambia, and Zimbabwe.[25]

In other words, the Chamber of Mines, through its Witwatersrand Native Labour Association (WNLA), was building a vast system of migrant labor to recruit, control, and house the hundreds of thousands of Black men whose work built the industry and made the mine owners rich. Conditions for unskilled workers in the mines were so dismal that recruitment initially proved difficult. Rural areas were often self-sufficient enough that Black men had no incentive to leave their families to work for grueling hours underground for extremely little pay. Therefore, in a stunning example of greed — and of white supremacist disregard for African lives — the WNLA set out to undermine the rural economies and to force recruitment through colonial land policies.[26]

The organization also collaborated with Portuguese colonial officials who guaranteed access to workers in Portuguese East Africa (again, Mozambique) in exchange for a percentage of profits on the rail transport line the WNLA built. That rail line would eventually carry about five million men between Mozambique and the Witwatersrand during the first half of the twentieth century. Its passengers were packed tightly into cars with little food or water and, as a measure of control, were deliberately transported at night to disrupt their sleep patterns.[27] Meanwhile, the WNLA bought airplanes to fly Black workers from Malawi to the mines. In most cases, contract workers had no control over where they would go or how they would get there. Once a Black worker signed a contract, it was a criminal offense to break it.[28]

"Taking on a contract," Andries Bezuidenhout and Sakhela Buhlungu write, also "meant being sucked into" another form of social control — the compound.[29] Closed, single-sex compounds housed male migrant workers in hostels, twenty to fifty to a room, next to the mines. Food was minimal and of such poor quality that it often led to protests. Both malnutrition and disease were common. Just a decade and a half after the discovery of gold, the compounds housed about one hundred thousand African workers, who were forbidden by law from entering white parts of the city.[30]

Amid this racially stratified urban revolution the idea was conceived in

1894 that Hillbrow should become the "most fashionable suburb" of the new city. On the brow of the mountain ridge that crosses through Johannesburg, it offered a scenic escape from the intense crowds near the core of the new city.[31] Influenced by Victorian ideas about fresh air, its developers began marketing it as a "healthy" suburb removed from the noise and grime of mining camps.[32] As in all other white sections of the city, only white people and their domestic workers would be permitted to live there. Samuel Goldreich, who was associated with the Transvaal Mortgage, Loan & Finance, issued flyers promising no shops or canteens (bars) and only one hotel would be erected in the district. These restrictions were a sign, write Paddi Clay and Glynn Griffiths, that Johannesburg's new, white middle class "did not want their estate to be attractive to riff raff."[33]

The term "suburb" carries a particular meaning in Johannesburg. The location for the city's original mining camp was on a patch of unfarmable land called Randjeslaagte, the northern apex of which overlaps with current-day Hillbrow. As Johannesburg's population grew and spread each new settlement was originally called a "township." Over time, townships occupied by white people became known as "suburbs" and the word "township" came to refer exclusively to Black residential spaces. That terminology would harden in subsequent decades, as overcrowded Black townships expanded to house tens of thousands and sometimes hundreds of thousands of people.[34] In the US, a suburb is typically a district that is independent from a city's jurisdiction and does not share a property tax base with the city. Therefore, Hillbrow is what in the US would conventionally be called a "neighborhood." The term "neighborhood" is less common in South Africa, although some researchers do use that term when writing about Hillbrow. We follow the lead of Alan Morris[35] and Tanja Winkler[36] in using "neighborhood" to avoid confusion with the more distant northern and southern suburbs.

Hillbrow never did develop into Johannesburg's "most fashionable suburb." Rather, it became an "affordable option" for the white middle class between ultra-wealthy Parktown, on its north side, and the increasingly impoverished Doornfontein, to its south. Early postcards, from 1906, show a scattering of one- and two-story spacious homes with plenty of visible green trees.[37] Until the end of World War I, some of Hillbrow's residents still owned horses and stables.[38]

But as Johannesburg's population surged, so too did Hillbrow's. It would become one of South Africa's most significant residential destinations. Hundreds, and then thousands, of Jewish people from Eastern and Western Europe settled in and around its borders during the early twentieth century. Buildings grew higher, streets denser. In the post–World War II years, Hillbrow became Johannesburg's "flatland" (place of tall building with numerous "flats," or apartments) and Germans, Slavs, Italians, Portuguese, and Greeks clustered in its new soaring residential high-rises. During the waning years of apartheid and following South Africa's transition to nonracial democracy, Africans from almost all regions of the continent restarted their lives in Hillbrow.

Race in South Africa

For eight decades, Hillbrow was legally zoned as a "white" suburb, after which it transitioned, informally, to a mixed or "grey zone," and then to one that is today 98 percent "Black African" (according to the terminology of the most recent census). To understand what this means, we examine how race was constructed in South Africa through colonization, capitalism, war, and legislation.

Nature does not build race; rather, empires, governments, modes of production, voting registries, media, and militaries do. Race is crafted through social, political, and economic forces. Science, too, built race, not because it discovered the biological fact of race as many scientists once claimed but because eighteenth- and nineteenth-century scientists, from Carolus Linnaeus to Johann Friedrich Blumenbach, built classification systems that reflected the racist European imperial orders in which they lived.[39] Thus, in the modern history of imperialism racial categories came to be justified as based in biology.

Ideas about racial difference empowered whites to aggressively monopolize land, resources, and political power, not only in South Africa but across the continent. During the same decade in which whites established a monopoly over the Witwatersrand goldfields, the European powers met in Berlin (1884–85) to divide Africa among themselves. King Leopold of Belgium's Force Publique systematically murdered ten million people in the Congo (now the DRC) in the process of extracting ivory and rubber.[40] Great Britain used divide-and-rule methods to, as Chinua Achebe would later describe it, scoop up large parts of western Africa, including Nigeria, like a "giant piece of chocolate cake."[41] From Algeria in the north to Basutoland (now Lesotho) in the south, and from Senegal in the west to Kenya in the east, the European empires would leave no part of Africa unclaimed save Ethiopia. Adam Hochschild argues that none of this would have been possible without inventing the idea of racial difference.[42]

Akil Kokayi Khalfani and Tukufu Zuberi's study of the South African census as it evolved from the first population count in 1911 over the remainder of the twentieth century is revealing. Though the state and cultural institutions claimed that race was both biological and obvious, we see instead that a series of contradictory, sometimes bizarre, and ultimately brutal decisions were made around how to classify people. The 1911 census listed three major race categories: "European or white," "Bantu," and "Mixed and Coloured other than Bantu." In 1921, 1936, 1946, and 1952, the category "Bantu" was replaced with "Native," but the label "Bantu" returned in 1960 and 1970; was changed to "Blacks" in 1980, 1985, and 1991; and finally became "Black African" in 1996 (the first census following the end of apartheid). During the years that "Bantu" was used as a term, the census also counted twenty-four subcategories within this group, including Basutho, Hlwangweni, Ndebele, Pondo, Swazi, Xhosa, and Zulu.

In a Kafkaesque attempt to define and control, the "Coloured" (or "mixed") category contained a curious arrangement of overlapping subcategories. The subcategories within the "Coloured" classification in 1911 somehow included "Afghan," "American Coloured," "Arabian," "Chinese," "St. Helena," "Syrian," "West Indian," and "Zanzibari." From 1921 on, the category "Asiatics" was added to and subsumed under the "Coloured" group. In that year, the census counted "Syrians" as "Asiatics" but later reclassified them as "white." In the 1936 census, respondents were permitted to choose a racial category, but the state changed their responses at will. "Here," Khalfani and Zuberi write, "the state gave populations the illusion of self-classification but did so only to appease those involved."[43]

After the victory of the National Party in 1948, racial classification and separation became a central obsession of the state. The Population Registration Act of 1950 mandated that every South African would acquire an identity card, on which their race would be enumerated as part of their identification number. Five military huts were set up in Pretoria to count the population and issue the ID cards. The Population Registration Act initially specified that there were three races: "European White," "Bantu," and "Mixed and Other Coloured." Those three classifications would evolve to four, with "Indians" added as a distinct race in later years. By the 1960s, each person's "race" was "stamped on the cards in bright red ink." Identification cards for "whites," "Coloureds," and "Indians" were small enough to fit into a wallet and bore the words "SA Citizen." Cards for the Black majority were glued to passbooks and, in place of "SA Citizen" was the word "Native."[44]

White people were given the label assigned to them by census enumerators, while "Coloured" and "Indian" people were often required to submit to "humiliating and frightening official examinations" by officials from the Department of the Interior who were focused on preventing "Africans" from trying to pass as members of those groups. Africans, meanwhile, were coerced into classification and acquiring passbooks through processes that were "often degrading and sometimes terrifying." By the late 1960s, the state had built a thirty-story building and hired hundreds of clerks to use IBM computers to count and classify every member of the population.[45]

Every person's ID number ended with two digits that disclosed their race. It is worth quoting Benjamin Pogrund's description at length. "Those vital two digits," he writes,

> were intended to, and did, affect life from birth to death, with every detail specified and fixed by law: in which hospital you could be born; in which suburb you could live; which house you could buy; which farm you could buy; which nursery school and school you could attend and which university or technical college; which cinemas and theatres you could go to; which buses, train compartments and taxis you could travel in; which bus stops, railway pedestrian bridges and platforms you could use; which beach you could swim from; which municipal pool you could use; from which library you could get books; which park bench you could sit on; in which restaurants you could eat; which lavatories you could use; in which hotels you could stay; whether you were allowed to enter a municipal hall; which jobs you could hold and how much you would earn; how much liquor you could buy and possess; who you could legally have sex with and who you could marry; how easily you could get a passport for travel abroad; how much your old age pension would be; whether you could vote; which hearse you would be carried in when you died; and in which graveyard you would be buried.[46]

After the first democratic elections in 1994, the new, democratic government determined that racial classifications would remain the same in subsequent censuses "because most people in the country recognised and understood the categories." This, too, reflects the ways that the imprints of history are hard to change. "African," however, was altered "to distinguish between Afrikaners [white descendants of the earlier Dutch-speaking Europeans], many of whom also define themselves as Africans, and indigenous Africans." The 2011 census — the most recent as of the writing of this book — uses five race categories: "Black African," "Coloured," "Indian or Asian," "White," and "Other." The census is now conducted every ten years.[47]

For readers outside South Africa, "Coloured" may be the least familiar of the above "racial" categories. While "Coloured" originally evolved to refer to the mixed offspring of Europeans and Africans at the Cape, the construction of this group in the 1911 census vividly illustrates the arbitrary nature of racial classification. It counted 678,146 people in a category that it labeled "Coloured or mixed." But a finer breakdown reveals that this category included Indians, Chinese, Mozambicans, and Malay (a term that had come to generically refer to people of Muslim background). There were also overlapping and seemingly inexplicable subcategories. For instance, among the 678,146 "Coloured or mixed" people, the census counted 435,288 people that it designated "mixed." Seemingly excluded from the "mixed" people but within the "Coloured" category were 8,695 Bushmen (San) and 38,074 Hottentot (Khoi), while there were 566,036 people in the "total Hottentot race." Thus, it was somehow possible to be a member of the "Hottentot race" but not be "Hottentot." Also among the "Coloured or mixed" were Korana (9,185), Griqua (7,759), and Namaqua (82) people, some of whom defined themselves as "Coloured" and some of whom did not. By the 1950s, Indians would be removed from the "Coloured or mixed" category and occupy a category of their own, while people of Chinese birth or background would be counted as "unclassified" and the Japanese would be considered white.[48] Such are the inconsistencies of the supposedly biological, but ultimately political, attempts to classify people by race. During most of Hillbrow's history, everyone in all of the categories above would have been prohibited from buying or renting property — except for "whites."

The Roots of the "Colour Bar"

Scholars still debate what led to South Africa's notorious and increasingly "rigid colour bar." Rodney Davenport and Christopher Saunders trace it to the first European settlements at the Cape of Good Hope, dating to the 1650s. The powerful and voracious Dutch East India Company (DEIC) initially viewed the Cape as little more than a way station for ships bound to and from its slave territories in the East Indies — the islands that would later come to be known as Indonesia. Cloves, cinnamon, nutmeg, and tea extracted from those islands were making the Netherlands one of the richest countries in the world, but the nearly 10,000-mile journey often left shipmates sick and malnourished. The company set up a hospital and a garden at the Cape in 1652 to treat the ill. The DEIC initially showed no interest in establishing a colony on the Cape but permitted some of its members to establish a few farms in 1657.[49]

These white-owned farms soon faced a labor shortage, which the DEIC chose to address by importing slaves. As the number of farms grew during the rest of the 1600s and into the eighteenth century, the practice of bringing slaves from East Africa, Madagascar, and the East Indies developed into a "continuous" one. Most slaves were privately owned by farmers, but the company also established a lodge where it housed hundreds of its own slaves. Thus, a pattern was set early: only "free burghers" — white Dutch "servants" of the DEIC and those who had been freed from service to the company — could own land in the new colony. Their numbers grew slowly, but by the end of the eighteenth century there were about sixteen thousand "free burghers" and a slightly smaller number of slaves.[50]

As the Dutch fanned out and settled more farms, they encountered the indigenous Khoikhoi and the San peoples. Both groups had migrated to what is now South Africa from the northern part of Botswana, about 1,500 years ago. The San were primarily nomadic, and the Khoikhoi lived in larger family units and raised cattle. Though the Khoikhoi launched a series of wars to fend off Dutch settlers, the Europeans had brought the lethal smallpox virus with them and it decimated the Khoikhoi population. Thereby weakened, the Khoikhoi lost their lands to Dutch military raids in the 1670s and largely ended up in servitude to whites. Further to the north, "trekboers" (traveling white farmers) encountered the San people who responded with frequent raids on trekboer farms and wagons. The Boers (farmers) massacred five hundred people in 1774, in a failed attempt at genocide of the San.[51]

During the eighteenth century, through settlement and slavery, the population of the Cape grew to include the remaining Khoikhoi and San, Xhosa, Bengali, Chinese, French, Dutch, British, Spanish, and Arabic people, and people from western and southwest Africa. From the beginning, members of these groups mixed with one another and some intermarried. In the context of slavery, sexual relationships among groups were largely determined by power and involved sexual assault. As Pumla Dineo Gqola has written, "the rape of slaves was an integral part of the architecture of slave-ordered Cape society." She notes that rape was extensive, but because it was the colonists who were recording events and telling the stories — and because raping women who were not white was not a crime — the exact scale can only be inferred. Evidence comes from anecdotes told in the journals and letters of the colonists. One such incident involves the reversal of a man's sentence for rape "when the judge realized that the woman had not in fact been a white woman." Rape would be "used as a weapon" by both the Boers and the British as they moved east and north into the interior.[52]

The "mixed" offspring of Europeans and other groups, who came to be known as "Coloured," were for the most part not enslaved; but because they were excluded from the social positions reserved for members of the DEIC, they "became the poorest group of the free people."[53] During the early nineteenth century, "Coloured" people on the Cape were "free" but forced to carry passes.

In 1795, with the DEIC heading into bankruptcy, the British Empire seized control of the Cape. Control over the colony would vacillate between the Dutch and the British until the British took permanent control in 1815.[54] Martin Meredith explains that the British did so reluctantly at first, with their primary aim being to establish and protect a naval base at the Cape. That base was critical to the transport of ships to and from Britain's own colonies to the east.[55]

The British set about "anglicizing" the colony, transitioning the official language of government and education from Dutch to English. British rule, writes Richard van der Ross, brought a "gradual liberalization" to the Cape. The government abolished pass laws for "Coloured" people in 1828 and emancipated all slaves in 1834, although freed slaves were required to perform a four-year apprenticeship. Both "Coloured" and "African" men who were landowners (there were a small number in each group) were permitted to vote after the 1850s. Nonetheless, in daily life, van der Ross writes, Coloured and African people were treated with disrespect by white public officials, the police, and members of the general white population.[56]

Despite this reputation for "liberalization," Gqola writes that from the 1830s the British used overwhelming violence against the Xhosa, burning their homes, driving them off their land, and frequently killing their children. She quotes Ania Loomba, who writes that some among the British colonizers wrote about the land as if it were a "naked woman" and described themselves as rapists of the land and the people. The British would deploy violence and rape against the Xhosa for a century.[57]

Some among the Dutch population found British rule intolerable. They bristled at the sidelining of their language and what they perceived as "moral laxity"—especially around what they denounced as the "leveling of the races"—in the Cape. While "trekboers" had moved about and settled in parts of the Eastern and Northern Cape since nearly the beginning of Dutch settlement, a new phenomenon emerged in the 1830s—that of the "voortrekkers." Unlike earlier trekboers, the voortrekkers organized in small groups with the intention of "emigrating" permanently from the Cape Colony. One group migrated far to the east in 1838, into what would become Natalia (later the Natal Province and today KwaZulu-Natal) and were killed en masse by the Zulu king Dingane. That same year, another small group of Boers battled with Dingane's army at Blood River and killed five thousand Zulus. In 1839, that group established the first Boer state in Natalia with a constitution that reserved voting rights for whites only. Davenport and Saunders note that exclusive white suffrage would become a defining feature—if not *the* defining feature—of all Boer republics.[58]

Another group of voortrekkers moved into the eastern Transvaal in the 1840s. Despite resistance from African chiefs who tried to stop the expansion of white claims over this sizable territory, the voortrekkers would declare it an independent Boer country — the South African Republic (SAR) — in 1852. As Davenport and Saunders phrase it, the Transvaal was "acquired through conquest in a series of conflicts extending over sixty years." The SAR's policy allowed any white man — with the stress on *man* — to claim and register "unoccupied" land. White men were allowed two farms of 3,000 morgen each (nearly 2,000 acres) as of right. Black people could not individually own land in the SAR, although a few missionary societies acquired about 800,000 morgen (50,000 acres) for Black chiefdoms. In a territory where Black people outnumbered whites three to one (about 900,000 vs. 300,000, respectively), only about 1 percent of land was reserved for Black people by the end of the nineteenth century. It was in this republic that George Harrison would discover the gold reef on which Johannesburg sits.[59]

The voortrekkers established poorly developed, sparsely populated republics, some of which lasted briefly and others which survived for decades. In the process, the Boers who created the republics had clashed for territory with the Ndebele Kingdom, the Xhosas, the Zulus, the Basothos, the Tswana, and the Griqua. The latter were a group of mixed descendants of European and Khoikhoi people who had departed Cape Town and had established their own semiautonomous republics in the interior: Griqualand East and Griqualand West. The voortrekkers in the Boer republics sometimes deployed "commandos" to kidnap young Africans whom they forced into labor. The British had granted independence to the Boers in the SAR (1852) and the Orange Free State (1854) on the condition that there would be no slavery. The Boers called the kidnapped Africans "apprentices" instead.[60]

The construction of racial hierarchies in South Africa intensified with the "mineral revolution." In 1871, fifteen years before the discovery of the Witwatersrand gold reef, prospectors discovered the largest diamond deposits in the world about 290 miles to the southeast of what is now Johannesburg. The resultant "diamond fever" gave rise to Kimberley, the "instant boomtown" whose racist labor patterns would in many ways serve as a template for Johannesburg's. The two Boer republics, the British-held Cape Colony, and the Griquas all claimed jurisdiction over the diamond mines, but the British initially conceded control to the Griquas. Griqualand West would soon become a British colony, as the British absorbed Kimberley into the Cape.[61]

Kimberley became known for its "diggers democracy," in which any white person could raise grievances in the public square. One of their most vociferous demands was for the right to control Black workers on the diamond fields. "They wanted black labour," writes Martin Meredith, "but they feared that black competition would undermine them." More than 50,000 Black migrants traveled each year to the diamond mines in Kimberley, often for weeks on foot, from Pediland (500 miles away), Zululand (506 miles), and Tsonga territory (1,000 miles). They worked for 5,000 white diggers who frequently used violence and abuse to control them.[62]

The British appointed a local administrator at Kimberley, Sir Richard Southey, who initially declared that Black and Coloured laborers should receive the same opportunities as whites to become claim owners and to buy and sell claims. Enraged white diggers responded by burning down the tents of Black claimants. White diggers' demands grew so vehement that the British acquiesced and agreed to a system of pass laws — like that which would later be instituted in Johannesburg — aimed at controlling the movement of Black people. Black men were forced to register as soon as they arrived in Kimberley, obtain a new pass each day until finding work, and then to carry a new pass signed by an employer.

Amid the diamond fever, Benjamin Disraeli came to power in Britain in 1874 and sought to extend the Empire's global reach, including taking more direct control over what is now South Africa. At the time, the territory consisted of "three British colonies, two Boer republics, and an assortment of African chiefdoms, including Xhosa, Zulu, Swazi, Pedi, Venda, Tswana and Sotho."[63] Consequential to these plans, a twenty-year-old Cecil Rhodes had arrived in Kimberley and over time successfully set about consolidating the South African diamond operations into one massive enterprise — the De Beers Corporation. Rhodes was an ardent advocate of British domination and set his sights much farther north with the objective of extending British control over all land with any potential of holding diamond deposits. His relentless drive eventually led the Empire to extend its reach for more than a thousand miles beyond Kimberley, into what first became known as Zambesia (now Zimbabwe and Zambia) and, in 1895, was named after himself: Rhodesia.

The British coexisted uneasily with the Boer republics and had already gone to war once with the Boers in the SAR, in 1880–81. But the discovery of the Witwatersrand goldfields "transformed the economic balance of the subcontinent," shifting the regional advantage from the British-held Cape to the Boer-controlled SAR. At the same time, amid the European scramble for Africa, the Germans began to challenge British domination in southern Africa. German chancellor Otto von Bismarck declared Southwest Africa a German colony in 1884. The following year, Germany would claim a sizable portion of East Africa (the contemporary countries of Tanzania, Rwanda, and Burundi became German East Africa in 1885). The Germans also eyed Zululand, and Pondoland, on what is now the South African coastline. Believing the Transvaal (SAR), with its vast gold mines, to be the key to controlling the region, the British began to "encircle" the Boer republic in the early 1890s.[64]

The British and the Boers went to war over the Transvaal in 1899. With an army of 40,000, the Boers started the war to seize the initiative against the British military presence of 15,000. British and other residents were briefly expelled from Johannesburg and most of them fled toward the coasts. As the city emptied out, the British resorted to scorched earth tactics in the countryside, burning Boer farmsteads and entire villages to the ground.[65] British soldiers erected concentration camps, forty-four for Boers and twenty-nine for Africans. About 20,000 Africans and 28,000 Boers died in the camps, many of whom were children under eighteen.[66]

When the British military arrived in Johannesburg in 1900 to reclaim the city from the Boers, Black Africans in the city were hopeful that British rule might bring new and better circumstances. Keith Beavon describes how some "stood on the pavements" to greet the soldiers, but in a gratuitous act of cruelty the British troops forced the Africans into the streets by resorting to an older Transvaal law requiring that only white people could walk on the pavements. The British immediately made it clear that they would enforce all racist laws that had existed when the colony was in Boer hands and, to add insult to injury, they slashed Black miners' already meager wages by as much as one third. In the years following the war, the British spent enormous sums developing the city's infrastructure but almost all of it went to "European" areas.[67]

The Johannesburg Town Council, for which only whites could vote, had "authority over the native and coloured inhabitants of the town" but no responsibility to those residents. After the war, the council massively expanded the limits of the city, making it one of the largest in the world in terms of land area. Because the council had the authority to remove Black Africans from the city limits, Beavon argues that the purpose of the expansion was to force Black people to distant areas on the city's far west and southwest sides. The city passed another law in 1903 requiring there would be no permanent residential areas for Black people within the city's boundaries. Nonetheless, recognizing that the city depended on Black labor, the council built compounds — similar to the mining compounds — for male Black workers who would serve as street cleaners and refuse removers.[68]

As Johannesburg's population burgeoned following the war, the British administration developed extensive plans for "slum clearance" from the poorest and most crowded areas near the city center. By 1904, Philip Harrison and Tanya Zack write, "more than 100,000 Black Africans, and large numbers of Chinese, were corralled in regimented single-sex compounds on mining property along the Witwatersrand."[69] But Black people were also finding jobs out-side the mining industry and living in crowded neighborhoods interspersed with poor and struggling whites. Susan Parnell writes that, despite the preva-lence of "white supremacist discourse . . . there was a tendency for workers of all races to live together in the inner-city slums."[70]

The Town Council was determined to quash residential race mixing and to remove the "volatile" white poor from the central city. An increasing number of impoverished, traumatized Afrikaners — white Boers — who had lost their farms during the war, were pouring into the city. They briefly found a niche as brickmakers during the housing boom of 1902–3 but were soon forced to the western edges of the city under the guise of improving public health. Mine owners were also intent on suppressing labor resistance by keeping the two elements of the white working class — Afrikaners and English speakers — apart, especially when the depression of 1906 led to a massive increase in the number of unemployed whites. Notably, during this severe economic down-turn, unemployed whites would receive assistance from the Rand Aid Society, while there would be "nowhere to turn for even temporary relief" for mem-bers of any other groups. In fact, many unemployed African men during the depression "soon found themselves either locked up in prison, or else seeking shelter in the disused mine shafts, prospect holes or abandoned houses on the city's periphery."[71]

One of the first, and most ruthless, acts of "slum clearance" occurred when a reported outbreak of bubonic plague gave the Johannesburg Town Council the pretext under which to remove people from the "Coolie Location," a site that had been occupied by a mix of Indian, Coloured, and African people. Troops surrounded the location on the night the plague was discovered, burned many of its 1,600 structures to the ground, and blockaded it with an iron fence. Its residents were taken in wagons to Klipspruit (which would later form part of Soweto), ten miles southwest of the town center. They were to be housed "temporarily" in shelters that had previously served as a concentration camp for Afrikaner women and children. Because the laws regulating the movement and living spaces of Africans were stricter, the Africans among this group were forced to stay in Klipspruit while the Indian population managed to trickle back into the city to find housing wherever possible.[72]

Perhaps ironically, the Town Council's efforts to clear slums from the city resulted in the development of new kinds of slum conditions — both inside and outside the city. The African settlement at Klipspruit sat near a large sewage works, and as the population grew, the child mortality rate reached a staggering 12.5 percent. Others in Klipspruit suffered from high rates of se-vere gastroenteritis. Because Klipspruit was so far from white-owned places of employment, the city constructed a railway station in 1906; but there were only two trains a day, commutes lasted an hour each way, and steep fares ate into the minuscule wages of Black workers. Therefore, many white employers demanded the council provide exceptions for their workers to stay in town.

Slums developed behind factories and in backyards. White homeowners made extravagant profits by renting their backyards to as many as sixty to eighty people and packing ten to twelve into hastily constructed rooms. Beavon notes the immense gap between the general quality of Black and white working-class accommodations. White people arriving in Johannesburg could pay between ten and twenty shillings a month for a bed in a private boardinghouse with clean surroundings, where they were served a daily meal for a small extra charge. African families, meanwhile, had to pay two to three times as much to occupy backyard slum "accommodations," where they had to cook and use the toilet outside and live separated from the next family by thin partitions. Beavon notes that there were a few hundred African, and a slightly smaller number of "Coloured," people living in "white" Hillbrow's backyards by 1915.

For further context, before the war there existed a "Coolie Location" and a "Kaffir Location" (pejorative terms for Indian and African people), but little by little the Transvaal government had whittled away parts of the African Location to house poor Afrikaner whites. In 1905, the remaining parts of the African Location were converted into a cemetery for whites. Africans who had moved into the Coolie Location lost their homes when it was destroyed during the bubonic plague scare of 1904. Africans who were not employed on the mines or living in houses as domestic workers faced three choices: move to the "Malay Location," move to distant Klipspruit, or live illegally in the hundreds of backyard and other slum locations.[73]

Davenport and Saunders maintain that the British, after taking control of the Transvaal, seemed initially willing to consider granting some rights to the colony's African, Indian, and Coloured people. But in Britain, public sympathy was building for the Boers who had suffered extreme losses of life and property during the war. The British became so attentive to addressing the "wrongs done to the Afrikaners" that all other groups experienced an erosion of the minimal rights and quality of life they had. The British agreed with Afrikaners that Africans would not gain the right to vote until, and unless, a majority of whites consented. Separation and segregation were becoming more and more entrenched.[74]

After the Boer republics and the British colonies formed the Union of South Africa in 1910, one of the conditions on which the Boer leaders insisted was that African and Coloured people would henceforth be prohibited from serving as members of parliament.[75] The resulting whites-only parliament would enact one profoundly consequential racist law after another. The Natives Land Act of 1913 prevented Black people from owning land outside of native "reserves," the often-arid parts of South Africa that accounted for less than 10 percent of the total land in South Africa (this would later be expanded to 13 percent). The intent of this act was to force members of the Black majority to the cities, where they would become workers for white-owned industries, or onto farms, where they would work white-owned land.[76]

The Native (Urban Areas) Act of 1923 declared that Black people would henceforth be considered temporary "sojourners" who had no legal rights to live in the cities. The intricacies of this act are worth exploring, considering how it would shape Johannesburg for decades to come. The Native (Urban Areas) Act required that cities wanting to "declare" themselves under the Act had to provide alternative accommodation for any Black Africans (the act applied only to Black people) who were moved. As the city began to force Africans to places such as Klipspruit, a lawsuit in 1927 alleged that it was doing so without providing other accommodations. The court ruled against the city and permitted those who had been removed to return to the suburbs from which they had been expelled.

At the time of the lawsuit, the Black African population (excluding the 100,000 people living in mining compounds) was nearing 100,000, almost one-third of whom were domestic workers living on their employers' property. Therefore, the city would have had to find accommodations for about 60,000 African people if it was going to comply with the law. So, the city tried to apply the act suburb by suburb, starting with the northern and eastern suburbs where the fewest Africans lived (excluding the domestic workers). There were three existing "freehold townships" on the western side of the city, where Africans could own land: Sophiatown, Martindale, and Newclare. The city provided no municipal water supply, forcing residents in these increasingly crowded communities to draw water from polluted wells. As subsequent amendments to the Urban Areas Act forced more people to relocate to these communities, more and more people were paying rent to absentee white landlords. Black residents who did own their properties struggled because their interest payments were higher than the rates that whites paid.[77]

The Slums Act of 1934 became the basis for moving even more Black residents to growing townships outside the municipal boundaries. Johannesburg developed rapidly during this period. Because the "reserves" were producing less than half of their subsistence food requirements, many African men were forced to migrate toward the city to earn enough money to send food home. Meanwhile, more and more Afrikaners who lost their lands to mining companies or to commercial farmers also headed toward the city. Fearing that desperate Afrikaners and poorly paid Black people would develop class solidarity, the city's elite decided to help only the poor whites by providing low-interest loans. It also used the Slums Act to clear neighborhoods such as Bertrams and build council housing for whites. Such actions effectively quashed any possibility of cross-racial class alliances.

Vertical Hillbrow

As the Native (Urban Areas) Act of 1923 and the Slums Act of 1934 shaped the city's human geography during the 1920s and 1930s, technological innovations began transforming Hillbrow's physical landscape. New technologies, such as reinforced concrete and elevators, enabled the neighborhood's first "massive growth spurt" by making it possible to construct multistory buildings. Height restrictions would keep most buildings relatively low until the 1940s, but a growing number of residential hotels would make Hillbrow an increasingly likely "port of entry" for many new (white) arrivals to the city.[78]

Meanwhile, skyscrapers were rising in the Central Business District (CBD), on the southwestern edge of Hillbrow, and architectural innovations from London, Paris, Vienna, New York, and Chicago were making their way to Johannesburg. By the end of the 1930s, Johannesburg boasted buildings taller than any in Europe or Asia.[79] While much of the world suffered from prolonged economic depression during the 1930s, gold mining in Johannesburg experienced a significant economic uptick. Investment funds poured into the city in 1937 and 1938, and much of it went to a "building boom" in Hillbrow and its neighboring communities: Joubert Park, Berea, and Yeoville.[80] Johannesburg's economy expanded even further when its factories began making war materiel for the Allies in the late 1930s and early 1940s.[81]

With millions of pounds being spent on new buildings in white areas, removals of African people were intensifying. By 1939, more than 101,000 people were living in the "African locations," such as Pimville and Orlando. In Orlando, residents rented homes from the city—structures with dirt floors and no kitchens, toilets, or water. They also had no electricity, despite being next to the power station that provided electrification to the white sections of the city. When South Africa entered World War II, construction on housing in new homes in Orlando came to a dead stop. Because Orlando's population was increasing rapidly, existing homes became extremely overcrowded and squatter camps—some led by political protesters—developed on the township's borders. Tens of thousands of desperate, angry—and organized—people filled up the squatters' camps and demanded better housing. One group named their camp *Sofasonke*, meaning "we shall die together." By the mid-1940s, such organizing led to the new suburbs of Jabavu and Orlando East. The city declared another emergency camp, called Moroka, in 1947.[82]

One of the few job niches for African women was the brewing of sorghum beer. To pay for the construction of African "housing" in the townships, the city took over and monopolized the brewing of this beer. While this cruel scheme deprived hundreds — perhaps thousands — of Africans and their families of income, it failed to generate anything close to sufficient revenues for the city. Beavon points out that if the city had placed a mere 1 percent tax on new buildings constructed in places such as the CBD and Hillbrow it could have raised about thirteen times the money generated by sorghum beer sales. But, he writes, the city did not want to touch any money "generated" by white people for African housing.[83] Such were the decisions made prior to the National Party's victory in 1948, which would usher in the era of apartheid.

Our Argument

The South African Broadcasting Corporation hosts a program called "The Big Debate," which enlists politicians, intellectuals, and members of the public to discuss major contemporary topics. In the "Big Debate on Racism" (2014),[84] the poet Lebogang Mashile says that South Africa "has endured 350 years of systemic violence, misogyny, and the racist exclusion of people." The host of the program, Siki Mgabadeli, notes that after the long struggle against apartheid and several decades of transformation, Black workers still earn only 13 percent of what a typical white person earns. This ratio has risen by only 1 percent since the formal end of apartheid in 1994. Mgabadeli's comments prompted political columnist Kay Sexwale, during this same debate, to remark: "We put a plaster [a Band-Aid] on a gunshot wound in this country."

In *The Roads to Hillbrow: Making Life in South Africa's Community of Migrants*, we explore a single neighborhood to understand how the legacy of 350 years of systemic violence, misogyny, and exclusion (in Mashile's words) shaped and continues to shape everyday life, consciousness, and patterns of social interaction in South Africa. Though the neighborhood, Hillbrow, has only existed for one-third of that time, the pattern of white supremacist domination forged during the two centuries before Hillbrow's founding molded the neighborhood's development and evolution.

White domination in Southern Africa relied on violence, including sexual violence, and racial separation to preserve almost all social and economic resources for the white minority. For much of its existence, Hillbrow was itself a resource. Its earliest developers marketed it as a clean, quiet space for whites to build homes away from the crime, chaos, and filth of the central city. During much of the twentieth century, Hillbrow would offer only white people safe streets with fashionable shops, restaurants, bars, and clubs; modern high-rise apartment buildings; proximity to some of the city's most elite schools; and centralized access to transport to the region's jobs. Its density also offered spaces and opportunity for the rebellious and unconventional to explore ways of living and expressing themselves that were not tolerated elsewhere in the country. Again, with few exceptions, these were resources and options exclusively enjoyed by whites until the late 1980s.

White domination was not confined to South Africa's eventual borders. All African borders, all bodies, were subject to white colonial violence, and the appropriation of massive tracts of land.[85] After the British colonized South Africa, they extended their rule north into Bechuanaland, Rhodesia, and Nyasaland (now Botswana, Zimbabwe, Zambia, and Malawi). Portugal had already claimed parts of what is now Mozambique and Angola, to South Africa's northeast and northwest, as early as the fifteenth century and continued to expand its colonial rule through the next 400-plus years. The Germans took control of Southwest Africa (now Namibia) in the late nineteenth century and committed the first genocide of the twentieth century when the Herero and Namaqua people tried to fight back.

Despite the wave of formal independence in Africa, which began in Ghana in 1957 and reached completion[86] with the formal democratization of South Africa in 1994, the violence of colonial rule continues to exert itself on the continent's institutions. In many cases, the imperial powers withdrew from their colonies only after lengthy wars of liberation that stalled development and shattered infrastructure. These struggles for independence were often followed by devastating civil wars, some of which lasted decades and killed hundreds of thousands or millions. The Cold War antagonists — China, the United States, and the Soviet Union — intensified the destructiveness of civil wars in places such as the Republic of Congo, the DRC, Mozambique, and Angola when they sent hundreds of millions of dollars in military equipment and armaments along with military advisers. In the case of Angola, the scale of the civil war magnified after independence in 1975 when the United States transported armaments from the war in Vietnam to the DRC border with Angola. These efforts helped the apartheid government in South Africa maintain its power in the region.

During the historical arc of colonization and decolonization, Hillbrow has occupied a position at once unique and illustrative of the challenges of living with the continued impact of white supremacy, violence, and patriarchy on the continent. For almost one hundred years (1895–1991), only white people could legally purchase or rent property in Hillbrow. But in a rigidly racially stratified and patriarchal society, Hillbrow was also notable as a space for immigrants, particularly Jewish immigrants, some of whom embraced the dominant racist paradigm while others devised counterhegemonic modes of thinking and living within a white supremacist context. The density of Hillbrow's constructed environment meant that it would continue attracting immigrants while also providing niche spaces — such as jazz clubs, cafés, bars, bookstores, parks — for countercultural, nonpatriarchal, and queer expression.

As apartheid gave way to formal democracy, tens of thousands of people affected by wars and instability on the continent moved to Hillbrow, along with people from the townships of Johannesburg and other parts of South Africa. People from at least twenty-five African countries now live in Hillbrow and make up about 43 percent of its residents.[87] It is, as Alex Wafer writes, a place of "super-diversity."[88]

We believe that Hillbrow provides an important lens through which to investigate South Africa's and the region's numerous political and social transitions. We wanted to understand how people lived in Hillbrow prior to and following its most significant transition — in 1994 — and how they interpreted and made choices about how to live in South African society. What circumstances led them to the neighborhood, what opportunities did it provide for them, and how did they view the political and social order? As the neighborhood's buildings and infrastructure severely declined in the 1990s, it nonetheless attracted more people than ever. We asked why these new arrivals came to Hillbrow, what they hoped to find by moving to Johannesburg, and how they built — or attempted to build — their lives in the city.

Our method involved interviews with more than one hundred people, including anyone who has or has had a stake in Hillbrow: residents, religious leaders and congregants, social workers and social service providers, small business owners, property developers, teachers, and frequent visitors. We kept our questions minimal to provide as much time and opportunity for each participant to discuss issues most significant to them. Oftentimes, the simple prompts "What led you to Hillbrow?" and "What does the neighborhood mean to you?" elicited quite detailed and substantial responses that required little additional prompting.

Some of our conversations lasted for only a few minutes, but others continued for one, two, or several hours. Respondents discussed such topics as reasons for leaving their place of origin, the challenges and emotions associated with adjusting to a new location, finding housing, the challenges of raising a family, economic possibilities and survival strategies, formation of networks, xenophobia, safety, finding and belonging to religious institutions, and developing friendships or sexual and romantic relationships.

Caroline Wanjiku Kihato[89] writes that most social science focused on Johannesburg has been written "from above," that is, focused on the level of policymakers, governmental institutions, or planners. Like Kihato, we believe it is important to understand the contours of South African society by focusing on the lives of distinct individuals and their everyday interactions. Their memories, reflections, and accounts of current challenges provide vital interpretive evidence.

That evidence points not in one direction, but in many. We do not attempt to reach generalizable conclusions, but instead strive to show the many-sidedness of life before and after apartheid in one compact geographic neighborhood. Many published descriptions of contemporary Hillbrow label it as "poverty-stricken" or "crime-infested." Though not inaccurate, these phrases flatten and homogenize understandings of the neighborhood. Our method of collecting stories aims to enable people who actually live or have lived in or near Hillbrow to describe it. We are interested in the way personal reflections tell us how a neighborhood is inhabited, how memories shape relationships to the neighborhood even as newer memories are being made, and how inhabitants (long-term, recent, and migrant — permanent and temporary) of the neighborhood are cocreating lives and experiences in the city.

Lebo Machile, in the "Big Debate on Racism," stressed that what is needed now is "deep, emotional work — loving work, for South Africans to genuinely talk and to listen to one another." We are not South Africans, and we recognize the limitations of our understanding as privileged outsiders. But we are inspired by Machile's poetic sense that redressing centuries of racism requires not only knowledge and discovery but the emotional, loving work of listening along with radical structural change. We, too, as people from the United States, grew up in a system built on white supremacy and capitalist domination, sustained by state violence. Though the histories of the US and South Africa differ in substantial ways, they bear many similarities. They began as slave colonies that consolidated their territories after extensive conflict and forced displacement of indigenous populations. Both developed legal systems of racial stratification that, during most of their histories, benefited only their white populations. The South African intellectual, Njabulo Ndebele, has even called the US and South Africa "twins born at different times."[90]

2

Hillbrow and Apartheid

Jewish Hillbrow, Nationalism, and the Decades Leading to Apartheid

Before it became a "port-of-entry neighborhood" for migrants from across the African continent, Hillbrow played a somewhat similar role — in the late nineteenth century and early decades of the twentieth century — for Jewish migrants from Europe. After the assassination of Tsar Alexander II of Russia in 1881, deadly pogroms (anti-Jewish riots) swept through the western part of the Russian Empire. One of the suspected co-conspirators in the assassination was Jewish and, in response, hundreds of vengeful mobs targeted Jewish communities across Lithuania, Poland, and Ukraine. The riots sparked a massive migration of Jewish people from Eastern Europe, thousands of whom headed to South Africa. A second, even deadlier, wave of pogroms roiled Eastern Europe again from 1903 to 1906 and led to even more migration.[1]

Jewish Eastern Europeans who migrated to Johannesburg during the 1880s and 1890s arrived virtually penniless. They settled in the "slums" of Ferreirasdorp and Marshalltown, near the original mining camps. In contrast, Margot Rubin notes, better-off Jewish people, largely from Britain and Germany, lived in what was at first the relatively "posh" Doornfontein — to the southeast of Hillbrow. Over the years, many would migrate to communities north and east of Doornfontein. Rubin describes Hillbrow, Yeoville, Berea, and Doornfontein as having all become "predominantly Jewish" by 1920.[2]

About seventy thousand Jewish Eastern Europeans immigrated to South Africa between 1880 and 1948 — the year apartheid was formally introduced as state policy. Most arrived extremely poor, but "South Africa offered [them]

civic freedom in all essentials, as well as upward economic mobility and ultimate prosperity."[3] Many Jewish Eastern Europeans who became more prosperous during the 1920s began moving from heavily Jewish Doornfontein to
other places, such as Yeoville, Berea, and Hillbrow.

In the 1920s, the southern part of Hillbrow, just north of Doornfontein, had
also become home to a substantial German population. As National Socialist
German Workers' Party (Nazis) organizing intensified in Germany during
that decade, some of the Germans in Johannesburg embraced Nazism and
anti-Semitism. The Gentile National Socialist Movement (more commonly
the "Greyshirts") formed in 1933 and held boisterous rallies in Johannesburg,
where they harassed Jewish residents. "The message of all these organizations," write Richard Mendelsohn and Milton Shain, was that "Jews con-
trolled the press, dominated the economy, and exploited Afrikaners."[4]

German Nazi mobilization in South Africa in the 1930s overlapped with
an increasingly anti-Semitic thrust among the Afrikaner population. In 1934,
D. F. Malan, the man who would become the first prime minister of the
apartheid era in South Africa in 1948, broke away from the United Party and
founded the Purified National Party (PNP). That party made "the Jewish
Question" a central plank of its platform, which labeled Jewish South Africans "unassimilable."

During the 1930s, Hillbrow had substantial populations of Christian German migrants, along with Jewish Germans and Jewish Eastern Europeans. As
fascism descended over central Europe, Katrin Zürn-Steffens shows, struggles
developed in Hillbrow over how to respond to Nazis. Zürn-Steffens writes
that Jewish and Protestant Germans in Hillbrow for a time had a shared sense
of identity. Some Jewish schoolchildren attended the German School (the
Deutsche Schule Johannesburg) in Hillbrow. There was also a dues-paying
German Club with about one thousand members from both religious backgrounds. It had been founded by Jewish Germans, but as Nazi sympathies
among Protestant Germans in Johannesburg grew during the late 1920s, anti-
Semitic expressions became increasingly noticeable. Jewish leaders were expelled from the club and in 1930 many German Christians in the club "ap-
plauded" when South Africa's parliament enacted the Quota Act restricting
Jewish immigration from Europe.[5]

The German School in Hillbrow remained independent from Germany,
but a teacher formed a chapter of the Hitler Youth and students were pres-
sured to join. The school's remaining Jewish students left and, in 1936, the
school celebrated Hitler's birthday.[6]

Even as open sympathy with the Nazis was roiling the Friedenskirche (the
German Lutheran Church) and the German School on Hillbrow's southern

side, the "mother synagogue" of Progressive Judaism in South Africa rose on the northern side. The two houses of worship were less than a mile apart. Progressive Judaism (called Reform Judaism in the United States) had emerged in 1926 in London to "promote modernity among the global Jewish community."[7] In 1933, one of its founders, Lily Montagu, recruited and personally paid for Rabbi Moses Cyrus Weiler to move to South Africa to head the movement there. He was a twenty-six-year-old Latvian who had just completed his rabbinical studies at Hebrew College in New York.[8]

Gideon Shimoni[9] writes that Jewish Lithuanian communities in South Africa developed a marked "conservative traditionalism." But the progressive movement under Rabbi Weiler took notably different positions. Even before a permanent site had been selected for worship, the movement adopted a constitution specifying that women would have "complete equality" in the congregation and "could serve on any committee." The constitution also declared that there "would be no hierarchies of privilege or assigned seats and that there would be a paid, professional choir, including women and non-Jews."[10] Mendelsohn and Shain describe Rabbi Weiler as "deeply sensitive to the plight of the black majority," but also note that he refrained from criticizing the racist government out of fear that doing so would put the Jewish community in a dangerous position.[11]

Temple Israel, as it would be called, was built in Hillbrow because most of the money for its construction was donated by James Kapnek, a wealthy member who lived in nearby Parktown. Hermann Kallenbach, a close associate of Mohandas Gandhi, designed the building. The initial plan was for a large structure in Parktown, but congregants further south in Doornfontein objected that a temple in Parktown would be inaccessible to them. There is also speculation that, during a period of rising anti-Semitism, Hillbrow was seen as a safer neighborhood for the new synagogue than ultra-wealthy Parktown. Rabbi Weiler, buoyed by the ever-growing Jewish progressive community in Hillbrow, insisted that Temple Israel be built with twelve hundred seats. Ultimately, Temple Israel was built with just over five hundred seats, and for many decades they regularly filled to capacity.[12]

Apartheid—1948

When World War II ended, South Africa entered a period of rapid economic growth. Mendelsohn and Shain credit South Africa's rising prosperity for a precipitous decline in anti-Semitism. Since the Anglo-Boer War at the turn of the century, Afrikaners living in Johannesburg felt marginalized and increasingly resentful among English-speaking whites. After the war, however, an Afrikaner middle class emerged—largely on the basis of a racist system of labor—and "their sense of competition with and fear of the Jew declined." Afrikaners also realized that they could not construct apartheid without help from other whites, including Jewish whites.[13]

The National Party's victory in 1948 surprised and alarmed South Africa's Jewish community. The party had taken an explicit anti-Semitic position in 1938 but had lost overwhelmingly to the more pro-British (and less anti-Semitic) United Party. The United Party might have gone on to win subsequent elections but was badly weakened by internal division over whether to send troops to Europe to support the British during World War II.

As the war came to an end, the South African Jewish Board of Deputies developed a "Nine Point Programme," with the first of the points urging Jewish South Africans to oppose racial discrimination or caste in all instances. The board retreated from this position after the election of 1948, however, and declared that Jewish South Africans were not morally required to oppose racial discrimination as that stance might lead to discrimination and retaliation against themselves. As a sign of the increasing *rapprochement* between the Jewish and Afrikaner communities, Prime Minister Malan declared in 1948 that the South African government would not discriminate against Jewish South Africans — as long as there was no additional Jewish immigration.[14] This was a terrible blow but a compromise to which many Jewish people resigned themselves.

Afrikaner nationalism is often compared to fascism. But sociologist Pierre van den Berghe notes the differences — some significant and some superficial. "The *ideology* of Afrikaner Nationalism," he writes, "is a complex blend of provincialism, isolationism, xenophobia, pastoralism, egalitarianism within the *Herrenvolk* [Afrikaner community], and deeply ingrained colour prejudice with a touch of condescending benevolence so long as the master-servant relationship is unthreatened." Like fascist movements, Afrikaner nationalism glorified the past and aimed to return to a previous "Golden Age." But unlike fascists, Afrikaners did not "idealize the supremacy of the State at the expense of the individual or stress the *Führer* principle." Nonetheless, van den Berghe writes, despite the differences in the ideology, the methods used by the nationalist government became increasingly fascist and violent in their character.[15]

Bill[16] is a white Jewish man who lived through this time. He was born in Hillbrow and remained there throughout his ninety years. He started leading Friday night services as a lay reader at Temple Israel in 1996 and was still doing so at the age of eighty-nine, when interviewed at his men's clothing and shoe store in Johannesburg's CBD in 2019.

He attended Hillbrow's Twist Street Primary School in the 1930s and Parktown Boys' High School in the 1940s, both of which he could walk to from his home. He describes them as "very nice" and has no memory of anti-Semitism at those schools. "But they were all white," he says. "There was no mixing of the races in the city at that time."

Because Hillbrow was already thoroughly segregated, he explains, the 1948 election did not bring much difference to everyday life in the neighborhood. After the nationalists came to power, he recalls, "everything in Hillbrow stayed the same — it was just more strict."

"I remember the 1940s very well. They were very good years," he says. He clarifies that by "good years" he means that the neighborhood was a pleasant, interesting place to live and seemingly conflict-free. But the phrase also reflects his status as a white person in a country that was developing one of the most racially oppressive systems in the world. "Hillbrow was all one- and two-story houses then — ordinary housing. But it was very popular. The 'internationals' [European immigrants, mostly from Britain, Germany, Austria, Italy, and Portugal] came after World War II, so Hillbrow had restaurants and cafés then. But the higher buildings did not come until the 1950s."

Bill married and moved into one of those "higher buildings" in the late 1950s and started attending Temple Israel in Hillbrow in 1957. He describes the temple then as always full during Friday night and Saturday morning services and "especially packed" during the holidays. He recalls Rabbi Weiler as an inspiring religious leader who left the congregation in 1960. "He went to Israel," Bill says. "He had lost two sons there. I was sorry to see him go."

"Hillbrow offered everything in those days," recalls Barry[17] of the 1940s. Barry, who is Jewish, was born in Cape Town. When his father joined the South African army in 1940, Barry and his mother moved to a boardinghouse in Hillbrow. After his father returned from the war in Europe, the family remained in the neighborhood for several more years. He remembers it as a period of intensive construction and change. For instance, his family lived near the Hippodrome Theatre, which was torn down in 1950 to make way for a department store. Many nearby houses and buildings met the same fate as ever-larger buildings arose all around them.

For a white teenage male, Hillbrow offered plenty of leisure activities. "On the corner of Kotze and Banket was a café called The Oasis," Barry says. "That was a great attraction for us teenagers. My friends and I also liked to visit the Golden Ray Coffee Shop, which became so popular that it left its first location on Kotze Street and moved into the Ambassador Hotel on Pretoria Street. The Ambassador was a very smart hotel in those days. It was next to the Curzon Theatre near the Florian Hotel. There is nothing quite like [that] Hillbrow now."

He met Eve, who would become his wife, in Hillbrow in the early 1950s. She lived in Benoni, a suburb nineteen miles from Hillbrow, but at the age of seventeen began working at an advertising agency in Hillbrow. An express train would take her directly to Hillbrow every morning. One of the couple's fondest memories of Hillbrow in the 1950s is of Exclusive Books, which became one of the city's first bookstores and a major draw.

Eve later began volunteering at a crèche (prekindergarten) in Hillbrow. Even after the couple moved to a northern suburb, she would remain with the same crèche for several decades, until the mid-2010s, as it began serving what became a far poorer community. Barry became a lawyer and a "stalwart" member of the Progressive Federal Party, and Eve joined the Black Sash, a white women's organization that held nonviolent protests against apartheid.

Clive M. Chipkin[18] is a white Jewish man (now deceased; at the time of the interview in his nineties), who became one of Johannesburg's most preeminent architectural critics. He authored two major volumes on Johannesburg history. He was born in Yeoville and never lived in Hillbrow, but many of his friends at King Edward VII School in Houghton were from Hillbrow.

"It was very English Empire," he says of King Edward VII. "It was very good then and is still good now. I finished school in 1946 and, sometime after that, Hillbrow began to change very, very rapidly. It was a total transformation. As a boy, and later as a young man, my friends and I took the tram to the CBD, which went from Yeoville through Berea and Hillbrow. We did not own cars—no one did. The center of attraction in the 1940s and 1950s was the CBD, but we always went through Hillbrow and sometimes we stopped there. There were all these restaurants and places with pinball machines. In those years, Hillbrow was not a high-density area—not yet. It was a medium-density area. You had a lot of Cape Dutch architecture and a lot of houses with corrugated iron roofs.

"Then there was a sudden transformation," Clive continues. "In twenty years, all the houses were torn down. There was chaotic change between the end of World War II and 1960. There was no planning. Industrialization in Johannesburg had started early—after the Boer War. But in the 1930s, the American cars came. Suddenly, we had traffic jams. We were so proud to have traffic jams!"

Clive explains that much of Hillbrow's transformation was guided by the work of Le Corbusier. Le Corbusier's plans for city living made heavy use of concrete slabs and modular housing and placed an emphasis on high-density living. The high-density construction in Hillbrow came to be known as the "Hillbrow Vernacular."

"That's a phrase used by Sir Nikolaus Pevsner," Clive explains. "Pevsner came from England to South Africa in 1952, when he was already a great scholar. He arrived in a country that had not been affected by the war and finds an unbelievable building boom in Hillbrow. It was all modernist architecture at a time when England had very little modern architecture. He began to call Hillbrow 'Little Brazil in the Commonwealth.' South Africa had made a lot of money during the war and much of that money went into real estate. In Hillbrow, it led to dense — but not yet very dense — modern buildings. In 1953, Pevsner wrote very dramatic descriptions of what he saw in Hillbrow."

Federico Freschi, Brenda Schmahmann, and Lize van Robbroeck explain that the Brazilian influence on South African architecture intersected with the rise of Afrikaner nationalism. When Afrikaner nationalists assumed total power over the state, they "commissioned buildings [that] generally had decorative programs that parlayed the blood-and-soil imagery of the 1930s into increasingly abstract forms that promoted new imaginaries of progress and achievement." Their objective was to portray a confident modernity to the world, and it was heavily influenced by the Afrikaners' belief that they were chosen by God to settle, and through their sacrifice, rule South Africa. In 1943, the University of Pretoria (then an Afrikaans-language university) had established a school of architecture which came to be heavily influenced by the *Brazil Builds* exhibition that was hosted in New York City that year. That exhibition was so influential that Brazilian architectural ideas — especially the emphasis on buildings of enormous scale — heavily influenced architects at the University of Pretoria and spread to Johannesburg.[19] That "enormous scale" is reflected in many parts of Hillbrow and Berea.

In his book, Chipkin writes that the "Hillbrow Vernacular," influenced by the *Brazil Builds* exhibition, reflected the "transporting of modern utopian ideas into the environment of anarchic land use, laissez-faire economics and the banality and indifference of speculative building."[20] There was a chance, for a while, that Hillbrow might have become a genuinely cosmopolitan urban space amid the totalitarianism of apartheid. But the building developers used shortcuts, cost-cutting methods, and short-term thinking. They produced what Chipkin views as a monotonous, alienating landscape of unimaginative high-rises. "As early as the 1950s," he writes, "people worried that overbuilding on the scale of the Hillbrow Vernacular would inevitably lead the neighborhood to become a 'vast future slum yard.'"[21]

Lael Bethlehem[22] did not live through the years of Hillbrow's primary building boom. But as someone who has worked for several agencies that redevelop buildings in Johannesburg, she has a perspective on Hillbrow similar to Chipkin's. "Because Hillbrow was planned from the 1940s as a hyper-modernist neighborhood in the Le Corbusier model," she says, "this has become an intractable problem. Hillbrow was built with massive towers and almost no green space. There are a handful of very small parks. But overall, it offers density without the pleasant, diverting, open spaces that would have made it a truly great physical space."

Queer Hillbrow Emerges

Martin J. Murray writes that during the 1950s Hillbrow "became a vast testing ground" for Manhattan-like urban living. He echoes Clive Chipkin's and Lael Bethlehem's criticisms when he writes that the neighborhood was marred by "feverish overbuilding" that led to structures that were "similar in style and uniform in size."[23] But it was this resultant density that enabled Hillbrow and Joubert Park (a neighborhood on Hillbrow's southwestern border) to produce South Africa's first "protogay" neighborhood.[24]

The first signs of a queer Joubert Park/Hillbrow[25] can be traced back to World War II, a few years before the building boom. During the war, the government built an army camp in Joubert Park. Men began to meet one another for romantic and sexual encounters in bars that served soldiers at the camp. The bars were not gay bars, but amid their otherwise "heterosexual clientele" men looking to meet other men developed ways of identifying one another. Similarly, in Durban and Cape Town, men began to meet each other around military ships in the harbor. After the war ended, the bars in Joubert Park closed but many of the people who moved to be near them remained.

With the proliferation of apartment buildings in the 1950s, Hillbrow and Joubert Park became neighborhoods for young, single people. The studio and small, one-bedroom apartments were seen as best suited for people — white people — who were starting their adult lives. Several buildings developed a reputation for having queer tenants. Mark Gevisser and Edwin Cameron (Cameron later became a justice of the Constitution Court, 2009–19) point to one building in Hillbrow called Reynard Hall as an example. By the mid-1950s, it housed so many lesbians and gay men that it became unofficially known as "Radclyffe Hall," after the lesbian novelist by that name. In the 1990s, Gevisser and Cameron interviewed a woman who lived in "Radclyffe Hall" during that time. "I had a helluva lot of parties," she told them. "There was always terrific music, and tens of beautiful women crammed into my little flat. I had very young people mixing with me. Because they were living at home and couldn't let their hair down, they used my place as a gathering point. As we say in gangster-talk, it was a 'safe-house.'"[26]

In addition to its density, and the preponderance of young, single people,

Hillbrow was also home to several theaters. Club 58 had opened in 1930 in the center of Hillbrow and was so successful that a few years later it opened an additional cabaret space on the second floor. That same decade, the Andre Huguenet Theatre opened on Kapteijn Street, and the Clarendon opened in 1940, followed by Cinema International.[27] Theaters attracted young people and a budding queer community. By the 1970s, Club 58 would become an explicitly gay space.

A Queer, but Whites-Only, Space

By the 1950s, Gevisser and Cameron note, South Africa's three major cities — Johannesburg, Cape Town, and Durban — had developed identifiable, if still largely clandestine, queer subcultures. Despite periodic crackdowns by the police, they were "relatively unharassed."[28] In Johannesburg, the queer male culture that developed after the war concentrated in a handful of bars such as those at the Carlton Hotel and the Waldorf. White women in South Africa earned less money than their male counterparts "as a matter of course." With less disposable income, lesbian subcultures in the 1950s were based on networks of friends, although by the 1960s the city had a handful of identifiable lesbian bars. Cape Town had a long history of "moffie" — a derogatory but sometimes positive self-identifying term for "gay" — culture based in the Cape Malay community, and there were plenty of same-sex encounters in Black men's worker hostels.

Black men also had ongoing relationships with other men at the mining compounds. Indeed, Isak Niehaus explains that male-male sex was "the dominant expression of sexuality" both in the compounds and in prisons. Men in both locations had limited access to women, even their own wives. Yet the male-male relationships were not merely, as the old trope claims, a matter of men making do with other men because of a lack of women. Niehaus believes that male-male sexual relationships presented and still present "a unique opportunity for realising intimacy and romance."[29] Men asked other, often younger, men to be their "mine wives." The younger man, the wife, cared for the older man, the husband, including completing traditionally female work such as cleaning, cooking, and sex. The "mine husband" gave his wife "lots of money," protection from the violence of other men, and "great kindness."[30] The couple sometimes even had a mine wedding and might stay together until they left the mine.

For young white and queer people, Hillbrow and other parts of the central city were increasingly places of promise and new possibilities for self-expression. For all other "racial groups," these areas were anything but. Gugu

Hlongwane writes that "for black, coloured, and Indian masses the city was a place of deep anxiety, entrenched segregation and often certain death." From the beginning of the gold rush through to the end of apartheid, she writes, "working masses who flocked to urban areas like Johannesburg . . . returned home with virtually nothing to show." They were enriching the mining companies while living in homelands and townships that were "wretched spaces of abandoned people."[31]

Year after year through the 1950s and 1960s, the legislative screws of apartheid turned ever tighter. White people could enjoy the flourishing economy and the increasingly cosmopolitan streets of Hillbrow while remaining largely oblivious to racism's deadly and deadening progression. In 1950, an amendment to the Immorality Act prohibited sexual encounters between "Europeans" and "non-Europeans." The Suppression of Communism Act of the same year allowed the government to "ban" persons for suspected communist activities — which, in practice, meant any "anti-government" activities.

The Group Areas Act of 1950 (GAA) mandated the confinement of all "races" to separate residential areas. It led to thousands of evictions of Indians, Coloured people, and Black Africans who were living in "white" areas and formalized and expanded the "townships" on the outskirts of cities. The GAA was complemented by the Population Registration Act, which forced Black people to carry a "dompass" (passbook) which contained fingerprints, photographs, and personal information.

The Bantu Authorities Act of 1951 established separate "homelands" for Black Africans, in rural areas far from the cities. In 1952, the Native Laws Amendment Act forbade anyone from leaving a "homeland" without government permission, enabled police to arrest any Black person caught without a dompass, and extended passbook requirements to Black women. The Public Safety Act of 1953 gave the government power to arrest and detain, without trial, anyone suspected of dissent. The Criminal Law Amendment Act of 1953 declared that anyone accompanying a person found guilty of committing an offense while protesting a law was to be presumed guilty themselves. The Bantu Education Act of 1953 established a separate education system for Black African students to be run by the Department of Native Affairs, with the primary objective of keeping Black South Africans out of white schools and training them to work only in "homelands" or to labor for whites.[32]

As apartheid's grip tightened, and in the "shadow of government violence," Loren Kruger writes, Johannesburg celebrated its seventieth anniversary in 1956. The 1954 Natives Resettlement Act had given the government the power to remove any Black African people who lived next to Johannesburg. One of the government's targets was Sophiatown, a mixed neighborhood known then as the city's center of Black African art, music, and culture. It had been zoned for four thousand people but housed more than ten times that number. In February 1955, the government sent two thousand police officers armed with rifles to begin removing Sophiatown's residents from their homes. People fought back with their own guns and with explosives. Over the course of the next five years, the government tore down the homes and businesses in Sophiatown and, in the 1960s, declared it an all-white neighborhood that they renamed "Triomf."[33] (The neighborhood, which is now 41 percent white, 27 percent Black African, 26 percent Coloured, and 5 percent Asian, was once again named Sophiatown as of 2006.)[34]

The Natives Taxation and Development Act of 1958 raised the minimum tax that all Black men in South Africa were required to pay and, for the first time, imposed a minimum tax on all Black women. The impact was that low-income Black South Africans had to pay a higher proportion of their income than low-income whites and were required to begin paying taxes at the age of eighteen, whereas members of other racial groups were not compelled to pay a minimum tax until the age of twenty-one. Remarkably, only Black African people could be imprisoned for nonpayment of taxes.

In 1962, the Terrorism Act allowed for indefinite detention without trial of anyone that a police officer suspected of terrorism. The Criminal Procedure Act of 1965 gave the state the power to detain anyone for 180 days if the government thought they might be able to provide evidence in a criminal proceeding, and to keep such persons in solitary confinement with no access to an attorney. That act also took away the ability of any court to order the release of a detainee.[35]

Sophie Mgcina is a performer, singer, theatrical director, and educator who recalls what it was like to perform as a Black African woman in Hillbrow during the 1950s and 1960s. From the age of nineteen, she began singing at a club called the Night Beat and was arrested almost every evening after her performances. She says she became used to walking into the police van, getting taken to Marshall Square, and then paying two pounds to get released, after which she would go back to Hillbrow and perform again. "It was work and it was a challenge," she says in a documentary called *The Man Who Drove with Mandela*, "but it made me feel that I was somebody. I needed to fight the system in some way." Mgcina was born in 1938 in Germiston, but the apartheid government had forced her family to move to the township of Alexandra. In her triumphant later career, she would perform in London and New York, translate songs from English to several African languages, and in 1994, be given the task of forming the National School for the Performing Arts in Johannesburg.[36]

Cecil Williams: The Man Who Drove with Mandela

Cecil Williams was a gay white man and communist antiapartheid activist who was arrested with Nelson Mandela in 1962.[37] His remarkable life, as recounted in the documentary *The Man Who Drove with Mandela*, referenced above, offers a revealing glimpse into the complex intersections of race, sexuality, political activism, and resistance during apartheid's first two decades. He was born in Cornwall, England, to working-class parents and moved to Johannesburg in 1928. Like many other gay men at the time, Williams had a sexual awakening when he met a man in Joubert Park while attending university. His politicization developed when he was a reporter for the South African Broadcasting Corporation, during World War II, while stationed in Rome. There, Williams learned sexual relations between men did not have to be hidden. He also realized that Black South African soldiers fighting in Europe were paid half the amount of their white counterparts and were supplied with only spears rather than guns. This realization led him to join the South African Communist Party.

After the war, Williams and his friends in the Communist Party were horrified to witness the coming to power of the National Party. Though these friends described him as a "bit aristocratic," they said he could also be a "street brawler" when he protested against apartheid. They also recall that they never imagined he might be a "homosexual." He moved onto the sixteenth floor of the Anstey's Building in Johannesburg's CBD where he lived a discreet gay life, surrounded as that building was by others populated with actors, set designers, and theater producers. Williams briefly became an English teacher at King Edward VII High School, where Chipkin (above) had been a student, but resigned in anger because he felt that the school's military-style discipline was raising children to become fascists. He later became a theater director and coached numerous actors, Black and white, including Sophie Mgcina (mentioned above).

Just as Williams's fellow communists had difficulty believing he might be gay, he himself wrote that it took him many years to realize Black gay people existed given, in his experience, their complete invisibility in queer white spaces. He had learned to search for other gay men in Joubert Park and discovered gay beach areas in Cape Town, but Black gay people rarely if ever had access to such places. Even those with passes to enter the city were not permitted to walk there after dark. There were no pubs and no private spaces for them in whites-only Johannesburg.

In 1955, the Congress of the People, a multiracial political meeting in Kliptown, Soweto, adopted the Freedom Charter and declared open resistance to apartheid. Cecil Williams began to host dinner parties for Nelson Mandela, Winnie Mandela, and members of the Communist Party. Nelson Mandela frequently visited Williams in his apartment building but was forced to walk up sixteen flights as only whites were permitted to use the elevator.

After the Sharpeville massacre of 1960 the government declared a state of emergency. It banned Nelson Mandela's organization, the African National Congress (ANC), and arrested a broad swath of white and Black antiapartheid activists. Williams was among those apprehended and confined in the Old Fort Prison in Hillbrow, where he entertained other prisoners by staging theatrical productions.

The widespread arrests of apartheid's opponents led Mandela to reconsider the efficacy of nonviolence. He, Walter Sisulu, and communist leader Joe Slovo formed the guerrilla organization Umkhonto we Sizwe in 1962. This organization would carry out acts of sabotage against government installations and critical public facilities, though with the intent of minimizing any possible deaths. Mandela then left for a tour of several African countries, where he met with leaders of newly freed states and raised funds. Because he was a "banned person" and wanted by the government for treason, when Mandela returned to South Africa he had to be smuggled across the border of Botswana (then known as Bechuanaland).[38]

The plan was to have Williams meet him in Botswana and then drive across the border, with Mandela posing as a chauffeur and Williams posing as his employer in the backseat. They managed to get through the border and drive to Durban. But on their way from Durban to Johannesburg, they briefly switched roles and Williams began driving for a stint. The police apprehended and arrested them both. They released Williams but detained Mandela, who would spend the next twenty-seven years in a series of prisons. Back in Johannesburg, a doorperson at the Anstey's Building warned Williams that police were waiting for him in his flat. He enlisted the help of a friend to drive him across the border into Bechuanaland, then to Bulawayo, from where he would fly to London and remain in the UK for the rest of his life.[39]

Bus Boycotts and the Sharpeville Massacre

As apartheid legislation grew increasingly severe, resistance — and the risk of resisting — increased. In 1957, tens of thousands of commuters in Alexandra, a Black African township north of the central city, launched a bus boycott in response to a 20 percent increase in fares. Their incomes were so low that the spike in fares presented a wrenching blow to their abilities to feed and house their families. In some ways mirroring the Montgomery, Alabama, bus boycott of 1955, Alexandra's workers began walking several miles to and from their job-sites. The effort quickly spread to other Black communities, including places such as Germiston and Edenvale, where residents did not face increased fares but walked in solidarity with the Alexandra boycotters.[40]

Mary-Louise Hooper lived in Hillbrow in 1957 and witnessed the boycotters walking along her street in Hillbrow morning after morning. "At first," she writes, "they came singing, or tootling on their penny whistles, especially on the lovely spring mornings. Later they slogged along wearily and silently. The daily trudging of nine miles to work and nine miles home again, after an eight-hour day, subdued their spirits even as it had worn out their shoes. Often they were caught in the sudden, violent summer storms . . . [and b]abies strapped on their mother's backs, wash-bundles balanced on heads, and precious shoes would all be soaked."[41]

A total of about seventy thousand people participated. The national government ordered the police to "crush the boycott," and officers harassed walkers by demanding to see their passes. About fourteen thousand people were arrested for pass violations. The police deflated the tires of bicyclists and searched the cars of drivers who offered rides to the boycotters. But after ten weeks, the boycott resulted in a "complete victory for the people," in the words of one of its organizers. The government reduced the cost of the fare and agreed to study the need for higher wages.[42]

In 1960, a group calling itself the Pan Africanist Congress (PAC) broke away from the ANC and decided to "launch a nationwide campaign for the total abolition of the pass laws." Its organizer, Stephen Sobukwe, emphasized that all actions against the pass laws should retain an "absolute commitment" to nonviolence as a path to freedom for South Africa's Black people. When a crowd of around five thousand unarmed protesters reached the police station in Sharpeville, a township forty-three miles south of Johannesburg, they faced three hundred armed police officers. The police would later claim that the crowd had begun stoning them, but an eyewitness reporter wrote that only three officers were hit by stones. The South African police often dispersed crowds of protesters with batons, but in Sharpeville they gave the crowd no warning to disperse and opened fire for two full minutes. The confrontation killed 69 protesters and left 180 seriously wounded.[43]

The Sharpeville massacre generated horrified reactions around the world. The British Commonwealth expelled South Africa in 1961. At first, the government was shaken both by the resistance and the international response. Ultimately, however, it turned the massacre to its advantage. It claimed to its white voters that stone-throwing protesters in Sharpeville were a sign of waves of violence to come if the government did not further suppress the Black African population.

Though the government expected global condemnation to have a negative impact on the economy, the next ten years brought South Africa's greatest economic expansion yet.[44] The country began attracting significant levels of investment from the United States (including by Halley's grandfather), and much of that investment went into Hillbrow real estate. Whereas the average height of a Hillbrow building during the 1950s was twelve stories, during the economic boom of the 1960s new buildings started at eighteen stories and rose much higher — to twenty, thirty, and forty stories. "The demand for Hillbrow accommodation seemed endless," writes Chipkin.[45]

Chipkin also notes that Hillbrow's cultural fare blossomed during this period. The jazz pianist Chris McGregor started bringing musicians from Black African townships to play at Hillbrow venues. As a result, the noted writer Can Themba began calling Hillbrow and Berea the "white Sophiatown."[46] Meanwhile, in 1961, Nelson Mandela was living underground and spent two months hiding out with the communist activist Wolfie Kodesh in his flat in Berea.[47]

During the 1960s, Martin Murray writes, Hillbrow became a place for newcomers — mostly people from the UK, France, Italy, Greece, Germany, and Portugal.[48] By the end of the 1960s, due to the new, high-density buildings, the neighborhood's population had ballooned to twenty-five thousand (although this is a fraction of what it would become by the end of the century).[49] Stadler and Dugmore write that about 30 percent of Hillbrow's residents in the 1960s were European immigrants or expats. They also note that the large supply of studio and one-bedroom apartments made Hillbrow one of the centers of Johannesburg's sex work industry at this time. Critics of Hillbrow who stigmatize the neighborhood today forget that sex work has been concentrated there for decades. Then, as now, sex work was a viable way for people to earn a living in the city.[50]

By the mandate of the Group Areas Act, Hillbrow was zoned exclusively for white people. However, the law granted one exception. Black African domestic workers were permitted to live in Hillbrow if they worked for white families, but their living conditions were highly regulated. A gratuitously cruel architectural feature emerged that would later become known as the "locations in the sky." Even today, a pedestrian walking through Hillbrow will notice a row of tiny windows on the top floors of most buildings, markedly smaller than the windows on all other floors. Domestic workers were required to live in cramped, shared quarters on the top floors. Windows were placed near the ceiling for ventilation, but their height and small size were intended to keep Black workers from partaking of the views that white tenants could enjoy.

Even under these tightly constrained circumstances, the government periodically cracked down on domestic workers living in Hillbrow. Hendrik Verwoerd, who was the minister of native affairs in the early 1950s and became the prime minister in 1958, was determined to reduce the number of Black Africans living in white central-city neighborhoods. About one in every ten people living in Hillbrow was a domestic worker at that time. Legislation in 1955, passed at the urging of Verwoerd, restricted the number of Black people living on the rooftops in Johannesburg to five per building. The total number of domestic workers removed from "these locations in the sky" was between eight thousand and ten thousand, although it is not known how many lived in Hillbrow.[51]

Queer Organizing

During the 1960s, queer organizing became more public and the queer presence in Hillbrow more visible. Simultaneously, crackdowns increased in South Africa. On January 22, 1966, the police raided a large party in the posh northern suburb of Forest Town. There were 350 people present, but they arrested nine men in drag for "masquerading as women," which was against the law. Gevisser and Cameron write that the National Party had been able to consolidate its power through its use of "bogeymen" or scapegoats, whether they were Black, English, or Jewish. It intended to do the same with the gay men in Forest Town. Previous antiqueer legislation had been aimed at public expressions of homosexuality, but this raid at a private home sparked fears that the government was moving into the private sphere. To persecute queer people, police proposed using informers to identify them.

One lesbian who looked back on the days after Forest Town told Gevisser and Cameron: "We were terrified. There was a rumor that women would not be allowed to live together." Just as they left England when the British Crown prosecuted Oscar Wilde for "posing as a Sodomite" in the late nineteenth century, many queer people began to leave South Africa after the Forest Town case.[52]

Ultimately, the raid had the opposite effect. It led to the Homosexual Law Reform Fund, which raised money to hire a lawyer against the proposed legislation. The organization held a public meeting in 1968 at a hotel in Joubert Park, which became the "first gay public meeting ever held in South Africa." Queer people began meeting, donating, and organizing. One informant told Gevisser and Cameron: "Suddenly, gay life flourished and there were more parties than ever before. People seemed to forget their differences." Another informant told them that by the 1970s there were so many queer establishments in Hillbrow that he had a gay butcher, a gay tailor, a gay grocer, and could visit gay-friendly restaurants all over Pretoria Street.[53]

Despite this flourishing of a (white) lesbian and gay subculture, Morris writes that the government also sowed the seeds of Hillbrow's physical decline during the 1960s. It had decided to curtail the development of housing and land for Indian, Coloured, and Black people, thereby creating a severe shortage of suitable places to live for these growing populations. As that shortage, and the resultant overcrowding, worsened, ever more people were desperate to move into inner-city housing. They would begin doing so in the 1980s, because no matter how crowded or neglected the housing in Hillbrow, it offered better alternatives than what could be found in the severely neglected townships.[54]

David — "I realized very quickly that I had gotten into the wrong place"

David,[55] a white Jewish man, was born in 1939 at the Queen Victoria Hospital on the Hillbrow/Parktown border. In the 1950s, David's father, Leopold Grinker, developed a reputation as a pioneer in South African architecture by bringing the Frank Lloyd Wright style to South Africa (large rooms, glass doors, stamped earth bricks). Several of Leopold Grinker's buildings remain in Hillbrow today, but David does not remember their names or exact locations at this point.

A website describing South African architecture notes that Grinker was a fierce critic of Le Corbusier's modernism and objected to its "arrogance." It quotes Chipkin: "He [Leopold Grinker] was by nature a rebel: an anti-establishment man in politics, anti-mainstream in architecture. Although he was regarded as an outsider for much of his life, it was only after he died in 1973 a disillusioned man that his eccentric views became more acceptable to a younger generation of architects."[56]

David went to live in Israel in 1955, when he was eighteen or nineteen. He had no interest in Israel or its politics at the time, he just wanted to live on a kibbutz and learn Hebrew. When he returned, he settled into a flat in Berea with his girlfriend.

"At the time," he says, "Doornfontein had already faded as a Jewish community. Yeoville really became the center of Johannesburg Jewry. Hillbrow was different. It was a mix of everyone. Though it had a large Jewish community, it was certainly not predominantly Jewish — whereas Jews were the solid majority in Yeoville. Also, Yeoville was more progressive. Hillbrow was larger and denser, so it had a greater range of people. They went from very progressive people to apartheid supporters to outright fascists. Yeoville was smaller, more Jewish, and more progressive. Everyone lived under the apartheid government, but in Yeoville they did not support it. One thing that was remarkable about Hillbrow was its blend of Jews and Germans. In 1957, I went into a German restaurant on Pretoria Street and saw that there was a picture of Hitler on the walls. I realized very quickly that I had gotten into the wrong place!"

When he married and had children, he moved to Yeoville and took his children to Hillbrow every Sunday. "The big draw for me was the bookstores — Estoril and Exclusive Books," he says. "I started working at Exclusive Books on Kotze Street in the late 1950s, before it moved to Pretoria Street. People came to Exclusive from all over. It and Estoril were really the only two bookstores in the city at that time, with the exception of CNA, which was really a magazine shop."

After David's wife died, he remarried. His wife, Edith, is a Xhosa woman who worked as a chef at Bella Napoli, an Italian restaurant and nightclub in Hillbrow. The couple continues to live in Yeoville, where David helps raise Edith's grandchildren.

Paul Davis — "Nice cafés and shady characters"

Paul Davis[57] is a white man and a doctor who was born and raised in Parktown. When he attended Parktown Boys' High School, from 1960 to 1963, many of his classmates lived in Hillbrow and he visited them often. He describes Hillbrow in the early 1960s as "an always vibrant and interesting place of which you were warned by your parents to be careful — not because of crime, but because of the edginess of the place. There was plenty of trouble to be gotten into. There were shady characters. It had a fascination for us all. There were very nice cafés, for instance. It was like Vienna but was too expensive for us to enjoy the cafés. Our parents would drop us off in Hillbrow with strict orders to behave."

When asked if, by "shady characters," he means drug dealers, Paul smiles and says: "No, they were not drug dealers. They were the sorts of people who could sit in the coffee bars all day and nobody knew what they were doing. Many were Greeks or other recent immigrants from Europe. It was cosmopolitan. There was also a lot of gambling going on in the coffee shops, most of it hidden — but some of the bookkeeping was in the open. The card games were in the open. There was also quite a lot of fencing — people bringing [stolen] goods from everywhere and selling them. There might have been some selling of hash from the stores, but I don't think there were any hard drugs at that time.

"But my parents were extremely worried about homosexuality," he continues. "They were Jewish, but it was the feeling of the day, the dominance of Afrikaner culture, which was all about masculinity. They were worried that you could be seduced by some randy male who might be hanging out in Hillbrow. Homophobia was so pervasive in South Africa. It was pervasive in all aspects of society. I did meet a homosexual couple there once when I was in my teens. That was very good for me to see. They were so supportive."

Paul also offers a more general sense of Hillbrow in the 1960s. "It was a waypoint for new arrivals—as it is now," he says. "Everything was there for them. It was also a place that Jews felt safe to move out of. They didn't need to stay in a shtetl as they did in Europe. As their fortunes rose, Jews could move from a place like Hillbrow to one of the northern suburbs without feeling any kind of threat. And there were African homeless people living on the streets, even then. There were plenty of beggars. And there were street cleaners, building workers, domestics, and municipal workers. So there was always a Black presence. Sometimes people would sleep on the streets because it was too expensive to go back home after work.

"Hillbrow was a melting pot," Paul continues. "It was the place where all the intellectuals hung out. It was really like the Algonquin Hotel. There were some bohemians in the 1960s, but they were not quite flower children—that was more at the university. Surely, there must have been some predators. The Florian Café was very sophisticated. It was like the days of old Vienna—with heavy, dark, wooden furniture—and it was smoky. But the owners were so welcoming. In fact, I think the wife [one of the owners of the hotel] made the strudel herself. The Crest Hotel was bought by Jewish owners who had left Rhodesia [now Zimbabwe] in the early 1960s. They had hotels, mostly for ex-Rhodesians."

Paul explains that when he started medical school at the University of the Witwatersrand in the mid-1960s he began spending much more time in Hillbrow. "The medical students hung out at the Quirinale Hotel, which had an interesting bar," he recalls. "It was close to the medical schools and the hospitals. And there was Lenny's, which was owned by a German immigrant of that name, which had great sandwiches on Claim Street. And, of course, there was the Porterhouse Steak House, an avant-garde American-style restaurant where even poor students could afford steak and chips. Then there was a German restaurant down the hill. We all knew of 'Charlie the One-Eyed Waiter' at that restaurant. They served a bowl of mandatory pea soup as a first course and then anything else you wanted. It was sometimes an offensive place. They celebrated Hitler's birthday and sometimes they had a swastika on the wall, which was eventually removed. They had big parties on the street — we never went there — but they were never violent."

While at medical school, Paul joined and became the chair of the African Night School. "There were two places in Johannesburg that the Group Areas Act had forgotten," he explains. "They were the Flower Market in Newtown, which became the Market Theatre, and the University of the Witwatersrand. So we started a formal African school, the African Night School, that held classes from 7:00 to 10:00 every night. Men and women — mostly the domestic workers and gardeners from Parktown and Hillbrow — came to take classes. I was the president of the school until it was finally banned. It was banned when the government ruled that no one could come onto the campus at night. Then it moved somewhere else in Braamfontein and was taken over by another group. But this is one of the things that the security police came to grill me about."

Paul elaborates on his encounter with the security police: "Three large men came to my grandfather's house one day and they took me to a building somewhere. At first, I thought it was a joke put on by my mates in school [like a fraternity hazing]. It would have been like them. My mother thought that was the case, too. But then I was held for four days. I was questioned about everything. They had every detail about what I had written. I was not tortured or beaten, but I was kept awake most of the four days. I was never officially in the Communist Party, but these security police were obviously focused on that. They wanted to know all about the African Night School."

Paul adds one more intriguing detail about Hillbrow during the 1960s. "The Summit Club [a large building on Pretoria Street] went up at the end of the 1960s and it was a turning point," he says. "It went up first as a hotel, but then it became a place for sexual encounters. It has this very imposing exterior, which makes you think it would be a formal and sophisticated place. But there were booths for sex, and you could rent by the hour. The swimming pool functioned a lot like a gay men's bathhouse — but it was not only gay. There were drugs. The owners must have paid someone off. But also, the government had infiltrated the Summit Club. The CCB [Civil Cooperation Bureau], also known as the 'death squads,' were called the 'assassins for the government.' The Summit became a place for them to get compromising material on their enemies. That's why there were always a strange contingent of Afrikaners there. It was an attempt at entrapment. And, you know, there were always big, homophobic Afrikaners that would wander around Hillbrow and beat up gay men. They would knock them around. They would accuse them of 'looking at my penis.'"

Paul wraps up his description of Hillbrow in the 1960s: "It was completely different to anywhere else in Johannesburg. The other places were all staid suburbs. The CBD died at night and Hillbrow stayed alive."

The Early 1970s

Gevisser and Cameron[58] write that the early 1970s brought the "pinking of Hillbrow." It started with the Butterfly Bar, a gay men's establishment that opened in the Harrison Reef Hotel on Pretoria Street and would eventually serve as an anchor for queer Hillbrow for the next two decades. But even as it provided space for an increasingly visible queer minority of white gay men, it actively upheld South Africa's racial and sexual hierarchy. During its first ten years or so, the Butterfly prohibited anyone who was not white from entering. It excluded women, white and of color, even longer, until 1994. A lesbian establishment, called the Together Bar, opened in 1974 at the Ambassador Hotel on Pretoria Street a block from the Butterfly. It would remain a lesbian bar until 1989.[59]

As a reflection of Hillbrow's growing urban edginess, Gevisser and Cameron write, the Butterfly was always "jam-packed" and "a notoriously rough place." There were sometimes knife fights at the Together Bar. Around the corner from the Butterfly, the sex trade was also burgeoning as "rent boys" (male sex workers) lingered on the street. "Rent scenes" were also developing in Hillbrow movie theaters. They were "ordinary cinemas" where men would have sex with one another while watching a film.[60]

Gary,[61] a white Jewish man in his late sixties, confirms the presence of an increasingly "rough edge" in Hillbrow starting from the early 1970s. Even as it remained one of the city's most popular destinations for restaurants, bookstores, and entertainment spaces, he says, "there were gangs in the area. The 'ducktails' were a [white] gang on motorcycles that terrorized pedestrians. The stores and restaurants on Pretoria Street had to pay the local mafia to operate. The mafia at that time were Greeks and they dominated the streets."

Whether Gary's memory of a Greek mafia is correct — we have also heard this from others but have discovered no further evidence — Hillbrow was certainly ablaze with activity. Taki Xenopolous had opened the Fontana Bakery in the Highpoint Tower in 1968 as South Africa's first twenty-four-hour store. He famously threw away the key during the opening ceremony and proclaimed that the store would never close. Through the 1970s, its roast chicken and rolls would make it a popular spot for clubgoers who would sit at its indoor and outdoor tables until dawn.[62] The Fontana remains open as a supermarket as of the writing of this book.

"By the early 1970s," Melinda Silverman writes, "Hillbrow had become an entertainment magnet for ordinarily conservative white suburbanites. The area offered clubs, jazz bars, late-night bookstores, record shops and ambience — Café Pigalle, Café Zürich, Café Wien, Café de Paris, Café Florian. Hillbrow was Johannesburg's equivalent of London's Soho or New York's Greenwich Village."[63]

Johannesburg's postwar industrial boom had expanded through the 1960s and into the 1970s, according to Silverman, providing full employment for Johannesburg's prospering white middle class. As a sign of white Johannesburg's rising fortunes, planning began in 1969 for a particularly extravagant symbol: Ponte City. Silverman calls this single, circular tower the "biggest, grandest, most swaggeringly ambitious residential block in Africa."[64] At fifty-four stories, it was large enough to alter the city's skyline and for many years it occupied a place in *The Guinness Book of Records* as "the tallest residential building in the world outside of America." When finished, it had 464 apartments — some of them occupying multiple floors — 54 shops, and 7 floors of parking, along with a swimming pool and a bowling alley. It was so large that several roads were realigned to make way for its construction.[65]

Silverman also explains that the building's architects became embroiled in a multiyear debate with the city's authorities over where the "non-European" or "Bantu" servants would live. As noted previously, the city required that Black African domestic workers in large buildings could only occupy rooftop quarters. Ponte's architects, on the other hand, envisioned barbecue terraces and sundecks on the roof and wanted to place "servants'" quarters at the base of the building. The two sides reached a compromise in which half of the roof would feature barbecue terraces and the other half would house forty-two domestic workers. Like other "locations in the sky," they built the windows in the workers' accommodations six feet above the floor.[66]

Ponte, however, would quickly become something quite different from the modern symbol of luxury the architects intended. It was completed in 1976, Johannesburg's ninetieth anniversary. The city's whites, who were the intended tenants, "were politically and materially powerful, and filled their city with their inflated colonial sense of belonging," writes Denis Hirson. "Yet 1976 was the year when they discovered that they were sitting on a volcano, as the children of Soweto and other townships in the country took to the streets to say they had had enough."[67]

3
Uprising and Change, 1976–93

On the morning of June 16, 1976, somewhere between three thousand and ten thousand schoolchildren gathered in Soweto to protest increasingly intolerable conditions. In 1960, the apartheid government had begun funneling resources away from Black townships to rural "homelands." Poverty intensified and many young children had to find work, often selling items such as fruits and nuts, to help their families survive. Despite a rapidly growing population, all new housing construction in Soweto ended in 1970. That year, the Bantu Homelands Citizen Act stripped urban Black South Africans of all rights of citizenship. At the same time, schools in Soweto reached new levels of overcrowding when, between 1972 and 1974 alone, secondary school enrollment increased by 300 percent. But because the government spent thirteen times more per white student than it did for each Black student, young learners in Soweto often met in rented, makeshift classrooms.[1]

The ultimate spark came when the government ordered many Soweto schools to switch from English to Afrikaans as the language of instruction. Teachers who had no fluency in, and in some cases no familiarity with, Afrikaans were now expected to begin conducting their courses in that language. The students believed that this imposition was intended to prepare them for a life of servitude to whites. Unprepared for the scale of the spontaneous demonstration, police sent one of their trained dogs into the crowd. When some of the marchers killed the dog, the police opened fire and fatally shot nearly two dozen of the children. Over the next two months, the number of Soweto protesters surged to 20,000 and the number of deaths rose to 575.[2]

The severity of the state's response shocked the world and drew condemnation from the United Nations. It also mobilized the ANC to launch protest actions nationwide and to call for international sanctions. Demonstrations erupted in other townships around Johannesburg, such as Krugersdorp and Tembisa, and hundreds of white students from the University of the Witwatersrand marched in solidarity through the CBD to register their objection to the government's brutality.

Though the government had faced challenges before, most notably during the Sharpeville massacre in 1960, the Soweto Uprising sent the first serious signals that white minority rule in South Africa might not last forever. Some observers speculated that it was only a matter of time until the National Party's rule would collapse, while others more cautiously predicted the government would need to reform apartheid to survive. In the immediate aftermath came a severe recession, triggered in part by the significant withdrawal of international investment in response to government brutality. The global recession following the oil shocks of 1973–74 also drained investment capital from South Africa.

Apartheid planners designed Soweto (an abbreviation of South Western Townships) to house as many as a million Black African people close enough to Johannesburg — about fifteen miles — to meet the city's needs for labor but far enough to keep them from participating in the life of the city. Despite its distance, however, the uprising in Soweto exerted a profound influence on Hillbrow. As Clive M. Chipkin writes, the events of 1976 "changed everything."[3] Prior to the uprising, demand for housing in Hillbrow had been so intense that tenants moved into new high-rises before their upper floors were completed. By the end of 1976, the frenzy of construction ground to a halt. As the 1970s drew to a close, landlords contended for the first time with mass vacancy.

Paddi Clay and Glynn Griffiths write that, in the 1970s, Hillbrow "became a very different place to the optimistic young suburb of the sixties."[4] Some observers describe the transition as driven by "white flight," but that phrase fails to capture the complexity of change. Ta-Nehisi Coates has argued that describing the white desertion of US central cities during the 1960s and 1970s as "flight" obscures the degree to which whites moved because the suburbs had been engineered for their benefit. Houses were newer and more spacious and there were lawns for their children and garages for their cars. Most important, the GI Bill and favorable mortgage terms provided them with the financial ability to move.[5]

Johannesburg experienced a similar pattern. Some whites did leave, or begin to avoid, Hillbrow out of fear. A high rate of violent crime had always been one of the costs of imposing white minority rule in South Africa, and whites worried that police protection was wearing thin. But they also left because the northern suburbs provided more desirable — and whites-only — housing and living spaces at a comfortable remove from the noise, dirt, and congestion of the city.

These were not the only reasons that Hillbrow's white population dwindled. Following the Soweto Uprising, the government expanded military conscription. Young white men who might have rented one of Hillbrow's thousands of "bachelor flats"[6] were deployed instead to contain protests or to destabilize newly independent Angola and Mozambique.[7] The government also repealed rent control laws in 1978, which led to "the immediate rise in the rental price of property" and therefore "an exodus of white residents from districts such as Hillbrow."[8]

A wave of emigration from the country also began in 1976 and was particularly pronounced among white Jewish South Africans. One of the two whites killed on the first day of the Soweto Uprising was a Jewish doctor and humanitarian activist who was stoned to death by protesters, sending shock waves through the Jewish community. Richard Mendelsohn and Milton Shain write that three thousand Jewish people left the country per year following 1976, largely bound for Israel or the United States.[9] It is not possible to determine how many of the emigrants had lived in Hillbrow, but it is certain that the neighborhood's Jewish population began to decline. At the same time, the steady flow of white Europeans that had fueled Hillbrow's residential construction boom during the 1950s and 1960s slowed to a trickle during the recession of the 1970s.

Conditions in the townships, meanwhile, pushed many Indian, Coloured, and Black South Africans to look elsewhere for living quarters. Under apartheid, Indian and Coloured townships were typically better living spaces than were Black African townships. Homes in Indian and Coloured townships were more likely to have electricity and indoor plumbing, and schools there were better funded. But the post-1976 recession led to severe government cutbacks in township construction and maintenance. Indian townships, such as Lenasia, and Coloured townships, such as El Dorado Park, experienced severe overcrowding. Black townships endured even more extensive overcrowding along with waves of violence due to police and military crackdowns and deadly rivalry among competing camps of the resistance movement: the ANC, the PAC, and the Inkatha Freedom Party (IFP).

Through the late 1970s and early 1980s, the housing shortages in Indian and Coloured townships intensified. Alan Morris writes that people were so desperate for accommodation that they were living in cars or anywhere they could find to sleep. Many had no alternative but to take the risk of looking for housing in white spaces. With the movement of whites out of Hillbrow after the Soweto Uprising, hundreds of units were vacant and landlords were desperate to fill them.

For a time, the local government tolerated the few hundred Black and Coloured people who moved into Hillbrow. This was, after all, helping alleviate overcrowding in the townships. But when *The Star* newspaper published an article about it in April 1978, right-wing groups responded with strong objections and the minister of community development ordered the new tenants to leave. Some were prosecuted in court and fined. By the end of 1979, there were so many cases filed against tenants who had violated the Group Areas Act that a special magistrate's court was set up to hear them. Members of the British-based National Front, a neo-fascist organization, began arriving in Johannesburg with the intent of creating an atmosphere of fear in Hillbrow that would keep "illegal" tenants out.[10]

Such tenants lived in constant fear of eviction, writes Morris. But in February 1979, several hundred people formed an organization called Actstop to fight back. Several dozen attorneys quickly volunteered to help anyone facing eviction for violating the Group Areas Act. Actstop was so well coordinated and effective that by 1981 there were members of the National Party calling for the legal recognition of Indian and Coloured tenants in Hillbrow. Noting that there were more than four thousand Indian families in Hillbrow, one of the National Party members of parliament even suggested formally declaring part of Hillbrow an "Indian area."[11]

A turning point came in 1982, when Judge Richard Goldstone ruled that evictions due to the Group Areas Act were unjust and had to be stopped. But that same year, members of the National Party broke away and formed an even more right-wing party, the Conservative Party (CP). The conservatives made Hillbrow one of their central causes, charging that the large presence of Indian and Coloured residents in the neighborhood was evidence that the National Party was betraying its principles. They began targeting landlords to prod them into evicting "illegal" tenants. But by 1985, the number of Indian and Coloured tenants in Hillbrow had increased so substantially — to about 25 percent of the total — that even the Conservative Party gave up on halting further integration. That same year, Black Africans began to move into the neighborhood in large numbers.[12]

Ponte City epitomizes a broader transition. The fifty-story colossus in Berea, near the border of Hillbrow, never filled with whites. By the early 1980s, Ponte's owners began to sign leases with anyone — mostly Indians and Coloured people — who could feasibly "pass" as white. They advised such tenants to adopt Greek and Portuguese names and, for a time, Ponte became a surreptitiously, if uneasily, integrated tower. By the early 1990s, it was often called

"Little Kinshasa" because it had become home for a while to several thousand migrants from the DRC. In subsequent years, many Nigerians, Zimbabweans, and Malawians followed. Over time, tens of thousands of people settled into the tower, though most moved on to other buildings, other neighborhoods, and even other countries.[13]

As investment dried up, many of Hillbrow's buildings fell into disrepair. The neighborhood became both seedier and, in many ways, more vibrant as it became a center of transgression in this rigidly conservative country. Even as middle-class and more affluent whites began leaving, the neighborhood maintained its upscale restaurants, shops, and cafés through the 1980s. Joubert Park, on Hillbrow's southwestern border, remained a popular and increasingly integrated destination. Both the sex and the drug industries became more pronounced and visible, and one by one, many of the residential hotels transformed into brothels. The queer population, which had long maintained a quiet presence, was now defiantly visible.

In 1984, P. W. Botha was elected president (having already served as prime minister from 1978 to 1984) and became known as "the Great Crocodile" for his hardline stance on apartheid. In 1983, as prime minister, he had successfully proposed a new constitution that created a house of parliament for Indians, and a separate one for Coloured people, but permitted no representation for Black people. Instead, Black South Africans were expected to move to homelands which the government claimed would become independent states. Bophuthatswana, Ciskei, and Venda became nominally independent, though the international community refused to recognize them because it was clear the "independence" was a ruse on the part of the apartheid government.[14]

South Africa became a pariah state in 1986 when Botha gave a speech in Durban pledging to the world that the country would never give in to demands for reform. A year later, he declared a state of emergency that resulted in several years of brutal police and military crackdowns, mass arrests, torture, thousands of deaths, and numerous "disappearances." Government security forces killed at least two thousand people and detained twenty-five thousand during Botha's time as president.[15]

The interviews that follow tell the story of Hillbrow's — and South Africa's — critical transition years. They include the experiences of a renowned Black actor, a Black switchboard operator who worked in the Ponte City tower, a multiracial Indian and Coloured woman whose first ventures outside the township of Lenasia were to Hillbrow shops and clubs, a gay Chinese man who found unexpected freedoms in Hillbrow, two white women who moved into Hillbrow-area flats, and a white doctor whose practice served numerous antiapartheid activists.

John Kani—"That was Hillbrow"

John Kani[16] is a Black African man in his seventies who has been called the "grandfather of South African theater" and has also starred in international films such as *Black Panther* (2018) and *The Lion King* (2019). He recalls Hillbrow in the 1970s as a place of some promise in an otherwise bleak political atmosphere. Ron Nerio and John Kani sat together to discuss Hillbrow near the theater that now bears his name (the John Kani Theatre) inside the Market Theatre complex. He was directing a staged version of Zakes Mda's previously unperformed drama, *The Dying Screams of the Moon*, exploring South Africa's intractable land tensions. That play is about an older Black woman who returns after many decades to claim land she saw taken from her family when she was a young girl. She faces down—or tries to face down—a young white woman who owns the deed to the land and is convinced that it rightfully belongs to her. The white woman's father paid cash for it to another white man who had seized the land in the first place.

"You see," John says, in his sonorous voice, "when our people left Sophiatown and they moved to Soweto, and when the glory of Alexandra Township became really like a third-rate suburb of Sandton, there was a strange migration towards Hillbrow. Hillbrow was the only place that could give you a postcard that would confuse you about South Africa's apartheid. You could arrive here in the 1970s and you would see a mix of people. Because Johannesburg was the economic hub of southern Africa, there was a little bit of a tolerance around Johannesburg. Apartheid wasn't as harsh here. You could even have reporters like Can Themba, like Lewis Nkosi, and dramatists, and poets, all migrating towards Hillbrow in the evening. This was the place where you could get a little bit of the Moulin Rouge, a little bit of the corner restaurant, a little bit of being allowed to do what you would normally not do."

Though the Black music scene in Sophiatown was crushed in the 1950s, John believes a small part of it was preserved in Hillbrow. He recounts that even before moving to Johannesburg he had heard that Black musicians had "little gigs in Hillbrow, in a little corner shop at night, for instance. Of course, the leader of the band was white, but there were guys like Allen Kwela and Kippie Moeketsi who had little joints. Things happened there. So when I arrived in Johannesburg in 1970, one of the first things I wanted to know is Hillbrow. Coming from Port Elizabeth, far down in the Eastern Cape, I knew that apartheid was segregation, separation, and not equal."

John recalls finding a hotel in Hillbrow that contrasted with his expectations of apartheid. "I remember we would stay at the hotel—I think it's not there now — the Moulin Rouge," he says. "It was so wonderful. And all the people would walk down the stairs and they would be dressed for the night."

John had achieved considerable fame in the 1960s, having cowritten and performed in many well-received plays in the Eastern Cape. He began living in Johannesburg in 1970, at a time when his plays were winning accolades around the world. In 1975, he traveled to New York to perform in *The Island* and *Sizwe Banzi Is Dead*, for which he won a Tony Award for best actor. Upon his return to South Africa, he was arrested and held in solitary confinement for twenty-three days.[17]

Two years later, in 1977, he joined the Market Theatre, which became known as the "theatre of the struggle." The Market Theatre opened in Newtown, about one and a half miles from Hillbrow, because the apartheid laws had inadvertently exempted only two places in the entire city from rigid racial separation: the Old Indian Market in Newtown (which became the theater complex) and the University of the Witwatersrand.

"I remember, in 1978," he recalls, "we were doing a production of *Waiting for Godot*, and we wanted to go have something to eat with the cast. Because the cast was white, we went to Hillbrow and there was a Greek restaurant. And it was so funny, because the Greek guy had a bit of a problem allowing me and Winston [another actor] in, being Black. But being Hillbrow, we just sat back and the customers insisted that we be let in. That was Hillbrow."

In 1982, John starred in a production of *Miss Julie* at the Market Theatre. The play called for him to kiss a white woman on stage and half the audience walked out. During the play's run, he received numerous calls threatening violence. During one assassination attempt, he was stabbed eleven times.[18]

Another controversy ensued when he played *Othello* in 1986. "It was the first Black Othello in South Africa, for which, oh my God, I was detained," he says. "I was questioned by the police. The performances were disrupted. There were bomb threats — hate mail to the girl who played Desdemona. She was Jewish. She even left South Africa. She was marginalized by all white institutions that employed white actors on television, because she played the wife of this Black terrorist masquerading around as an actor. That was me — with a Tony Award and an Obie Award. You could tell anyone around the world, but in South Africa, I was still not recognized as an actor, because an actor was not a profession defined in the Labour Act for Black people."

During the late 1980s another theater, the Windybrow, opened in Doornfontein on Hillbrow's southern border. "It was a wonderful old house that was left by some rich Randlord[19] and it became a meeting place for artists," John says. "That's where we met people like [Nigerian playwright and essayist] Wole Soyinka. American writers would come down there and filmmakers from England, and we would have discussions at the Windybrow about the direction of the arts, where things were going. People . . . would create new music there. We had a strong relationship with the Market Theatre, here in this building, with Mannie Manim and the late Barney Simon."

John describes the Market and Windybrow Theatres as places "where all people of this country, all artists, could come and not avoid issues, and talk about the fact that 'you're white and I hate you for what you have done all these years,' and for white people to say, 'I apologize for inheriting the problem of the Dutch that I don't even know. I'm inheriting the sins of our fathers, which surely have nothing to do with me. I should be judged by who I am, by the content of my character. You can't judge me because my grandfather was white and was a racist.'"

John here offers the perspective of some whites, which seems to suggest systems molded in one historical epoch may "have nothing to do" with the descendants of those who established them. But data show clearly that the racial inequality built from the seventeenth to the twentieth century remains stubbornly in place well into the twenty-first century. The legal, social, and political systems that created and advanced white supremacy continue to make South Africa one of the most unequal societies on earth. White South Africans still benefit from a system that has long granted them unequal access to education, professional employment, land ownership, and other forms of white privilege, just as their counterparts in the United States benefit from similar patterns of inequality.

"Our target audience was Hillbrow," John elaborates. "Our banners were around Hillbrow, and our advertising, because that was where the audience would be that would find it easy to come to the Market Theatre — a multiracial audience."

South Africa's "Stonewall"

Though South Africa's first ever queer political meeting happened in Joubert Park in 1968, Mark Gevisser and Edwin Cameron[20] write that through the 1970s, queer organizing took an "accommodationist" stance toward apartheid. White queer people, they explain, were largely conservative and tended to avoid any talk of "rights." Even as Hillbrow became a "clearly identifiable 'gay neighborhood'" most of its participants remained apolitical.[21]

In the late 1970s, the government began cracking down once again on queer people and places. Suspected gays and lesbians were expelled from universities and well-known political figures began making public anti-gay proclamations. The powerful Dutch Reformed Church announced that it would address "the homosexual problem." In Hillbrow, police raided queer nightclubs. Over the New Year celebrations of 1978/79, a particularly visible and aggressive raid occurred at a bar called the New Mandy's. Mandy's was the bar of choice for the famous and queer Granny Lee who passed as white, discussed below. "I'm going to Mandy's where everybody loves me!" she would regularly shout.[22]

Gevisser and Cameron write that patrons at Mandy's on the night of this particular raid were "manhandled, verbally abused, and kept locked up in the building until morning." The police singled out Black men in the club for the worst treatment. Because some of the patrons fought with the police, this incident came to be known as South Africa's "Stonewall." The Stonewall Inn is a bar on Christopher Street in New York that was raided on June 28, 1969, and where dozens of patrons fought back with such intensity that the police barricaded themselves inside for protection. The Stonewall rebellion is often credited as the catalyst for the modern "gay liberation" movement of the 1970s.[23]

Following the raids in Hillbrow, queer organizing in South Africa became somewhat more politicized. The Gay Association of South Africa (GASA) formed and gradually added branches in many cities and towns. In 1983, GASA opened its national headquarters in Hillbrow. But Gevisser and Cameron judge the queer political organizing of this era to have been a failure. This is because GASA never built bridges to the Black liberation organizations that were blossoming at this time.[24]

The pivotal experiences of Simon Nkoli, perhaps South Africa's best-known gay activist, illustrate the chasm between queer white organizing and the general struggle for liberation in South Africa during the 1980s. Nkoli grew up in Sebokeng, a Black township thirty-three miles south of Johannesburg. Nkoli is the first person Nerio visited upon arriving in South Africa in 1990, when he went directly to Sebokeng.

When Nkoli was fifteen, he became an antiapartheid activist. At nineteen, he revealed to his mother that he was romantically involved with another man. His mother spent a year taking him to *sangomas* (traditional healers), some of whom proclaimed that he was bewitched while others assured his mother he was not sick. A psychologist then advised him to accept himself. In 1983, he became the first Black African person to join GASA. Membership perks were supposed to include discounts at Johannesburg's gay clubs, but Nkoli found that when he presented his GASA card several clubs told him that they did not admit Black people. He responded by forming the Saturday Group, a "Black interest group" within GASA that mostly held meetings in Soweto, but occasionally met in Hillbrow. The GASA office in Hillbrow was often less than welcoming, even floating a proposal to limit the number of Black people who could attend at any given time.[25]

Nkoli's life took a dramatic turn in 1984 when he attended a funeral for an antiapartheid activist in Sebokeng. He was arrested with twenty-one others in what would become known as the Delmas Treason Trial. His friend Bev Ditsie, a Black woman from Soweto, describes this as a period during which the state was "detaining every antiapartheid leader in the country." They were determined to execute Nkoli and his codefendants.[26] Nkoli was held and tortured at the infamous John Vorster Square Police Station,[27] where detainees were often held for weeks or months without trial and where several men died in custody under suspicious circumstances.[28]

Ditsie reports that people who knew him recall Nkoli as someone "totally without fear."[29] He chose to "come out" to the other detainees, some of whom responded with fierce homophobia. Many objected to being tried with a "known homosexual," and others sought to prevent him from taking the witness stand as his presence might prove a stigma too difficult to overcome. Nkoli writes: "I felt I had to testify because of my indictment. The primary charge against me was murder: I was alleged to have thrown a big rock. I was adamant that I had to take the witness stand to defend myself, as I was innocent." Over time, most of his codefendants overcame their opposition. Terror Lekota, who was jailed with Nkoli and later became a major figure in the ANC, credits Nkoli with the organization's decision to include language outlawing discrimination on the basis of "sexual orientation" in the constitution. That constitution became the first in the world to do so.[30]

Nkoli remained in prison for four years. In 1988, he and sixteen codefendants were set free. Five others were sent to Robben Island, where Nelson Mandela was serving his twenty-fifth year of imprisonment. After Nkoli's release, he quickly launched the explicitly political, antiracist Gay and Lesbian Organization of the Witwatersrand (GLOW) and became a "cause célèbre" for antiapartheid groups in many parts of the world.[31] Meanwhile, the apolitical, mostly white GASA disbanded. As one of GLOW's most active members, Bev Ditsie says of her years in the organization: "It was the first time in my life I was happy. There were meetings, rallies, and parties all the time."[32]

Queer hopes were high when GLOW held the continent's first Lesbian and Gay Pride March in 1990, which started in Braamfontein and traversed through Hillbrow. Ditsie would go on to speak at the 1995 UN World Conference on Women in Beijing. There, she told the thousands assembled that "lesbian rights are women's rights." Thirteen years later, in 2008, the intersection of Twist and Pretoria Streets in Hillbrow was renamed "Simon Nkoli Corner." On that day, banners with Nkoli's name were unfurled on two Hillbrow apartment buildings to uproarious applause.[33]

Nkoli died of AIDS-related causes in 1999. His obituary provides a sense of his impact:

> There is a Simon Nkoli Street in Amsterdam; a Simon Nkoli Day in San Francisco. He has an international name recognition few other South Africans share. But the best place to see Simon's legacy is the vibrant black gay subculture in South Africa's townships. These young men and women are the Nkoli Generation; they saw articles about him in the press, they flocked to him. He made something of a political home for them, giving them an ideology that fused the freedom struggle with a sense of how they might find redemption from their families' rejection through gay community and activism.[34]

Ditsie, however, experienced the limits on queer hope when she left GLOW soon after her return from the World Conference on Women in Beijing. In a documentary about her relationship with Nkoli called *Simon and I*, she recalls this painful decision. Violence against women, and especially against lesbians, was increasing in the 1990s, but GLOW seemed more and more exclusively focused on the social and political rights of gay men. By the mid-1990s, Ditsie no longer felt it was safe to walk alone as a woman anywhere in Johannesburg — even in Hillbrow. Tragically, however, male members of the organization seemed uninterested in the emergency facing South Africa's women.[35]

Matthew Krouse — "The clubs were absolutely astonishing"

Queer environments in Hillbrow involved more than activism on the one hand and racism on the other. Matthew Krouse describes the queer culture and leisure spaces that developed in the neighborhood. Matthew is a tall, broad-shouldered, white Jewish man in his early sixties with a shaven head. He has been a scriptwriter, a director, a performer, a journalist, an activist, an art gallery manager, and now operates a bookshop. When Nerio and Matthew Krouse met near the bookshop in Victoria Yards, an industrial space in the inner city that has been converted into a sprawling network of galleries and artists' studios, he explains that he "fled" to Johannesburg from the small city of Germiston when he was a teenager. He enrolled at the University of the Witwatersrand, in Braamfontein, a neighborhood on Hillbrow's western border.

"Hillbrow was a high-rise playground for us whites in those days," he says. "By the late 1970s and early 1980s, it had become daring and seedy. I moved to Braamfontein in 1982 and met my first boyfriend, who lived in Yeoville. So I had to walk through Hillbrow every day to get from where I was living in student housing to see him. I loved those walks, because I could stop in Hillbrow's bookstores and record shops and other spots on the way. Every store of interest was in Hillbrow at that time."

Matthew can barely contain his enthusiasm as he reflects on the Hillbrow of the 1980s. "The clubs were absolutely astonishing," he says, with a look suggesting he remains astonished by what the clubs were able to get away with. "In the 1970s, there was a lesbian bar called 'The Together Bar,' but from the late 1970s on, a huge range of bars and clubs opened. They were mixed in among all the Jewish places, some of which dated back to the 1940s. The Jews had opened a number of eateries and kosher groceries, but they had also moved into the hospitality industries and had many hotels and resorts in the neighborhood.

"The government tolerated these places [the clubs]," he continues, offering an interesting analysis of the government's role. "They hated it, but it [the government] did not want to be seen as so extreme that it was isolated among countries. So it permitted an alternative culture to develop, provided that it was confined to Hillbrow—and to a certain extent Yeoville.

"You have to remember, disco was quite political in its formative years. It allowed people to break out of their cocoons—especially their racial cocoons. In the 1960s, Hillbrow's clubs were still about dinner and dance. They were stiff and formal. But then came disco and the clubs became increasingly outrageous!"

During the 1970s, Matthew explains, Black and white people were forbidden to dance or drink together. But at 11:00 p.m., the official closing time for all clubs and bars, most of the establishments would shut down and quickly reopen as speakeasies. They would lock their doors and bouncers would peer through small windows to see who was outside, waiting to be admitted.

"We were underage," Matthew says, "but they let us in—because we were 'the bait.' There was a mythology developing. The clubs wanted to develop a mystique by admitting young people and an increasing number of Black people. Big Afros were in and radical hairstyles were important. They were symbolic of challenging the extremely stiff order in the rest of the country.

"By the end of the 1970s, there were several gay bars: Chaparral, La Poupette, and Barbarella among them. Barbarella had the first bubble machine in the country, and also the first 'cages' where men danced. People drank and did drugs to excess. There were still frequent raids, but the patrons were fairly defiant. The bars developed a system. If they did not have liquor licenses— and many did not—patrons got a number when they entered. They placed the number on a sticker on the bottles and they used the same number all night—where they could refill their bottles as often as they liked. During the raids there were regular arrests of people for 'masquerading' in the clothes normally worn by the other sex, and they were also arrested for 'cross-racial drinking.' But during the raids, people could place their bottles behind the bar and reclaim them later by using their identifying number.

"By the late 1980s, there were more gay bars: Garbo's, which was bombed in the early 1990s, Gotham City, Club 58, and Mandy's. There was also Studio 54 in the Diplomat Hotel. The raids continued until the late 1980s, but patrons blithely disregarded the danger. Some of the places, especially Club 58, had backrooms. Gotham City had regular 'dick size' contests. There was a large board with holes in it through which men would place their penises and judges would examine them from the other side. One day, the board fell over, onto the judges, injuring them and leaving the other man standing, mostly naked!"

Matthew then recalls Granny Lee, who had achieved almost legendary status in South Africa's queer history. "Granny Lee became a staple," he says. "She was a 'Coloured man' who lived as a 'white woman.' She had vitiligo [a condition that causes the loss of skin color]. The newspapers would call her the 'disco granny.' This is during a time when everyone was going out—everyone was getting outrageous. Granny Lee wore elaborate female clothing. She never missed a single night. As the years wore on, she became more and more unstable. She was falling down on the floor at times, drunk from alcohol, shouting things like: 'I need cocks!'"

The documentary *Metamorphosis: The Remarkable Journey of Granny Lee* provides more detail on this legendary figure. It notes that she was always at the bar demanding, "Young man, please buy me a drink!" People recounted that she was a heavy drinker but never had to pay for her drinks. Sometimes she passed out on the floor, and at least one observer states: "We really expected her to drop dead!" Notoriously garish herself, she was always surrounded by a group of adoring, beautiful young men. But if she did not want to talk to someone because she was tired, she would take out her dentures and put them in her glass as a sign to leave her alone. She was eighty-one when she died following a car accident, in 1989, but she almost certainly would rather have died on the floor at Mandy's.[36]

Toward the end of the 1980s, Matthew says, he became more political and more left-wing. He joined the Communist Party, which he says frowned on decadence. "They weren't into flaming queens," he laughs, "so I gradually, but not completely, withdrew from the Hillbrow bar and club scene."

Matthew achieved a certain level of success in 1985, but it was often problematic for him. He was mentored by the famous playwright Barney Simon (a close colleague of John Kani) and began writing film scripts. He wrote and produced two movies within a several-week time span. One, called *Famous*

Dead Men, was a "gay porn romp" caricaturing Hendrik Verwoerd, the architect of apartheid. The movie outraged the Verwoerd family, who lobbied to have him jailed and induced the government to hold a show trial against him.

The ANC approached him at this time when he was in dire financial straits. They asked him to house a Black man from Soweto, who was part of the struggle and was trying to escape the police. The man hid out in Matthew's Braamfontein flat and shared a bed with him. The man came to him one day and said: "I heard you are a queer! Don't you love your mother?"

Matthew was aghast but recognized that it was a common trope in South Africa that men are gay because they dislike their mothers. He wrote his second film, *While You Weren't Looking*, about this incident.

Matthew places Hillbrow's vibrant queer scene in context: "You have to understand that the police strife in the 1980s was enormous. The stress on the country — with massive violence, the boycott, bombings, and the state of emergency — was overwhelming. It drove people to extremes. There were also many, many scars [traumas] caused by mandatory conscriptions. The South African Defence Forces were fighting on multiple fronts, especially in Angola."

Matthew himself was conscripted into the military. He grimaces and explains that his family could not afford to send him abroad, as "most families with 'unusual sons' did" in order to help them avoid military service. Though it was a very homophobic society, he says, the government could not afford to exclude gay, or any white, men who would otherwise be regarded as incompatible with military life. So he was drafted and sent to a "queer platoon."

"It was extremely stressful for everyone," he says. "It was not comfortable, as one might be tempted to imagine, to be in a platoon with other 'queers.' The word was broadly interpreted to mean 'strange' or 'weird,' so many of those who were conscripted were extremely unhappy or antisocial people."

Matthew was stationed in Pretoria. One night, he and a few friends cut a hole in the fence and stole away to Hillbrow for a few hours. He had no clothes other than his military uniform, so he wore an army track suit. They visited a jazz bar called "The King of Clubs" (not a gay bar).

"Simba Murray, the famous jazz musician, was playing," Matthew recalls. "It was an integrated place. But when I ordered and sat down, someone threw a bottle at me — because of my military clothes and crewcut. Murray said to me, gently, 'Perhaps this is not the best place for you.'"

Gevisser and Cameron also point out that a "quiet revolution" began in Hillbrow's queer spaces in the mid- to late 1980s. The all-white bars in the neighborhood became more and more integrated. The Butterfly Bar, for instance, had been an exclusively white space since it opened in the early 1970s. In 1987, it moved upstairs in the Harrison Reef Hotel and changed its name to the Skyline. It became "almost exclusively" Black from that date on.[37]

Hillbrow and the Queer Vote

In 1987, Hillbrow became the center of a remarkable, unexpected struggle over gay[38] voters. The National Party, which ruthlessly opposed homosexuality, surprisingly fielded a pro–gay rights candidate, Leon de Beer, in Hillbrow. This was not a sign that the party was becoming more progressive; rather, it was a sign that the party suspected gay white voters were becoming more conservative and hoped to lure them away from more progressive parties.

Much of the ANC's leadership was in exile in Europe and in other parts of Africa, and it had called on whites to boycott the election altogether and support the resistance to apartheid. The gay newspaper *Exit*, however, supported de Beer's campaign because it thought doing so would increase (white) gay political power. Until 1987, it was all but unthinkable that the National Party would support a pro-gay candidate. Homosexuality had always been a *bête noire* in Afrikaner discourse, and the National Party vigorously opposed all attempts to decriminalize same-sex encounters. But the political ground was shifting.

Facing a severe recession, growing international hostility, and the surging power of the antiapartheid movement, the government was desperate to preserve what it could of white unity. Part of the right wing had already broken away from the original right-wing National Party in 1982 and formed the far-right Conservative Party (also briefly discussed above). The CP objected even to the small concessions the National Party had made to apartheid's opponents. In 1984, it made a national issue out of integration in Hillbrow and vowed to clean up the "Hillbrow cesspool."[39] Facing a surging right wing, which had siphoned off the most conservative voters, the National Party thought that its best play at white unity in Hillbrow was to adopt a gay rights platform.

Hillbrow had been a stronghold of the opposition Progressive Federal Party, but by 1987 whites realized that demographics were changing so quickly that they were about to become a minority in the neighborhood. Leon de Beer courted their vote by promising to protect "minority groups," by which he meant both gays and whites. Gay (white) voters, meanwhile, were surprised to find themselves openly courted by any political party. De Beer appealed to their desire for recognition while also stoking racial fears by promising to support "law and order" and to get rid of "the criminal element in Hillbrow."

When de Beer won the election, he helped increase the National Party's vote count in parliament. *Exit* drew widespread condemnation for its role in supporting de Beer's victory. The gay students' group at the University of the Witwatersrand expressed its "profound disgust." Lesbian activist Julia Nicol wrote in a letter to the paper that it "was a moral outrage." Edwin Cameron, who chronicled lesbian and gay lives with Mark Gevisser and who would later become a Constitutional Court judge, called it a "debasement of the gay cause."[40]

By the time of the next parliamentary election, in 1989, half of Hillbrow's white voters had left the neighborhood. De Beer lost his seat to the progressives.

Paul Davis — Doctor of the Left

Paul Davis[41] (also discussed above) moved his medical practice to Hillbrow in 1974, two years before the Soweto Uprising. "Nineteen seventy-six," he says, "changed things more drastically. There was the banning of people and there was the birth of the Market Theatre, which became one of the central nodes of antiapartheid activism in Johannesburg. For a while, a number of my patients were from the Market Theatre — both Black and white."

He explains that the government permitted doctors to treat both Black African and white patients, but required them to have separate waiting rooms. He refused to comply with this law. Most of his white patients were liberals or members of the broad political left and they never objected to his integrated waiting area.

"I became sort of the Doctor of the Left," he says. "There was a lot of worry among activists about spying at the time, and Jewish doctors had a reputation as being safe — that we would not give people's names away — so they came to us. Medical staff were not seen as a threat [to the government] but there were communists and socialists among us. The activists were harassed like hell, but you could still escape into Hillbrow. It was densely populated enough to hide in. We always suspected that people were taking pictures of us and of our patients."

When asked if he noticed any evidence of residential integration in Hillbrow during these years, Paul's response is emphatic. Apartheid authorities allowed Black patients to visit his office, he notes, but there were so few Black pedestrians that they stood out. "The segregation," he says, "was not only residential but in every other way as well."

In 1980, he moved his practice again, this time to a building called Medical Hill, on Kotze Street in Hillbrow. He estimates that one-third of his practice consisted of patients whom he usually treated free of charge because they were unable to pay. He used pharmaceutical samples, where appropriate, because they were free. Many of his white patients were on medical aid. He had Indian patients, who all paid cash. There were also several "political patients," or well-known ANC members who were injured — not necessarily in political battles but also in car crashes and other incidents.

White patients who needed hospital attention went to Johannesburg General, while all others went to a nearby "non-European" hospital. Although both hospitals were government funded, the differences between them were sharp. The funding allocated for each white patient was about three times that for every Black African patient.

A sharp spike in commercial rents in Hillbrow led Paul to leave Medical Hill after only two years. He relocated the practice five kilometers away in Auckland Park.

"I still did house calls into Hillbrow, which was still a common practice then," he explains. "General practice was also very different then. I performed a wide array of medical services, from surgery, to obstetrics, to counseling."

While at the Auckland Park location, Paul consulted many people who had been detained and tortured by the police. He and his colleagues formed the Independent Doctors Panel (IDP) to make themselves available to former detainees and to compile as much information as possible from them. The IDP later became part of the Detainees Support Committee.

"When detainees were released," Paul explains, "we took very detailed reports to document evidence of torture. If someone had very clear signs of torture, the police would kill them — throw them from a window, for instance — but in the case of the patients who came to us, it was a forensics issue. Then, in 1986, the new state of emergency was declared and five thousand people were arrested at once, willy-nilly. But the government had not correctly complied with the law, so all of those arrested had to be released. We were flooded, and we could document more evidence of recent torture."

Paul also helped form the Emergency Services Group, which provided care to people injured during demonstrations in Johannesburg, Cape Town, and Durban. "Police would shoot people with buckshot and then go to hospitals to arrest anyone who showed up with buckshot," he explains. "Soon, protesters began avoiding hospitals. So, we made contacts with nurses and doctors. We would meet them at a safe house or clinic. If a hospital was necessary, we found a way to bypass the front entrance. We gave lectures to nurses on how to deal with injuries. People would try to remove buckshot themselves and cause more injury. We taught them how to do it safely or where it could be done properly."

There was no unrest in Hillbrow during these years, because most major protests occurred in townships or in the CBD. But, Paul says, a number of residents in Hillbrow were harboring the injured or other activists.

"Then, in 1990, things began to change," Paul says. "The government's tactics against the ANC began to change. There were many people who died on lonely roads under suspicious circumstances."

Philip—"We were not allowed to stroll"

Philip[42] manages Constitution View, a seven-story, 136-unit apartment building in Hillbrow that once served as the Johannesburg Blood Bank. He is a tall, slim Black man who stands very straight. Though he speaks softly and has a slightly reserved, gentle manner, he has a bright smile and the quiet authority of someone who has known Hillbrow well for many decades.

Ron Nerio and Philip walk together from Constitution View to a corner restaurant called the Jozi Takeaway. This cheery fish and chips shop has a bright interior and floor-to-ceiling windows open to the sidewalks. It is an oasis of normalcy surrounded by buildings such as 74 Klein Street, a mammoth, vacant, eighteen-story tower with jagged shards of glass lining every window frame. The charred remains of a department store occupy the entire ground floor.

Despite the foreboding presence of 74 Klein Street, the scene at the Jozi Takeaway is one of reassuring urban life. Even with their backs exposed to the sidewalks, no one seems apprehensive. Customers place their orders with the smiling young people behind the counter and walk off into the crowds headed in all directions. As we take our seats at one of the restaurant's indoor picnic tables, Philip begins to recall a different Hillbrow.

"I came to Johannesburg in the early 1980s, from Tzaneen, a small village in Limpopo," he says. Limpopo is a mostly rural province in South Africa's northeast, bordering on Zimbabwe, Botswana, and Mozambique. Tzaneen is about 250 miles from Johannesburg. "I was looking for work. I found a few casual jobs here and there, working in buildings around Hillbrow. Then I became a switchboard operator in Ponte in 1983 and moved into the building. It was very difficult then. You had to have a pass with you at all times."

The Native Laws Amendment Act of 1952 (briefly discussed in chapter 2) required all Black Africans over the age of sixteen to carry passbooks. They were a form of internal passport containing the photograph and the fingerprints of the holder, along with information about the holder's employment. An "employer" could only be a white person, and a Black person found in the city without a pass could be arrested.

"I had to go to the Home Office on 80 Albert Street to get my pass," Philip continues. "They would urine-test you. If you wanted to travel in the country, you had to go there and get a pass for that, too. If I wanted to go home to Limpopo, I would have to get a pass—and a urine test—and then stop there for another pass to reenter the city. Cops would randomly stop Black people to see their passes until 1986. Then, after 1986, fraudsters would hang outside of the Home Office Building and tell new arrivals from other countries—or people who did not know better—that they had to have passes in addition to their ID documents. These criminals would tell people that they still needed passes to walk around the city and they would sell them passes."

When asked about Ponte's reputation for having become a residentially integrated building in the 1980s, Philip says he does not remember it that way.

"The building was all whites," he insists, "or almost all whites, from Germany, from Brussels, China, Israel, and Egypt—from many nations. There were exactly five flats with Black tenants and they all worked in the consulates of Nigeria and Congo. So it was not an apartheid building in the strictest sense, because if it were there would not even have been those five flats of Black tenants. But the rest of the building was all whites in the 1980s."

Like other Black employees at the time, Philip had to live in one of Ponte's "locations in the sky" on the roof. "I had a room with a bed in a unit with five other men," he elaborates. "There were shared bathrooms and a small area to cook food. We were not allowed to go for a stroll in the city, as that would have been breaking the law. And we could never go out at night. Black people were not allowed to be out at night without a night pass."

Philip says that it was not until 1990 that the building began renting to a sizable number of Black tenants. "In 1990," he says, "many Nigerians were coming and renting the apartments to do 'funny businesses.' They opened small shops in the building on many different floors. They were splitting phone cables and running phone hotlines, calling everywhere in the world. Then the building ended up with a one-million-rand phone bill, because they were splitting the cables and not paying. The management simply could not control this. Eventually, in 1996, they shut down the switchboard. That is when they fired all the switchboard operators and I was out of a job."

As we talk about the early 1990s, Philip seems intent on recalling the spectacular deaths that happened in the building. To this day, something about Ponte's dizzying circular structure, great height, and brooding gray façade seems to elicit stories of death and suicide.

"There was a Portuguese boy who had been left alone by his parents," he says. "That was in Room 4006, on the fortieth floor. He was playing by the window and fell. That was in 1991. In 1991 or 1992, a white man who did not live in the building called the SABC [South African Broadcasting Corporation] to tell them he was going to jump from the top of the building. The SABC did not know if this was a joke or not, but they parked their vehicles in front of the building to find out whether it would happen.

"There were many businesses in the building, including the famous bowling alley," he continues, "and one of the businesses happened to be an escort agency — a fully legal business — on the fifty-first floor. The man went to the agency and walked inside where he was greeted by several women from many countries. He claimed that the view was beautiful and that he would like to see it. They thought nothing of the request, but he stepped up to the window and jumped. He was wearing a yellow suit. The impact was so severe that his body parts scattered. His arm landed in a park and one hand was found in a tree. Many parts were never found. It was later reported that he was having family problems."

Philip and Nerio sit alone at Jozi Takeaway for about thirty minutes. Nerio had arranged another interview with Bianca, a white woman who used to live in Yeoville. Bianca joins the two men at their bench at the Jozi Takeaway. She and Philip share their recollections of Hillbrow from the 1980s and early 1990s.

"Even after the scrapping of the pass laws," Bianca notes, "the police harassment did not end — not by any stretch. Hillbrow bars and restaurants were slowly starting to integrate, but Afrikaner cops would randomly pull up in front of a restaurant and hang out. As soon as they would see them, Black patrons would disappear — either on their own or because the owners would urge them to leave. If the cops felt like it, they would punish a particular restaurant or establishment by doing this every night.

"You have no idea how afraid of the Afrikaner cops I was," Bianca says. "They had such a belligerent attitude. It was really a neo-fascist atmosphere. There were two kinds of cops. There were the more professional members of the police force and they were more respectful. But many Afrikaner men would leave school in Standard 8 [eighth grade], the year beyond which school was no longer compulsory, and they would absolutely rule over the sidewalks and the railway stations as their fiefdoms — especially the railway stations. They were uneducated and tyrannical!"

Illuminating the fact that integration happened in stages, Philip recalls that Hillbrow was at its most integrated in the early 1990s, before the formal end of apartheid. "That was also when it was the most fun," he says. "On Christmas Eve and New Year's Eve, all of Pretoria Street was shut to traffic and there were huge celebrations. Blacks and whites mingled together and played games, including cricket.

"Then came 1994," he says, "when the habit of throwing furniture from the upper floors began. In 1995, I was walking with a friend, back home to Ponte, when a huge package whizzed down from somewhere above. It nearly killed us. It was a box full of bottles, some of them full. It hit a car and caused huge damage to that car. But these crazy New Year's Eve celebrations stopped fifteen years ago, due to the SAPS [South African Police Service], which began heavily pamphleting Hillbrow and warning people to desist from throwing refrigerators and furniture or any other objects from their buildings. They even used the army for a while to assist in breaking this habit. The last furniture that fell from the buildings was in 1999 or 2000, but poor Hillbrow is still tarred with that image. It's been eighteen years!

"But everything changed in Hillbrow in 1994," Philip continues. "The whites moved out of town. The last white people left Ponte and all the businesses left Hillbrow — and I mean *all of them.*"

He emphasizes by gesticulating with his arms, as if pointing to every part of the neighborhood at once: "I'm really talking about *all* of them. Crime was increasing. Everyone started to feel afraid. A lot of flats started to rent out by the night. Muggings became very common. Companies were just protecting their workers when they left the area. But I never left. After I lost my job at Ponte, in 1986, I moved to 48 Eselen Street in the Neville Building. A little while later, I met my current employer and now run his building for him."

Wendy—"You could not freak out Hillbrow"

Wendy[43] is a white woman, now in her early sixties. She graduated from a teacher's college in 1981 and moved into a flat in Joubert Park that same year. "The park was very safe [in the 1980s]," she says. Her memory, of course, is from the perspective of a white person with no reason to fear arrest or harassment and who was never required to carry a pass. "There was a public greenhouse with the most luscious plants. Joubert Park was like Central Park. It was the center of the city. The Johannesburg Art Gallery was there. There were chess games. There was also a huge chess game that people could play. No one was afraid of anybody else. You could meander and talk to everybody else."

Both the Johannesburg Heritage Portal and Pinterest provide historic photographs of Joubert Park from the 1950s through the 1980s. They show a neatly trimmed landscape with trees, an expansive lawn, winding pathways, and a small pond with fountains. Among the park's many pleasant attractions are well-manicured rows of flowers, a Victorian greenhouse, and, as Wendy mentioned, the sprawling Johannesburg Art Gallery. Though Joubert Park is smaller in scale, Wendy's comparison of it to New York's Central Park seems apt.

But in its century and a quarter of existence, the park has evolved through a considerable arc of change. It was built in 1893, two years before Hillbrow was formally established as a neighborhood. The Johannesburg Art Gallery opened within its boundaries in 1915. The city formally declared it a whites-only space in 1953.

The current condition of the park reveals much about the stresses facing the inner city. By 1998, hundreds of people had begun sleeping in Joubert Park and the neighborhood had become known as one of the region's epicenters of crime.[44] At that time, the Johannesburg Art Gallery fell into "heavy decline." In 2002, someone stole R20 million (about US$1,364,000) of copper roofing from the building. The city seriously considered moving the museum to Newtown, on the other side of the CBD, but ultimately opted to keep it in its present location. The greenhouse, too, fell into disrepair but was partially restored between 2002 and 2004.[45]

But there are signs that the park continues to provide enjoyment, even if it is badly neglected. A YouTube video from 2017, for instance, shows many Black African children, some in their school uniforms, laughing and playing on brightly colored playground equipment. The narrator, a young girl, even mentions that the park was a "colonial structure" where Europeans once could go to feel they were at home. "Today," she says, "it is where we play."[46] Another video from 2012 shows a group of Zulu and Xhosa men (according to the video) intently concentrating on the gigantic chessboard that Wendy mentions. The chess pieces are broken and, in some cases, only small bits of them remain. But the men nonetheless make do.[47] The park is still green and lush, but the museum is a ghostly place with few visitors and the greenhouse is once again vacant, all of its windows missing.

When asked about Joubert Park in the 1980s, Wendy responds, "Our building, Lorna Court, had no Black people. The residential buildings were still whites-only. But in the park, there was a total, healthy respect for everyone of all kinds and all colors. It was the first area to relax and ignore the pass laws. It was *the* most cosmopolitan area in the country.

"There were whites-only benches, yes," Wendy continues, "but we never paid attention to that in Joubert Park. Everyone could sit where they wanted. Even bottle stores [liquor stores] were required to have separate Black and white entrances, but we did not pay attention in Hillbrow. The post office was the same, with separate entrances, but no one in Joubert Park paid attention to the regulations by then [the 1980s]."

When asked whether she recalls there having been a gay presence in the neighborhood, Wendy responds that she had a close gay male friend. "He took me to a cruising ground," she said, "and we watched from a distance.

There were men meeting each other and picking each other up. He wanted me to see it. But it wasn't always safe for them. There were several murders of gay men at pickup places — not just in Joubert Park but in places like Zoo Lake. No one ever knew for sure whether they were robberies or homophobic attacks.

"I was brought up in a nonjudgmental environment," Wendy explains about her willingness to accompany her friend to a gay cruising area. Then she flashes a broad smile and says, "But you also have to know that anything went in Hillbrow! If you tried to be your most freaky in Hillbrow you would just fit in instead. You could not freak out Hillbrow."

What stands out most in Wendy's memory is the cosmopolitan nature of Hillbrow and Joubert Park. "Hillbrow was a totally international place," she exclaims. "I became a master backgammon player by learning from a group of Turkish men who used to hang out every day at Café Wien [on Kotze Street, Hillbrow]. And there was a place called the Perfumed Garden — a popular Indian restaurant. It had all these wonderful curtains and fabrics. They had a dish called 'honey chicken,' or 'j'iji imir.'[48] It was the gastronomic experience of my being!

"There was also a Thai restaurant in Hillbrow called Cranks, owned by a German man with a Thai-Australian wife. The place was decorated with nets across the ceiling, and in those nets were 'perverted' dolls, in all kinds of positions — some of them bonking each other. It was all for a laugh. And there was a huge cow-jumped-over-the-moon clock. It had the best Thai breakfast! Eric, the owner, had such a talent for running a restaurant. The service was impeccable and it was so joyful. And they had a tuk-tuk outside to take people home. The culture of Africa is one of storytelling and Eric was no exception. He could tell such stories! It was wonderful."

When asked what apartheid meant to her during her childhood, Wendy responds, "My parents were humble. I didn't know about apartheid until I realized my friends could not go to the same school as me. I didn't understand it much. I could understand the idea of racial separation, because that is what we had. But then I thought: the math was wrong! Why no special parks for Black people? Why only for whites?"

Wendy backs up in time to speak about her family background. "I only learned a piece of the puzzle last week, about how my family came to South Africa," she says. "I learned this during my uncle's funeral. My father was of Jewish descent, but I did not know that. His father was Jewish. I learned they were Russian Jews who escaped from the czar and ended up in London, then came down to South Africa. My father was born here. His father had met a Catholic woman and they decided to raise the children Catholic — which caused my grandfather to be shunned by his own family. Then he died early and left my grandmother with many children. I have a Jewish surname, but I know nothing about Judaism. Our family was so Catholic.

"My mother's side was part Irish and part English," she continues. "They went to Rhodesia and became tobacco farmers. The Irish side came down early. Africa was heralded as a place where you could 'make it happen.' Some of them stayed in Rhodesia and they lost their farms during independence — and rightly so! My maternal grandparents, who lived in Rhodesia — they did not understand how sophisticated Zimbabwean culture was. What a shame! We should be very ashamed. When I look at what we [whites] did in Zimbabwe and in South Africa, I think 'How dare we!'

"And I've always said there are few white South Africans who do not have some Black parentage." She points to her skin: "I am white but I had dark, curly hair when I was growing up. I am a 'darker beige.' There were more male than female Europeans in South Africa from the beginning. What was going to happen?"

Wendy's grandfather moved to South Africa and became a miner at the age of thirteen, in the 1940s. He was not literate, but had a strong desire to learn to read. He had an image of retirement as being an age during which to spend time reading. Wendy started to write short pieces for him to read, and she kept producing more and more lessons for him over time. In his honor, she started to teach reading at mining hostels.

Wendy grew up in Mondeor, which at the time was a new suburb in the south of Johannesburg, close to Soweto. She laughs and says: "Imagine, in life we roll the dice. We were given a choice of Mondeor in the south, or Bryanston in the north. We didn't know which to choose so we picked Mondeor. Our fate would have been very different if we had picked Bryanston!" Bryanston is a northern suburb and now one of the wealthiest communities in the region.

At teacher's college, Wendy met a Lebanese man who would become her partner. The couple moved in 1981 to a building with a pink façade and spacious balconies, called Lorna Court (mentioned above). Several sources describe the building, which was built in 1931, as an "architectural jewel"[49] that once "encapsulated all Johannesburg's supposed potential to become the next Manhattan."[50] Racine Edwardes describes it as "the beautifully-designed building in the city where chauffeur-driven Rolls Royces passed nightly, as the fabulous people of the city . . . made their way to and from soirées and social gatherings."[51] It now sits abandoned and in ruins. A fire ravaged the building and killed several tenants in 2001, after a man set his wife alight.[52] This type of destruction epitomizes the gendered violence that torments much of South African life.

But Lorna Court's difficulties began several years before the fire. Wendy explains the process. "In 1986, when the Group Areas Act was repealed, Hill-brow just changed within weeks," she says. "I wasn't scared. But you soon had seventeen people living in a flat. In 1987, I became the chairman of the body corporate at Lorna Court. There was a fight in a flat and I had to investigate. I saw there were seventeen people living there. They needed to live like that to be close to transit. But the infrastructure could not cope. Lorna Court saw its demise very quickly. My car was broken into five times within a week.

"Then I was violently hijacked," Wendy continues. "I had a gun in my mouth and another to my head. And I looked at these guys and I thought, 'crime has a career path.' If your sister is starving you could commit crime, too. The first time it happens you are petrified, but the next time you are not as scared. One of the men was so nervous, he was shaking. I knew at Lorna Court when my car was broken into that they were people in need. Circumstances make us who we are. They make us do the things we wouldn't normally do. I stayed in Lorna Court because I thought it was important to keep the building operating, to be integrated. If we did not have integration at an apartment level, at a community level, we would have no chance as a country."

By 1989, however, crime had become so pervasive that Wendy and her part-ner, Yusuf, no longer felt able to remain at Lorna Court. Wendy had become an executive at IBM by then, and the company moved its headquarters from the Johannesburg CBD to the northern suburb of Sandton. Shortly after, she and Yusuf also moved near to Sandton.

Sam—"That was the level of oppression"

Sam[53] is a bubbly, exceptionally charming woman with a buzz cut and a quick wit. Like Wendy, she has fond recollections of Joubert Park. But as the daugh-ter of an Indian father and a Coloured mother, apartheid guaranteed that her experiences of the neighborhood were quite different.

Sam was born in Randfontein, a mining town twenty-five miles west of Johannesburg, in the mid-1960s. She recalls Randfontein as having been quite ethnically mixed until the government began more aggressively enforcing the Group Areas Act at the end of the decade. Everyone except the white residents was forced to leave. Because her parents were of two "different races," her family was given the choice of moving to a Coloured township or an Indian township. Her mother chose Lenasia, an Indian township south of Soweto, because she thought it would be the best option for raising children. Sam was five when the family moved in 1971.

"In Lenasia," she says, "we were extremely sheltered. It was especially strange for us because my father was in the apartheid police force. He did not allow us to speak or think about politics. We were isolated and kept to ourselves because he was a cop. But this was not just us. There was a law in place—the Informations Act—that meant you could not speak about apartheid. In Standard 4, I did a project about the police, because my father was on the force, and I was reprimanded. They failed me and told me I had to do it all over. The teachers used me as an example of what not to do. It was the first time I found out that information was banned."

The authors are unable to confirm the existence of an "Informations Act," although Sam may be referring to any number of pieces of legislation, such as the Official Secrets Act of 1956 or the Censorship Act of 1963. The novelist Nadine Gordimer wrote in 1972 that there existed in South Africa a general atmosphere, backed up by numerous laws, aimed at suppressing questions about apartheid and "the way of life" it engendered.[54]

"Apartheid," Sam emphasizes, "was the oppression of your complete self. It was the oppression of your social, political, linguistic, and informational self. It was the oppression of your ability to move about. We never left Lenasia in the 1970s. I never knew that anything else existed. It was the oppression of everything. Our thinking was oppressed. Our lifestyles were oppressed. Imagine—at train stations, there could be hundreds of Africans and one lone white police officer. But if he said 'stop!' they all did. They never thought to defy him. That was the level of oppression."

Sam was eighteen or nineteen when she traveled to Hillbrow for the first time, in the mid-1980s.

"When I first saw Hillbrow, I was shell-shocked!" she recalls. "I had no idea that such a place existed in South Africa. It was overwhelming and it was wonderful. Joubert Park was beautiful. It was bigger then than it is now."

In sharp contrast to Wendy's description, Sam adds, "We could go in the park and wander around freely. But we could not sit down. The benches all said, 'whites only!'"

Though it was a long drive from Lenasia, she began to visit Hillbrow frequently. "It was a different world!" she says. "It was so cosmopolitan. It offered a chance for people to escape their quiet, sheltered suburbs. There was truly nowhere else like it. Before I saw it, I never thought that such a place could exist in South Africa."

Over time, Sam became more and more comfortable walking about in Hillbrow. "But truly," she emphasizes, "we did not know how to socialize with other races. We did not even know that you *could* socialize with other races. It was a thrill for us to go to Hillbrow, but we also felt awkward because of this. We stayed together. Apartheid made us all feel uncomfortable around one another."

Sam recalls that she and her friends from Lenasia could visit some of Hill-brow's clubs, but they did not feel secure enough to walk into a restaurant and sit down. "It was too risky," she says. "There was a chance of being turned away. We did not know how to behave around whites. By 1984 or 1985, there were some clubs in Hillbrow that were 100 percent Indian or Coloured. There was the Pink Cadillac and the Thunderdome. That is where we felt comfort-able. By the time I was twenty-one or twenty-two, we [my friends and I] started to feel like grown-ups. We started going to Hillbrow all the time. It was the first place in the country to offer late-night shopping. Though we did not go to sit-down restaurants we loved to go to the Fontana grill and order chicken [discussed in chapter 2]. It was a famous, twenty-four-hour deli that served food any time. Though it was primarily a takeaway, people could sit at tables and have their chicken and socialize."

Dickie—"We never knew how we would be treated"

Dickie,[55] a Chinese South African man, came out as gay in 1977—to himself and some of his friends, but not to his family. He was nineteen. "The gay spaces were all, or mostly, in Hillbrow," he recalls, "so that is where I went."

The clubs that he can remember were the Skyline, Scants, and, in nearby Doornfontein, a bar called After Dark. He befriended a white man named Tom who lived in Highpoint, a massive tower on Pretoria Street. Tom had a Coloured boyfriend who lived across the street. Dickie stresses how unusual and exciting it was to know that a Coloured man could be living in Hillbrow in 1977.

"There was no [residential] integration yet," he says, "but the landlords sometimes turned a 'blind eye' when they could. And it was easier for Co-loured people to pass as white than it was members of most other groups."

Dickie's family often struggled under the apartheid laws. The laws recog-nized only four racial groups: whites, Africans, Indians, and Coloureds. Chi-nese South Africans, he says, were considered "unclassified," and they faced uncertainty.

"Our role as Chinese South Africans was to *comply, concede, and conform,*" he recalls. "We were treated in many ways as an invisible minority."

His parents settled in the largely Black township of Lady Selbourne, near Pretoria, and had eleven children during the 1940s and 1950s.

"We were not allowed to live among whites," Dickie says, "but as non-Africans, we did not entirely belong either. But Lady Selbourne was one of the only locations anywhere in South Africa where non-whites were allowed to own property."

Then came the Group Areas Act of 1950. This act rolled out gradually, but eventually forced the Black African population to leave Lady Selbourne. Dickie's family owned a small business trading goods in Lady Selbourne and depended heavily on selling to Black South Africans. Sales began to dry up and they soon found themselves unsure of where to go. In the midst of the population removals, Dickie's father died and left his mother alone with eleven children. She was forced to close the business.

"There was no Chinese neighborhood for us to go to," Dickie explains. "So we went to a white neighborhood in Johannesburg to look for housing. Since we were unclassified the government did not know what to do with us. We had to go to every house on the block and get written permission from the white families saying that they were okay with us living there.

"Not wanting to bring attention to ourselves," he says, "you felt compelled to be compliant and follow in the customs of our 'benefactors.' So, what the ruling party — the whites — did, we felt almost obliged to follow their lead. They went to Catholic school, so I went to Catholic school. They were Catholics, so I became a Catholic. We just did our best to fit in. Like I said, *comply, concede, and conform*. It was too dangerous to deviate in any way. We were Chinese and we had to blend in and have no identity of our own and no personality."

But in the late 1970s, Dickie found a job at one of several stores owned by Helen de Leuw, a white woman credited with transforming the culture of design and aesthetics in South Africa. He began making friends and connections through the company.

"Hillbrow was always the place to go to meet up with friends, especially gay friends, in the late 1970s," he says. "By the early 1980s, it was becoming very relaxed. It was liberal and friendly. There was nowhere else like it in South Africa that I know of. There was a flow. There was a lot of conviviality. We could have a good time walking around."

Dickie pauses and echoes some of the same reservations that Sam, above, expressed about Hillbrow in the 1980s. "We [people who were not white] could go to clubs and mix," he says. "But that was partying. We did *not* go to the restaurants. It was one thing to go to a bar and hang around, but sitting down in a restaurant and having a meal would have been too uncomfortable. To go into a formal setting like that felt too risky. We never knew how we would have been treated — and there was always a possibility that we would have been told to leave."

Dickie believes that almost every other group has had its stories popularized in novels, nonfiction, memoirs, plays, and poetry. There have been some works by Chinese South African authors, such as *Colour, Confusion and Con-*

cessions by Melanie Yap and Dianne Leong Man; *All Under Heaven: The Story of a Chinese Family in South Africa* by Darryl Accone; and *Paper Sons and Daughters* by Ufrieda Ho. Sociologist Yoon Jung Park has also written *A Matter of Honor: Being Chinese in South Africa*. But Dickie wonders "when the Chinese narrative will be popularized" to make Chinese stories known to a broader South African audience.

"The Chinese South African experience is still hidden from view," he notes. "I wonder about my mother's experience, for instance. She was born in South Africa and then moved with her family to China when she was eight. When she was a teenager, she moved back to South Africa and I don't know why. What was the connection between her family and South Africa? My older sisters might know, but I have never figured it out. I never felt a part of the Chinese community given the fact I was sent to a boarding school from an early age. There were so few in my age group that I never established a social network amongst my own kind. Furthermore, being gay meant that I was a minority within a minority group. There was a Chinatown in the CBD but the only thing that brought us to that part of town was to get Chinese commodities and produce. To my knowledge, it was for trading, not for cultural edification."

Goren—"That place was not for the family man"

Goren's[56] memories of Hillbrow during the 1980s are wildly different from those of Sam and Dickie. He is a white man who describes a rowdy, mostly white, place where people drank heavily and frequently fought over territory. He had moved from Serbia (in what was then Yugoslavia) in 1985 at the age of twenty-four. The government paid for 80 percent of the cost of his airfare as part of the National Party's plan to boost the size of South Africa's white population.

"You had to have some skills to come in under that program," he explains, "but really anyone could come. They were lax about it because they wanted whites. It came with a provision. If you did not like it, within the first months, they would pay your fare home."

For Goren, a talkative man with a shaven head, the choice was easy. His brother, Mishko, had already moved to Johannesburg ten years earlier. "It was a form of economic immigration," he explains. "That was during the time of [Prime Minister] Tito and the [Yugoslav] economy had stagnated. Mishko heard there were opportunities in South Africa. He first lived in a town 80 kilometers [50 miles] south of Johannesburg, where he found work in the construction industry. By the time I came here, he had already moved to Hillbrow."

The two brothers shared a flat in the Cape Agulhas Hotel, near the Moulin Rouge, a hotel with a famous nightclub. "I paid only R125 a month to live in the hotel," he laughs, "with most meals included! I lived on one rand a day! That bought me chicken liver, onion, and bread. Beer was thirty-five cents. That's how I lived."

Goren briefly found work in a platinum mine. "It was an extremely racist operation," he says. "They provided me with a Black man as my assistant to carry my toolbox. What was in the toolbox? Nothing but alcohol! They called us [whites] skilled workers but what skills did we have? Nothing!"

In 1985, Goren says, "Hillbrow was 95 to 100 percent immigrant. There were immigrants from Scotland, Greece, Portugal, England, the Netherlands, Austria, and Serbia. It was a drinking environment where everyone hung out and drank enormous amounts of alcohol. There were so many clubs everywhere and it was simply impossible to avoid alcohol. They all became alcoholics. That place was not for the family man! It was men who broke away and wanted to drink."

Goren pauses and his expression becomes serious, almost grave. He goes on to describe a shocking incident in which we see how the white power structure and the individuals supporting it treated Black African lives as if they had no value. "On the third or fourth day after I first moved to Hillbrow — I will never forget it for the rest of my life," he says. "Me and my brother went to a nightclub owned by some Yugoslav guy by End Street. We were not drunk but not sober either. We left around 3:00 a.m. Three Black guys were walking. We were being driven by our friend, a white man, who had a car. He hit one of the Black guys who was on foot. It was an accident. Our friend, the driver, saw that there was a cop car nearby and we signaled for it. We walked over to the cop car and told him what had happened. The cop told our friend: 'This is what you do. Go back and run over the body again. Make sure he is dead. If he lives, he can sue you. But he can't sue you if he is dead.' My friend did not do this. He just drove away." Goren's story is a reminder of the profound system of violence against Black lives throughout South Africa's history of colonization and apartheid. From such a history comes the everyday racist brutality Goren describes, where a Black pedestrian's life had no value to the police officer, who actively supports the murder of this person, or to Goren and his friends, who leave him there, potentially to die.

Goren goes on to describe a neighborhood that was, from his point of view, a lawless terrain of bars and clubs, ruled by ethnic conflicts, gambling, and a burgeoning sex trade. "Hillbrow was 70 percent white in those days," he estimates. "But they had what were called 'multi-clubs.' These were mixed clubs.

At first the 'mix' only included Coloureds and Indians. Africans were excluded but they started joining the mix later, gradually. By the end of the 1980s, the best clubs were in Yeoville. They were all shabeens which just means they did not have liquor licenses. There was always plenty of cocaine. The White Horse was a nice nightclub in Hillbrow owned by Greeks. I was young and stupid and got in a fight with the security guards at the White Horse. They knocked my teeth out! It was all whites fighting whites."

When asked what the fights were about, he says: "Fuck, I don't know! We were all drunk. We fought for no reason. Didn't you ever get into fights when you were young?"

When Nerio tells him that no, he had never been in a physical fight, Goren looks baffled. He seems unable to imagine a young man who did not get into occasional brawls.

"The fights were sometimes about money," he says, "but they were more about manliness. There was not much crime, but in 1986, three Black men pulled a knife on me. They got my money but there wasn't much of it. It was daylight, the afternoon. That was the only time I was ever robbed [in Hillbrow]."

Goren describes a general level of violence that seemed ever-present to him in Hillbrow in the late 1980s. "It could happen at any time," he says. "It was like fights between nations. Groups of Lebanese would fight the Portuguese. Serbians would fight the Greeks and on and on. I don't mean one-on-one. I mean groups of ten or more on each side. In Nedbank Plaza [on Pretoria Street] there was a pizza place. I was there one day and saw a Black worker stab another Black worker in the neck. That one was a fight about money.

"There were also gay bars," he recalls. "The Skyline, for instance. No one minded. There was plenty of [male] prostitution around there, around the corner from the Skyline. And there were also plenty of nice places: Café Wien, Café Zurich, Café Paris. But there was a lot of gambling. Café Zurich had a back room where people gambled. It had Greek owners—Nick and his son. There was also a Chinese takeaway on Pretoria Street that was a high-stakes gambling place. Roma Pizza was two doors down from Café Zurich and they also had gambling. At Café Wien, we went one night at 3:00 a.m. after we lost our money gambling somewhere else. Five Black men came in and robbed the place. They went table to table taking what they could get, but when they got to our table we didn't have one cent. They didn't know what to do with us. Eventually, they left us alone."

Goren recounts the famous, rowdy New Year's Eve parties that were a staple in the neighborhood for decades. "New Year's in Hillbrow always meant big parties," he says. "People broke into cars and rolled the cars over. Sometimes they set them on fire. They were all white people doing this. Eventually, New Year's became too dangerous."

In 1990, Goren moved from Hillbrow to Berea and lived there until 1992. "That's when the crime really started to increase and I felt I had to go," he explains. "They broke in twice that year and I was at home both times. I was able to get out the other door. But I didn't want to live with that anymore. So I moved to Northcliffe [an upscale, northern suburb] where I was robbed almost immediately. There were four more home invasions after that. Each time, the men who invaded had guns. I gave them everything and they let me live."

Goren opened a food market in the CBD in 1993, around the time he moved to Northcliffe. "The CBD was already regarded as dangerous by then," he says, "but it was the only place I could afford to open a business. It was too expensive in the suburbs. I sold that food market two years later, in 1995. Three days after that, gunmen came in and shot the new owner."

Claudine — "There were lots of strange people around"

Claudine,[57] a white Jewish woman, was twenty-two years old in 1988 when she moved into a flat on the corner of Twist and Eselen Streets. She had completed a degree in English two years earlier and had begun teaching at Malvern High School. On her motorbike, she could reach Malvern from Hillbrow in twenty minutes.

"Hillbrow was a tourist center then, with a good economy," she recalls. "It was completely integrated. My building, and the buildings around it, were very mixed and there were lots of strange people around."

Her eyes twinkle when she says the words "strange people," and it is clear that she uses that term affectionately. "There were many clubs in the area, and there were also drugs, prostitution, and runaways. I loved it," she adds. "Hillbrow had a good social life. It was exciting. The flat below me was a trans brothel. The other tenants in the building were young people who did not know where they were going in life and some were elderly."

A few elderly people had begun to avoid Hillbrow in the late 1980s, Claudine says, but its "vibey-ness" was still attractive to young people like herself. Joubert Park, on the other hand, had by then acquired a greater reputation for crime. Some of its residents had begun to feel like "prisoners in their own homes." But in Hillbrow, Claudine had no sense that there was anything to fear. She fondly remembers that she used to walk home with her boyfriend from midnight movies on Pretoria Street.

Claudine was born in 1966 to white Jewish parents who lived in Mayfair, a community then zoned exclusively for white people. But given its location on the border of Fordsburg, Claudine says, the residents of Mayfair were exposed to more diversity than were residents in other white areas. Fordsburg was also zoned as a white neighborhood, but it had become home to a significant number of Indians from the 1930s on. Marc Latilla writes that by the 1940s and 1950s, Fordsburg "also had a reputation of being on the cutting edge of black urban culture defined by its four bioscopes [movie theaters] and various jazz clubs."[58] By the 1980s, Mayfair became a broadly diverse community, much like Hillbrow, and is now the center of Somali life in Johannesburg and one of the most important locations in the city for members of the Muslim faith.[59] Claudine says she reveled in the diversity that was developing around her.

At eighteen, she moved into a residence hall in Jeppestown while working on her university degree. She began teaching math at Malvern High School, in 1986, and recalls a city experiencing rapid change. Malvern High was zoned for whites only but experienced a precipitous drop in enrollment — from eight hundred students to four hundred students in the mid-1980s — as the white exodus from the city's central neighborhoods began. By 1987, most of Claudine's students were Angolans and Mozambicans. They were African, she explains, but because they had "white" (Portuguese) surnames they were able to enroll.

On Christmas Eve, 1991, a handful of children attacked Claudine in the lobby of her Hillbrow building. She describes them as "street children," mostly from Soweto, whom she had often provided with food over the previous two years. While usually gathered on the sidewalk, the children were waiting inside the building on that day. It was easy for them to gain access, as there was no security gate. During the scuffle, one of the children stabbed her.

"It was only a flesh wound," she says. Like so many Johannesburgers, Claudine has a way of shrugging off nonfatal violent encounters. "It did not affect me because I had already been mugged several times. The first time, I was seventeen and was walking home from the main library in the CBD. I was also mugged by the Absa Bank office in Hillbrow and once near Highpoint. You just go on."

Her decision to leave Hillbrow, in 1992, was not related to any sense of fear. As a teacher, Claudine received a housing subsidy and wanted to purchase a flat. She found one for a good price on the border of Berea and Yeoville. She had taken a new position at a technical college in Doornfontein, only six blocks away from her flat, but she felt that Doornfontein had become a bit unsafe for walking. Her motorbike helped her reach the school every day without incident.

Most of the students in the technical college were recent arrivals from the

DRC, the Republic of Congo, and Uganda. Many others were mid-career South African adults, sent by their employers for additional training. "There was a nice, constructive atmosphere," she says, "but the management was Afrikaans and they still had an apartheid mindset. They treated the students poorly, even though they were adults."

During the late 1990s, Claudine experienced a series of health problems. Her lungs collapsed, and eventually she had to have a tracheotomy. In and out of the hospital over the course of several months, she lost her job at the technical college. She found work at Greenside High School, her alma mater, even though she struggled with her voice. The Anglo-American Corporation (a mining house) sponsored her to run a math clinic at Greenside, which she describes as the most racially integrated school in all of Johannesburg — up to the present day.

By the early 2000s, Claudine's doctor advised her to move to the Cape Peninsula. It offers the only type of microclimate suitable to her lungs. Without such a move, he told her, she would be shortening her life.

Claudine's experiences after leaving Johannesburg for the Cape Town area provide a glimpse into the evolving diversity of South Africa. She followed her doctor's advice and moved to Muizenberg, on the shore, but explains that she was unable to find work in a government school: "They are simply not going to hire an older white teacher with chronic health problems."

She makes a daily two-hour commute from Muizenberg to teach in an Islamic school in the suburb of Athlone, in the Cape Flats. At 237,000, Athlone's population is 81 percent Coloured, 6 percent Black African, 5 percent Indian, and less than 1 percent white.[60] "The students are very poor and most are sponsored by an organization in Egypt," Claudine elaborates. "Most of the staff are not committed to secular education — even those teaching secular subjects. There are many behavioral problems, but the religious orientation of the school prohibits diagnosing learning disabilities or psychiatric conditions."

Claudine observes that the lives of the children she teaches are marked by numerous obstacles and considerable chaos. Sometimes gang members block their path to school and they are unable to attend for a day or more at a time. On other occasions, parents keep their children home because they have heard there may be gang activity.

"I love Muizenberg," she says. "The sea is my front garden and the mountains are my backyard. But it is also showing signs of going the way of Hillbrow. There is still wealth, but many more people are now sleeping in the parks, doorways, and under the bridges. It is not as violent as Hillbrow, but I feel that is coming. My friend's home was burgled seven times."

Claudine lives in a boardinghouse that she says is home to "a lot of people who have dropped out of life, basically. There are some teachers and taxi drivers, and there's even a filmmaker living there, but the rest are alcoholics."

Claudine believes that Cape Town's structural problems may ultimately be more insurmountable than Johannesburg's. "Foreign money has been pouring into the city," she reflects, "mostly to buy real estate on the coastline. This fuels the inequality. Meanwhile, apartheid created a group of people, the Coloureds, who are now the poorest paid and the least likely to be employed. This has created a terrible bitterness. There is so much alcoholism. The educational system is failing because the teachers are so poorly paid. The issues I face in my classroom, in the Cape Flats, are similar to what I saw in Malvern: so many parents in jail, so much drug addiction."

Throughout the interview, Claudine maintains a gentle smile, but her projection for the future seems to grow ever bleaker. Nonetheless, she ends our conversation on a note of hope. "Earlier this year, I interviewed at a school in Khayelitsha," she says. Khayelitsha is one of Cape Town's largest townships. "I saw something wonderful," she smiles. "There was overcrowding. There were classrooms in shipping containers. But there was such commitment and energy! The school was going from strength to strength. It was just blossoming."

Paul Davis — "It was a country in a state of ferment"

Paul Davis,[61] mentioned earlier in this chapter, points out the immense changes driving South Africa's political environment beginning in 1990. That year, Nelson Mandela was freed after spending twenty-seven years in prison. His release was greeted with joy and hailed as a milestone in much of the world. But the next years would be difficult ones for South Africa.

The early 1990s was an extremely tense period. Rodney Davenport and Christopher Saunders write, "Annual deaths from civil strife had actually risen from between 600 and 1,400 in the 1980s to between 2,700 and 3,800 in the early 1990s. Mortalities from political violence in 1994 more than tripled those during the Soweto uprising of 1976–7."[62]

"It was a country in a state of ferment," Paul recalls. "Right-wing Afrikaners knew they were losing control of the country but they were trying to impose themselves. The right wing was pushing for violence and the military had many right-wing elements — and they were skilled. There were provocateurs initiating violence. The ANC's goal, meanwhile, was 'to make the country ungovernable.' On top of all of that, the Inkatha Freedom Party was also getting money from the government to foment violence against the ANC. There were a lot of arms everywhere. A lot of obstructionists wanted to stop the process [of democratization]. Others wanted revolution.

"And 1990," Paul continues, "is also when the taxi violence started [in Hillbrow and other parts of Johannesburg]. Taxis were one of the only business sectors where Blacks could own their own businesses. Not only were the taxi drivers and owners in competition with one another, but the drivers were also divided by ideology and party. Some supported the Pan Africanist Congress, some the ANC, and some the Inkatha Freedom Party. The big violence was over money. Taxis were vital to people for getting around locally and for going home to other parts of South Africa."

In the early 1990s, no one was sure whether a peaceful transition would really happen or whether things would spiral out of control. The year 1993 was especially tumultuous. On April 10, a right-wing Polish immigrant shot and killed Chris Hani, the charismatic leader of the South African Communist Party and head of the ANC's armed wing, Umkhonto we Sizwe. Mass protests followed, but after Nelson Mandela appealed for calm there was no violence at Hani's funeral. A little more than two months later, the militant right-wing leader Eugène Terre'blanche tried to disrupt negotiations between the National Party and the ANC by smashing his armored vehicle into the building where the negotiations were being held. Later that year, some radical Black activists held demonstrations chanting "one-settler, one-bullet" and staged a handful of violent attacks on white restaurants and a church.[63]

"The police and the military had a tight grip around the time of the elections," Paul stresses. "If they had wanted to, they could have stopped the election [in 1994]. But at election time, the police and military took a pledge to protect the constitution. The whole world supported the truce. It was a world event! And there was jubilation! It was the very best time for me here in South Africa. Everyone was positive. But it was easier for whites to be positive, of course, because they had not suffered. There was always a population that believed wrongs had not been righted."

One Day I Will Write about This Place

In his memoir, *One Day I Will Write about This Place*, the late Kenyan journalist and queer activist Binyavanga Wainaina provides a sense of South Africa's transformations during the early 1990s. He writes about Hillbrow mostly from afar but tells of the roads migrants from around the continent began taking toward Johannesburg during these years. Briefly, he was one of them.[64]

Wainaina's mother left Uganda in the 1970s, during Idi Amin's reign. He grew up in the comparative safety of Kenya but with vivid nightmares about the murderous dictator, Amin. His family lived uneasily, monitoring the steadily eroding situation their relatives faced in Uganda while enduring the xenophobic comments of their Kenyan neighbors. They lived through a brief coup in Kenya, which was put down within a day but not before thousands of people across the country were killed.

In describing his route to South Africa, which began in 1990, Wainaina helps us see some of the many factors pushing people to leave their homes to migrate and some of the pulls drawing them to South Africa. When the International Monetary Fund (IMF) imposed a structural adjustment program on Kenya, it forced the government to end subsidies for the nation's universities. Wainaina stresses that this was a tragic turn for the country. "Since the 1950s," he writes, "all the Kenyans who did well in exams have not had to worry about money. The idea was that this was the way to make new people. The children of dirt-poor peasants could become doctors. This is where my parents came from. Now, the IMF has insisted that we stop spending so much government money on education. It is truly the only thing that works in Kenya. . . . Our schooling machine, nationwide, merit-based, proud, and competitive — Kenya's single biggest investment — is falling apart."[65]

Parents began selling whatever they could in order to send their children to universities abroad. One of his friends left for the US to study and Wainaina decided to enroll in the University of Transkei, in one of South Africa's "homelands." Two of his uncles were professors at that university.

Wainaina arrived in Transkei, in 1991, a year after Mandela's release from prison. He found himself, he writes, at a school where "students regularly shut the campus down, over one or another political issue" and "liberation talk" was everywhere. Nonetheless, he was distressed to hear people ask him, every day, if he was from "Africa." In a taste of the xenophobia that would become a prominent theme in twenty-first-century South Africa, they insisted to him that "South Africa is not Africa."[66]

Like much of the country, he was captivated by the ubiquitous music of Brenda Fassie and saddened by the way media portrayed this era of her life. Fassie had been dubbed the "Madonna of the townships," and the "queen of pop," but her life was a "roller-coaster" of great highs and terrible lows. Wainaina connects this low point in her life with the symbolism of Hillbrow's transformation. "They [the scandals] are fast and furious now," he writes. "She was seen playing soccer with young boys on the streets of Hillbrow, Johannesburg. Then she shocks the conservative country by announcing she is a lesbian. . . . Brenda is where sex and struggle politics met. *She is Hillbrow* [emphasis added], in Johannesburg, where tens of thousands of illegal immigrants find themselves selling and trading and changing and dying and making money and losing money. Where Black meets white, drugs meet dreams, and music soaks it all in. Hillbrow is where she always seems to end up when she is down on her luck."[67]

In 1993, Wainaina moved off campus and stopped taking classes, an action that made him an "illegal immigrant" in South Africa. Uncertainty and violence gripped the country during this time. "Bodies pile up in Zululand," he writes. There were widespread expectations that the country would "explode."

The end of the Cold War was upending the political order on much of the continent. "We are children of the cold war," Wainaina writes, "We came of age when it ended; we watched our countries crumple like paper. It is as if the Great Lakes [in Eastern Africa] are standing and rising above the map and tilting downward, and streams of Rwandese, Kenyans, and others are pouring into Congo, Tanzania, Kenya. Then Kenya shook and those stood and poured into South Africa."[68] The economy worsened in Kenya at this time, especially amid widespread allegations of election rigging. Doctors from the country began "flooding South African hospitals to work."[69]

In 1995, Wainaina decided to return home to Kenya and his family sent him a ticket. As part of his journey, he took a packed bus to Johannesburg, from which he would fly to Nairobi. In Johannesburg, he met his friend from the University of Transkei for a night of partying in Hillbrow. The two men were taken through the neighborhood by a Zambian taxi driver and during the ride they heard "guns and screams."[70]

The Zambian driver let them stay at his apartment in nearby Yeoville. "There are mattresses spread on the floor," Wainaina writes; "there must be fifteen or twenty people staying in this apartment."[71] When he awakened in the morning, he saw some among this crowd rustling plastic bags of curios to sell at flea markets. Two of the tenants were schoolgirls dressed in their uniforms and another was a security guard.

Wainaina offers a glimpse of what he believes is a transformed Hillbrow. After spending a month back home in Kenya with his family, he returned to South Africa to finish his degree, in late 1996. He writes, "Once Struggle Central, now Hillbrow is the drug-dealing capital of Africa, where the broken are robbed by the new and hungry." Brenda Fassie's romantic partner, Poppie Sihlahla, died of a crack cocaine overdose in a room at the Quirinale Hotel that year. Fassie was lying next to her, in the same bleak Hillbrow hotel room.[72]

4

Hillbrow in a New Country, 1994–99

With the inauguration of President Nelson Mandela on May 10, 1994, South Africa began its arduous and uneven transition from apartheid toward broadly inclusive democracy. In 1997, the ANC-led government adopted one of the most progressive constitutions in the world. After three hundred years of white supremacist rule, the new constitution promised a democratic state founded on human dignity, nonracialism, and nonsexism. The people of the country, it proclaimed, "believe that South Africa belongs to all who live in it."[1] Many observers and organizations would, over the years, interpret that line from the preamble to include the many nonnationals who would take up residence in the country. Many others have questioned whether the negotiations between the ANC and the National Party could right the wrongs of colonization and apartheid.

Even as the developments of a new government and constitution received global acclaim, the country encountered numerous obstacles on the way to meeting South Africa's ambitious goals of democracy. The ANC had made bold claims. It promised to construct a million new homes, redistribute land, and provide clean water for everyone during its first five years in power. It would soon discover, however, that the former white minority government had left the coffers bare after decades of arming the police and military to crush domestic opposition and of funding rebel movements to destabilize Black-led governments to the north (especially in Mozambique and Angola).[2] Expectations for the Rainbow Nation were high, but by the turn of the century, wariness was spreading through most sectors of the society.

Many of the challenges facing postapartheid South Africa were reflected or amplified in Hillbrow. White minority rule had resulted in the development of only limited parts of the country — primarily those where whites lived — and the deliberate underdevelopment of much of the rest of the country. As apartheid crumbled, millions of people who had been confined to economically desolate rural areas and severely overcrowded townships looked toward the cities with hope. In 1991, the scrapping of the Group Areas Act, which had separated the population into four distinct racial groups, freed people to move to any area they could afford.

As the economic powerhouse of the country — indeed, of sub-Saharan Africa — Johannesburg seemed to offer access to everything previously withheld: jobs with the potential for upward mobility, formal housing with modern amenities, a well-developed infrastructure, and an extensive cultural life. With its central location, soaring high-rise buildings, and relatively low-cost flats, Hillbrow was the logical first stop for many new arrivals to the city.

From its earliest days as a neighborhood, Hillbrow had offered middle-class comfort, urban excitement, and a bracing taste of modernity to residents and tourists. But by the 1990s, Johannesburg started to change in ways that made Hillbrow far less hospitable. The end of the global boycott brought new investment to the metropolis, but the economic center of gravity shifted northward into the sprawling, still largely white, suburbs. As capital withdrew from the inner city, Hillbrow's property owners could no longer secure loans for maintenance, and many of its vast blocks of flats spiraled into decline. At the same time, the city's political and economic leaders were determined to make Johannesburg a "world-class city" by luring high-tech and professional employers. Though the region did gain sixty thousand well-paying, high-skill jobs, it also experienced the staggering loss of one million blue-collar jobs. Richard Tomlinson, Robert A. Beauregard, Lindsay Bremner, and Xolela Mangcu attribute the loss of stable, working-class jobs to South Africa's entry into the World Trade Organization (WTO), after which the country dropped tariffs on imports.[3] Local industries that were poised to benefit from the end of boycotts against South Africa found themselves struggling in an economy swamped by cheap imported goods. The "world-class city" plan did little or nothing for job seekers in the townships and the inner city, who had few options but to turn to the informal sector, where work was insecure and sometimes dangerous and often barely paid survival wages.[4]

Tens of thousands of people made their way to Hillbrow during this period but found a neighborhood with increasingly neglected housing where most had access only to insecure, poorly paid jobs if they found work at all. According to the census, the neighborhood's population grew by about 3.5 percent per year during the 1990s and early 2000s to reach a total population of 74,000 by 2011.[5] Other sources suggest the actual population grew much higher. Carrol Clarkson, for instance, estimates that by 2003 Hillbrow was home to 100,000 people during the week and 200,000 on the weekends. The additional 100,000 in Clarkson's estimate consisted of people who regularly drove into the neighborhood and stayed a night or two before they transported goods back to Zimbabwe, Malawi, Mozambique, and other outlying areas.[6]

South Africa's shift toward nonracial democracy signaled to the rest of the continent that the country was ready to receive other Africans. Johannesburg beckoned to people in regions experiencing tumult, war, repression, or economic stagnation. On South Africa's northeast border, for instance, Mozambique's civil war lasted from 1974 to 1992 and left its infrastructure severely eroded and its economy underdeveloped. According to the United Nations' *Human Development Report* of 1992, Mozambique's population by the end of the 1980s was the poorest in the world with an average income of only US$80 per year.[7] Though Mozambicans had formed a major part of Johannesburg's industrial labor force for much of the twentieth century,[8] the war forced an additional 6 million people out of their homes and sent 1.7 million fleeing to neighboring countries. Though Malawi received the greatest number of those who fled Mozambique, South Africa received the second-highest at about 350,000.[9] About 100,000 of those made their way to Johannesburg.[10]

Angola has some of the greatest concentrations of natural resources in the world, including diamonds, bauxite, and uranium, and the second-largest oil reserves in Africa. Had it developed differently, it might have prospered; instead, its war for independence from Portugal lasted more than thirteen years (from 1961 to 1974). Almost immediately after this war ended, the country was engulfed by a civil war, stoked by South Africa's apartheid government. That war dragged on for a grueling twenty-seven years, destroying 98 percent of Angola's bridges, 80 percent of its factories, 60 percent of its hospitals, and 80 percent of its schools. As rivals in the Cold War, the US, the Soviet Union, Cuba, and China all sent heavy armaments and military advisers, thereby heightening the destructiveness of the conflict.[11] As a result, Angola soon had and continues to have more land mines than almost any country in the world (with about 100 million square meters of land still contaminated).[12] A third of Angola's population was displaced and 450,000 Angolans ended up in refugee camps in neighboring countries. Several thousand moved to Johannesburg.[13]

Three thousand miles to the north, Nigerians also looked to South Africa for better economic prospects. This was especially true for members of the Igbo population, who felt the Nigerian government had blocked them from opportunities at home. Likewise, as Zimbabwe began its economic descent in the mid-1990s, tens of thousands and then hundreds of thousands migrated to Johannesburg. As many as 700,000 Zimbabweans entered South Africa in 1995 alone.[14] In 1997, civil war erupted in the Republic of Congo and, a year later, the second Congo War, also referred to as the "African World War," broke out in neighboring DRC. Each of these developments sent large numbers of people on routes that would lead to South Africa and in many cases to Hillbrow. They were joined by Burundians, Ethiopians, Zambians, Rwandans, Somalians, and Tanzanians.

Though it was the continent's industrial and corporate powerhouse, apartheid had left Johannesburg with severe structural imbalances that made it ill suited to absorb so many people. Property and wealth were concentrated in a small number of hands. For many decades, the primary purpose of its police force had been to protect the white minority and to crush political resistance. Under democracy, that police force, poorly paid and used to the violent suppression of the Black African, Indian, and Coloured populations, was expected to reorient itself to serve the entire population (more than five times the number of people). It had to do so with almost no additional personnel, little new training, and few new funds.[15]

Johannesburg had world-class hospitals, schools, and infrastructure, but the landscape of apartheid meant that only parts of the city, and some of its people, enjoyed such facilities. White rule had left all South African cities surrounded by townships that had informal housing, unpaved roads, poorly equipped schools, and little access to health care. Keith Beavon shows that, for much of the twentieth century, the Johannesburg Town Council had grown ever more aggressive in preventing Black people from starting or owning businesses or owning homes; under such conditions no Black wealth could develop. Even as Soweto exceeded one million people, its Black residents were forbidden to own laundries, bookstores, tailor shops, doctors' offices, and lawyers' offices. Only the selling of basic necessities, such as fruits, vegetables, milk, bread, and assorted sundries, was permitted. After prohibiting Soweto from developing an industrial or commercial base of its own, the Town Council officially "excised" the townships to prevent them from receiving infrastructure funds. Even as some of these laws were gradually relaxed after the Soweto Uprising of 1976, the template of geographic inequality has been extremely difficult to undo.[16]

Perhaps the greatest difference between Hillbrow's first ninety years (1894 to 1984) and years since 1984 is the extent to which trauma pervaded the lives of its residents. Until 1991 with the scrapping of the Group Areas Act, Hillbrow was zoned as a whites-only residential area. Not only did its white residents during that time benefit from an economic system that restricted most opportunities to members of their "race," their government also shielded them from the state violence that pervaded the everyday lives of most other South Africans.

It is impossible to overstate the extent of the state brutality used by the white minority government to enforce its will over more than 80 percent of the population. It did so by creating a climate of humiliation and terror. Antjie Krog writes that she and other South African reporters became physically ill for weeks at a time — rashes, vomiting, hair and teeth falling out — when they covered the Truth and Reconciliation Commission hearings (1996–98). They confronted evidence of state-sponsored kidnappings, disappearances, and often gratuitously gruesome killings. They heard from grieving parents whose children had disappeared and who wanted to know what the police had done with their remains. They listened to stories about security force members keeping human body parts in jars on their desks. Krog writes that the white population — including herself — not only had been protected from this kind of violence but had been shielded from even *knowing* that it was going on all around them. Black South African reporters, on the other hand, were well aware.[17]

State brutality was not the only systemic violence that left its imprint on the society. By the 1980s, many of the townships surrounding Johannesburg were engulfed in deadly confrontations between rival resistance parties: the ANC, the PAC, and the IFP. Many of the first Black South Africans who moved to Hillbrow were trying to get away from these conflicts. It was not only adults who were fleeing; some refugees were children as young as eleven who made their way to Hillbrow alone. Jill Swart spent years talking to children in Hillbrow during the 1980s. Many of them confided to her that they felt safer living there on the streets than in the townships. A fifteen-year-old boy named Francis, for instance, told her: "I am here because of all the fighting in the townships. I don't like all the violence. When it is quiet, I will go back."[18]

Jonny Steinberg also shows that thousands of young men were recruited from rural areas by parties such as the ANC and IFP to fight in the struggle against apartheid. They were trained to use guns and explosives and to think of people as targets. When the fighting ended, they were left without resources or assistance. Many of them drifted to Johannesburg and other large cities where they ended up unemployed and often homeless and desperate.[19]

This chapter examines the expectations and experiences of people in Hillbrow during the immediate postapartheid years. Our interviews illustrate the complexities involved in moving to, surviving in, and sometimes succeeding in Hillbrow. Some arrived expecting a pleasant and exciting environment that would enable them to prosper. Others arrived having steeled themselves for life in a difficult place. Through their own words, and those of social workers, religious leaders, and housing developers, we learn why people chose to move to Hillbrow, how they found housing and work, and how they built families and networks.

The Fleeting Promise of a "Post-race" City

Lindsay Bremner captures the sense of promise and possibility that the transition to democracy brought to Johannesburg. In 1994, she writes, many hoped for the birth of a "post-race kind of city." With de jure apartheid consigned to the historical dustbin, the city that began taking shape "produced new ways of imagining and being."[20] De facto apartheid would, however, remain a stubborn reality.

Bremner takes issue with the scholars who eyed Johannesburg at the time and used phrases such as "fragmented," "degenerated," and "disintegrated" to describe the postapartheid city. Those terms, she argues, rely on the premise that "order" is desirable. She reminds us that the prior order was brutal, exclusionary, and rested on persecution and torture. Johannesburg may indeed have negated the old sense of order, but it did so in the process of creating a "dynamic vision."[21]

In a similar vein, Martin J. Murray writes that when apartheid ended, there was a "brief and exhilarating historical moment" when the city seemed ready to overcome the terrible legacy of extreme racial separation. But that moment quickly gave way to uncertainty as city planners found themselves caught between two contradictory aims. On one side was the enormously challenging task of meeting the needs of the vast majority who had suffered under apartheid, a large portion of whom had been born into and trapped for their entire lives in poverty. On the other side was a desire to distance Johannesburg from the past and affirm its status as a "world-class African city." To do so would require the kind of infrastructure, technological capacity, and retail and entertainment facilities that could lure tourists and attract global business owners and professionals. The city barely had the resources for either one of these aims; it did not have enough for both.[22]

No matter how great the potential for "new ways of imagining and being," the architects of apartheid had left a landscape of inequality and structural violence that would not soon be overcome. Townships constructed before and during apartheid surround much of the city, from Alexandra and Tembisa in the north to Soweto, Tokhoza, and Kathlehong in the south. During and following the last years of apartheid, even more new townships have arisen. Orange Farm, in the far southeast, was settled by thousands of unemployed squatters during the severe housing shortage of the 1980s,[23] and Diepsloot, in the far north, was established in 1995 and quickly grew to exceed 100,000 people. Because parts of it have developed considerably, Soweto stands as something of an exception. But most townships, which together house millions of people, remain places of "widespread material deprivation" that lack even the basic amenities found in traditionally white areas of Johannesburg.[24]

The needs of the poor and the extremely poor in the townships were often sacrificed to the goal of transforming Johannesburg into a "world-class city." Murray's central argument is that while the end of apartheid gave birth to an officially deracialized Johannesburg, the city—indeed, the entire region— never actually desegregated. A Black African middle class emerged, but the majority of the Black urban poor has become even more economically isolated. Wealthy and middle-class Black people joined their white counterparts in moving from townships and inner-city neighborhoods such as Hillbrow, Berea, and Yeoville to northern suburban districts where they could feel safer behind high walls patrolled by private security companies.

Owing to residential disinvestment and flight from one neighborhood to another, Murray observes, the city rapidly reshaped itself in the 1990s. It "has metamorphosed into a sprawling megalopolis, a fragmented, unsettled, and multicentered conurbation without fungible boundaries or rules." To compare Johannesburg to what happened to US cities during and after the urban crisis of the 1970s, Murray quotes the sociologist Michael Sorkin, who wrote that US cities became like "swarms of urban bits" without centers.[25]

Hillbrow changed so rapidly that Murray characterizes its post-1994 incarnation as a "hyperghetto" or an "outcast ghetto," where most dwellers were cut off from the formal economy. Many who could, left, and new arrivals had to cope with "almost unbearable pressures." Those pressures included fear and wariness, and the sense of loneliness that results from distrust. As economic marginalization increased, Hillbrow and its surrounding neighborhoods, such as the CBD, Yeoville, and Berea, became home to "high densities of con artists, thieves, and other social predators."[26]

In this chapter, rather than using blanket terms such as "hyperghetto," we speak to the people who have lived in, worked in, or spent considerable time in Hillbrow in order to provide the sense of daily life amid challenging conditions. Murray frequently uses the term "battlefield" to describe Hillbrow, in particular. The battlefield is a result of low incomes, high rents, and municipal and national governments that often fail to adequately deliver even the most essential basic services.

At the same time, Murray believes Hillbrow is manifesting "embryonic signs" of an "antighetto." If it is "now a dismal and unforgiving place," there is also a complexity that suggests better possibilities and other, more optimistic futures. Even in such a desperate environment, he writes, "new kinds of sociability and cooperation continuously develop in the cracks and crevices." It is a neighborhood "full of surprises," in which faith-based organizations, social organizations, networks, families, friends, and relatives struggle to build community. "The inner city is a 'multiplicity of places,'" he writes.[27] We seek to capture that complexity, multiplicity, and desperation, and the potential surprises of Hillbrow.

John Kani — "The melting pot, the challenges, the excitement"

John Kani,[28] the "grandfather of South African theater" (also discussed in chapter 3), reflects on the complex transitions in Hillbrow. In the 1970s, John was lauded in many parts of the world for his plays depicting the bleak realities of apartheid. In the 1990s, he saw both fresh possibilities and difficulties emerging as a new society was born. The apartheid government had arrested him for the crime of acting while Black — acting was a profession forbidden to Black Africans under apartheid — and he had been stabbed during an assassination attempt for kissing a white woman on stage. Now, a new president and a new constitution promised equality and opportunity for everyone.

Hillbrow seemed on the verge of becoming a genuinely African cosmopolitan space. At the same time, John recalls new tensions developing within and over that space. Black South Africans, he notes, had organized and struggled for decades, and they believed they were about to gain full access to a city from which they had been excluded by forced removals and pass laws. Meanwhile, other Africans were eyeing Johannesburg as the new continent's aspirational city.

"Mandela gets elected," John says in an interview, "and suddenly the borders with Africa are open. Mandela removed the six thousand–volt fence that ran for thousands of miles, closing down South Africa from the rest of Africa. It was a humanitarian act. The animals were dying. It was also a way of saying 'now the borders of Africa are open.' And thus came the new migration of people from all over Africa, of people from conflict areas, from economically depressed areas, and also just for the excitement of coming to South Africa.

"And that, to me, is Hillbrow — the melting pot, the challenges, the excitement," he continues. "Now, with the influx of Nigerians, Somalis, Ethiopians, the DRCs [sic], Zimbabweans, Malawians, Mozambicans — Johannesburg has become a true African city, with all the modern amenities, all the technology and accessibility to every business situation that could promote you. But there is still a slowing down to soberness, an African rhythm. People stand in Hillbrow. They just stand and the world moves around them. They talk to their friends and they see friends across the street. I walk around Hillbrow and I go to Shoprite, the little supermarket, and I listen to six different dialects of the African continent."

The transition from closed, white city to open, African city is one that John savors. Nonetheless, he stresses that it has not always been a smooth transition.

"The first time, it did unsettle most of us," he recalls. "There was almost like a second colonization, a second invasion of South Africa. We Black people of this country, who had suffered for over three hundred years — when Mandela became president in 1994, we thought, 'It is our turn now to sample the fruits of freedom.' And suddenly there were these brothers and sisters of Africa also flocking, also wanting a piece of this small pie."

The transition to African cosmopolis might have been a smoother and more equitable one had South Africa's other structural imbalances not been so severe. Successive governments had spent centuries depriving the Black majority within the country of adequate education, of gaining the skills that would have enabled them to prosper, and of starting or owning businesses. As noted earlier, they had built housing for Black South Africans that lacked even basic amenities in townships with cramped conditions, unpaved roads, and few or no recreational spaces. And those who moved to Hillbrow in the 1990s often faced landlords who stood to profit by allowing their buildings to deteriorate, because it freed them to rent one- and two-bedroom units to numerous occupants.

"Suddenly employment became a major issue in South Africa," John adds. "And suddenly accommodation became a major issue in South Africa. At that stage, about 1999, it seemed the stepping down of Nelson Mandela and the coming in of a new president [Thabo Mbeki] resulted also in the out-migrating of white people from the city center businesses. They left the residential areas of Hillbrow and around Hillbrow — Yeoville, Observatory, Braamfontein — and started moving to the northern suburbs. They started building huge malls in Sandton, in Rosebank, in Hyde Park, all over, just to move away from what the reality is."

It should be noted that the history of the border fence is somewhat more complex than what John recalls. His belief that Nelson Mandela tore down the electrified barrier and opened the borders appears to be widespread in South Africa, but this is a fundamental misunderstanding. While many South Africans believe that the doors were opened and people from across the continent "flooded" in after 1994, the reality is that South Africa never opened its borders. What is true is that South Africa's borders were heavily patrolled under the apartheid government, which used electrified fences, the military, and commando units to keep antiapartheid guerrillas from entering the country.[29] The apartheid government acknowledged that the fences at the Zimbabwe and Mozambican borders killed more people in just four years (1986 through 1989) than were killed at the Berlin Wall during its entire twenty-eight years of existence (1961 to 1989). The Catholic Bureau of Refugees reported in 1990 that South African border fences had killed about two hundred people during the 1980s, which was more than twice as many as the government admitted.[30]

The voltage in the fence at the Mozambique border was indeed reduced in 1990, after the government freed Nelson Mandela, and much of the fence between Mozambique and South Africa was either removed or knocked over by wildlife.[31] Jonathan Crush and David A. McDonald write that while the new government ended the *racist* features of immigration policy — which welcomed white-skinned people from other countries and largely excluded everyone else — it preserved most other aspects of previous immigration law. The ANC-led government believed that its priority was to "redistribute the cake to newly enfranchised citizens, not to allow others in to take an undeserved slice."[32] Accordingly, in 1995 South Africa's new government strengthened the apartheid-era Aliens Control Act and provided new powers to police unauthorized crossings at the borders. It also sharply reduced the number of new immigrants legally permitted to enter the country to less than ten thousand per year. The fence along the Zimbabwe border does not appear ever to have come down, though a 2020 video shows streams of people stepping through broken parts of the fence near Beitbridge.[33]

Local politicians and the media frequently overestimated the number of undocumented immigrants in the country, routinely reporting that nine million people (which would have been about 20 percent of South Africa's entire population) had entered illegally. They often implied that cross-border migrants were entering for economic, or criminal, reasons and generally dismissed stories of political oppression or life-threatening turmoil. Teresa Dirsuweit writes that elected officials, newspapers, and televised media sources routinely attributed rising levels of crime to "foreign" migrants, even though only about 1 percent of suspects arrested during the late 1990s were from outside South Africa.[34]

More sober analyses show that about 500,000 undocumented migrants were in fact living in the country at any given time during the second half of the 1990s. In any case, under Nelson Mandela's presidency the government began a vigorous campaign of deportations. In 1995, it forcibly removed over 157,000 migrants — a higher number than in any year during apartheid. Altogether, Mandela's government removed about 600,000 people between 1994 and 2000 (a number that reflects the fact that many people experienced multiple reentries and deportations).[35]

The wildly inflated media reports of nine million undocumented migrants living in South Africa, combined with the loss of hundreds of thousands of industrial jobs, set the stage for the simmering xenophobia that would mark the 1990s and beyond. Oddly, however, the ANC government chose to pre-serve another element of apartheid — the contract labor system that permitted mining companies and farmers to import labor from neighboring countries at will. Even as the mining industry shed 50 percent of its jobs, it continued to recruit workers from across the borders — thereby depressing wages.[36]

Moving to Johannesburg, Moving to Hillbrow

It is difficult to know exactly how many people moved into and out of the central city (including Hillbrow) after 1994. Most new arrivals came from townships or from rural areas, but increasing numbers came from beyond South Africa's borders. Many crossed borders without authorization and are more difficult to count. Between 1994 and 1997, almost 25,000 people formally applied for political asylum in South Africa — though it is not known where they settled. Angolans constituted the largest group (about 4,000), followed by Nigerians and Congolese with (nearly 3,000 each). Alan Morris cites one study indicating there were 23,000 Congolese living in Johannesburg by 1995. He estimates that about 3,000 Nigerians had moved to Hillbrow and Berea by 1997.[37] In other words, most cross-border migrants living in Johannesburg had not gone through a formal asylum-seeking process; according to the state, they were breaking South Africa's laws.

Morris conducted household surveys and face-to-face interviews in Hill-brow during this time. His respondents who had left other countries gave him three reasons for moving to South Africa. The top priority was the desire to pursue higher education in the country. The second and third most frequently cited reasons were fear of political persecution and a lack of job opportunities in their home countries.

He interviewed nine Nigerians living in Hillbrow, all of whom had moved to escape political persecution. Two had left Nigeria when the annulment of the 1993 elections led to widespread crisis. The leader of the Social Demo-cratic Party had won the election but was overthrown months later by the mili-tary, which installed General Sani Abacha as president. Abacha's rule became infamous for widespread human rights abuses.[38] The seven other Nigerians whom Morris interviewed left for South Africa after Abacha's government exe-cuted the writer and environmental activist Ken Saro-Wiwa for protesting the large-scale dumping of petroleum waste into the Niger Delta. Their friends or family members had been detained or threatened for protesting Saro-Wiwa's hanging. One of Morris's interviewees had had her house bombed.[39]

Morris also interviewed ten people from the DRC living in Hillbrow. Most had fled to South Africa in fear of political persecution. A young man named Yves told Morris his mother and father had been killed when the government found out he served as an adviser to the opposition. He feared he would be targeted next.[40]

Mike Dick—"Hillbrow is the most popular place in the city to live"

Mike Dick[41] is a white South African who was twenty-two in 1994. At that time, he observed that whites were leaving the inner city so quickly that entire buildings were left empty. He sensed both crisis and opportunity.

"In the mid-1990s," he says, "the property market completely bombed out. People were paying others to take their buildings. There was panicked emigration—back to Portugal, back to Italy. There was massive [white] movement out of Johannesburg and out of South Africa. The only people moving into the city were perceived to be poorer people. Sons did not want their fathers' properties, so many of them were just abandoned."

Mike emphasizes that white attitudes were central to the collapse of the real estate market. "Racism was huge," he says. "Whites in South Africa are afraid of Blacks. Even those who think they are not racists are afraid of Blacks. It was part of our education and it was taught to us by everyone around us—the fear of Blacks. For years, no one would invest."

Though others could not see the turnaround that was about to happen, Mike did.

"Before 1994," he reflects, "10 percent of the population could own 100 percent of the property. Now everyone could own property. Black people were getting jobs and moving from the townships into the city. A property boom was certain."

When he was twenty-six, he and his friends began buying buildings. They named their company Vuka Jozi (Wake Up, Johannesburg).

"The worse the area, the cheaper the property and the higher the return," he says. "We cornered the market. We grew up in the [poor white neighborhoods of] Rosettenville and Turffontein. We were used to rough areas."

As Mike predicted, a property boom did develop, but it took some time. "It came in about 2003," he says. "And it changed the game. People realized there would be no civil war. Vuka Jozi bought two huge Doornfontein buildings [next to Hillbrow] for R750,000 and R2 million, respectively, to start" (about US$50,000 and US$133,000, respectively, in 2021 values).

He emphasizes that Hillbrow, despite what many outsiders believe, became and remains "the most popular place to live in the whole city, because of transit. All transit goes to it and through it — whether it is going to Soweto, Sandton, Germiston, the CBD, or the Midrand. Transit eats a lot of money for the average earner — 30 to 40 percent [of their income], if you need a transfer. Living in Hillbrow allows you to cut one leg of the journey. So, in Central Johannesburg, Hillbrow has the highest rents. We can't get that kind of rent in Doornfontein or the CBD."

Crime in the 1990s

One of the causes of the rapid exodus of the middle class from Hillbrow was a sharp increase in criminal activity. The fear and the fact of crime became a major challenge for people living in — or moving into — the neighborhood during the 1990s, especially as criminal activity shifted from mostly property crimes toward more violent crimes. Alan Morris, who interviewed the captain of the Hillbrow precinct at the time, writes that the Hillbrow police believed criminal activity had become far worse during the late 1990s than earlier in the decade. In 1997 alone, there were 96 murders, 576 robberies, 48 cases of burglary, 324 automobile break-ins, and 504 vehicle thefts within Hillbrow's boundaries.[42] That same year, a survey revealed 20 percent of residents reported that they had been mugged in the neighborhood at least once, and 10 percent had been mugged more than once. During the first half of 1998, the police were recording an average of six muggings per day.[43]

In this section, we explore the literature that portrays or tries to come to terms with the rise in violence that would, from the 1990s, become associated — and to many, synonymous — with Hillbrow. Long-term residents, new arrivals, visitors, journalists, and social scientists alike would struggle to make sense of this particularly painful reality of life in the neighborhood. Not everyone felt the same level of fear about walking along Hillbrow's pavements. Many residents hesitated to leave the safety of their flats, Morris writes, and some began to carry guns for protection. Others felt no sense of danger at all.[44]

Though Hillbrow in particular became associated with crime in the local imagination, the entire city and the country at large were undergoing a complex evolution in patterns of criminality and violence. International media sometimes portrayed Johannesburg as the most dangerous city in the world.[45] According to Teresa Dirsuweit, in 1997 the International Criminal Police Organization (Interpol) reported Johannesburg had "the highest per capita rates of murder and rape, the second highest per capita rate of murder and the fourth highest number of serious assault and other sexual offences" of all the cities in the 110 countries in its international survey.[46]

In the early 2000s, the journal *Urban Forum* dedicated an entire issue to examining the causes and consequences of crime in Johannesburg. In her introductory essay, "Johannesburg: Fearful City?," Dirsuweit explores several theories attempting to explain the pervasiveness of violent crime in the 1990s. The "culture of violence thesis," she notes, posits that by the time apartheid repression had reached its apex in the 1980s, violence had become the dominant mode of political expression both on the part of the state and among the organizations opposing the state. As apartheid crumbled, according to this thesis, political violence transformed into criminal violence. Another theory suggested that all highly repressive societies experience a temporary increase in criminal behavior as they begin their transformations into democracies and repressive controls are lifted. Some observers believed that the postapartheid state was investing far too much in strengthening the criminal justice system and not enough in measures that may have prevented crime in the first place, such as job creation, education, and health care.[47]

Lindsay Bremner examines the proliferation of violence throughout the fabric of the entire city. "What we see in Johannesburg today," she writes, "is an evolution from the political economy of apartheid to a criminal economy of violence. This has many roots—the militarization of society under apartheid and its lingering effects . . . [and] a police force effective in defending white rule, but under-resourced and under-skilled in taking on regular police functions, [and] the failure to effectively integrate ex-combatants (across the entire South African region) into society."[48]

Bremner notes that violence in Hillbrow reached such a level of intensity that the government called out the military in 1997. Members of the Defense Force began patrolling the streets.[49] The filmmaker Clifford Bestall describes Hillbrow's transformation in the starkest of terms. In the mid-1990s, he says, "a realm of darkness descended, of rape, murder, human and drug trafficking. The depth of crime had no limit. Even entire buildings were stolen."[50] Bestall is speaking from the perspective of a white person who grew up in Hillbrow during the 1980s, when the neighborhood was safe for white people. During that decade, however, many of Johannesburg's townships were beset by state-sponsored murder, rape, and kidnapping.

Ivan Vladislavic, who has written several novels about Johannesburg in the 1990s and the 2000s, ties the widespread crime in the city to the nation's extreme inequality. In 1998, for instance, three hundred cars were stolen every day nationwide. At the same time, he notes, corporate directors were earning sixty times what they were paying shop floor workers—and those were the workers lucky enough to have work in a nation with an unemployment rate hovering around 30 percent. Crime was costing the country an estimated eighty million dollars per day but, in a country unable to provide stable jobs to the masses, certain criminal activities offered economic opportunities that exceeded average daily wages.[51]

Jonny Steinberg's edited volume *Crime Wave* offers another attempt to explain the intensity of crime and violence that descended during the 1990s. The book opens with an observation by Nadine Gordimer, who says that "you don't need to be a sociologist or a criminologist to identify the reason for the prevalence of crime in South African cities — it is unemployment." Many thousands of people who trekked into the cities, year after year since democracy, found little work. Gordimer notes the logical next step: "When the humiliation of begging fails, desperation offers one way to survive — crime."[52]

But Steinberg believes that joblessness is only part of the story. South Africa's poorest provinces have the lowest crime rates, while many armed robberies and hijackings are committed by well-off people who live in suburbs and have good educations. He states that, in many urban areas, crime has become hegemonic. It is no longer countercultural but normal, he writes, and is a reflection of the "past's animosities." While observers marveled at how South Africa transitioned from apartheid to democracy without civil war or "widespread rage," Steinberg argues that widespread rage is in fact happening. But instead of civil war, that rage has been translated into crime and victimization.[53]

Imprisonment and early death, Steinberg states, were once the fates of heroes and martyrs under apartheid and in subsequent years remained attached to popular images of masculinity. "Nobody is foolish enough to argue that young men like going to jail," Steinberg writes. "The argument is far subtler than that. It says that people are seduced into crime by a richly imagined world of masculine virtues: fearlessness, bravery, the capacity to wield power."[54] Likewise, Pumla Dineo Gqola attributes high levels of sexual violence to "the violent masculinities and war talk" that pervaded South African society from the earliest days of colonization to the present.[55] Alec Russell concludes that "centuries of race-based repression, applied for the last half of the twentieth century with scientific, and brutal rigor, embedded a culture of violence" that the country still lives with.[56]

The police often blamed foreigners for the surge in crimes in the 1990s, although foreigners were as likely as anyone else to be victims. When Alan Morris interviewed recent arrivals from Nigeria and Congo living in Hillbrow, he found that all of them had either been victims of crime or were worried about crime. The victims, he writes, suffered from both minor and major incidents. Surprisingly, he counted instances where victims were surrounded by numerous men carrying knives as "minor"; major crimes, on the other hand, included the increasingly common problem of being kidnapped and held for ransom. Nigerians, in particular, had strong fears of being kidnapped. The police reported that thirty Nigerians had been kidnapped during a single two-month period in 1996 alone because they were perceived as likely to be carrying large amounts of cash. All of Morris's Nigerian and Congolese participants told him they had never worried about crime in their home countries.[57]

The Police

In *Crime Wave*, Steinberg argues that the police must be understood in the context of apartheid. For decades, the South African police existed not primarily to fight crime but to protect white people and enforce white supremacy. By the mid-1990s, "police discourse changed abruptly [to account for the rights of all] . . . but there was no organizational reform."[58]

Gareth Newham, who spent fifteen months studying the Hillbrow Police Station during 2000 and 2001, chronicles the obstacles to building an effective police force after 1994. Though the National Party's police force had been notoriously corrupt and brutal, Nelson Mandela's Government of National Unity agreed to a "sunset clause" in which the same police officers were permitted to keep their jobs for five years. At the same time, the equally corrupt "homelands" police forces — which had been assembled by the National Party as part of the "grand apartheid" plans to force the entire Black African population into rural "bantustans" — were folded into the new South African Police Service (SAPS). As a result, the postapartheid SAPS was a force that spoke many different languages (but often not a common language), had different uniforms, generally lacked much education, and had little training. Newham cites a 2001 study that showed that one-third of the new police force was functionally illiterate; 30,000 of its members had no drivers' licenses; and 20,000 had criminal records. In the year 2000 alone, 14,600 police officers had active criminal charges against them "ranging from murder, rape, armed robbery, assault, theft and bribery to reckless driving."[59]

Hillbrow's residents, especially those from other countries, paid the price for such widespread corruption. The Hillbrow Police Station officially had a "zero tolerance" policy toward misdeeds among individual officers, but Newham and other researchers found evidence of "collusion between police members and other criminal syndicates." In some instances, police officers were accepting bribes from drug dealers and other criminal organizations to suppress their competition. Some members of the Hillbrow Police Station even reported that they had seen officers from other police stations coming into Hillbrow "with the express purpose of preying on the drug dealers, prostitutes and foreigners living in the area." Newham found widespread skepticism among police officers about the effectiveness of the zero-tolerance policy, because the potential gain from corruption almost always outweighs the penalties. He also found that managers at the station find it too risky to confront corrupt officers.[60]

Undocumented migrants are particularly vulnerable to corrupt police officers, who see them as "ATM's." Newham quotes a study in 1999 which found that many of Hillbrow's residents — especially migrants, drug dealers, and sex workers — refer to bribery as a "street tax" they must be prepared to pay at any time. Police detain, or threaten to detain, migrants who refuse to pay the "tax." Even fully documented refugees are vulnerable, because the police would threaten to destroy the documents of those who would not surrender a bribe.[61] Steinberg believes that South Africa's leaders will have to put forth a strong moral vision before the culture of policing is likely to be reformed. But since Steinberg's book was published, the national leadership of the police has been marked by constant scandal. Jackie Selebi, the minister of police from 2000 to 2009 (in charge of the police force for the whole nation), was sentenced to fifteen years' imprisonment on corruption charges. His successor, Bheki Cele, was suspended amid corruption allegations. Cele's successor, Riah Phiyega, was suspended for her role in ordering the mass shootings of striking miners at Marikana. Her successor, Khamotso Phahlane, was arraigned, with his wife, on fraud charges in 2018. Remarkably, the disgraced Bheki Cele was reappointed to replace Phahlane and remains in his post as of the writing of this book.

Legacy: Coming of Age during Apartheid's Violence

In *Midlands*, Jonny Steinberg traces the ways in which apartheid created a foundation for enduring patterns of violence. He argues that young Black men who came of age in the 1980s experienced a different reality from their forbears, who largely dealt with whites by "trying to carve out just a little more room to breathe." After the Soweto Uprising, defiance spread across the country. The ANC turned away from non-violence and embraced an increasingly militaristic response. Liberation movements enlisted adolescents in the struggle and young people moved in large numbers from the countryside to the cities to fight in what Steinberg calls the "urban insurrections."[62]

During South Africa's industrial revolution, in the 1950s, jobs were plentiful and almost anyone could find work. Three decades later, as South Africa entered a deep and lasting recession, it was not work on the mines or in the factories but fighting for IFP or the ANC that became a top vocational option.

By 1991 or 1992, Steinberg observes, awareness set in that a large problem was being created. Tens of thousands of young men had been trained in guerrilla warfare, he says, but the liberation movements had not developed plans for programs helping them transition back to civilian life.

"What is a bandit?" asks Steinberg. "He is somebody who has retained the revolutionary's disrespect for the law. He sees shops and post offices and banks and police stations, and they are nothing but potential targets. The bandit calls himself an entrepreneur. He says that the world has not given him any opportunities, so he will create his own." Though the violence in the urban areas attracts the most attention, rates of violence in the rural areas (not to be confused with the rates in poor provinces, which we discuss above) can be even higher. In rural KwaZulu-Natal, for instance, murder is so frequent that mortuaries are overwhelmed. There are also many suicides. In most cases, Steinberg writes, the murder and suicide victims are "young, unemployed, and black."[63]

But it was not only former combatants who moved from rural areas to cities, often with little education, no applicable training, and almost no opportunities. In general, children of farmworkers since the 1990s have been unable to find work in agriculture. "They went to the cities to look for new lives and new identities," Steinberg notes. "Some find work, build city families, and seldom return to the farmlands of their childhoods. Some live in single-sex compounds in the cities eleven months of the year. . . . But most find nothing in the cities. They live strange, transient lives, wandering between town and countryside, but they belong to neither. In the cities, they are jobless and live in the vast shantytowns on the edges of the metropolis."[64]

Changes

Marc Latilla[65] has chronicled the changes in Johannesburg's architecture in his book, *Johannesburg Then and Now*, and in his extensively researched blog *Johannesburg 1912*. He has also written about the history of some of Johannesburg's nightclubs, including some of its LGBTQ clubs. During Nerio's conversation with Marc, they realized they had both lived in Hillbrow in 1990.

Marc first moved to Hillbrow with his mother and stepfather in 1987, first to police flats behind the government mortuary and then to the historic Art Deco building Clarendon Place. His stepfather worked at the now demolished mortuary, which was owned by the South African Police. Marc recounts a wrenching story of what it was like to get the occasional ride to school in his stepfather's car. To reach the car, he and his stepfather had to walk through the morgue building to the carport on another level. The mortuary was often overflowing, particularly on Monday mornings. There were so many bodies that some of them were stacked in the corridors.

These were sometimes the corpses of protesters who had been killed by police and sometimes they were of people who had been partying and had been stabbed or shot during a confrontation. The worst part, Marc recalls, was seeing the bodies of people who had been "necklaced."[66] His stepfather would advise him to "just keep walking [past the bodies] and keep your mouth shut."

"Hillbrow in the 1980s," Marc says, "was like New York in the 1980s in terms of the casual violence and the grittiness."

In the early 1990s, Marc became a DJ at the famous Bella Napoli nightclub on Pretoria Street in Hillbrow. Most of Hillbrow's most popular businesses — the coffee shops, the cafés, bookstores, and clubs — began to permanently close around that time. Bella Napoli held on until 1994 and Marc remained with the establishment until six months before it permanently shut its doors.

"It closed," Marc says, "because Hillbrow was no longer a melting pot."

From his point of view, Hillbrow had become a "melting pot" from the early 1980s, when large numbers of South Africans of Indian descent had moved into the neighborhood and were living among large numbers of Europeans. When they were joined by Black South Africans, the melting pot reached its highest level of development. Then the middle class, he says, "panicked and left, taking their businesses with them."

"Hillbrow was cheap," Marc recalls. "I could live there [in the early 1990s] and have a two-bedroom flat on a waiter's salary."

The cheap rent at the time, he says, can be partly traced back to the Soweto Uprising: "Many [European] immigrants and South Africans left the country in the aftermath of the violence and international outrage. In Hillbrow, there was an oversupply of flats. In the early 1990s, banks 'redlined' Hillbrow and would no longer lend to inner-city property owners or new potential buyers. Some body corporates [co-ops] remained strong, and others did not. [Flat] owners started using letting agents to get whatever rentals they could as they could not sell. Some buildings got worse and worse and some were abandoned by their owners. Then the hijackings started to happen. There was a famous hijacking, at the old Florence Nightingale. It was a nursing home close to the Quirinale Hotel. The whole building was stripped. It is still hijacked."[67]

Marc moved out of Hillbrow in 1995, when he felt the environment became too dangerous to remain. He was never personally affected by a crime, but the turning point for him came when he witnessed the shooting of a man outside his building. He had walked up to the sixth floor, where he was living, and heard noises coming from the street. He looked down from the landing and saw two men holding up a third man. As he watched, one of the men shot the victim point blank in the chest. Marc does not know whether this was a robbery or perhaps a revenge killing.

Nonetheless, Marc continued working in Hillbrow. He had found a job at a book and music store called Look and Listen. He never felt unsafe working there, but by that time he would step only from his car to the shop and back to his car. It was no longer safe to stroll casually on the street. Half of the store's efforts, he says, became devoted to theft prevention. Marc was transferred to another branch in 1999 and the Hillbrow store closed in 2009.

He reflects on the older white generation who say negative things about Hillbrow, especially those who make comments on web pages. "They are all moaning," he says, "about how 'in my day, Hillbrow was so wonderful' and how it has deteriorated now. They blame the Blacks for the downfall, but it was apartheid that caused this. People risked their lives to move from the townships to Hillbrow to be closer to work and amenities. Whites had it easy and didn't put themselves in their [Black people's] shoes. . . . Hillbrow is not much different to how it was in its heyday. It's still mostly full of regular people from all over the world with big dreams trying to make a better life for themselves while trying to navigate this complex city."

Kagiso Patrick (Pat) Mautloa[68] is a Black visual artist in his sixties who lives in Alexandra township. He has had an art residency at the University of Johannesburg as well as residencies in Belgium, Botswana, Switzerland, and Cuba.

During the 1980s and part of the 1990s, he used to enjoy transiting through Hillbrow on his route between the University of Johannesburg and the township. He would often stop in the neighborhood to eat or have a walk.

"I was mugged a couple of times, but I still felt comfortable," he says. "But then something extraordinary happened. And now I shy away from Hillbrow." Sometime in the late 1990s, he was walking on a sidewalk when he was accosted by a group of young men. They lifted him off the ground and hoisted him into the air. While he was aloft, they pulled off his shoes and took his wallet, along with everything of value. He was not hurt but it was so disturbing that he rarely returns to Hillbrow, although he has created artwork about it from afar.

The Reshaping of Jewish Hillbrow

For almost a century (from the 1890s to roughly 1990), Hillbrow had maintained a strong Jewish presence. Most of its buildings were built by large and small-scale Jewish "venture capitalists," according to Melinda Silverman.[69] Many of its entertainment and cultural hotspots, including places such as the Florian Hotel and the Crest Hotel, were once popular meeting spaces for Jewish residents. Many elderly Jewish people bought flats in Hillbrow in the 1960s and 1970s with the intension of retiring and living in them for the remainder of their lives.

But a pronounced pattern of Jewish migration from Hillbrow, Berea, and Yeoville began after the 1976 Soweto Uprising and increased in subsequent years. As noted above, Mendelsohn and Shain report that an average of 3,000 Jewish South Africans left the country per year after the uprising. Overall, the number of Jewish people in Johannesburg remained fairly stable at about 60,000 as those who emigrated were largely replaced by others who moved from smaller cities and the countryside during the 1970s and 1980s. Nonetheless, the overall decline in population hit Jewish philanthropic and cultural organizations hard and their revenues dropped precipitously.[70]

Within Johannesburg, many Jewish residents left inner-city neighborhoods and moved north to locations such as Glenhazel, Sydenham, and Norwood. In Hillbrow and Berea, the emigration of younger Jewish South Africans led to a "major crisis in eldercare" as residential hotels that had once provided room and board closed.[71]

The Chevrah Kadisha (Jewish Burial Society, also known as Jewish Helping Hand in South Africa) began looking out for isolated and elderly Jewish residents in Hillbrow, Berea, and Yeoville. Adele[72] explains that many of the people reached by Chevrah Kadisha were living in badly deteriorating buildings. Not only were the buildings unsafe, but in some cases their elevators were no longer working and residents had to climb as many as twenty flights of stairs to reach their flats.

Kosher Mobile Meals worked with Chevrah Kadisha to regularly deliver prepared food. Together, the organizations spent several years locating all of the remaining elderly Jewish people in Hillbrow buildings. Those who agreed were relocated to the Vistaero, a secure building in Berea, or other buildings funded by Chevrah Kadisha. The organization continues to look for any elderly Jewish people in need of help as of the writing of this book.

"They were often very disoriented," Adele says, "and no longer knew where they were or what was happening to them. They could barely care for themselves. Sometimes there was no water and no food. Many of them were over eighty or ninety. There was one that I know of who was 101. In most cases, they did not want to leave and it took a lot of effort to persuade them. Usually, though, they were not in danger of being victimized from crime. There is a strong tradition in African culture of respecting the elderly, and people in their buildings looked out for them and would not let them be hurt. But often they could not care for themselves."

Adele helped organize a Wednesday lunch program at the United Jewish Women's Center. The Center hires a bus to pick up people in the neighborhood so that they could have a hot meal and time to socialize once per week.

As discussed in chapter 2, Temple Israel in Hillbrow once regularly seated hundreds of attendees. It had opened in 1936 and became the first Progressive (Reform) shul in the country. Reeva Foreman, its executive director, recalls that in 1994 the progressive movement sent a rabbi from London to take over rabbinical and management responsibilities for the temple.

"He took one look around at the neighborhood," she says, "and he decided that the temple should be closed and sold off."

That is when Reeva, who had grown up in an Orthodox shul in Doornfontein, decided to put all her efforts into keeping the temple open. At that time, she estimates, there were still about sixty attendees at Friday night and Saturday morning services.

Though it has taken enormous effort and persuasion, Reeva has managed to keep open the temple. The rabbi returned to London and Reeva asked David Bilchiz, a gay man and a legal scholar, to serve as the congregation's lay rabbi. The congregation grew smaller and many of the older white members left or passed away, but the temple began to attract a small number of younger Jewish Black Africans.

The "Hijacking" of Buildings

It became common from the 1990s on to speak of the "hijacking" of buildings in Johannesburg, especially in Hillbrow and the CBD. Accounts of armed gangsters taking over high-rise towers dominated newspaper headlines and alarmed the public. United Artists even released a film about hijacking in Hillbrow called *Gangster's Paradise: Jerusalema*. Media depictions of hijacking added to a generalized association of inner-city Johannesburg with a place of lawlessness.

The reality behind the "hijacking" phenomenon, however, is complex and often quite different from common perceptions. Margot Rubin shows that the phenomenon started with a severe debt crisis among landlords. During the 1980s, there was a massive jump in interest rates that left many property owners unable to pay their mortgages. Soon they were in arrears to the municipality because they were also unable — or unwilling — to pay their water, electricity, sewage, and trash collection fees. Many tried to pass on the extra costs, but tenants were often equally unable to afford these additional expenses. Residential and commercial owners alike began walking away from their buildings. In sectional title buildings (co-ops), owners also deserted their units, leading eventually to the shutting off of electricity and other vital services to entire buildings. By the end of the century, the impacts multiplied and left "large swathes of the inner city uninhabited." The buildings were then "taken over by informal dwellers, who used the spaces for residential purposes or unregulated businesses."[73]

"'Hijacking' is a sexy, sensational term," Nic Barnes,[74] the director of a residential development company tells us. He occasionally uses the term himself, but stresses that it is a shorthand and should not necessarily be taken seriously. "There *have* been some proper hijackings. But it mostly happens in buildings that are not properly run.

"Look, the inner city is tough," he continues. "But I want to emphasize that the common perceptions of Hillbrow are not accurate. There is a great deal of exaggeration. When it comes to hijacking, I must tell you that the reputation exceeds the reality. In the last twenty years, there have been only about twenty incidents of actual hijacking. Usually, there are two scenarios in which 'hijacking' otherwise happens. In the 1990s, there was a growing demand for housing, combined with a rapid outflux of original tenants. The buildings were badly maintained and managed as a result of the middle class leaving. New tenants formed their own tenants' associations, their own committees and withheld payments in lieu of repairs. But these large buildings are so capital intensive that if only twenty percent do not pay their tenants' association fees the body corporate is no longer liquid. That's when the building severely degrades, and overcrowding happens. The other scenario is that a 'silky-tongued' individual comes and says, 'you should pay the rent to me. I will take better care of the building.' The tenants start paying rent to this person, but he doesn't do any maintenance and a cycle sets in."

Such a "silky-tongued" individual is at the center of *Gangster's Paradise*. The film's protagonist, Lucky Kunene, is based on the real-life "sartorially elegant gangsters who parked expensive cars outside of seedy apartments" and managed to appropriate them. Kunene is inspired both by the US gangster Al Capone and by Karl Marx, the German philosopher who he believes wrote that all private property is theft.[75] He is frustrated with the unfulfilled promises of the new South Africa, which have left so many impoverished and denied him any possibility of getting a scholarship to attend business school. He believes that stealing buildings owned by whites is a form of "affirmative repossession" and he ends up building an empire of "hijacked" buildings across the inner city.[76] Though intended to demonstrate the lingering impact of apartheid, the film was widely criticized for its sensationalized depictions of car chases and shoot-outs.

Jono Wood,[77] a professional photographer who has worked in several Johannesburg buildings, shares his perspective. "We don't use the word 'hijacking' unless we have incontrovertible proof that a gang has hijacked a building," he says. "What tends to happen is that a landlord neglects a building or the body corporate no longer functions. A 'committee'—which can be a euphemism for a gang—senses an opportunity and comes along to 'organize' the tenants in the building. The tenants are often relieved that someone is actually doing something to at least ensure they will get some services. But once a building starts to lose light and water because the city turns them off for nonpayment, then the building slides very, very quickly into chaos. It is stripped of all metal, including the metal around the door frames. The lift shafts are totally stripped—one of the first things to go. The shafts are then used to dispose of waste (people throw the waste down the shaft into the basement of the building). People start erecting shacks in the corridors. They build barricades around the windows [because most of the windows are broken]. They essentially recreate the building and improvise in any way possible."

Jono and his colleagues use the term "dark buildings" to describe structures that, through neglect, have lost services such as electricity and basic maintenance. He worked intensively with a team visiting one such building over the course of two years. There were hundreds of people living in the severely deteriorated structure and the team spoke to everyone in the building. "It was frightening at first," he says, "but you eventually become quite adept at it. You learn how to talk to people. If you are polite, people will cooperate with you. The team surveyed everyone in the building and the PhD student [who headed the team] determined that only two percent of the residents in the building were involved in crime. But that two percent, of course, has a strong impact on the rest of the tenants. The problem is that as soon as a building becomes 'dark' the city turns its back on it. That is the exact opposite of what they should do."

Jono himself is white and grew up in a white suburb during the 1990s and early 2000s. "I had no sense of the city," he says, "because my mother kept telling me: 'We don't go there because it is too dangerous.' But once I became a photographer and met many other kinds of people who did not live a sheltered white existence, I began to change my mind. The city is a fascinating place that is far less dangerous than I had been told. I was so happy to break out of my white bubble.

"This is not to make light of the neighborhood's problems," he cautions. "There are so very many muggings. I lived in Ponte City for seven years and saw many dead bodies in the park outside. I have personally seen four suicides since I started visiting other buildings. Living in the neighborhood is very, very tough. But it is a resilient city."

Matthew Wilhelm-Solomon has written frequently about "dark buildings" in Johannesburg which he also calls "unlawfully appropriated buildings," "hijacked buildings," "bad buildings," or "slum buildings." In policy discourse, he writes, the city refers to them as "bad buildings." Residents often call them "dark," as "*umnaya*" (darkness) in isiZulu and isiNdebele refers not only to the lack of light but to a metaphysical fact or misfortune. A dark building is therefore much like a haunted building. Inhabitants face not only overcrowding but a lack of sanitation (such as overflowing toilets), rats, fires, structural collapses, and the possibility of attack and victimization. Nonetheless, residents also develop "forms of engagement and sociality" by listening to music or attending churches together, watching sports, and sharing stories with one another.[78]

Wilhelm-Solomon also points out that "hijacking" is a matter of perspective. He offers the example of a building named Chambers, in Doornfontein, which a property management company called Affordable Housing and Retail Spaces in Johannesburg, also known as "Afhco," purchased when the building's owner went into liquidation. Though Afhco, which is privately owned, viewed the residents as squatters, the building's numerous occupants saw Afhco's attempts to evict them as a form of hijacking. "Questions of legality and illegality and order and disorder," Wilhelm-Solomon writes, "are socially situated and not given. From the perspective of the residents of Chambers, the property company represented disorder and an illegitimate use of power." Notably, many of the residents had started living in the building as legal tenants before it fell into disrepair. After a four-year battle, all of the occupants — including numerous blind Zimbabweans — were evicted.[79] Ironically, the aim of the evictions was to pave the way for Afhco to transform the building into low-income housing.

Afhco was founded in 1996 and, with over eight thousand units, has since become the leading developer of low-income housing in Johannesburg. According to its website, it is dedicated to working with its tenant base to maintain safe, clean, and comfortable buildings. Its social responsibility mission has led it to develop parks and a school, and to sponsor a sports team and clothing drives.[80] Margot Rubin argues, however, that as property developers like Afhco restore "bad buildings," they have also displaced thousands of the city's very poorest residents.[81] We explore the Bad Building Programme in more detail in the following chapter.

Xenophobia in the 1990s

Xenophobia — the fear of, or hostility toward, "foreigners" — has become a central concern in South Africa's postapartheid political landscape. Though it was not until 2008 that the world began to focus on violent attacks on non-nationals in South Africa, Alan Morris shows that as early as the 1990s many migrants to Johannesburg arrived with concerns about xenophobia. His interviews with Nigerian and Congolese people living in Hillbrow in 1997 revealed that they faced xenophobic discrimination in their everyday interactions. "All the informants," he writes, "alleged that they had experienced verbal abuse whilst walking in the streets of Hillbrow or when using public transport."[82]

Media and political leaders often abet negative sentiments against foreigners, especially Nigerians. Mangosutho Buthelezi, who had founded the IFP and headed it for decades, became democratic South Africa's first minister of home affairs. He stated publicly, in his official capacity, that *all* Nigerians were drug traffickers and criminals. Perhaps as a result, Nigerians were more likely than other immigrant groups to be targets of police brutality because the police, too, perceived them as drug dealers. Many Nigerians were forced to pay bribes to corrupt police officers.[83] West reported that foreign nationals in Hillbrow often felt so exasperated that they longed to return to their home countries. They were afraid of crime, they feared xenophobic discrimination, and they were often unable to find work.

Phaswane Mpe's now classic postapartheid novel, *Welcome to Our Hillbrow*, focuses on the deepening expressions of xenophobia. His main character, Refentše, moves to Hillbrow in 1991 to attend university. A few years later, he has become a lecturer and still lives in the neighborhood. He finds himself often among people from Zambia, Zimbabwe, Congo, Nigeria, and Mozambique and understands that they have moved to Johannesburg for the same reason he has: to search for "greener pastures." Many of his compatriots, however, feel differently. They call Africans from other countries *makwerekwere*, in what they believe to be an imitation of the sounds their "incomprehensible" languages make. His former love interest, Refilwe, has come from his hometown and believes Hillbrow is full of immoral people, not least because many of them are foreigners whose "sinful acts" are spreading AIDS.

Refentše's cousin is a police officer and blames the *makwerekwere* for all Hillbrow's problems: crime, grime, drug dealing, physical decay, moral decay, and AIDS. Refentše tries to reason with his cousin by comparing such xenophobic thinking to the racism of the apartheid era. His cousin seems always to forget the widespread violence of the very recent past — some of which he witnessed with his own eyes — and is determined to focus his fury on migrants. The cousin and his colleagues on the force harass and sometimes terrify foreigners by picking them up in their squad cars and driving them around for interminable hours while taunting them that they will never see the outside again. In Mpe's telling, other police officers who picked up foreigners sometimes demanded sexual favors.[84]

Not everyone remembers the 1990s as a time of widespread xenophobia. Barbara,[85] for instance, moved to Johannesburg from Bulawayo, Zimbabwe, in 1998. The city proved to be difficult for her, but xenophobia was not one of the reasons. She was twenty-two when she arrived to join her husband and her sister, both of whom had moved to the city two years earlier to find work. Barbara, her husband, and her sister had numerous family members in Zimbabwe counting on the money they would send home.

"I was very, very excited," she says. She lights up as she recalls the day she boarded a bus in Zimbabwe. "Everyone told me I was going to a very nice place with tall buildings. They made it sound as if everything was going to be easier. But I was shocked when I arrived. Zimbabwe was much better. Yes, there were tall buildings, but . . ."

Her voice trails off, as if to say that there was nothing about those tall buildings that could provide her with a better life. She and her husband moved into her sister's small home in a Soweto[86] township called White City. Her sister had chosen Soweto "because it was much cheaper and much quieter than Hillbrow." Barbara gasps at the memory of how expensive Hillbrow was.

"I expected everything to be different [in Johannesburg]," Barbara continues. "But Soweto looked like Bulawayo. It was just rows and rows of houses. The only difference was language."

Barbara and her family members spoke isiNdebele, and in Soweto no one understood her. When she tried to speak English, most people asked her why she was not speaking isiZulu to them. But their reaction, she is certain, was not due to suspicion or hostility.

"No, there was no xenophobia then," she says. "People were happy to meet a foreigner. They wanted to ask questions and understand your life and your country. The xenophobia came later."

Barbara and her husband worked and saved every penny. She found a job at a clothing store in the CBD owned by a Pakistani family. After a year of saving, the couple was able to move to a flat on Banket and Caroline Streets in Hillbrow. Whereas traveling from Soweto to the CBD required a long, two-fare commute, she could walk to the shop from Hillbrow in only fifteen minutes.

She still lives in the same building with her daughter. They live in one room of a two-bedroom flat that has been subdivided to accommodate several families.

"I'm used to Hillbrow now, but I miss the cleanliness of Bulawayo, and the quiet," she says. "I miss walking without being scared."

5

Hillbrow in the Twenty-First Century

Hillbrow is not like it was ten or twenty years ago, when there were lots of woozy, spaced-out criminals high on drugs. Now it is a place of organized, violent crime syndicates. Hillbrow is not London on a bad day. Hillbrow is Afghanistan on a bad day.

— ALAN CHILDS, THE (NOW FORMER) DIRECTOR
OF MES,[1] INTERVIEWED IN 2018

Hillbrow is safer than anywhere else I have ever lived.

— KEVIN, FROM ABA, NIGERIA, WHO LIVED IN HILLBROW
FROM 2010 TO 2018, INTERVIEWED IN 2014

I am an African, whose heart is everywhere in the continent. I fight to create such ideals [of pan-Africanism] in the city. It would be hopeless to move into anywhere else, into any other part of the city than Hillbrow, Berea, or Yeoville. There is no culture in the [northern] suburbs. They are betraying the Rainbow Nation.

— SANZA SANDILE, PROPRIETOR OF A RESTAURANT
IN YEOVILLE, INTERVIEWED IN 2018

I would call it [Hillbrow] hell. When I first saw it — yes, I would say I thought it was hell. My sisters were here for years before I came, and they were fine. But everything about it looked like hell to me. I still feel the same way. It will never change. There is nothing I like about it. I am only trying to survive there.

— MARIE, FROM THE EASTERN CAPE, WHO HAS LIVED IN
HILLBROW SINCE 2012, INTERVIEWED IN 2019

Hillbrow is safe. It is bad at first, but you create friends. If you create lots of friends, nothing happens to you. . . . And Hillbrow is fun! It has everything. It is all about entertainment, entertainment, entertainment! If I were to move to Sandton [an upscale, and largely white, suburb] it would be so boring. Anyone who has lived in Hillbrow could not be in Sandton. They would find it so boring. If I moved to Sandton, probably I would go to Hillbrow every night.

> — VUSI, A TAXI DRIVER FROM DURBAN WHO LIVED IN YEOVILLE FOR SEVENTEEN YEARS AND NOW SHARES A THREE-BEDROOM FLAT IN HILLBROW WITH HIS BROTHER AND SISTER, INTERVIEWED IN 2018

Many people come to this country looking for freedom, and those who do leave their countries and come to Johannesburg are "astonishingly open-minded." They are looking for many kinds of freedom: economic, cultural, gender, and sexual freedom. They want not only to be free of the economic strains and political tumult of their countries, but they want to be free of the traditional ties that bind and restrict them. They end up in Hillbrow, en masse. They are an en masse population of the young.

> — MATTHEW KROUSE, JOURNALIST AND OWNER OF A BOOKSTORE, INTERVIEWED IN 2018

Xenophobia has never affected me. It does not come into Hillbrow. It happens in Alex [Alexandra Township] and Soweto, but it does not come into Hillbrow. I feel very good about that.

> — DAVID, FROM ZAMBIA, WHO HAS LIVED IN HILLBROW SINCE 2004, INTERVIEWED IN 2018

The brief quotations above show a range of perceptions and attitudes our respondents hold about Hillbrow during the twenty-first century. The neighborhood continues to attract large numbers of people from within South Africa, including those from smaller cities, townships, and the countryside, as well as thousands of cross-border migrants. Despite high levels of crime, many people find ways to navigate the neighborhood's spaces, build connections, and feel safe.

As South Africa confronts one of the world's highest unemployment rates, many arrivals have no choice but to seek work in the informal sector that offers little pay, no security, and frequent risks — including harassment or extortion at the hands of the police. They often cope in ingenious ways, not only supporting themselves but also providing family members back home with money for rent, food, and school fees.

Alan Childs[2] may not be exaggerating when he compares Hillbrow's violence rate to Afghanistan's; some statistical measures do support this claim. During our interviews, everyone we spoke to said they worry about the potential of being victimized. But what Matthew Krouse points out is also important. The fear of crime, no matter how real or pervasive, does not prevent people from moving to Hillbrow in search of certain freedoms and from seeking the means to build those freedoms for themselves. Sanza Sandile captures the impressions of many when he notes that, whatever the challenges of life in Hillbrow, it offers the chance of a genuine African cosmopolitanism. Like Sanza, Vusi sees the potential for fun and excitement in Hillbrow and only sterility, if not outright betrayal, in the richer northern suburbs. Hillbrow, David observes, can also offer a bulwark against the xenophobia that frequently haunts other parts of the city. A year following David's comment, however, Hillbrow did face a serious wave of xenophobia, but the neighborhood responded by keeping xenophobic attackers at bay.

In this chapter, we try to capture the scope of experiences, difficulties, and hopes for a better future among those who call Hillbrow home during the twenty-first century. Tanja Winkler, who has written frequently about Hillbrow, points out that it is a neighborhood of sharp contrasts. It has a reputation for "decay and chaos," and is "demonized by the city council, many Johannesburg citizens and South Africans in general." Nonetheless, it remains popular because it is the first port of entry to Johannesburg for more people than any other part of the city.[3]

Given their numbers, migrants and immigrants are able to build networks based on language and culture. But in a broader environment of simmering xenophobia and high unemployment, Hillbrow is also, as Winkler writes, a "zone of great vulnerability." Many who live there wish for somewhere safer and more secure and hope their residency in the neighborhood is only temporary.[4]

The Twenty-First Century—Johannesburg as Africa's Aspirational City

Though the pace of change in central Johannesburg was rapid in the 1980s and 1990s, Loren Landau shows that even larger numbers of people moved into and out of the area in the 2000s. He cites one survey that shows that by 2003, 25 percent of inner-city residents had moved to Johannesburg from another country. Even more remarkably, fully 68 percent of people who lived in the inner city in 2003 had moved to their residence within the last five years. In some parts of the inner city, 42 percent had done so during the past year. While some had relocated from other parts of the city, such as the townships, hundreds of thousands had moved from rural parts of South Africa and from countries to the north.[5]

So many people moved to Johannesburg during the last few years of the previous century and the first few years of the new one that, as Landau writes, it became a city "in which no single group can claim indigeneity." The high degree of transience, he argues, partly explains the simmering tensions between nationals and nonnationals. South African citizens, who also might have just arrived in Johannesburg, use labels such as *makwerekwere* (the degrading word for "foreigners" mentioned in the previous chapter) to establish a connection with one another by scapegoating a "dehumanized and foreign 'other' that becomes a target." Arrivals from other countries often respond to such xenophobia by defining themselves as people who are only passing through South Africa en route to a better place.[6]

The economic crisis in Zimbabwe during the 2000s deserves special attention, as it helped make South Africa the recipient of one of the highest numbers of asylum seekers in the world.[7] Human Rights Watch estimated that by 2008 about 1.5 million Zimbabweans had crossed the border to live in South Africa.[8] Sarah Chiumbu and Muchaparara Musemwa make clear that Zimbabwe was, in fact, facing not only an economic crisis but a series of interconnected and mutually reinforcing crises. Eighty to 85 percent of Zimbabwean adults were unemployed by 2008, but the population also faced an electricity crisis, a cholera crisis, a water crisis, and a health-care crisis.[9]

All these crises were compounded by a political crisis. The Zimbabwe African National Union (ZANU), which had once constituted one of the major liberation movements during white minority rule, formed a government in 1980 and, Chiumbu and Musemwa write, "inherited the repressive and violent machinery of the Rhodesian state." The increasingly authoritarian government of Zimbabwe cracked down on political opposition, causing journalists to leave the country "in droves." During the height of the unemployment crisis, the government also cracked down hard on the informal sector, causing an additional 650,000 to 700,000 people to lose their homes and their livelihoods. By 2008, fully one-quarter of the Zimbabwean population (about three million people) had left the country for Europe, Australia, the United States, and, especially, South Africa. Whereas migrants from Zimbabwe during the 1990s were most likely to be men traveling alone, by the 2000s they were increasingly likely to be women — including women traveling with children.

Fifty percent of Zimbabwe's urban families depend on the money these expa-triates send home.[10]

Nic Barnes[11] (also discussed in chapter 4) tells us that by the twenty-first century, Johannesburg had become Africa's "most aspirational city." He claims that more people in sub-Saharan Africa look to Johannesburg as a potential place to build better lives than to any other city on the continent. But its very status as the continent's biggest draw may also be exacerbating some of its biggest problems.

Johannesburg, in part because of its early industrialization, remains the wealthiest city in Africa, with a reported net worth of US$248 billion. That is almost double the wealth of Cairo ($129 billion), the richest city on the continent outside South Africa. Africa's largest city, Lagos, with a popula-tion of 21 million, is four times the size of Johannesburg but has a net worth ($96 billion) less than half that of Johannesburg. At a distant third, Nairobi ($49 billion) is Africa's only other city outside South Africa with a net worth close to $50 billion. In South Africa, Cape Town ($133 billion) and Durban ($54 billion) also have high net worth. If Pretoria's $45 billion is added to Johannesburg's wealth — treating both nearby cities as a single conurbation — the resulting megacity approaches $300 billion in wealth, dwarfing all cities on the continent.[12]

But if Johannesburg's wealth is a draw for aspiring migrants and desper-ate migrants alike, numerous structural problems severely restrict its capacity to meet their needs. Both the national and the local economies have stag-nated and are growing more slowly than the population. By the end of the 2010s, global ratings agencies such as Standard & Poor's and Fitch Ratings had downgraded South Africa's economy to "junk status" (or "noninvestment grade"), making it more difficult for the country to attract foreign investment and to meet its high debt obligations. The national public utility, Eskom, faces severe difficulties in meeting the country's electricity demands due to years of corruption and underinvestment. Eskom has been forced to institute "load shedding" measures, resulting in regular, planned blackouts. The frequent power outages strain small and large businesses alike and create a drain on economic growth. Further, some high net-worth individuals, often white, are emigrating from the country, taking their wealth and skills with them; others are "financially emigrating" by moving their wealth to other countries while physically remaining in South Africa.[13]

Most important among the city's structural problems, however, is the ex-treme inequality that resulted from colonization and apartheid. More than half of South Africans (55.5 percent) live in poverty, and one-quarter (25 per-cent) live in extreme poverty. "Extreme poverty," or what South Africa labels "below the food poverty line," refers to the inability to afford even a basic diet of 2,100 calories per day. The percentages for both groups in poverty are growing, after having fallen for a number of years around 2006, when two-thirds of the population was living in poverty.[14] In an extensive review of the literature, Carl-Ulrik Schierup shows that the proportion of people living on US$4 per day or less in South Africa in the 2010s was double that in other "middle income" countries such as Mexico, Peru, and Brazil. Moreover, two population groups most likely to be living in poverty were South Africans in the former rural "homelands" and cross-border migrants who were living without documentation. Schierup does not believe that South Africa's inability to significantly reduce poverty is entirely unintentional. The same neoliberal policies that have led to immiseration for so many migrants benefit mining and other companies by depressing wages, disempowering unions, and enabling "accumulation-through-dispossession."[15]

Poverty rates exceed 70 percent in the poorest provinces, the Eastern Cape and Limpopo, and many people move from such provinces to Gauteng, where Johannesburg is located, and where the poverty rate hovers at about 33 percent.[16] Thus, at the same time that Johannesburg attracts migrants from across the continent it also exerts pull factors on people who live in South Africa's poorer cities, rural areas, and less developed townships.

Within Johannesburg itself, wealth is unevenly spread. Most new construction occurs in the northern suburbs. The suburb of Sandton lies twelve miles north of Johannesburg's original CBD, but these two "downtowns" bear almost no resemblance to one another. The older CBD resembles a miniature Manhattan in layout, with hundreds of skyscrapers built on a street grid that provides easy access for pedestrians. But many, perhaps most, of its buildings now bear the marks of extreme neglect and in many cases are abandoned. Former prestige buildings, such as the Carlton Hotel and the Johannesburg Sun, have been mothballed for years. Meanwhile, the new "downtown" in Sandton glitters with new glass and steel towers spaced apart from one another in pedestrian-unfriendly fashion. The landscape reminds Nerio and Halley of Mike Davis's famous descriptions of "Fortress Los Angeles," where the architecture is designed to restrict pedestrian access and recolonize space. The streets are jammed with vehicles, but sidewalks are empty.[17]

Still newer construction is sprouting further north of Sandton, stretching deep into the Midrand and reaching toward Pretoria (fifteen miles and thirty miles from Hillbrow, respectively). This ever-northerly development places employment opportunities even further out of reach of those who live in inner-city neighborhoods and southern townships. A shimmering high-speed rail system called the Gautrain opened in 2012 at a cost of 25 billion rand (about 1.5 billion dollars). The Gautrain can whisk passengers from central Johannesburg to Sandton or the Midrand in minutes but is priced far out of reach of the average commuter.[18]

Housing in the Inner City

Ivan Turok describes South Africa's history of urbanization as a "tortured" process, driven for a century by the single-minded determination of successive white governments to control and prevent the movement of Black Africans into the cities. Given these "extreme policies of socio-spatial engineering" in the past, he writes, the postapartheid government has been understandably hesitant to develop an "explicit urban policy or programme." The lack of such a policy, however, has left cities without effective approaches for housing the urban poor. The government has built housing, but it has done so mostly on or near the very same townships created by the apartheid government. Not only are the townships distant from urban centers, but they are often on flood-plains or on contaminated land. Even with their large populations of potential low-wage workers, the townships have also failed to attract capital investment that would translate into jobs. These conditions, and the enormous pressure on people to seek accommodation in the urban centers, Turok writes, have "resulted in thousands of people occupying abandoned buildings."[19]

Section 26 of the new Constitution guarantees access to housing, but Stuart Wilson, Jackie Dugard, and Michael Clark show there have been numerous legal battles over how to interpret and apply this right. For instance, what does it mean to have "access" to housing if one does not have sufficient resources to afford such housing? How should the state balance the rights of occupants of structures with the rights of the owners of those structures? In the new century, these questions became especially critical in the inner city of Johannesburg, where "hundreds of buildings left fallow by their owners became an obvious low or zero-rent option for people excluded from the formal urban housing market." What are the rights of municipal governments or private developers to evict those living in such buildings, and what obligation do cities have to find alternative housing for mass evictees? Though the Constitutional Court has generally sided with tenants, Wilson et al. find, it has done so on a case-by-case basis, leaving tenants "substantially in the dark about what 'housing' or 'adequacy' are."[20]

The Centre on Housing Rights and Evictions (COHRE), an international nongovernmental organization (NGO), investigates mass-scale evictions in many African cities. In the early 2000s, it assembled a fact-finding team to examine the scale and impact of evictions in Johannesburg. COHRE wrote that, in spite of the new government's efforts, 7.5 million people in South Africa still had no access to adequate housing, and most were living in cities. In Johannesburg, they were living either in the numerous shack settlements on the outskirts of the city, or, in the inner city, in "bad buildings," in backyards, under bridges, or on sidewalks. COHRE praised the South African government for the progress that it had made: building 1.5 million new houses, providing subsidies for an additional 1 million new homes, and transferring hundreds of thousands of title deeds to tenants in the townships so that they had secure ownership of their own homes. But it also found that, in Johannesburg, the Department of Housing had created a subsidy program that almost entirely excluded the very poor. Its "low-cost" housing projects were available to those earning what was then between R1,250 and R3,500 a month, far above what most workers in the informal market can hope to earn. Likewise, several hundred NGOs offer "transitional housing" in the inner city that is priced far out of reach of the many — the very poorest residents.[21]

COHRE emphasizes that living in "bad buildings" is not a choice but a necessity for most who inhabit them. Buildings labeled as such are generally structures where the management has broken down — or no longer exists — and where payments for water and electricity are seriously in arrears. Occupants tend to view these buildings as their best possible choice of accommodation for the moment, but the city views such buildings as "sinkholes" that must be shut down. In response to media portrayals of the inner city, including Hillbrow, Berea, and Yeoville, as lawless places, the city undertook a succession of regeneration programs that included plans for multiple mass evictions. COHRE, however, found a range of conditions in "bad buildings." There was a "sense of community" in many of them, and the occupants themselves often engaged in maintenance and cleaning of communal areas. Evictions might have cleared out problematic buildings but did not leave those evicted better off. COHRE found that the city seldom met its obligations to find evictees alternative accommodation.[22]

The Better Buildings Programme attempted to convert several dozen "bad" buildings into more livable environments. Through this program, the city takes possession of buildings that are seriously in arrears, writes off some or all of the debt, and converts them into social housing or sells them to private developers who rent them as "low-income housing units." The program results in better-managed, more hygienic, and secure units for thousands of individuals and families. However, both social housing and "low-cost" housing remain priced far out of reach of most of those working in the informal market. The needs of the very poor are sacrificed to the needs of the merely poor or the stable working class.[23]

Looking down on Banket Street (photo by Lesley Mosweu)

View from the Manhattan Building (photo by Bongani Nduvana)

From atop Mimosa Hotel (photo by Bongani Nduvana)

Highpoint, Pretoria Street (photo by Bongani Nduvana)

Idlewild Flats: a "hijacked" building (photo by Bongani Nduvana)

Young man sitting by Tygerberg Building, Berea, with Ponte City in background (photo by Bongani Nduvana)

Making a home wherever possible, Olivia and Joel Road, Berea (photo by Bongani Nduvana)

Crowds on Pretoria Street (photo by Bongani Nduvana)

Enjoying drinks on the balcony at The Base, a club on Kotze Street (photo by Bongani Nduvana)

Fruit sellers on Pretoria Street (photo by Ron Nerio)

Mono, aspiring rap artist, sitting at the "Ghost Building" (photo by Bongani Nduvana)

Sports at eKhaya Park (photo by Bafikile Mkhize)

Mass at the Cathedral of Christ the King, practicing COVID-19 distancing (photo by Bafikile Mkhize)

Meeting of Migrant Woman's Voice (photo by Richa Kamina Tshimbinda)

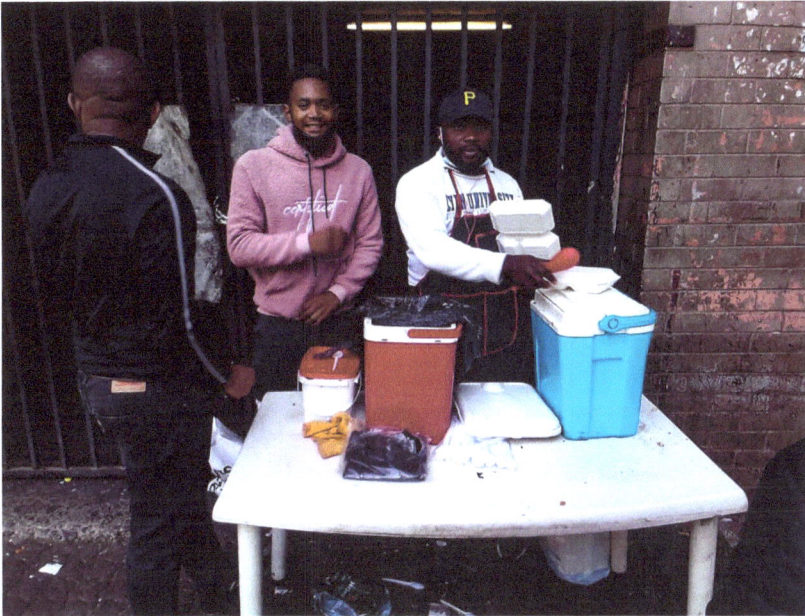

Lesley and Mike at Mike's Kitchen, which has been moved outside due to COVID-19 distancing (photo submitted by Lesley Mosweu, taken by Praise Siphali)

Liz, Bafikile, and Megan at the Christ the King soup kitchen, following its post-COVID reopening (photo submitted by Bafikile Mkhize)

Bongani Nduvana, photographer, overlooking Hillbrow (photo by Ikwezi Zulu)

Smit and Wolmarans Street, with the former Wolmarans Shul in the background (photo by Bongani Nduvana)

Sleeping rough on Clarendon Street (photo by Bongani Nduvana)

Banket Street (photo by Bongani Nduvana)

Pretoria Street (photo by Bongani Nduvana)

Pretoria Street (photo by Bongani Nduvana)

South Hillbrow, from the rooftop of Mould, Empower, Serve (photo by Bongani Nduvana)

Joel Road, looking toward Hillbrow (photo by Bongani Nduvana)

Kapteijn Street (photo by Bongani Nduvana)

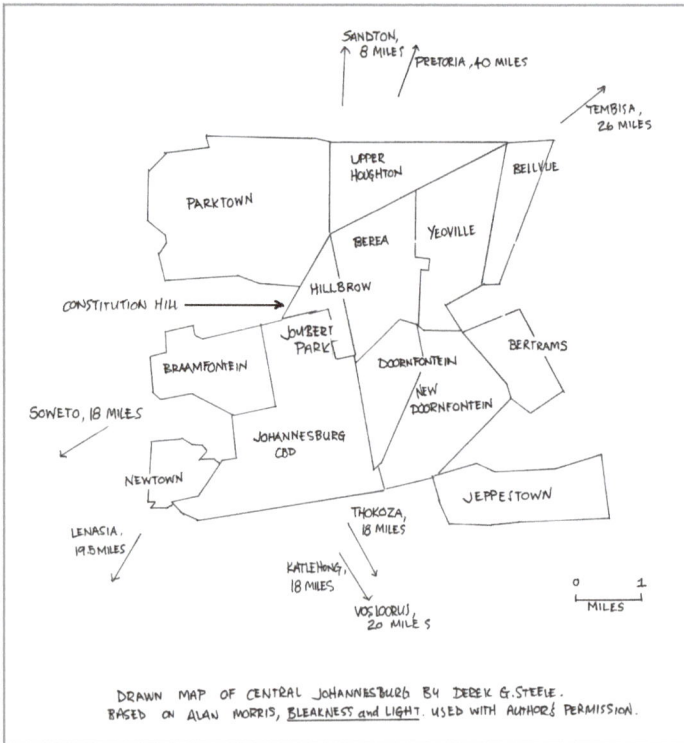

SANDTON,
8 MILES   PRETORIA, 40 MILES

TEMBISA,
26 MILES

UPPER
HOUGHTON   BELLVUE

PARKTOWN

BEREA   YEOVILLE

HILLBROW

CONSTITUTION HILL

JOUBERT
PARK

BRAAMFONTEIN   DOORNFONTEIN   BERTRAMS

NEW
DOORNFONTEIN

SOWETO, 18 MILES

JOHANNESBURG
CBD

NEWTOWN   JEPPESTOWN

LENASIA,
19.5 MILES   THOKOZA,
18 MILES

KATLEHONG,
18 MILES   0   1

VOSLOORUS,   MILES
20 MILES

DRAWN MAP OF CENTRAL JOHANNESBURG BY DEREK G. STEELE.
BASED ON ALAN MORRIS, BLEAKNESS and LIGHT. USED WITH AUTHORS PERMISSION.

Map of Hillbrow and Johannesburg, drawn by Derek Steele with permission
from Alan Morris (author of *Bleakness and Light*)

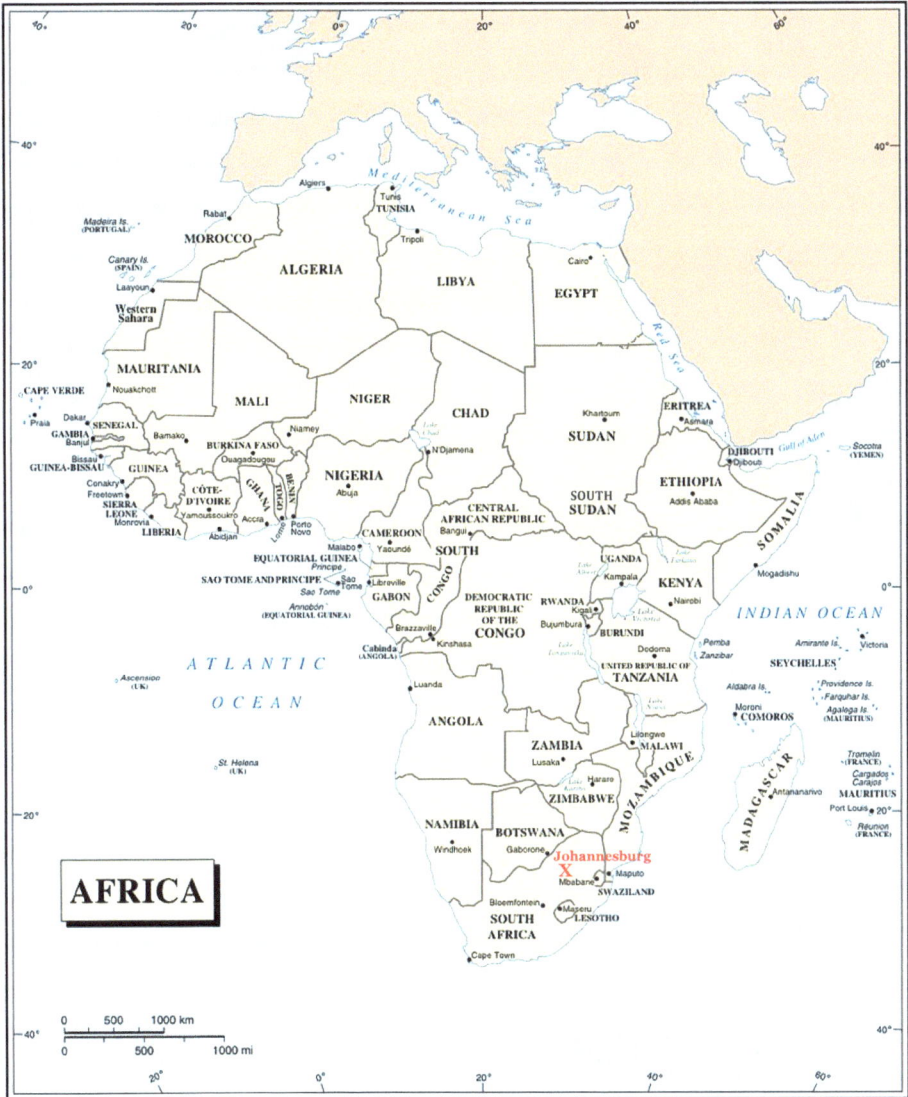

Map of Africa from the Creative Commons

COVID-19 clothing and food distribution at Temple Israel (photo by Marion Bubbly)

Doctors Without Borders (*Médecins Sans Frontières* or MSF) began assisting "survival migrants" in Johannesburg starting in 2007, partly in response to Zimbabwe's economic collapse and the resulting flow of migrants into South Africa. The organization estimated that by 2011 there were 1.5 million Zimbabweans living in the country. Their report that year cites the City of Johannesburg's estimate that a substantial portion of the 1.5 million, about 250,000 people, were living in 1,305 "slum buildings" in the inner city of Johannesburg (including in Hillbrow).

MSF conducted its own survey of eighty-two "slum buildings" in 2010 and found that about fifty thousand to sixty thousand people were living in them. They described the living spaces as subdivided and "warren-like," and the conditions as "appalling." Many of the homes, they reported, fell substantially below those used by international organizations to rate refugee camps during "major humanitarian crises." MSF found that 38 percent were sharing a single water tap with more than two hundred people and 7.5 percent had no access to water in their buildings. Nearly three-quarters of the occupants were sharing a toilet with more than twenty people and nearly half were sharing a toilet with more than one hundred people. Nearly 85 percent of occupants in the MSF survey were living below the minimum standard of three and a half square meters per person and 22 percent were living with less than one square meter of space per person. Seventeen percent were sleeping on a floor with no mattress.

MSF found that residents sometimes self-organized to remove waste from their buildings. In one case, the organization helped residents remove waste from the exterior of their building after it had been cleared from the inside because the city had left it outside for weeks without collecting it.[24]

Many of the former commercial buildings in the original CBD have been converted to residential buildings or have filled with squatters. They house some of the city's poorest people, often migrants, in overcrowded, unsanitary, and dangerous conditions. Jonathan Torgovnik, a Cape Town–based photojournalist who has worked in Cameroon, Rwanda, Burma, and Central America, tries to provide a sense of the living conditions in central Johannesburg. In 2015, he spent a year photographing migrants living in "abandoned inner-city high-rise buildings" in the CBD. He met people, mostly men, from Malawi, Tanzania, and Zimbabwe, and a smaller number of people from Kenya and Nigeria. They had all come hoping to send money back to their families in their home countries. Their dreams, he reports, had largely been shattered by the lack of access to work. He describes the living conditions in these buildings as "the worst urban poverty I've seen in all my travels around the world."[25]

Hayley Gewer and Margot Rubin caution against an overemphasis on bleak depictions like those offered by MSF and Torgovnik. They note that Hillbrow offers an extensive range of housing options, and for people who arrive with nothing it is important to have a place where they can live with nothing. Hillbrow's accommodations range from "sleeping rough" in streets, parks, and empty buildings, often for no cost; sharing a bed, with up to three people in the bed; sharing a room, while sleeping on the floor, for about R500 a month; sharing a room, while sleeping on a bed, for R2,000 a month; sharing a room in social housing or illegal accommodation for R10 a night; living with a family in a flat; or renting a one-bedroom flat in formal housing for R2,500 or a two-bedroom for R4,000 a month.

In 2015, they interviewed twelve Hillbrow residents: six from Zimbabwe, three from South Africa, and one each from Kenya, Uganda, and Zambia. "Most respondents," they write, "contend that people come to Hillbrow confident that they will be able to access some form of accommodation from the extensive choice in the suburb. . . . No matter the income level, there is always an option for accommodation."

Gewer and Rubin speculate that Hillbrow's population may have peaked in 2006 at 89,500 (according to the City of Johannesburg's estimates) and began to fall slowly in subsequent years. They attribute the drop-off in population to the greater controls imposed on the number of people permitted to live in some of the buildings. These controls relieve overcrowding in some buildings but exacerbate it in others.[26]

Robert Michel—"A big economy" with "Great Depression levels of unemployment"

"A country with a big economy attracts," says Robert Michel,[27] the white CEO of the Outreach Foundation, a nonprofit that provides job training, counseling, and other services to people who live in Hillbrow. "But South Africa is no longer that. It is shedding jobs. Population growth last year [2019] was 3.8 percent, but economic growth was only .8 percent. That means the per capita income is shrinking."

Robert warns that the implications of a shrinking economy are dire. Economic stresses lead to and exacerbate other problems. "South Africa's economy is in free fall," he says. "Unemployment is at an all-time high. If the unemployment in South Africa is thirty percent, it is forty to fifty percent in Hillbrow. Many buildings in Hillbrow are in ruins, where people are without water and lights. Violence and crime are at all-time highs. When there are ten to twelve to fifteen people living in flats, that breeds violence, especially gender-based violence. There is a huge amount of family violence. We run workshops to sensitize males and females to gender stereotypes. We try, but it is an uphill battle."

Despite this bleak assessment, Robert adds that he is not about to give up. He believes that one-on-one relationships and social connections can make a difference.

Robert has worked in international development for twenty-five years and has spent time in thirty African countries. "I've worked in Kinshasa, Lagos, and Nairobi," he says. "But Hillbrow is different. There are people from twenty-five nations living in Hillbrow. It is more like New York was in the late nineteenth century. Many are transient and they move on. Some go to other parts of South Africa. Others go to third countries, like Canada and the US, although they are a minority."

He is visibly moved when he speaks about difficulties faced by long-term asylum seekers. "Many are here for ten to fifteen years," he says. "But they are never made refugees, so they cannot work. The government has completely failed. The government has signed on to treaties, but it ignores them."

Robert's observations correspond with those of the United Nations High Commissioner for Refugees (UNHCR). The UNHCR reported in 2015 that South Africa has the largest number of pending asylum-seeker claims in the world. With 1,057,600 awaiting processing in 2015, South Africa holds nearly one-third of the world's 3,200,000 unprocessed asylum seekers. During one particularly severe period of crisis in Zimbabwe, from 2007 to 2010, South Africa received more asylum seekers than any other country, with almost 150,000 Zimbabweans seeking asylum in 2009 alone. In addition, the UNHCR reports that 41,500 Somali asylum seekers and 32,600 asylum seekers from the DRC are living in South Africa.[28] It should be noted that AfricaCheck, an independent fact-checking organization, refutes the UNHCR's numbers. It estimates, instead, that the number of unprocessed asylum seekers is closer to 400,000. Even that lower number would leave South Africa with the second-highest number of asylum seekers in the world, behind Germany's 420,625.[29]

In any case, the number of asylum seekers from Zimbabwe may be increasing again as the country entered another period of ongoing extreme crisis in 2019. The UN Special Rapporteur on the Right to Food reported in November of that year that 60 percent of the country's population was facing food shortages and 90 percent of children aged eighteen to twenty-four months were consuming a minimal diet. News reports indicated that South Africa's neighbor was "on the verge of starvation."[30]

As the executive director of a large residential real estate development company in Hillbrow and Berea, Nic Barnes[31] (also discussed in the previous chapter) places South Africa's migration and economic pattern in context. "South

Africa has had Great Depression levels of unemployment for ten years," he says. "In the United States, during the Great Depression, unemployment was at twenty-nine percent for ten months. We have had that level for a decade now — and it is probably rising."

Despite such daunting numbers, the national statistical service of South Africa, Statistics South Africa, shows that the overall number of migrants — not just asylum seekers — steadily and sharply increased during that decade. The total foreign-born population increased by about 63 percent from 2.1 million to 3.6 million. The agency estimates that 80 percent of foreign expatriates are employed, with 60 percent working in the formal sector and 18 percent working in households. If accurate, those numbers suggest that foreign migrants have employment patterns equal to or better than those experienced by native-born South Africans. Such a higher employment rate may contribute to xenophobia. In any case, remittances sent home to Zimbabwe, Lesotho, Mozambique, and Malawi "have been key in the survival and education of relatives back home."[32]

On Crime and Violence in the Twenty-First Century

It is important not to overstate or sensationalize crime in Hillbrow, but the potential to be victimized remains a grinding reality. Crime and the possibility of violent attack make everyday life feel precarious. Oscar Hemer offers a small taste of how vulnerable anyone who lives in or visits Hillbrow might feel. He stayed in Hillbrow for a week during the 2010s when he was researching his book *Fiction and Truth in Transition*, about the ways in which literature mines the past in formerly oppressive societies such as South Africa and Argentina. He later recommended to a friend that he stay in Hillbrow on his visit to South Africa. That friend was mugged three times on his first day in the neighborhood. One of those times was at gunpoint.[33]

Hemer's friend's story resembles that of Kaze Emile, a young gay man who left his home in Burundi after he was discovered to be in a sexual relationship with another man. Expecting to be sentenced to prison in accordance with Burundi's law forbidding same-sex contact, he fled to South Africa. After traveling 1,616 miles, he arrived in Johannesburg with nothing more than his wallet. According to an exhibit on the lives and histories of LGBTQ+ people in Johannesburg, Kaze Emile was mugged three times in succession on the streets of Hillbrow.[34]

In 2015, Bheki Cele (also mentioned in chapter 4), South Africa's minister of police, compared South Africa to a "war zone." He notes that, after a few years in the early 2010s, when crime rates appeared to stabilize and even decline, the murder rate had returned to the high levels of the late 1990s and early 2000s. The year that Cele made his comparison, South Africa had a murder rate of 36 per 100,000, the fifth highest in the world. Only actual war zones had higher rates of murder: Syria at 212; Yemen at 62; Afghanistan at 40; and Iraq at 40.[35]

But violence is concentrated in some areas more than in others. The South African Police Service reported that, after the number of violent crimes stabilized and even fell during the mid-2010s, the country was experiencing another uptick during 2018 and 2019. The Hillbrow precinct registered the second-highest number of contact crimes — a category that includes sexual assault, attempted murder, robbery, and assault with grievous bodily harm — nationwide. Only Johannesburg Central (the CBD), the precinct immediately to its south, had a higher number of contact crimes.[36]

By way of contrast, Brooklyn's seventy-seventh precinct had New York City's highest murder rate in 2019 with 15 homicides (compared to Hillbrow's 111 that year). Its population of 90,744 is roughly equivalent to that of Hillbrow. The New York City precinct with the highest overall crime rate was the tenth precinct (Manhattan South, which includes Times Square). With about one-fifth of Hillbrow's population (but an extremely high number of tourists), it had 2,252 total crimes[37] (compared to Hillbrow's 20,441).[38]

Such are the overwhelming numbers confronting people who live in Hillbrow. Nonetheless, Rajohane Matshedisho and Alex Wafer write, the perceptions of Hillbrow's residents toward crime are complex. The informants in their study "constantly" referred to fears about crime, and the authors conclude that "anxiety associated with public space" has become one of the "organizing principles" of the neighborhood. However, their respondents also believe "in unison" that conditions are improving and are hopeful that such improvements will continue.[39]

Observers have argued that the local government often responds to crime with tactics that are both heavy-handed and ineffective. Christopher McMichael writes that when he began researching Johannesburg's public safety policy in 2013, he noticed consistent references to "blitzes" in official reports. Given that "blitz" means a sudden military attack or aerial bombardment, this gave him pause. He spent the next two years interviewing city officials and building a chronology of media and government uses of the term "blitz." He discovered that Johannesburg's officials had modeled their plans for blitzes on the "zero tolerance" approach adopted by Rudolph Giuliani when he was the mayor of New York (1994–2001).[40]

McMichael argues that the term "blitz" has become "ubiquitous" in the city government's attempt to impose order and pacify urban spaces. In 2000, Johannesburg launched "Operation Crackdown" in Hillbrow, Berea, and Yeoville. Though officially intended to clear urban spaces of criminal organizations, this action led to indiscriminate arrests and the detention of many innocent people. The following year the police launched a coordinated air and ground blitz on the Mimosa Hotel in Hillbrow, alleging that this former residential hotel had become a major locus for criminal activity and drug sales. The "Mayoral Clean Sweep Initiative," in 2013, was a series of blitzes intended to clear out "bad buildings." Police were observed "using whips and dragging people out of vehicles." As many as six thousand street traders, many of whom had formal licenses to trade, were evicted from their spaces on the streets. When the Constitutional Court ruled the city's actions illegal, the police nonetheless used rubber bullets on the traders as they reoccupied their spaces. The spokesperson for the Johannesburg Metropolitan Police Department (JMPD) told McMichael that police blitzes "always will be used when there is a need for it."[41]

In more recent years, McMichael observes, the city's policy-makers have divided between "doves" and "hawks." The hawks continue to advocate zero tolerance. Doves stress the need to create safe and inclusive spaces. In any case, McMichael argues that the city continues to use military-style crackdowns, most of which are aimed at asylum seekers or "places where black men gather."[42] Claire Bénit-Gbaffou writes that zero-tolerance policies in Johannesburg end up targeting populations the state considers "undesirable." They displace crime, rather than preventing it. The state, she argues, would be more effective in reducing crime if it concentrated on the kinds of programs — e.g., education, health — that deter people from turning to crime in the first place.[43]

Aphiwe — "My welcome to Hillbrow was a rape"

Aphiwe[44] describes how Johannesburg can be a city of both aspiration and victimization. She was born in King William's Town, a small city in the Eastern Cape, the poorest of South Africa's nine provinces. Her mother had moved to Johannesburg when she was very young, so she grew up thinking of her grandmother as her mother.

As she reached her teenage years, Aphiwe grew tired of living in a village with no electricity. When she was fourteen, she decided to leave the village and join her mother in Johannesburg. She recalls being impressed by the glittering lights as her bus approached the city after a twelve-hour journey. She made her way to the building in Hillbrow where her mother was living. She would spend most of the next eighteen years living there with her mother, and eventually a daughter of her own, until her mother died in 2016.

Aphiwe's first encounter with the city, however, brought trauma. "My welcome to Hillbrow was a rape," she says.

In the village where she had grown up, she explains, all elders are considered to be like parents and are permitted to discipline any child who misbehaves. "Parents appreciate that," she says. But this custom also led her to believe she should never defy an adult who spoke to her. A man began speaking to her shortly after her arrival in Johannesburg, as she was walking through Braamfontein. He posed as a police officer, complete with a fake badge.

"I believed that police officers are there to protect you and that you should not disobey elders," she winces at the memory. The man ordered her to follow him and then warned her that if she were to do anything "wrong" he would shoot her. He walked a long way with her to a forested area of a park on the outskirts of Hillbrow and sexually assaulted her. She saw that people were living in the park, but no one tried to help her.

After this brutal introduction to Hillbrow, she feared that the man would reappear and follow her again. Worried about her daughter's safety, Aphiwe's mother sent her to live with her uncle and aunt in the Northwest Province. She returned to Johannesburg after a year to live in Hillbrow but found herself wishing — as she still does — that she could live in Soweto or somewhere other than the inner city.

"Today," she says, "Hillbrow means high population, crime, and poverty. They rob you in the daytime now."

Her daughter is ten and Aphiwe has warned her never to speak to strangers. "My daughter and I are friends," she says. "We are close. We talk about everything. She doesn't go out after school. She stays home reading because she knows the parks are not safe. This means it is hard for her to make friends. She has heard so many stories, so she is afraid to go out."

After her mother died, Aphiwe moved into her sister's apartment near Pretoria Street in Hillbrow. The two adult siblings live with Aphiwe's daughter, an adult cousin and her child, and an adult friend of the family in a one-bedroom flat.

Despite the worries she has for her daughter because of crime in the neighborhood, Aphiwe says she has come to feel safe walking in Hillbrow alone now. "I can never be robbed," she declares. "I know the street men who sleep around Shop-Rite [a supermarket on Pretoria Street]. I give them a few rand, and they walk with me and carry my packages. They always volunteer and will take my packages in a trolley."[45]

On Moving to Hillbrow

Carol[46] is a warm, outgoing woman from Bulawayo, Zimbabwe. In 1995, amidst the economic jolts imposed on the country by the IMF's Structural Adjustment Programme, her parents decided that her mother should move to Johannesburg in search of income. The plan had been for her father to remain in Bulawayo and for her mother to send most of her South African salary home so that, together, the two parents could support themselves and their four children.

Carol's mother found work in the city and a living space, in a shared flat, in Hillbrow. A year later, in 1996, her eldest daughter, Carol's sister, joined her. In 1998, Robert Mugabe's government began seizing large white-owned farms and giving them to inexperienced Black farmers. Food production in Zimbabwe, once considered the "breadbasket" of southern Africa, began to fall, and high inflation rates set in. Amid these multiplying pressures, Carol's father joined his wife and daughter in Hillbrow. Together, Carol's parents and older sister sent money home to the remaining members of the family.

In 2000, after two decades of steadily rising inflation, prices shot up another 50 percent. Carol was nineteen and had just finished school when she decided to join her family in Johannesburg. Her two brothers followed, one in 2002 when costs in Zimbabwe rose by 200 percent, and another in 2003 when prices climbed by another 600 percent.

The six family members moved from one flat in Hillbrow to another until they settled into a two-bedroom unit in 2000 on Claim and Paul Nel Streets, where they have remained ever since. Though the building is a high-rise, surrounded by other high-rises, Carol says the family enjoyed the area because it was relatively quiet and feels safe. Over most of the 2000s, she felt conditions in the neighborhood improved and became even quieter. The building was well kept, and the water, electricity, and lifts were reliable. The other tenants in the building were all from Zimbabwe and, Carol says, they could rely on each other.

But in 2018, the family discovered the building had been "hijacked." As mentioned in the previous chapter, there are many forms that a hijacking can take. In this case the tenants discovered that the "landlord" to whom they had been paying rent since 2000 was not the legal owner of the building. This made little material difference during the first several years as the "hijacker" maintained the building and made certain to keep the services operating so as to continue extracting rent. No one has been able to find the deed holder, who likely abandoned the building sometime in the 1990s.

As so often does happen in such a situation, the hijacker eventually stopped paying for the utilities. He absconded in April 2018 and has not been seen since. He left the building with 1 million rand in arrears for the water bill and 1.5 million in arrears for the electricity bill. He had also stopped paying for the building's security guard.

The tenants had only discovered the hijacking after the water stopped running, earlier that same year. They were forced to buy water for cooking and drinking, and sometimes resorted to using the fire hydrant on the street. The building has over ten stories, meaning some of the tenants must carry water and sewage up and down multiple flights.

"The people in the next building over have been very kind and understanding," Carol says. They have sometimes permitted people in her building to fill water bottles and buckets. "We are surviving without running water, but if the electricity goes, we will probably have to move."

The tenants have banded together to keep the building clean. They pooled money to hire their own security guard. Most important, Carol says, they have hired a lawyer. The tenants continue to pay rent into an escrow account while the lawyer searches for the original deed holder of the building. Their hope is that they will be able to recover the arrears from that person, and that life will return to normal in their flat.

Carol has worked at an upscale restaurant in Melrose Arch (in the northern suburbs) for twelve years. She said she enjoys it "very much" and is happy working there. However, the pay she receives for her twelve-hour shifts is barely enough to support herself. All six of her family members are working and they pool their money together, but they are scarcely making it in their shared two-bedroom flat. "We have just enough money for food, rent, bills, transportation, and some clothes when needed," she says. "And now there is the lawyer bill."

Nonetheless, she assures Nerio that not everything is a struggle. She enjoys her family life and has a large circle of friends from Zimbabwe. On her days off, they get together to have a "braai" (a South African barbecue tradition). There are several places in Hillbrow where they can buy meat and grill food on the premises while they spend time socializing. Carol appears to enjoy her life in Hillbrow.

When Nerio spoke to Carol again in 2019, Carol's worry that her building would lose electricity had been realized. Her family, however, had not moved. Though the tenants continue to pay their lawyer, he has had no success in locating the original deed holder. The family has adjusted, she says, by making the most of daylight hours and learning how to socialize in the dark. They use candles and kerosene lamps when needed but try to conserve. Though Carol makes it clear that their lives have become more difficult, she seems resolved to keep as positive an attitude as possible. She still seems optimistic that their legal case will eventually yield results.

Lindiwe[47] also moved to Johannesburg from Bulawayo, but she is much less sanguine than Carol about the years she spent in Hillbrow. She arrived in

2009 and stayed with her aunt in the Nedbank Plaza, on the corner of Pretoria and Twist Streets. Once one of the premier locations in Hillbrow, home to the famous Café Zurich and several levels of shops and restaurants, this soaring tower of flats was in a state of serious decline by the time Lindiwe first laid eyes on it. Most of the former shops were vacant, with their windows broken or missing entirely. Even some of the glass in the residential section of the complex was shattered. The structure was eventually shuttered and remains empty as of the writing of this book.

"When I first saw the building," Lindiwe recalls, "it was something scary. It was bad. I lived with my aunt, and her husband, and their two children. But they were used to it [Hillbrow]. It took me a long time before I would even walk outside. The elevators never worked. It was a twenty-one-story building, but we were only the fourth floor."

Eventually, she dared to venture out onto Pretoria Street. She says she became comfortable enough that she could enjoy going for a walk, provided she was with friends. "There are many other people from Bulawayo, so I met many people," she explains. "It is hard for them, but they had no choice — no choice but to come to Johannesburg. Even now it does not feel like home to me."

Lindiwe reports that she was robbed twice during the years that she lived at the Nedbank Plaza, once by a man with a knife and on the other occasion by a man with a gun. She shrugs almost imperceptibly as she talks about these incidents. "Anything can happen," she says. "Everyone I know has seen terrible things happen in front of them."

When the Nedbank Building was shuttered, Lindiwe's aunt moved with her husband and two children to Braamfontein. By that time, Lindiwe had given birth to a baby girl and had a boyfriend who was earning an income. She decided to move with her daughter and boyfriend to Braamfontein too, and found it "safe and quieter" but much more expensive than Hillbrow. A year later, she and her boyfriend separated and Lindiwe found herself with no choice but to move back to the more affordable Hillbrow. She had a sister who was living in a building near Claim and Goldreich Streets, and her sister offered to help with childcare. "I hated it," Lindiwe says. "I did not feel safe. But my sister was older. She was fine with it."

Through acquaintances from Bulawayo, Lindiwe found a job working at a restaurant in the fairly affluent northern suburb of Birnam. The money she has earned has enabled her to move to Bedfordview, a suburb several neighborhoods to the east of Hillbrow. Asked to describe Bedfordview, she is almost wistful: "It is safe. It is quiet and the transit is good. But there are no shops nearby. In Hillbrow, there is everything — all shops, and the taxi ranks, everything."

In contrast to Carol, who reports that she is no longer interested in ever returning to Zimbabwe, Lindiwe travels home once or twice per year. Her daughter, now eight, even lives with Lindiwe's mother in Bulawayo.

"Her school is very good," Lindiwe says. "It is good for her to be there now. But soon, maybe in a few years, I will bring her to Johannesburg. She can get a job here and maybe finish school here. But I would love to move back to Zimbabwe someday. I would like to be surrounded by the people I love."

As this conversation comes to an end, Nerio asks Lindiwe if she has ever seen or felt what she interpreted to be xenophobia in Hillbrow. "No, not really," she says. "Not in Hillbrow."

Then, in contrast, she adds the devastating news that her brother had been assaulted and stabbed in a xenophobic attack in Alexandra Township. She does not describe the details of this event or divulge its outcome.

Kevin — In Search of Greener Pastures

Kevin[48] is a tall, wide-shouldered, and gregarious Igbo man who was born in 1971 in Aba, Nigeria, as one of five siblings. Over the years, as Nerio and Kevin became acquainted with each other, they would warmly greet with an embrace. Nerio wondered whether Kevin, obviously a strong man, felt safer than Lindiwe because of his size.

Kevin attended the University of Port Harcourt and earned an accounting degree. Upon graduating, he started a small business in cellphone sales, but the store was robbed so many times that he came to believe it was not possible to run a business in Nigeria. He moved to South Africa, first to Rustenburg, a city northwest of Johannesburg, and then to Hillbrow. He sees Hillbrow as a place specifically for foreigners.

"Most South Africans who move to Hillbrow leave for Soweto," he says, "because they find Hillbrow too expensive. Or they move to Soweto in the first place. Everyone wants to come to Johannesburg, but South Africans avoid Hillbrow and the CBD because they cannot afford it. They can find cheaper accommodations elsewhere. Now Hillbrow is more Zimbabwean. It is [now] more Zimbabwean than Nigerian, and this has meant that Rockey Street, in Yeoville, has become the real center of Nigerian life in Johannesburg. It is not Pretoria Street in Hillbrow anymore."

When Nerio asks him if he generally feels safe in Hillbrow, he flashes a big smile and says that he has never felt safer anywhere else. He says this is especially true since he moved from a smaller building to Highpoint, one of the tallest and most-storied buildings on Pretoria Street. He praises the building's management and its "very good security." Unlike the Nedbank Plaza down the street, which frightened Lindiwe, Highpoint has a vibrant plaza of shops on its first two levels, which Kevin enjoys, and is across the street from many entertainment places — including places to gamble.

Kevin even praises Hillbrow's police officers. "The police response is very fast, very good," he says. He recalls an incident during which he was sitting in a car with his friend, stopped at a traffic light, when two men approached the car on foot and smashed the windows on either side. "But the police came quick! They stopped it [the attempted robbery]."

When Kevin first left Nigeria for South Africa, he moved to Rustenburg on the recommendation of a friend. "Rustenberg is not like Johannesburg," he pronounces. "It is much tenser and more racist." In contrast, he says, he is proud to live in Hillbrow.

Kevin was born into a Catholic family and raised in that faith, although before he left Nigeria he had joined a Pentecostal church. But he had always been curious about Judaism because he had heard that many Igbos had once been Jewish. One of his university friends who was also living in Hillbrow offered to take him to services at Temple Shalom, a synagogue in one of the northern suburbs of Johannesburg. Kevin says he was "overjoyed" by the experience.

He began to attend services every Friday night and every Saturday morning while taking both religious conversion and Hebrew lessons during the week. "People can see how serious I am," he says. "I never miss a service or a class."

Kevin thinks about returning to Nigeria one day, but he is not optimistic about its future. "It is a generator-driven society," he says, "which does huge damage to the economy. Until there is full electrification, Nigerians will not be able to invest, plan, and grow the economy. At least in South Africa, there is capital. You can work, invest, and save."

When Nerio met Kevin again,[49] a year later, he was in a much less buoyant mood. His small cellphone shop in the CBD had been robbed, along with four other shops on the same premises. "They were expert robbers," he says. "R135,000 was taken. They were caught, but the security guards kept most of the money for themselves and the police kept all the rest. The shop owners recovered only R7,000!"

The robbers, he says, stayed in jail for only two days. He attributes their release to collusion between the police and criminals. More ominously, he adds, "the robbers sometimes return to the scene in order to kill their victims." But he insists he is not afraid. He still leaves his flat in Hillbrow for the CBD at 7:00 a.m. and walks home at 7:00 p.m., even when it is dark.

But he feels that Johannesburg in general is becoming less hospitable. "Many Nigerians are frustrated," he says. "They sold their businesses to come here, but it is not what they expected. And they can't go back empty-handed. . . . More and more avenues for immigrants to South Africa [are drying up]. For instance, the government is taking away citizenship from foreigners who divorce. They can only appeal *after* they leave the country. And now, an immigrant must know their intended spouse for two years before marrying. With the disappearance of marriage as an option, only asylum is left. But the government provides no assistance for asylum seekers. They are on their own. Home Affairs raids in Hillbrow are becoming more common. Sometimes they are blocking streets in Hillbrow in order to search those who walk by!"

Kevin's remarks resemble Gareth Newham's observations (above) that migrants and immigrants refer to a "street tax" that they often expect to pay in the form of bribes to police.

Two years later, Nerio met Kevin[50] yet again. He insisted on going to the same McDonald's on Pretoria Street for "old time's sake." He seemed to have recovered some of his joyful manner. He dismissed the robbery of two years earlier with a shrug of his shoulders. It was a one-time incident that he hopes will never happen again. He has also moved to a one-bedroom flat in the CBD, into a freshly restored building with a gym. In Highpoint, he had adult roommates, but in the new building he is able to afford living alone. But he returns to Hillbrow often because it is livelier than the CBD. "All of my friends are still in Hillbrow," he says. "In my new building, I don't go outside after dark. I stay in. It is too quiet at night."

Kevin has returned to calling Hillbrow the "safest place I have ever lived." Unfortunately, he mentioned this just before he and Nerio walked outside together and two men approached and snatched Nerio's cellphone. They ran in different directions so that it was impossible to tell which one of them had the cellphone. Kevin ran after one of them, leaving Nerio to stand on Pretoria Street urging Kevin not to risk his safety. Kevin returned a few minutes later, deeply dejected that he had failed to rescue the phone.

Solo—"War came to the city and we had to run away"

Civil war led Solo[51] through a long, circuitous route, to Hillbrow. In 1994, he enrolled in the University of Brazzaville (Republic of the Congo), intending to complete a law degree. During his third year of studies, on June 5, 1997, he says, "war came to the city and we had to run away."

Solo left Brazzaville, the capital, with his parents, brother, and two sisters. They fled to Nkayi, the city where they were born, about 217 miles west of Brazzaville in the region of Bwonza. They stayed in Nkayi for four years but fighting occasionally broke out there as well. During such times, the family had to seek shelter in the small village of Voka.

"At one point," he says, "we tried to start a small business selling things in Voka. It was very difficult. Both of my parents died because conditions were so bad. There were no medicines during the war. My mother died first. My father died a year later, but he was living in another village by then, 199 miles away. We could not reach him. He died and we did not find out for a full year."

"My sisters and I stayed in Nkayi, because it had become calmer," he continues. "We stayed until the end of 2001. Then it became worse. It became so hard to survive. We started to look for options. My brother was a doctor and he left for Gabon. My sisters and I went to Pointe-Noire [Republic of the Congo's second-largest city]. I tried to find a job but it was very hard — very, very hard."

The family owned two small plots of land in Nkayi that had been left to them by their mother. Solo approached his sisters and asked if they could sell the land so that he could leave the country for work and send money home. They agreed.

Solo hoped to go to the United States or France, but a friend advised him to go to South Africa because he could connect Solo with people there. He had first to go to Kinshasa, DRC, to get his passport, because all the government offices in Brazzaville, Congo, were shuttered as the war continued. He met a woman who traveled regularly between Pointe-Noire and Johannesburg to sell goods and, in 2003, he decided to travel with her.

"We flew on TAAG Angola Airlines from Pointe-Noire to Luanda [Angola] and then to Johannesburg," he recalls. "The woman was renting a flat in Hillbrow. It was in Kennedy Place, on Beatrice Lane, and I stayed with her for three months. There were several other people who were living in the same flat. I still remember their names: Patrol, Cherry, George, and Amul."

"Hillbrow," Solo emphasizes, his eyes growing wide at the memory, "was *dangerous*. I was not prepared for this. You could not walk. I soon realized that I had run away from war only to see war here. There were gunshots every night. I wanted to go home. I never saw such a dangerous place. You could not leave your flat until 9:00 a.m. because the *tsotsis* [criminals] were around until then — but the police were around too. I was robbed, but the police caught him. When you woke up early in the morning, you saw blood everywhere."

He began to realize that people in Kennedy Place were stealing his money — the money he still had from the sale of his mother's land — and after three months he decided to leave. He moved to another building, Berlin Place, in Hillbrow where he found a bachelor flat that he shared with two other men from the Republic of Congo. He had only a bed.

Solo says that he looked everywhere for work in Johannesburg but could not find a job. He chose to leave for Durban on June 16, 2003. He had met someone who was heading there, and he thought he would give it a try.

"Durban *was not good*," Solo says, shaking his head as he recalled South Africa's third-largest city. "It was quiet and peaceful in the city and by the beach you could walk anytime. But there were no jobs. I met an Indian guy with a big truck, and we delivered goods to all kinds of shops. I had no choice. I worked for him for two years, until late 2005."

Because the delivery job paid very poorly and was physically draining, Solo says, he chose to return to Johannesburg and try again there.

"I knew some Congolese guys," he explains, "and one of them, Peter, told me I could stay with him for a few days. I had saved money from the delivery job and I wanted to look for a room I could rent on my own. I stayed with the guy on Muller Street [in Yeoville] for two months. There were three of us living in one room. I shared the bed with Peter, and the other guy, Donald, stayed in the other bed. We were paying R300 each" per month (about US$50 in 2005).

Solo soon found work in a restaurant in Eastgate (about 4 miles east of Hillbrow). He moved into the Ponte City tower in January of 2006. He was relieved to have a bedroom of his own for the first time since the war had begun in Brazzaville. He was sharing a two-bedroom flat on the twenty-fourth floor with a man from Zimbabwe, each paying R850 a month.

When asked what Ponte was like at that time, he says: "Not good, not bad. But it is closer to the restaurant where I was working. There were only two lifts working in Ponte then. One went to the twentieth floor and the other went from the twentieth floor to the top. The lifts were one of the main reasons I left. I could spend thirty minutes just waiting for a lift. But Ponte was very safe. There was plenty of security. It was wonderful for safety."

Solo's recollection of Ponte is similar to that of many of our interviewees who live or have lived there. It contrasts sharply with depictions in the popular press of Ponte as an extremely dangerous place. Anna Hartford, for instance, discusses the association of Ponte with lawlessness and fear in the minds of many white people who live in the northern suburbs.[52]

In 2008, Solo met his wife, Regina. They now rent a four-bedroom house with a cottage in the back, in Bellevue East (the neighborhood just east of Yeoville). The couple rents all but one of the rooms to subtenants. "This is African style," he says. "It is common and expected."

David—"It is my home and we will stay here"

When David chose to leave Zambia for South Africa in 2004, many people he knew told him that Johannesburg was both a "dangerous place" and the best destination for a young Zambian looking for opportunities. When he boarded the bus for the 994-mile journey, their warnings were fresh in his ears. He knew no one in the city and he arrived in Hillbrow prepared to encounter a frightening place.

"All buses [to Johannesburg] go to Hillbrow," he explains. "The ride lasted two days. I got off the bus and went to the Joburg Hotel, but it was too expensive. I looked at the Safari Hotel, which rented rooms by the week. It was safe inside, but I heard gunshots at night. During the day, there was no problem. The hotel had working toilets, water, electricity, and security. I stayed at that hotel for a year.

"My first experiences in the city were okay," he says. "It was better than I expected—safer and better. But I expected to find more opportunities in Johannesburg than existed. Many people told me that it was a land of opportunity, but that was not the case. It was a struggle to find work—any work. But now it is home for me. It is safe for me here. I know how to get around and what to do."

David trained as an engineer in Zambia and hoped to find work in that profession when he moved to Johannesburg. He had secured a sponsorship with a South African firm, but, he says, "that visa fell through" when he arrived in the country. As he waited for his paperwork to be sorted out, he found work in the food service industry. Weeks of waiting turned into months and then years, until he came to accept that he would never work as an engineer in South Africa.

Nonetheless, David felt it would be economically wiser to remain in Johannesburg than to return to Lusaka (the capital of Zambia). He says there are several agencies in the CBD that link potential employees with the hotels and restaurants of the northern suburbs. Through one of these agencies, he found work at a restaurant in Hyde Park and was there for nine years, until it went out of business. His third and current employer, a restaurant in Melville, recently promoted him to manager.

When asked if he enjoys working at the new restaurant, "Oh yes," he says, "They treat me very well. I work so they will love me. I work hard for everyone and they do love me. If I work hard, I can stay."

He takes his family home to Lusaka every year at Christmastime. David says that city has "developed a lot" in the years since he left. "It is very beautiful. There are restaurants, shops, and malls. But I do not feel at home there anymore. I feel a strong attachment to Johannesburg. It is my home, and we will stay here."

A Heartless Place

Perfect Hlongwane's novel *Jozi* provides a searing look into the ambivalence of many who moved to Johannesburg from rural areas, smaller cities, and other countries. Hlongwane opens the book with a judgment on what Johannesburg has become. "Jozi, the Johannesburg we know," he writes, "of the inner city — Braamfontein, Joubert Park, Hillbrow, Berea, Yeoville — is a heartless place. It is a monster that swallows people whole. A place that chews them up and spits them out as lifeless mince. An unforgiving fire turning bones into ash; a furnace whose flames lick hungrily at the particles of humanity as they dance, lost in the wind."[53]

Implicated in the suffering evident in Hillbrow is a failed transition to a nonracial society. Black people have offered the "hand of reconciliation," Hlongwane writes, only to see it spat on. The whites have become not partners in transition but "the spoilt children of this new democracy, squealing and criticizing and cursing while they continue to wallow in privilege." The failure of the whites to participate in the building of a genuinely inclusive city, he writes, has made half of the Black people angry and the other half filled with grief.[54]

Jozi's narrator, Frank, moved to Johannesburg from an unnamed location in 1991 after hearing it so often described as "the city of dreams." He spends his first few years in the city living in Hillbrow, surrounded by friends who love jazz and enjoy arguing about philosophy. They harbor "high hopes and grand dreams" of becoming professors, bank managers, and writers. Hillbrow, he writes, "was throbbing with the novelty and promise of the new South Africa."[55]

Everything changes for Frank one night when he walks out of a jazz pub with his five friends and is attacked by a very thin man with a knife. He speculates that the assailant was suffering from hunger or perhaps drug withdrawal, and he punches him in the jaw as an act of self-defense. The man staggers to the ground and falls on his own knife, and the group leaves him lying in a pool of blood. Frank is from then on haunted by nightmares and a lingering fear that he may have killed the man.

As the neighborhood becomes more and more marked by violence, his friends start leaving for the suburbs. They advise him to do the same to escape the "undesirables" who are moving into the neighborhood. One of them offers him a room, warning him that Hillbrow has even begun to smell bad.

"I too, can see what is happening," he tells them. "I see the influx just as you do. I see the prostitutes, the unemployed youth hanging around the street corners. I see the invasion of Zimbabweans and West Africans, escalating every day. I also see human beings, people like you and me, trying to scrape out a living as best they can."[56]

Frank stays through the end of the 1990s and into the 2000s. But one evening, when his friends come into Hillbrow for a reunion at a jazz club, Frank gets too drunk and wanders outside alone. He is attacked by two men, one of whom stabs him in the shoulder. Frank retaliates against the man by attacking him with a broken bottle. The man's accomplice hits him over the head with a heavy rod, leaving him to die in an alley.

Kingsley — "That is where everyone goes"

Kingsley[57] was born in Nigeria in 1971, just after the Biafran war devastated his home state of Ahoada. More than a million people died in the famine that accompanied that war. Igbo families, including Kingsley's, were forced to flee to the eastern part of the country in massive numbers. When they returned, they found their homes and property had been auctioned off. No Igbo family was compensated more than twenty pounds. Many took this minuscule sum and used it to start small businesses, particularly in trading.

After the war ended, Nigeria's Igbos faced what Kingsley describes as "total economic strangulation and discrimination." The government barred Igbo children from attending school until 1975. It enforced harsh laws making it difficult for Igbo people to find work in any sector well into the new century.

Kingsley attended college and completed a master's degree in 2001. It was an accomplishment that made him proud but, he says, for an Igbo in Nigeria at that time it turned out to be worth very little. Unable to find work, he flew three thousand miles south in search of "greener pastures" in Johannesburg. Like so many others before him, Kingsley went directly to Hillbrow.

Many people had warned him about the neighborhood before he left Nigeria. "And when I arrived," he says, "I saw that it was very, very terrible. But that is where everyone goes. That is the system. No landlord anywhere else will rent to you. And without papers, you can't open a bank account — so everyone has cash in their apartment. There are so many robberies."

For Kingsley, the South African dream became a reality. He found work in a private security firm and was promoted over time. After many years of saving every rand, he was able to buy a home in Houghton, one of Johannesburg's most historic and prestigious neighborhoods. He lives there with his wife and their two children.

Kingsley still visits Hillbrow. "You have to," he explains, "if you want to find Nigerian grocery stores or restaurants. But I pray to God every time I go there . . . for safety."

He says he worries about the many other Nigerians who arrive in Johannesburg every year. "There are cartels that bring them here, often under false pretenses," he explains. "They often say they will take them to Australia or the US, but they take their money and they leave town. They did not want to go to South Africa, but to America. Then, they get dropped off in Hillbrow."

Crossing the Border and Living without Documents

Sizwe[58] is a social worker who works in the Counseling Center at the Outreach Foundation in Hillbrow. She also provides support and advice for migrants when they need to visit the Home Office in Pretoria or have trouble with immigration authorities.

"I would like to open an office in Musina," she says, referring to the small town on the South African border with Zimbabwe. It lies across the Limpopo River from Beitbridge, the crossing point in Zimbabwe where people often line up for four or more hours to cross the border. "That is where the action is happening. There is so much need. This is especially true with the children. Many children are now trying to come in alone.

"The trauma is so severe and widespread," she continues. "And when they get here people tell them: 'You don't belong here.' People with severe trauma are even sacrificing their children in the Limpopo [River]. They are pursued or they cannot get across and their children are lost. Then they get here, and they find no jobs. They can't fit in. They realize they could be caught one day."

Sizwe recalls one incident where she was sitting with a young Congolese woman, whose family had been killed in political violence. "She picked up and brought her children from the Congo [DRC]. She did not even have time to get her documents. She had to make a split decision. And she arrived here and there is nothing for her."

When asked how people are prepared to travel all the way to South Africa on a moment's notice, Sizwe provides an example. "One child, a sixteen-year-old," she says, "told me she saw a huge rash of people in Kinshasa running toward the South African trucks. There had been several killings and there was violence and she was injured. She just ran toward the trucks and got on one. She was bleeding. All the way to Johannesburg, she was bleeding. And she arrived with no one. Her friend's mother was an activist who was killed in her home and she knew she had to leave."

Sizwe then introduces three people whom she has worked with: Koko, from the DRC; Thokozile, from Malawi; and Doreen, from Zimbabwe.

Koko[59] says he entered South Africa from the DRC as an asylum seeker nineteen years ago. Nearly two decades later, he remains an asylum seeker, which puts him in a quasi-legal situation. His status means he is legally permitted to reside in South Africa until he is declared a refugee. But until such a declaration, he is unable to work.

Koko was born in Kinshasa in 1974 and left the DRC in 2001. It was the year that President Laurent Kabila, who had been in office for four years, was shot to death. Koko describes this event as unleashing widespread unrest and a broad search for possible accomplices in the assassination. Dozens of people, including children, were rounded up and several were jailed.

Koko was a soldier and living in a military compound at the time. "Everyone had to leave the compounds because they were raided," he says. "We had to run. I went to Brazzaville [in nearby Republic of the Congo] by boat. Then I took a plane to the border with Angola and crossed into Namibia. From there, I took a bus to the border with South Africa.

"I thought South Africa had the best human rights and job opportunities," he explains. "Only South Africa—nowhere else. In Namibia, I had to stay in a refugee camp close to Windhoek [the capital and largest city]. As a refugee, you can't leave the camp and go into town. You have to get a pass."

Koko is pointing out what many others have noted: refugees in most African countries are confined to camps and have little freedom of movement. South Africa, despite widespread reports of xenophobia, is notable for permitting refugees to live within and integrate into society. It maintains no refugee camps.

"I was there for four months, in Osire Camp for Refugees [in Namibia]," Koko elaborates. "I gave money to a guy in the camp to get me out. Then I met some Congolese pastors who gave me money and told me how to get to Johannesburg. At the border, I posed as a Namibian who was going across the border to shop for the day—because Namibians can cross without a passport to shop. Then I took a bus from the border to Johannesburg."

The pastors had given Koko an address in Bertrams, a neighborhood close to Hillbrow. In an extraordinary act of generosity, the man who lived at that address allowed Koko to stay with him for some time. After a while, Koko began to feel like a burden as the man not only housed but also fed him. Koko met another pastor, who worked for a church in Hillbrow called the "Word of Life Assembly." He was able to find work at the church and move to Hillbrow.

Koko later attended the University of South Africa. At the time, he studied music and learned how to play the piano. He now works for a nonprofit, teaching piano lessons and music theory. Unlike many, Koko is fortunate to get a little bit of support from this organization. The nonprofit charges students only R200 (about US$15) a year for three one-on-one classes a week. Most of Koko's students are South Africans, but the courses are open to anyone, with or without documents. Meanwhile, he still awaits formal declaration as a refugee.

Thokozile[60] left Malawi for Johannesburg in 2005 at the age of twenty-two and is now thirty-eight. She chose to leave Malawi because, when she finished high school, she was admitted to university but her father was unable to pay. He had recently retired and had no funds. She took a seasonal job for the Tobacco Association of Malawi, which she held from 2000 to 2005, but its pay was so low and irregular that there was no possibility she could pay for university herself.

A friend of hers had moved to South Africa and told her she was earning much more money as a domestic worker in Johannesburg than Thokozile was making at the Tobacco Association. "I was seeing people coming [back to Malawi] from Johannesburg carrying nice blankets and clothes," Thokozile said. "I went to apply for a passport and then I moved in with my cousin, who was living in South Africa."

But the cousin was living in a rural area and Thokozile was unprepared for what she saw. "It was a shock!" she says. "There was no toilet, only a latrine. And no electricity. I wanted to go back!"

Instead, she left for Johannesburg and started working as a domestic. She lived in Hillbrow and worked for a family in a northern suburb. Her first salary was R800 a month, which she considered good, but she had to work twelve hours a day. When she found a job living in a family's home in Houghton, she earned similar wages but was able to save on housing.

In 2007, she met a Malawian man who proposed to her. They had a traditional wedding in Malawi, and he paid lobola (a groom's payment to a bride's family out of gratitude for permission to marry). He had been working for a white woman from the UK who was living in the upscale neighborhood of Observatory. The woman allowed Thokozile and her husband to live on the premises. The couple had a son in 2008 and a daughter in 2015. Thokozile had a daughter from a previous relationship who was living in Malawi, but she had joined her mother and new stepfather when they moved into the Observatory house. The British woman helps pay for the three children's school fees.

Though her economic situation has improved, Thokozile continues to live with an asylum seeker's status rather than a refugee status. She visits the Department of Home Affairs every six months in hopes of becoming a permanent refugee. She describes these visits as arduous, humiliating, and occasionally dangerous. The Pretoria Office is now the only Home Affairs office in the country that processes the cases of migrants and immigrants.

Thokozile, Doreen, and Koko explain that applicants must pay R150 (about US$10) to travel in each direction from Johannesburg to Pretoria. The lines are long, and people begin lining up at 4:00 a.m. There is no protection from the sun, the rain, or the cold—an oversight that they suspect is deliberate. Because there are no security guards until 8:00 a.m., *tsotsis* (thieves) join the line and try to steal cellphones and other items.

"I went once with my baby at 3:00 a.m.," Thokozile recalls. "I could feel she was freezing. We didn't even have food [with us]. They opened at 8:00 but they [the workers] just sit there talking to each other and ignoring you. They make you wait until 4:00 p.m. and then tell you to come back tomorrow. They don't even give you a paper to say that you have been waiting and that you can go to the front of the line the next day.

"Another time," she continues, "I went there, and they made me wait. Then they told me that the computer system said there was something wrong. I could no longer stay in the country. I must go home. They said there is no hunger or war in Malawi. I said: 'Have you ever been there before? Do you know what I had to eat before? Why are you telling me to go home?'"

Thokozile said standing up for oneself sometimes works. In this case, the worker told her to go back to Johannesburg and come back to the office in thirty days. She believed the worker was quietly permitting her to evade the system because the worker surely would know that Thokozile would not return in the allotted thirty days only to be subjected to the same treatment.

"They just want to frustrate you," Koko adds. "They get you to go outside and bribe someone."

"And you can't even leave the country without papers!" Thokozile says. "So we are trapped."

Sizwe says: "We teach people their rights. 'Don't let fear control you!' we tell them. I tell everyone to make certified copies of their passports. Police do steal passports and papers. Sometimes the police will come and take money from your purse and then give the [empty] purse back to you and say: 'You must leave the country.'"

Sizwe's comment prompts Doreen to say, "One morning the JMPD [Johannesburg Metropolitan Police Department] took me. The van came and picked me up. If you don't have any money, they hand you a phone and tell you to call your family so that they can come and pay the bribe."

"When I came here in 2005," Thokozile says, "they kept my passport. They said asylum seekers must not have their passports with them as they cannot leave the country. I was so scared to leave my passport. My friend had a cae-sarian section at the hospital, at Johannesburg Hospital. And they would not give papers to the child because she didn't have papers. She had to go to a private hospital and pay R2,700 (about US$153) to get papers for her child!" Such a sum can amount to several months' income for some people living in Hillbrow.

"The Home Office abuses you," Koko says. "It is all to discourage you."

"They tell us to go back to our countries and fix things," Doreen says. "We can't! We can't even cry in our country. There are spies everywhere."

Thokozile says that she was given a Zulu name at birth, even though she was in Malawi. "The nurses knew," she smiles, "that I would be coming here!"

Thokozile's recollection of her friend's experience at the hospital seems to line up with what is described in some of the literature. Rebecca Walker, for instance, notes that the migrant women whom she interviewed reported extreme neglect or abuse in health-care settings. One woman, Christa, who moved to South Africa from the DRC in 1999, told her that while she was giving birth to her son in a hospital the "nurses slapped her and referred to her as *kwerekwere* [a derogatory word for "foreigner," also sometimes spelled *makwerekwere* or *amakwerekwere*] while she was in labor." The nurses also told staff members not to feed her because the food "was not for foreigners." They would not clean her stitches or treat her child. Another woman, Patricia, from Zimbabwe, told Walker that a doctor accused her of coming to the country while pregnant and causing herself to give birth prematurely, thereby causing problems for the doctors.[61]

Sex Work in Hillbrow

In the popular imagination in Johannesburg, Hillbrow is often associated with sex work. In our snowball sample (participants in our study connected us to other people they knew and who we then asked to participate and be inter-viewed, thus our sample grew through these connections), we did not meet people who told us they were or are involved in sex work. Many other scholars have addressed this important area of work. Sex work includes payment for sexual acts, but also includes everything from stripping to phone sex. It some-times involves the exchange of sex for rent, food, and children's school fees (tuition). It generally pays better than other work in the informal economy, but "few women are making a large profit." According to Walker, current research estimates that most sex workers in Johannesburg are either internal migrants or nonnationals who have crossed the border.[62]

Elsa Oliveira also studied the lives of sex workers in Hillbrow. She conducted a participatory workshop in collaboration with the African Centre for Migration and Society at the University of the Witwatersrand, the Sonke Gender Justice Movement, and the Sisonke Sex Worker Movement. These organizations, with Oliveira, invited eleven women who sell sex in Hillbrow to take photos showing their perspective and to display such photos for the public. The participants were lent cameras and journals and given photography lessons. Six of the eleven women were migrants from rural parts of South Africa and five were from Zimbabwe.[63]

One of Oliveira's findings was that the women had all arrived in Johannesburg with high hopes and excitement but largely found disappointment. Nonetheless, disappointment was not the only thing they found. Many had left abusive situations in rural areas of South Africa or in Zimbabwe and found in Johannesburg a city of risks — but a city, even so, that offered many things to do. Some said that, while the city was noisy and confusing and complicated, it provided them with a level of self-determination and freedom impossible to find at home. Hillbrow proved to be a lonely place, but it enabled them to be more independent from men. As one woman said: "In Jozi I can be whoever I want. I don't have to be married."[64]

Oliveira cites earlier research that found sex work in Johannesburg paid three to five times what many migrant women could likely make in other jobs. Domestic labor often pays less than is necessary for survival. Many sex workers, meanwhile, send money home to take care of extended families in their places of origin. Ten of the eleven women in Oliveira's study said they had entered the field voluntarily, while one said that she had done so to pay back a driver who had brought her from Zimbabwe to Johannesburg. All respondents spoke of danger and violence as everyday realities in Hillbrow, but they also spoke about the emotional support they received from others, about the strength they drew from spiritual practices or religious organizations, and how they found a layer of protectiveness in social spaces such as bars and clubs. Moreover, as of 2017, there were three clinics specifically for sex workers in Hillbrow. The police, on the other hand, were seen mostly as a source of exploitation, and sometimes of violence. Officers frequently extracted bribes or even took sex workers to jail where they would rape them.[65]

Greta Schuler[66] used another cutting-edge, arts-based methodology to learn about sex workers in Johannesburg. She spent three months in Hillbrow, in 2012, with five female Zimbabwean sex workers in creative writing workshops. The Sisonke Sex Worker Movement helped recruit the women who spent the three months writing their stories, which then became the basis for Schuler's interviews with them. One of the prompts was to compose a "Letter to a Young Sex Worker," which elicited a range of reflections and advice.[67]

Because sex in exchange for money is criminalized in South Africa, those who work in the industry providing that kind of sex work must devise ways to stay hidden. Migrants without legal documents who are sex workers are doubly vulnerable, as the need to stay hidden is even more acute. But Schuler is careful to note that participants' responses extended well beyond vulnerability. They write of themselves as able to make choices, take control of their lives, and achieve independence. One author, Clara (a pseudonym), wrote in her "Letter to a Young Sex Worker" that she entered sex work after leaving her abusive husband. Beforehand, she struggled to find a small room to rent with her two children but was unable to find a job. Their stomachs were "empty" then. She began selling sex at the age of twenty-two and by the age of thirty-seven, when she wrote the letter, she described herself as making plenty of money and being "happy and healthy."[68]

Skara, another participant, described her life as both "dangerous and nice." She warns the imagined young sex worker: "In this business you can get a lot of money in different ways and if you are not clever you die fast." All the participants emphasized the duality between danger and opportunity. Schuler titled her work "At Your Own Risk" because that is exactly what the women described: making the choice to enter an occasionally dangerous field but being in control over their own decision-making.[69]

Rebecca Walker interviewed women from the DRC, Mozambique, and Zimbabwe who sell sex in Johannesburg. Sex work provided quick access to a good income for women without documents or struggling to obtain their documents from the Department of Home Affairs, and it was "one of the multiple ways that they negotiated the challenges of a largely hostile and complex city." They all insisted, however, that while they sold sex they were not "sex workers"—as they were only engaging in sex work temporarily. They also insisted that they had entered the field by their own choice and had not been forced.[70]

Unlike Schuler, Walker did not make her connections with participants through the Sisonke Sex Worker Movement, as she wanted to understand less-studied aspects of sex work in Johannesburg. She started with one sex worker, Heather, a woman from the DRC, whom she met at a women's shelter. Heather enabled her to build a snowball sample of more than a dozen women. She spent twenty-four weeks interviewing the women in a neutral space.

Walker notes that much research and writing about selling sex for money has divided between an "anti–sex work" or "prostitution" discourse and a "pro–sex worker" discourse which sees most participants in sex work as making choices and having agency. The women with whom she spoke emphasize that they were, indeed, making choices, given the limited opportunities available to them. But Walker urges that care be taken to not "homogeni[ze] a diverse and fragmented group of people under an umbrella term 'sex worker.'"[71]

Sex work is often situational, and many people begin to sell sex while in the process of selling other items in the informal economy, such as food, clothing, and domestic cleaning. Sex work, Walker writes, often follows other thwarted attempts to find work. One woman, Patricia, from Zimbabwe, arrived in Johannesburg in 2000 and moved to Hillbrow to look for employment. She worked in a restaurant that treated her very badly because she did not have papers. When she found a job in another restaurant, they did not pay her and told her she had no recourse without papers.

Walker explains that Heather had fled the DRC at the age of twelve when both of her parents and her brother were killed. She found work on a farm in Zambia until another brother paid for her transport to Johannesburg in hope that she would find steadier work. But she often found herself struggling to pay rent and was forced to move eight times in one year when "landlords" charged her between R2,000 and R3,000 a month for subdivided spaces in small rooms. One of them kept all her belongings, as well as all the items belonging to her young son, until she could pay him back.[72]

One of the women Walker spoke to, Miriam, first engaged in transactional sex at the age of sixteen when she ran away from home in the DRC. To cross the border into South Africa, she provided the van driver with sex. She was hoping to go into the modeling industry in Johannesburg but even the agencies that wanted to hire her told her she would get nowhere without being able to speak English. To pay her rent in Johannesburg, and to provide for her children, she sold sex.[73]

One writer who uses the word "prostitution" instead of "sex work," Perfect Hlongwane, does so very pointedly in his novel *Jozi* (also discussed earlier in this chapter). His main character encounters his friend, "the Poet," who frequents a brothel on the border of Hillbrow and Berea. The narrator tries to tell the poet that "sex worker" is a more acceptable term than "prostitute." The Poet responds: "I spend a lot of time with these girls. They know what they're doing, and they know what it makes them. If you try to give them the impression that what they're doing is not so bad they will never trust you, because they know just how much it sucks; they don't imagine the degradation of their occupation, they experience it."[74]

The poet is disturbed because he has just learned that the women at the brothel, and others like them, are trapped by their life circumstances. "You know what I found out?" he asks the narrator, "Let me tell you: with most of them, nearly all of what they make is sent home to KwaZulu, Eastern Cape,

Limpopo, Swaziland, Zimbabwe, Mozambique, Zambia, and so on. That money is feeding and burying grandmothers, fathers, aunties, you name it. So, you see, many of them are never going to get out."[75]

Self-Organized Agency

Lindsay Bremner[76] takes issue with those who would call postapartheid Johannesburg "disorderly," given that the previous order was one based on violent and cruel racism. Nele Dechmann and her coauthors note that a new type of order is evolving. "After the fall of apartheid and further abatement of the city's manufacturing base," they write, "a new period of self-organized agency began to emerge." They write that squatters were a sign of this new self-organization. "Low-income migrants began to occupy inner-city infrastructures, adapting them to suit their needs and gradually developing a powerful, informally regulated economy. . . . Enclaves of Ethiopians, Nigerians, and a plurality of other nationalities began to emerge. They commonly resided on the upper floors of buildings, sold wares on the ground floor, and conducted small-scale manufacturing in between."[77]

Wendy—"I have this friend . . . who said to me, 'I will show you how it all works'"

Wendy provides a sense of how this self-organized agency functions. After Wendy[78] and her partner left their flat in Joubert Park (discussed in chapter 3) for Sandton in 1989, she became involved in the textile trade. Though her primary employment was with IBM, she helped a friend open a factory in the CBD that employed forty-five people during the late 2000s. Her experience with that business provided her with considerable insight into the complexities of life and work in the inner city.

"The people coming to Johannesburg today have depth and skills," she says. "I know a Malawian man, Mr. Elias, who can identify any garment pattern and make it. I used to watch him in absolute awe. He worked from the gut."

With a statement that seems to border on racial determinism, Wendy adds, "It's like industriousness is part of their DNA. People from Zimbabwe and Swaziland have a more formal education than Malawians, yet Malawians work from the gut, from the heart. They make so much. There is such innovation to make things—like jewelry—to send home."

"Mr. Elias is a gardener and cleaner," Wendy continues, "but he has so many projects. He buys things in South Africa and sends them back to Malawi to sell. It is a very sophisticated network. He sends so much to his mother. A truck comes on the twenty-eighth of every month to the factory [the factory that Wendy co-owned] and leaves on the tenth and takes a load to Malawi. It makes door-to-door deliveries of things like bikes, furniture, food items, even cash. Only once in all the years did some money — R1,000 (about US$75) — go missing. There is a whole network, a whole other world of solidarity that people in this restaurant [where we are sitting] have no clue about. The informal network is much more reliable than SA Mail."

Wendy smiles as she recalls her days in the business. "I have this friend Gary," she says, "who said to me: 'You are coincidentally streetwise, but not formally streetwise. I will show you how it all works.' He is from Zimbabwe. He took me to a building in Hillbrow at 11:30 p.m. There were twenty trucks lined up against the building. It was a hive of activity. Depending on the destination, a truck leaves at a precise time — to Zimbabwe, to Malawi, to Zambia. They go without documentation and they do it with border guards who know them. That is why they have to leave at a very specific time, because they know they must reach the border when the guard is on duty.

"You see," Wendy explains, "clothing comes into South Africa at 40 percent duty. Gary gets the clothes in with no duty. He works with people from Dubai and places like that — Malaysia. Mandela always talked about a united Africa, but it is much more united in this way than people can dream — united through the informal network."

Xenophobia, 2019

Wendy describes the profound connections that people build in central Johannesburg. In contrast to Wendy's description of a united Africa, xenophobia challenges the city's connectedness, its social fabric. One of the most severe waves of xenophobic violence occurred in September and October 2019. Most of the attacks happened in townships or in Jeppestown, an area of the inner city with a number of single-sex hostels for male laborers.

Johan and Sizwe[79] (also mentioned above) provide counseling and other services to migrants in Hillbrow at the Outreach Foundation. They recall the details with grief and worry about the future.

"Last year was different," Sizwe says. "We had a problem. Instead of people fighting, there was much more looting. People were taking things from stores. Is it really about hatred if you are going into stores and taking things?"

"It was the first time I was afraid of Hillbrow," Johan says. "I thought, 'this beast is swallowing us whole.'"

When asked what that expression means to him, he sounds somewhat overwhelmed. He speaks not only of xenophobia but of a general loss of order: "It

[Hillbrow] has become uncontrollable," he says. "The city cannot control it but they have tried their level best. There is no order in the city anymore. [He mentions Broken Windows theory and then adds] broken windows tell us a building has been hijacked. And the city can't do anything about it."

"It was terrible," Sizwe adds. "The Children's Theatre Festival was going on at the same time that the xenophobic attacks were happening. The worst thing is that there were no police. Later, only one van drove around. Many people went to the UN offices and just wanted to leave [South Africa]. One of our clients was found hanged in his flat. We don't know if it was a killing or a suicide. His family suspects he was killed. More recently, a policeman was killed in Diepsloot. The police went there immediately. They did not want another explosion [there]."

Speaking of explosions, Sizwe adds, "This [xenophobia] is a wildfire. Anything could spark it. A blanket has been thrown over it, but there is so much tension. Immigrants have businesses that don't employ locals, only their countrymen. It makes people bitter. So many people graduate and have no jobs. So, they go and fight Zimbabweans."

"There is no one Hillbrow community. There are many," Johan says, edging toward blaming the victims. "Nigerians stay to themselves. Zimbabweans stay to themselves. It makes it very difficult to build a community and reduce the tensions. There is no program to create social cohesion."

Asked what such a program would look like, he replies: "It would be, one, stereotype reduction. Two, community integration. People should welcome the refugees. I saw reports of Germans going to [Syrian] refugees and personally welcoming them and supporting the arrivals. That would not happen here. And three, economic inclusion and poverty reduction."

"The government officials need to be educated," Sizwe says. "Some of them in the Home Affairs will tell refugees to go to the embassy of the country they have come from! Can you imagine? They ran away from that country and the Home Affairs tells them to go to that country's embassy. You can't go there! At Home Affairs I have seen security officers literally push people."

Simon,[80] from the Republic of the Congo, believes xenophobic tensions are multiplying in the country at large. Nonetheless, he feels that Hillbrow is still mostly immune to them. He recalls the incidents of 2019 with intense, but calm and eloquent precision.

"No flares happen here, no attacks," he says. "But foreigners cannot live in the townships anymore. They're moving out of the townships. It's getting terrifying. They're moving to places like Hillbrow, Berea, Yeoville, and Rosettenville, because they are safe."

While Simon feels grateful that no attacks happen *within* Hillbrow, he notes that for the first time there was a series of attacks *on* Hillbrow during September and October 2019.

"At the height of the xenophobic attacks, some of the guys [from hostels in Jeppestown, a nearby neighborhood] came up Twist Street [into Hillbrow]. Hillbrow residents — locals and foreigners — formed a human chain to stop them. They had bricks. The attackers had sticks and machetes — and a few guns. It was a huge fight."

He shakes his head in obvious grief at the memory: "It was an epic battle. The guys just ran at each other. The Hillbrow resisters were fed up. They were so angry at all the attacks that they put their lives on the line. They managed to disperse the attackers, who ran everywhere. Looters attacked the Hillbrow Spar [a supermarket]. If the human chain had not happened, the looters may have gone into the buildings and occupied them. It could have been very deadly, and I hate to think of what could have happened. The Hillbrow resistance must be praised for what they did. The police came and the looters finally dispersed. But they later returned with more comrades for vengeance. They came back.

"I really felt I was going to die," Simon, who lived through the civil war in the Republic of the Congo, continues. "They were right up to Kapteijn Street. The police were everywhere, trying to stop it. The attackers had machetes and they were chanting: 'We are going to kill these lowlifes [foreigners]. We will cut their heads off.' The Hillbrow residents said: 'Come! We are fed up!' The resistance repelled the attackers and they went to the CBD instead and attacked many, many people."

When asked what precipitated the attacks of 2019, Simon says that all the tensions and provocations can be traced to the continuously worsening economy.

It started, he says, when "a group of taxi drivers in Pretoria got fed up with being paid so little that they staged an illegal strike. They began sending out messages that migrants had invaded the transport and truck industry and that it was because of them that locals were earning so little. One incident initiated it: In Pretoria, a taxi driver was gunned down by a drug-dealing Nigerian who sold drugs to homeless people. The driver had been confronting the dealer when he was shot and killed. The drivers said: 'You have killed one of ours. We will kill a million of yours.' All of Pretoria became a no-go zone. Zulu taxi drivers put word out across the country and called for vengeance against Nigerians. They began sending out messages on social media: 'If you see a foreign driver, pull them out and decapitate them.'

"Drivers all over Durban were attacked," he says. "In one case a Nigerian man and wife were mutilated. He had his genitals cut off and she was sliced open. Many, many people were burnt in their trucks. It got so bad that some drivers started retaliating against South Africans north of the border, in Zimbabwe and Malawi. The hate is so overwhelming. I feel really sad. The occupants in the Cape Town Church [Central Methodist Mission, which housed six hundred migrants for several months] got out of the townships at the last second. They don't want to go back [to the townships]. They have seen the hate."

When asked how he feels about the current state of tensions, Simon says: "It started calming down after a little more than a month. But foreigners are not lulled by this. They are moving from the townships. We must live together. It increases our chances. In September, when my wife was at work, she would get reports of planned attacks and would call me and tell me not to go out for anything. It started calming down in October. The authorities were alert. Arrests were made with no bail. South African celebrities took to social media to try to calm the situation.

"But some locals started spreading fake stories that foreigners were capturing children and they were planning on killing them [the children]," Simon recalls. "The stories were that foreigners were going into Soweto and kidnapping children. Imagine! This is unthinkable! No foreigners would go into Soweto. It is too dangerous [now]. Some sympathetic locals started to believe it. They started losing their sympathy. People were also saying that Somali shopkeepers were poisoning the bread!

"In October, it had calmed down but I was still worried," Simon stresses. "I had to go to Newcastle [a small city in KwaZulu-Natal Province] for my sister-in-law's wedding. I was so scared. But I had to go because I had to show support. I did not want the family to think I was not supportive because I am a foreigner [Simon's wife and her family are South Africans]. My wife and I sat in the van and my sister and her daughter came too. We sat in the van and did not speak a word of English. I didn't breathe until I returned to my flat in Hillbrow."

When asked how whites can sit in a minibus taxi and speak English without worrying about being attacked, Simon responds: "Everyone expects whites to speak English, so they ignore it. I think a lot of South Africans still fear whites. The South African educational system has produced so much inequality and social distance. They would rather attack a Black middle manager than the whites who are at the top. And most white areas are protected. They are affluent and they have walls. They also sponsor local police stations and the police feel indebted. Corruption has crippled South Africa. The leaders are walking away with billions of rand and people are angry at them, and they channel their anger elsewhere — at foreigners."

In November 2019 Johannesburg mayor Herman Mashaba stepped down from his position after only three years in office. He left a legacy of xenophobia at the highest level. During his time in city hall, he was known to tweet out lists of arrests by nationality so as to give the impression that almost all violent crimes were committed by foreigners. A careful analysis of the records shows nothing of the sort. He also implied that foreigners were bringing "Ebolas" [sic] to the country.[81] According to the US Centers for Disease Control, South Africa has only ever had two cases of Ebola, both of which were reported in 1996.[82] The former mayor's tweets were gratuitous and spread false information during a period of extreme vulnerability for the foreign-born population.

The police, too, seem to contribute to the overall atmosphere of xenophobia. The South African Broadcasting Corporation (SABC) reported on a late-night police raid in Hillbrow on August 13, 2019. Officially, the police were targeting sellers of counterfeit goods. But a video of the raid posted on YouTube shows them checking immigration status. One of the officers the SABC interviewed said that seventy-eight foreign nationals were apprehended in the raid but insisted that police were only trying to target criminality and not foreign nationals.[83]

Doctors Without Borders works with thousands of migrants per month at their clinic in the CBD. In one survey, 70 percent of respondents reported that they had experienced violence at the hands of the police. The report specifically traces the climate of violence against migrants to Minister of Police Bheki Cele's 2010 crime crackdown initiative.[84]

"The Hillbrow Hooligans"

Three of our informants introduce us to a group of men they affectionately call the "Hillbrow Hooligans." This is their unofficial name for a "gang" of twelve or so young men who hang out together near an intersection across from a park.[85] In contrast to popular images of a "gang," this group is a loose network of young men who struggle and survive together, and their use of the term "gang" is at least a bit tongue-in-cheek. The five "Hooligans" present on this occasion greet our companions with warm handshakes and brotherly hugs.

Our informants eagerly chat with the men, as if catching up with them after a long absence. They prompt the "Hooligans" to describe their lives as members of a Hillbrow gang. One of the men opens his shirt to reveal a stab wound on his shoulder. Another lifts his shirt and shows scars from stitches that stretch from below his navel to the middle of his chest. They came from a bullet wound, he says.

One by one, the men each say that they feel unsafe at all times. They use the phrase "survivalist Hillbrow" to help us understand why, they say, everyone must steal. A truck idles nearby with five large oxygen tanks piled in the bed behind the cab. The driver sits behind the wheel, staring blankly. One of the Hooligans says: "If the driver were not there, someone would take those, just for the sake of stealing them — even if there was nothing they could do with them."

They speak of grabbing cellphones from passersby and show how it is done with a quick motion. "Hillbrow is the land of the split-second decision," someone says.

When they learn that we are writing a book about Hillbrow, one man asks: "Is this place known in the [United] States?"

Another exclaims: "Of course it is! It is the most dangerous place in the world. Everyone knows about it!"

Simon, the oldest and best-dressed of the Hooligans, says that there are no other options in Hillbrow. "You look for a job," he says, "and you can't get a job. You can't get an interview. If you get an interview, you can't get money for a haircut. You say, 'Fuck it! I have to steal.'"

But Simon also makes it clear that the imperative to steal is linked to broader expectations of masculinity and acceptance. "If you are not stealing phones in school," he says, "and not using weed, you're not cool. Girls won't date you, because you're a pussy. You don't have money to buy them nice things. Males look at you and think you are a pussy."

As we walk away, Nerio asks our informants how they know the Hooligans. "We used to jack with them," Bandile, who is an aspiring musician, says. "We started stealing phones with them in high school. You need cash. You need to eat."

It was their love of art and music that led our informants away from stealing. Thabo adds that it was a sense of compassion that made him stop. "You start thinking about what it means to take something from someone else," he says. "That girl's mother might have saved up to buy her a phone and now you have just taken it from her, and she has to tell her mother. And you feel bad. But when you are in the mode of stealing, sometimes you justify it. You say, 'Well, her mother can afford it anyway. She will just buy her a new one. It is the pressure of circumstance.'"

Mpho tells us, "There is a community of gangsters. The hardest gangster can be very soft inside. He may take everything from someone, like from a white person. But then, when you are behind closed doors with him, he can be very sweet to you."

On another occasion,[86] the "Hooligans" tell us that most of them live in a low-rise abandoned structure that they have dubbed the "Haunted Building," or in informal shacks behind that building. Those who were born in South Africa receive small monthly government allotments, but the several who are from Zimbabwe receive no such assistance. In any case, the men tell us, their ability to survive is always tenuous. They have no choice but to engage in occasional acts of theft. Some of them have lived at the intersection by the "Haunted Building" for several years or decades.

Mandla came to Johannesburg from Bulawayo in 1998. He is an Ndebele and he says he was seeking to escape police brutality in Zimbabwe, where Ndebele are a persecuted minority.[87]

"I thought South Africa meant freedom and opportunity," he elaborates.

Mandla rode in a packed van to the border, then walked across the Limpopo River, because he and the other passengers were crossing without documentation. The van, meanwhile, drove through the checkpoint and waited for the passengers on the other side.

"The water only comes up to the chest in the winter," he says, holding his hand across his ribcage to illustrate the depth, "and sometimes it is even lower than that. We paid a guy to check the water first to see if it was okay. We made it across the river and then saw a crocodile on the other side. A year before I came, my friend tried to cross the Limpopo and was killed by a crocodile."

Mandla speaks matter-of-factly about the crocodiles. He says that his fellow travelers evaded the potentially lethal reptile, reboarded the vehicle, and rode the rest of the way to Johannesburg. The van let them out in the City Deep, a dense industrial neighborhood about ten kilometers south of the inner city. He immediately set off in search of his brother who was already living in Hillbrow.

When asked if he ever found his brother, he answers in the affirmative but shrugs as if to say their reunion provided him with little succor. They have not maintained much of a connection over the twenty-two years that Mandla has been living in Hillbrow.

Mandla lives in a flat behind the Haunted Building and says that he is happy in Hillbrow: "I have a lot of friends here. It is better than Zimbabwe."

Charles, whose clothing suggests that he might be somewhat more economically secure than Mandla, came from Bulawayo in 2002. He also crossed the Limpopo in the winter and says the water was "very, very low." He holds his hands just above his ankles to show the water's low level.

As the van in which he rode neared Johannesburg, he says, "the city looked like heaven because of all the lights. But then I saw all the crime. I realized it would never be easy."

Like Mandla, Charles had a relative who had already moved to the city. His father had left Zimbabwe for Johannesburg in 1992 but "found another woman and married her." Charles's family had lost contact with his father, but Charles had decided to look him up. He did succeed in finding him, but the reunion was brief and not warm. They have not spoken in years.

He soon made his way to the intersection where the Hooligans hang out, but rather than the Haunted Building or one of the shacks behind it, he lives in a fully functioning building where he pays rent. But, he says, the rent bills are increasing much faster than he can manage.

"There are no jobs and I survive day to day," he says.

Unlike Mandla and Charles, Kagiso was born in South Africa and moved to Johannesburg from a village in the province of KwaZulu-Natal. He came to the city several years ago but, he says emphatically, "there is no work. I receive a grant, but it is very little. It is not enough to live on."

Simon, likewise, is a South African. Unlike other members of this group, however, he moved to the city not alone but with his entire family, who are from a small town in Limpopo. He was two years old when they came. He has been living with the Hooligans since 2013. Because he stays inside the Haunted Building rather than behind it, he pays a small amount of rent whereas, he says, those who live behind the building pay nothing.

After a few minutes of talking, Simon stares hard and says: "We live in an evil place. Hillbrow is hell. The things that go on here at night—you can buy the cops. If you give them R50 [about US$3.50], you can get away with anything."

Sandile—"I give a shout-out to any kids who lived here and did not get into gangs"

Sandile[88] is a soft-spoken man with a kindly disposition. He explains how circumstances can lead young people in Hillbrow to become involved in crime.

Though most of the members of his tight-knit circle of friends are South Africans, Sandile moved permanently to Johannesburg from Bulawayo when he was twelve. But he has a longer history of traveling back and forth between Bulawayo and Hillbrow. In fact, his mother had moved to Hillbrow in the 1980s, several years before he was born. She and her sister worked for an organization that traveled through Southern Africa educating people about how to protect themselves from HIV/AIDS. Their route had taken them through

Botswana and Angola, but when they arrived in Hillbrow they realized that many of their friends had moved there and they decided to stay. Her sister, Sandile's aunt, eventually moved to London to teach at a school and his mother stayed behind in Hillbrow.

Several years later, Sandile's mother met his father. They moved to the township of Orange Farm in 1996, when Sandile was one year old. The family stayed in Orange Farm until Sandile was five, at which time they moved back to Hillbrow, near the Hillbrow Theatre. They lived in a flat with Sandile's mother's relatives, which meant that Sandile was living with his cousins. But he explains that his cousins spoke isiTsonga and he spoke isiNdebele, "so we never really connected."

His father drove a minibus taxi and soon saved enough to buy a metered cab, so he had two vehicles and rented one to other drivers. "He started to make a lot of cash," Sandile recalls, "and with the cash came women. Our family started to see less and less of him, because he was spending all his time with these other women."

The couple separated when Sandile was six and just starting primary school. His father moved to another Hillbrow flat and Sandile and his mother moved to Berea. Soon, his father had a "new family" and his connection to Sandile faded.

"My grandfather sent for me to live in Zimbabwe," he says, "because there were better schools. So, I went to live in Bulawayo. I stayed there until 2007, up to grade seven. Zimbabwe had many hungers then. Eventually, it was all fucked up and you couldn't live there anymore."

He returned to Johannesburg to live with his mother, who had moved to another Hillbrow flat.

"That is when my life began," he says. "In Zimbabwe, we are on the farm. There was so much space. Everyone could have their own room — a big room. In Hillbrow, we are all crowded into tiny spaces."

His mother was thirty years old when he returned. She was no longer working as a health educator, but as a domestic. But that same year she began working for a Dr. Wright in his clinic. "He was a famous medic," Sandile says, "who saw her capabilities. She started reading the clinic's and the hospital's materials on health conditions and health issues. So, she went from being a maid to a personal assistant. Amazing things happen, you know."

Sandile says his mother started speaking with Dr. Wright about his clients and their conditions. She shared her perspective and he seemed to respect it. She advised his clients to be assertive with their health care and to make sure they received the attention and the treatment they needed. Soon, she started working in the neonatal ward.

But everything changed when Dr. Wright moved to Australia. Sandile's mother took a paid job at a neonatal intensive care unit and decided to go back to school.

"I was in grade ten when she started nursing school," Sandile says. "Money became much tighter. She asked me to start working and contributing. Now the socioeconomic issues were getting to me. I knew I had to start doing something. Living in Hillbrow was so hard."

He pauses and lifts his right hand to his heart and says: "I give a shout-out to any kids who lived here and did not get into gangs. For me, it happened in 2009. I had a cellphone. I was walking around with two friends and we were approached by a man in a van who offered us R300 [about US$30 at the time] each to move some boxes into the van. It was a huge amount and it sounded great."

It was such a large sum of money that his friends did not trust it: "'Come on, we should leave,' one of them said."

Sandile smiles ruefully. "I looked at them and said, 'What do you mean, we?'"

He persuaded both of his friends to stay. The man showed them a stack of boxes and it seemed like a reasonable task. Then another man approached and asked if he, too, could help in moving the boxes, and the first man immediately agreed to pay him R300 as well.

"They stole our phones and our money!" Sandile exclaims. "We came to realize that the other man was part of the scam. They were working together. We went to the police and the police struggled not to laugh at us. We told the officer at the desk what happened, and he tried not to laugh. But then he said to another officer: 'Did you know what happened to these boys?' The officer told them and then everyone laughed!

"That scam changed my life," Sandile continues. "I learned: don't trust, be sure. It exposed me to the world of scams. I was more impressed than angry. I started wondering about how these men had worked it out to get other people's money and belongings.

"I went home and—look, we are a Black family," Sandile pauses for emphasis. "The punishment is *harsh*. My mom whipped me so hard. I lied to her and told her we were robbed rather than scammed. I wanted her to feel sorry for me, but she whipped me anyway! After that, [my friends and I] were angry and decided we wanted revenge. We wanted to find the men who took our stuff. The next day, we wanted to get them. So, we went to the one-rand guys, the men who look after your vehicle for one rand. They told us who the robbers are and who knows who. Now, I'm making friends with people in the industry of stealing phones.

"Then we got scammed again by one of the one-rand guys," Sandile continues, "who said he would help. He said he knew where my phone was. He took me somewhere and introduced me to these guys."

Sandile says the men were quite "scary." They took his school bag and told him that if he wanted it back, he would have to go to school the next day and leave the gate open near the cloakroom. Students are required to pile their belongings in this cloakroom each day, and the men were determined to gain entry to steal their cellphones while they were in class.

"I saw the direct line between crime and the stress of the city," Sandile says. "You become willing to do what it takes, so quickly. The way people have to cope with stress in this city — especially because you have to send money back home."

Sandile pauses for emphasis. "Do you see how many babies are in the flats here? That was not their [parents'] plan. They wanted to come [to South Africa], make money and go home. But they stay too long. Then they can't leave. You are forced to do things. No one wants to do bad shit. I meet thieves, but they are not thieves. They are just doing what they have to, to survive. Those are not thieves. The thieves are the people who steal *big*. But people here are just looking for something small just to maintain themselves. There is so much stress."

Mono — "You had to hide from the white owners"

Mono[89] is an aspiring rapper who has recorded a few tracks with a recording company that has not yet succeeded in marketing its artists. Several months have passed since we first met him, and I ask him how life has been since then. "Life is turbulent," he says, with a knowing, almost bashful smile. "But I am enjoying it, broke as I am. It's about winning the world one ear at a time. It's more about the message, but the crowds, the masses, just want to have fun."

He explains that it has been difficult for him to catch a break. His music, he emphasizes, plumbs the depths, and therefore does not always appeal to crowds in Johannesburg who want easy entertainment. "But people might change their playlists if they saw us," he says. "It's all about getting stage time. There have been some clubs here and there where I could perform — but not many at this time. There is one club in Hillbrow, the Base Club, on Twist and Pretoria, where I have had good results. It takes a while for people to understand us. We are trying to push a message forward."

Mono speaks of the artists who have influenced him. Prokid, a Soweto singer who died from pancreatic bleeding in 2018, has been his main influence. He admires Zola 7, also from Soweto, and Yugen Blakrok, who is from Queenstown in South Africa's Eastern Cape.

"She was raised in Yeoville," he says of Blakrok. "You can really feel her. She's a Xhosa female and one of the greatest MCs of all time. Now she is touring the world, but she never toured South Africa. Why? Why don't we know her? They took her away from Africa — it's so frustrating. They go study overseas and they don't come back. When they do come back they charge crazy prices. Once we have a flavor that's blooming, they take it. Even when [Yugen Blakrok] comes back, she doesn't perform here. She has been touring for seven or eight years, but she doesn't perform here.

"She performs in English," he says. "If she comes here, will people listen deeply? She did not sell out — but she didn't buy in. She knows Yeoville. She knows what it's like. How many others here could walk through that same door? Her message is 'not impossible.' She makes words seem like they are hers, like she owns them. Like they come from a mind state. How far can a mind go? She pushes her mind. Oh my God, she is really amazing! Her greatest line is: 'I spat on God's face, for the lives he wouldn't take, suffering for suffering's sake.' It is about homelessness."

Mono begins to tell his own story and what led him to Hillbrow. His birth-name is iKhwezi, which means "morning star" in isiZulu. He was born in Nqutu, in KwaZulu-Natal (about five hours from Durban by car) in 1996. During most of his early years, he lived with his father and stepmother, whom he describes as "abusive." In 2001, his birth mother told his father that she was going to take him on holiday to Johannesburg. Mother and son did not return from their "holiday."

He has a clear memory of their arrival in Johannesburg. They went straight to a neighborhood called Mountainview, where they lived in a "very large mansion." Mono's mother had found a job performing domestic labor in that house.

"We lived in the basement," Mono says, his face curled in displeasure. "It looked like a concentration camp. You had to hide from the white owners. They must not see you. You were in a mansion, but you could not go outside of the basement!"

Mono started attending nearby Yeoville Boys Primary School. He was placed in the third grade but soon encountered difficulties. His father had been a teacher but had instructed him solely in isiZulu. As a result, he was forced to go back to a preschool classroom to begin learning English.

His mother had somehow found a way to enroll him at this prestigious school, where he was one of only three Black children. To be closer to school, he moved in with his grandparents in Yeoville. "I made friends with two white boys named James and Robert," he recalls. "They had everything! And I saw their houses! They were shocking [in their grandness]!

"After a while," he says, "I realized we were not rich. I started stealing toys from Shoprite. Yeoville Boys School had a militant perspective. They had tight rules and were very strict. I liked that. Mr. Allman, who was white, was a great principal. We had to wear a uniform all the time. It was beautiful. Everything was clean and neat — showing strength. But I had no older brother to go to when I had problems in Yeoville. My mother would go away for weeks at a time — she was a cleaning woman — and I had only my grandparents. The other kids had money. I had nothing. So, I stole toys and sold them. I was not caught until the sixth grade. I stole toys every day! My mother bought me clothes, but never toys. I couldn't go to the swimming pool, which cost R10 (less than US$1) — plus chips and snacks — so I sold toys to get in."

His grandparents moved with him to a one-room flat in Yeoville. When his mother was in town, all three adults and Mono stayed in the same room. His grandfather walked several kilometers a day to Greenside to work as a gardener for a white family.

"He never took a cab," Mono says, "no matter what the weather."

Mono started visiting his father in KwaZulu-Natal. "My stepmom was *so* abusive," he says. "I grew up fast because of her. I understood things. She made me feel bad about women, sometimes — about what a woman could do."

Back in Johannesburg, he found school easy once he had become fluent in English. With homework presenting little challenge, he focused on stealing. "In the fourth and fifth grades," he says, "I was always the kid who the other kids knew was having toys to sell. I became paranoid of other people stealing from me. It was addictive for me to steal. I was handling money from a young age. I became very materialistic. I bought watches. I hid money for my grandmom to find in her coat."

At the same time, he was developing a strong love of words.

"Beginning from grade four," he says, "I would walk to Eastgate [a suburb east of Yeoville] to play video games. I would play for the whole day — I wouldn't even stop to go to the toilet. But by the seventh grade, I was also starting to make music. I was printing out songs. My friends and I were writing music and printing it out. Hip-hop was not much in SA at the time, although people knew Tupac. It was more local music — Kwaito — or house. Now, all the Kwaito-heads are into hip-hop."

He was caught trying to steal drawing pencils from the Shoprite toy section when he was in the sixth grade. He was caught on another occasion trying to steal kitchen supplies for his aunt. At the memory of it, he performs a quick demonstration of how to steal effectively: tear out the bar code and squeeze behind another shopper. On one occasion when he was caught, someone asked him for his receipt. He tried to talk his way out of it, rather than to run. But the guard took him to the security office. Mono lied and said he had no parents and lived with his brother on the streets.

"The woman in the office melted to my story," he says, "but the male manager called the cops. They took me to the station and kept me nine hours. My grandmother came to the police station to report that I was missing, and she saw me there. My grandmother sweet-talked them into releasing me."

Mono's grandmother grounded him for a month, but he was out within two weeks. "That led to an 85 percent decrease in my shoplifting," he says. "I didn't need toys anymore, anyway."

In the eighth grade, he started Barnato Park High School in Berea. "Now there were drugs," he recalls. "Now there was alcohol, and weed, and girls. I got there and owned who I was. The other boys were intimidated by the girls. But now I was stealing phones. I could listen to any music I wanted. I was seen as one of the naughty kids, but I always did my work. I could write fast. I was in the top ten when I finished in 2015. I just did enough to get by.

"I was making R7,000 to R8,000 [about US$500 to US$575] from stealing phones, but I used it to buy weed, vodka, to hand out to my friends and girlfriends, and to pay for studio time," Mono says. "Okay, I didn't really pay for studio time, but I wanted to. I stole from teachers, too — laptops and phones. I even had a spreadsheet of customers with what they wanted — calculators, memory cards. I had a contract with customers, and when they signed the contract they agreed to buy stolen goods. They could not come back and complain. Even the student leaders were coming to me to buy. I was only called to the office once. I showed the teacher that the girl had signed the contract!"

This contract seemed to be enough to get Mono out of trouble.

"We fought a lot in high school, too," he says. "We were a dominant force — me and my three friends. We did so much destruction. It worked out best for me. I was the only one of my friends who got a matric certificate [high school diploma]. There was a lot of sex on school grounds — so much sex at school — and a lot of pregnancies. Sometimes there was sex in the classrooms when they were not in session — and in the maintenance sheds. It was addictive. Everyone knows you. Even now people know me from then. But people were getting more vigilant. We were like 'hyenas,' scavenging everything. I've walked every part of the city, every hour. We needed real money. We were young kids — but young kids who are going to kill you. We had that mentality. I see you as a feast coming toward me. We saw them, young or old — and we felt powerful.

"As soon as we took our uniform off, we transformed," he recalls. "We would drink. Then we would need more drink and finally have to find another person to steal from. We never carried a weapon. We were just too physical. We beat the shit out of resisters. Some of them would pull out a gun and pull it on us — and we would say, 'No, we weren't doing anything. We are just passing by.' One morning, at 7:00 a.m., we tried to attack a kid. We got caught by the police, but there were no charges. We just had to replace the kid's phone.

"We also started going to concerts to steal phones," he says. "I went with a group of seven. We would walk away with forty phones. We would go to Ellis Park [Stadium] or Soweto. Sometimes there would be mob justice. Twenty people would start beating up on someone who stole a phone. We had plastic covers for phones and buried them in a hole, so that people who were trying to track their phones couldn't find them.

"Some of my friends would get caught or beaten up," he elaborates. "But they were consoled by knowing that I had the phones. They would hand them to me during the concert. I was the one who collected them. They would come to me later to get them.

"One day I had twenty phones," he says. "I was held up in a minibus taxi. Everyone in the taxi was held up. Someone put a gun to my head: 'Give us your phone or wallet or we will shoot you.' I had hidden the phones below the seat. Even the driver's stuff was stolen. Everyone in the taxi was crying. They had no money left and no phones, no wallet. The driver was pissed off! I took my bag of phones and walked home through Hillbrow at 3:00 a.m. My share was only R1,500. The total take was R30,000.

"Then, finally, I decided, this is too much," he says. "It will hinder me from getting what I am destined for. The feeling is amazing, the adrenaline rush. You become an adrenaline junkie. But music was my love. I would look at the singers and just cry. And here I am stealing phones. It was 2016 or 2017, and I just woke up. I stopped."

He believes that, though he left a life of crime behind, Hillbrow is beset by even worse problems now. "There is more violence," he says. "People are shooting for phones. Five people were killed in Hillbrow just recently. My friend was shot outside there on the corner [by the Berea Tabernacle]. He was shot dead last month."

But Mono's music career has proved difficult to establish. "There has been no money and only closed doors," he says. "So, I put on beats and I rap *very loud*, in the streets of Berea and Hillbrow, every day. A lot of females are attracted by that. If I want to dance, I just dance. It's addictive. I'm in a zone, like nothing else exists. It is like there is a ball of fire in my chest. If I don't rap it out, I don't feel good. I have had five or six friends tell me I am so good, so close to making it. Two are dead now. One was shot by the police for stealing phones.

"But people stop their cars and look and listen," he says. "They are thrilled when they hear me. I will rap like it's my first and last time. Without emotions, it's just another sentence."

When asked what language he uses when he writes his music, Mono responds that he writes mostly in English. He will occasionally use an isiZulu word or phrase but has recorded only one track entirely in isiZulu. "I will not use isiZulu in any song with a curse word," he explains. "I respect it. I exploit English for what it is. I can be rough with it. But Zulu is for the heart and the home."

Mono generously performs for us in the one-bedroom apartment where he lives in Doornfontein, with other members of his musical circle. When he begins to rap, a noticeable energy infuses his body and his movements seem to cover the entire emotional landscape from fury, to love, to grief, to release. He mines the words on the spot. Drawn by the poetic intensity, several of the seven friends who live with him squeeze into the room with us to listen. Thumelo sits at the keyboard and begins to play while Valentino joins with gentle, almost mournful, backup lyrics.

Hillbrow and Queer Space in the Twenty-First Century

Hillbrow no longer boasts numerous visible queer commercial spaces, as it did from the 1970s to the mid-1990s. In fact, while Cape Town subsequently developed flourishing queer enclaves, such as Die Waterkant, Johannesburg no longer has any such equivalent. Marius Pieterse explains that in the twenty-first century "Joburg's white gay 'scene' came to be diffused and scattered across northern suburbia, where it gradually, though never completely, de-racialised."[90]

Aside from the "well-resourced" and "consumerist" venues in the northern suburbs, Pieterse writes, the inner city has a few taverns "whose patrons regularly face harassment" from passersby. Black lesbians, in particular, "overwhelmingly bear the brunt of such homophobic hate crimes." Pieterse points to an incident in which two lesbians were raped by a gang of men during the Gay Pride march in Braamfontein in 2000. In 2012, a Black lesbian was beaten by security guards for kissing her girlfriend at the Carlton Centre, in the CBD.[91]

Hugo Canham interviewed several Black lesbians who describe the challenges of negotiating urban spaces in Johannesburg during the 2010s. Those

over forty compare their earlier experiences with the present. Boledi, for instance, recounts the time she spent at the Skyline Bar in Hillbrow in the 1990s.
"It was a paradise," she says, "and made me believe I was okay. And then I
really started having girlfriends."[92]

Now, Canham writes, Black lesbians struggle to create small pockets of
safety in an otherwise daunting urban landscape. One of the women he spoke
to, Randi, says that when she was raped everyone knew what her rapist had
done but allowed him to escape punishment because his victim was a lesbian.
But Randi finds — and makes — places to feel safe. She says that Gay and Lesbian Memory in Action (GALA), a queer archive in Braamfontein, is "like a
personal heaven — your little space. And you find people who will not judge
you at all. . . . It brings meaning to who you are." Most of Canham's respondents describe the wealthy, northern suburban community of Sandton, with
its malls and plazas, as one area where Black lesbians can feel safe enough
to relax, socialize, and show affection to one another. But, Canham writes,
"Black working class bodies are . . . only guests in that space as the cost of
living and consuming there are prohibitive."[93]

The occasionally tumultuous history of queer pride marches in Johannesburg offers a sense of the shifting dynamics of queer space. The first lesbian
and gay pride march on the African continent progressed through Hillbrow
in 1990 with the slogan "Unity in the Community." By 2002, Johannesburg
Pride moved away from the inner city to the posh suburb of Rosebank. The
march did return to the inner city again in 2004, but that year a participant was
severely injured when someone atop a building threw a bottle into the crowd.
Johannesburg Pride returned to the northern suburbs the following year.

Pieterse sees the defensive move of Pride to the northern suburbs as rep-
resenting a "loss of the right to the city." Fear was leading organizers and
participants to concede the possibility of queer space in Johannesburg except
in the economically comfortable — and largely white — neighborhoods such
as Rosebank and Sandton. But the queer community in the northern suburbs,
he writes, shows little interest in the lives and the struggles of inner-city queers.
Meanwhile, Soweto started to develop its own vibrant and overtly politicized
pride celebration in 2004 and has continued the tradition ever since.

The tensions roiling Johannesburg's queer landscape boiled over in 2012.
That year, the One in Nine Campaign, an NGO dedicated to protesting sexual violence, staged a demonstration in the middle of the Joburg Pride event.
The One in Nine Campaign alleged that Johannesburg Pride, now marching
in Sandton, had demonstrated indifference to the systemic sexual violence
facing women in South Africa. Members of the NGO lay down in the street
and blocked the progress of the march, leading some participants in the Pride

parade to believe the march was being assailed by antiqueer counterdemonstrators. Members of the two groups confronted each other, and a few of them came to blows. Some of the participants in Joburg Pride hurled racist slurs at the One in Nine demonstrators.[94]

After this event, the Pride Committee disbanded. In 2013, some of the organizers urged a "back to the city" pride march that would begin and end in Newtown (on the opposite side of the CBD from Hillbrow), but decided to cancel the event before it occurred due to "safety concerns." A splinter group called "Johannesburg People's Pride" formed that same year. They decided to hold a march that retraced the route of the very first parade in 1990, by starting at Constitution Hill and proceeding through Hillbrow and Braamfontein. The People's Pride march was "multiracial and self-consciously political," with a tribute to the late activist Simon Nkoli, a "silent walk to honor lesbians who had been murdered in townships," and a general protest against sexual violence.[95]

Johannesburg People's Pride continued to host marches through Hillbrow and Braamfontein for the next three years. Meanwhile, Johannesburg Pride reconstituted and held marches in the affluent community of Sandton. Johannesburg Pride has continued to march in Sandton from 2014 on, with a new platform called "Pride of Africa," which seems more self-consciously devoted to inclusivity.[96]

Matthew Krouse,[97] whose extensive memories of Hillbrow's queer spaces in the 1980s are described in chapter 3, claims that the very concept of "queer space" has been transformed in Johannesburg since those years. "If you want to meet LGBT people now," Matthew, who is white, explains, "you have to just approach people. There are no gay spaces in Johannesburg anymore — or very, very few. That is because it is becoming an African city, and quite rightly. There is a different conception of public space. There are networks, instead. 'Gay space' is a reflection of privileged liberal values. But in an African setting, you adjust to whatever happens. If you have an effeminate son, for instance, you move him into the kitchen. They may knock him around for a while first, trying to toughen him up. But eventually, it if it does not work, they put him in the kitchen, they assign him other tasks — like take care of the children. In that sense, there might be *more* integration in such networks than there is in the western notion of 'gay spaces' now."

Research by Marian Nell and Janet Shapiro suggests a complex range of reactions to queer children in South African households. They conducted focus groups and interviews with queer youth in and around Johannesburg. Many participants reported feeling isolated and rejected, and some had been expelled from their family homes. Some were told by their parents that they were disgusting and that no parent would want a queer child. At least one participant who had been raped was told by a parent that she "deserved it" because of her sexual orientation. "However," Nell and Shapiro write, "we also found that in many homes homosexuality seems simply to have been accepted without surprise and even with relief."

South African schools, they found, "are rife with violent bullying." Homophobic bullying, in particular, is considered normal behavior and often receives at least tacit support from teachers. Nonetheless, Nell and Shapiro also found that most of the queer young people with whom they spoke described their coming out experiences as positive.[98]

Matthew continues, "I don't go to Hillbrow anymore, because there is not much of a social life for me there anymore. I only go there to pick up and drop off my boyfriend, who lives there. My last four boyfriends have lived in Hillbrow. When I come to think of it, my entire love life has been in Hillbrow!"

Matthew reflects on what the city offers to young people today. "Many people come to this country looking for freedom," he says. "And those who do leave their countries and come to Johannesburg are astonishingly open-minded. They are looking for many kinds of freedom: economic, cultural, gender, and sexual freedom. They want not only to be free of the economic strains and political tumult of their countries, but they want to be free of the traditional ties that bind and restrict them. They end up in Hillbrow, en masse. They are an en masse population of the young and they are mostly single men. They are looking for a life."

He pauses and says, "So now we come to the delicate part of this discussion."

Seeming to acknowledge the power differential, Matthew explains that he dates "nice, strong African men. They have nothing to offer the local women [economically], so they often look for 'husbands.' Many, but not all, are LGBT, with an emphasis on the 'G.' I met my current boyfriend in Nando's. He is from the Congo and lives in Hillbrow."

Again recognizing the power gap, Matthew describes the men he meets as: "living alone in the city, often struggling and coping — like everyone else in Hillbrow — with the fact that there have been less opportunities than they expected. They want proper structure. They want boyfriends and friends. It's not about money, but about decent meals, theater, etc. They are not looking for a roll in the hay. They want to see you again. Structure is very important to them. It is about going to the same restaurant, having the same meal, at the same time, on the same day of the week.

"When I meet someone, I want to know the person is honest, funny, conversant. They may have girlfriends, too, if they can. I am not jealous like that.

Why would I get jealous at this age? The boyfriend I had before this — he was an extraordinarily beautiful man from the Congo. We met at the KFC. He was with a woman. She was a white woman of means who seemed to have made a similar arrangement. She doted on him. He was living in Berea and was a cocktail barman. He wanted to be a model [here Matthew shows a picture on his phone of a shirtless man with six-pack abs, staring into the camera]. "He was working in an international hotel. He had quite a number of male suitors."

When asked if he ever feels fear when he approaches random men in the city who may or may not be open to his advances, Matthew responds: "No. Not at all. If you are respectful and kind and friendly, there is no danger."

Mbulelo[99] is a soft-spoken Xhosa gay person who moved to Hillbrow in 2012. He was born in the small city of King William's Town, in the Eastern Cape, in 1993. With friends, he often uses the name Marie. When we discuss fluidity with pronouns in the United States, Marie indicates a preference for he, him, his.

"It was very free in King William's Town," he recalls, with a smile. "I was a dancer. I was always dancing. Xhosas are very closed to homosexuality. They see it as a disgraced condition. The whole community condemns it. I grew up knowing I was gay, and I decided I would be who I am. I never told my parents about it, but they were very kind to me. I had six siblings and I was the youngest boy. No one ever insulted me or gave me any problems. They never said anything bad to me about being gay."

Marie's two older sisters were the first in the family to move to Johannesburg, and they found a flat together on Pretoria Street in Hillbrow. Marie decided to join them in 2012, when he was seventeen.

"I was so excited about coming to Johannesburg," he recalls. "I wanted to come for a job and to start a new life. When I arrived, I was so nervous. It was very different from what I expected."

When asked what he thought when he first saw Hillbrow, his response is emphatic: "I would call it hell. When I first saw it — yes, I would say I thought it was hell. My sisters were here for years before I came, and they were fine. But everything about it looked like hell to me. I still feel the same way. It will never change. There is nothing I like about it. I am only trying to survive there."

When asked if he has any friends in Hillbrow, he brightens up and says: "Oh yes, I have many, many friends in Hillbrow. Many of them are gay. But they don't enjoy Hillbrow. They are just trying to survive it."

In contrast to Matthew Krouse's description (see above), Marie explains that there are several places in the inner city where queer people socialize. In the

CBD, Marie points out, there is a popular queer club called the Underground and he believes there are two gay churches. About the Underground, he says: "It is very big. Huge! And very mixed. Many lesbian and gay people go there. But it is mixed — for everyone. It is safe because the bouncers keep it safe. I use Taxify [a car service like Uber] to get there and I meet my friends there."

There is a smaller club in Hillbrow, called Maxhoseni. "It used to be big," Marie says, "but it's been renovated. Now it is very small. It's in a big building, but it is very small. It's just north of Pretoria Street."

Marie's experience contrasts with that of Johan (see above), who believes that Hillbrow's population is divided along national and ethnic lines. Maxhoseni, Marie says, "is very mixed, nationally — with Xhosas, Zulus, Sothos, but also people from Zimbabwe and Malawi and other foreigners. No one makes a distinction and there's no separation. They communicate in Zulu, Xhosa, or English."[100]

Marie met most of his friends while dancing at the Underground. All of them are South African, but his boyfriend, whom he met on Facebook, is from Eswatini (formerly Swaziland). The boyfriend lives in Newtown (about 3 miles from Hillbrow) and the two see each other by taking a minibus taxi service, which costs around R6 (US$.50). Marie's boyfriend travels home to Eswatini every December to visit his family, but his very religious mother does not know he is gay.

"Our relationship is getting very serious," Marie confides. "I would like to move to Swaziland with him. He's an architect."

When I ask Marie about the general level of acceptance for queer people in Johannesburg, he takes several moments to think about his answer. In contrast to Mathew Krouse (above), who reports feeling no sense of danger, Marie responds to this question by saying: "People think we have a good life, a fancy life. But it's not like that. We live in fear every day. We are not safe as gay people, even though the country gave us the freedom to be gay and to get married. Robbers think you are a target. They call you names and say you are disgraced. They think it's okay to rob you because you have a disgraced identity. This is not nice — not a nice way to live."

When asked what "apartheid" means to him, as someone born in 1993 (a year before the birth of formal democracy), he responds that he does not think much about it — only what came after. "We are supposed to be free," he says, "but not much has changed. There is a big lack of jobs. Even people with degrees cannot get work. They feel they wasted their money getting their degrees. Without jobs, there is no freedom. And no political party, no political leaders, is doing anything. I don't have faith in any of them."

Marie works at a call center for Standard Bank in Bryanston, a distant northern suburb. "It is not such good work," he says. "The pay is not good, but I do have friends there." In 2020, he moved from Hillbrow to Newtown to live with his boyfriend from Eswatini.

Keval Harie[101] is the executive director of Gay and Lesbian Memory in Action (GALA), the archive mentioned as a safe drop-in space by Randi (discussed above). For many years, this organization offered queer history walking tours through Hillbrow but phased them out in 2016. The former guide has left the organization and Keval says GALA is still deciding whether to revive the walks with another guide.[102]

"We are thinking about restoring them in a meaningful way," he says. "Most people do not have a memory of Hillbrow as a significant queer space anymore."

Keval was born in Kensington in 1982 but grew up in an Indian community in the West Rand (west of Johannesburg), in a small town called Azaadville. He has no memories of Hillbrow as a queer space himself, although he did make frequent visits to Hillbrow during his childhood. His grandfather had a tailor shop on Pretoria Street for many years. Keval remembers visiting him in the shop when he was a young boy. He remembers being impressed that his grandfather "had clients from all across the racial divide." By the mid-1990s — Keval is not certain of the year — his grandfather was forced to close the shop because "it just became too dangerous."

In the early 2000s, Keval began attending the University of the Witwatersrand, whose campus is in Braamfontein — on the other side of Constitution Hill from Hillbrow. During his years there, in which he completed a law degree, he became aware of GALA. He never visited the organization during his undergraduate years, as he was only beginning the process of coming out. But he says that just knowing that GALA existed was helpful to him. Hillbrow, however, had by then long since lost its identity as an overt queer space.

After graduating in 2007, Keval moved to Cape Town and by that time had developed a strong interest in constitutional law and human rights. He entered private practice and found himself able to provide legal services to student activists as the Rhodes Must Fall movement erupted at the University of Cape Town. This was a protest movement that would eventually extend to almost all universities with the goal of decolonizing the curricula, diversifying the still mostly white faculty, and, under the guise of an offshoot movement, Fees Must Fall, lowering the cost of attending university so as to provide more access.

"This was a defining moment for me," he says, "because it reminded me of why I was in law in the first place. Then I saw a post for GALA and applied. It was not for the executive director's position, but to my surprise GALA asked me to apply for that position instead."

Asked whether any particular location in Johannesburg has replaced Hillbrow as Johannesburg's queer center, he says that no such place exists. Perhaps akin to Matthew's thinking (above), he explains that the city is a different place now, and the very notion of queer spaces — and who they are for — has evolved.

"Some people feel sad at the loss of Hillbrow," he remarks, "but there is a [queer] presence in Melville. There are remarkable social spaces in Johannesburg — in Soweto, and in the suburbs. Some think of Cape Town as the queer capital now, but it is only so for some.

"Soweto Pride, which is organized by the Forum for the Empowerment of Women (FEW), is amazing," he says. "It is very family oriented and right in the heart of Soweto. Thousands of people attend. There are no counterprotesters. Joburg Pride has religious counterprotesters but they are not threatening. Many churches have become welcoming now. Holy Trinity Church, in Braamfontein, has a support center for queer migrants. GALA is doing a book on it, called *Seeking Sanctuary*. But this is really something — a Catholic Church in the heart of the city supporting queer migrants. Religion is often very important to migrants. They seek it out. But it is also important for them to see allies too. The priest at Holy Trinity instituted the center after two parishioners told him about the needs of queer migrants in the congregation. South Africa has created space for religious tolerance, because of leaders who speak out — including in the Muslim community."

Asked what kind of role GALA plays in the city, he responds: "Visitors are from across the spectrum. We get about twenty-five to fifty a week. I find the idea of a 'safe space' problematic, because what are we saying about other spaces? But this is a place for tolerance. We don't always have the resources to meet all needs. There is no safe house in Johannesburg. We get migrants who have been kicked out of their families and fled their home countries, for instance. We don't always have the ability to serve them. Sometimes people 'smooch' in the library because they have nowhere else to go. Every Thursday we have a GALA Youth Forum, which is mostly students from Wits — mostly Black students who meet each other and discuss topics. We hosted a screening of *Paris Is Burning* recently. The students were so engaged — critically engaged, asking deep questions.

"We have a remarkable archival collection that provides opportunity for queer visibility in an African setting," he says. "We are still dealing with the trope that homosexuality is not African. We have recorded documents to show that it most definitely is. We are gentle activists wielding soft power — the power of stories. We have been through twenty-five years of democracy but there is still so much violence. But people live their lives with love and joy the best that they can. We offer the possibility of visibility in an African space — the possibility of a vibrant robust, in-your-face queer resistance."

Holy Trinity, which Keval Harie mentions above, is a historic Catholic church founded in 1899, one year before the second Anglo-Boer War started. It occupies a stately building with majestic stained-glass windows built in the 1930s. Though not in Hillbrow proper, it can be reached by a short walk past Constitution Hill into Braamfontein. Its website prominently advertises the church's LGBTQIA+ Ministry, which meets every other week. A message on the ministry's website from the archbishop reads: "You belong to the heart of this Church. And there is nothing that you may do, may say, that will ever rip you from the heart of this Church. There is a lot that has been said to you, about you, behind your back, that is painful and is sinful. . . . We have to find a way to talk to one another."[103]

The journalist Ndileka Lujabe[104] visited the ministry in 2017 and learned of the almost unimaginable lengths that those in attendance have taken to seek safety in Johannesburg. Rodney, for instance, fled Zimbabwe for South Africa not once but twice. He said he had experienced years of persecution, physical violence, and depression in high school. He reached out to Gays and Lesbians of Zimbabwe (GALZ), the country's best-known queer rights organization, but was told that because he was under eighteen, he was too young to join or visit. He confided to his mother that he was gay and his family "disciplined" him with beatings. A potential suitor reported him to supporters of former president Robert Mugabe, after which a crowd pursued him, tied his hands with electric cable, and took him to the police station, where he had to bribe officers before he was released.

He left for South Africa at seventeen but was unable to find work. Discouraged, he returned to Zimbabwe but still felt unsafe. After several years, he decided to try South Africa again. "I did not have a cent in my pocket, but I made it here," he told Lujabe. "I begged and walked all the way [from Zimbabwe]." As of 2017, he was still struggling to find a job and a permanent place to live.

Dumisani, an activist and the leader of the ministry, moved to South Africa in 2011. He says he feels safe at the church, where about 60 percent of the full congregation is from outside South Africa and many are refugees. The LGBTQIA+ Ministry provides advice on how refugees may access their rights and get treatment at hospitals and clinics, which often discriminate against foreigners. The group also works with other organizations, such as the Jesuit Refugee Service, which assists asylum seekers with their papers and helps them pursue work.

Lujabe notes that GALZ continues to work "tirelessly" for queer rights in Zimbabwe but has faced a declining membership after so many people have left the country for South Africa. GALZ's own website states that, while religious and political leaders in Zimbabwe have "whipped up a climate of hysterical homophobia," tolerance in the country is nonetheless growing. "The problems facing lesbian and gay people are," the website reads, "by and large, the same as those facing Zimbabweans as a whole: oppression, lack of freedom of expression, fear of the state, fear of rampant inflation linked to increasing poverty, scant regard by national leaders for the rule of law and a declining health service in a country with one of the highest prevalence rates of HIV/ AIDs in the world."[105] Zimbabwe's media, however, continues to single out queer people by airing frequent antigay comments from the country's leaders. Mugabe, president until 2017, for instance, referred to queer people as "worse than dogs and pigs."[106]

Dumisani cautions that life is not decisively easier in South Africa than it is in Zimbabwe. "The only thing we're holding on to," he told Lujabe, "is that the Constitution protects LGBTI rights here. But the plight of LGBTI refugees is double."[107]

B Camminga, who lives in Hillbrow, has written a book about transgender refugees in South Africa. Camminga interviewed twenty refugees from Central, Southern, and Eastern Africa. "It is unsurprising that, since its inception," Camminga writes, "those fleeing persecution have made their way to the country that is widely considered the most multicultural and egalitarian state on the continent" and that is "gay friendly." Sometimes this message is spread unwittingly by homophobic churches that denounce or pray for a South Africa that they believe has been "infected" with the perversion or sinfulness of "homosexuality" that comes from the West.[108]

Camminga's participants describe harrowing incidents and extremely arduous journeys to reach a South Africa that they imagine to be safe and free. Some have left because their parents have beaten or threatened them, such as Alex from Central Africa, whose parents tried to inject them with petrol. Others were supported by parents, who provided them with the funds to get to South Africa. Some left their home communities because they felt their presence put their families in danger. Camminga is very careful not to disclose actual names, details, or precise names of home countries.

Kelly and Daniel, from East Africa, were "locked in compounds, hidden in safe houses, forced to empty their bank accounts, beaten, chased, or threatened and slashed with machetes." Akram was seventeen when she left her home country in East Africa. Her story provides an example of just how difficult it can be to reach South Africa, and how determined one can be to survive. She had always been taunted in her country as a "ladyboy," and as she approached adulthood she "faced two options: tell her father her feelings about being a woman and face the very real possibility of being killed for embarrassing the family, or run away." She took US$100 and went to a safe house where she found herself among seventy other migrants waiting to leave — many of whom also now called her a "ladyboy." The migrants ended up on a crowded fishing vessel headed for Yemen, where Akram fled with a smaller group of ten people to the Saudi border. In Saudi Arabia, guards shot at them and one of the people next to her was struck and killed. Akram surrendered to Saudi authorities and was placed in a vermin-infested jail cell until she was deported back to her country.[109]

There, her mother quietly arranged for her to leave for Kenya where an aunt would shelter her briefly. With her mother's money, she reached the Kenyan border with Tanzania and bribed a guard to gain entry. She took a boat and then a bus to reach Maputo and then a taxi to reach the Mozambican border with South Africa. She slipped through a fence, where she had to abandon all her belongings. Once in South Africa, she hired a taxi driver who left her stranded in a remote location in Limpopo. She searched for another driver who would take her to Cape Town. Once there, she tried to connect with an aunt and cousins who were living there. The relatives beat her and told her never to come back, which effectively meant being cut off from her national community of origin in that city. She eventually moved to Johannesburg. Like many others who had taken extreme measures to get to South Africa, Akram followed the requirement to apply for asylum at the Home Affairs Office within fourteen days.[110]

Most of Camminga's participants reported difficulties at the Home Affairs Office. The locations of the Refugee Reception Offices (RRO) were often unclear and were sometimes changed abruptly. Applicants often found themselves having to join queues for more than fourteen days — longer than the maximum allowed period during which to apply. They sometimes waited on line for a full day only to realize that the office was serving only members of other nationalities that day. Transgender asylum seekers were sometimes harassed by others in the queues, even to the point that they were pushed to the back of the line. They often did what they could to "fit in" or obscure what might have been perceived as gender nonconformity. Nonetheless, when they finally reached the front of a queue, they found that the clerks were also likely to humiliate them by demanding to know "what are you?" or calling other clerks over and tell them to "come and look." Clerks also accused some transgender applicants of fraud because the sex listed on their passports did not correspond to their physical appearance. Transgender applicants worried that providing clerks with their chosen names might lead to accusations of fraud.[111]

In cities such as Johannesburg and Cape Town, transgender refugees struggle to find a sense of community and belonging. After Akram left Cape Town for Johannesburg, she found a job. Unfortunately, other people who knew her from Cape Town were working in the same place. The boss liked her, but they insisted to the boss that she was "gay" and, therefore, not a good person. She was fired and then assaulted by a group of conationals who were determined to kill her, but a passing truck driver rescued her and took her to a hospital. When she later found a room in a hostel, other people from her country identified her and told the owner of the hostel to evict her lest Allah punish her.

Another interviewee, Alex, told Camminga they went to a church in Johannesburg wearing a touch of makeup and the minister called them in front of the congregation and told everyone present that Alex had an "evil spirit."[112]

Camminga notes that the participants in their book were "by necessity, extraordinarily resilient and creative." They have found ways to survive. But they have not found the kind of life they imagined South Africa would offer them. Presumably to protect their identities, Camminga does not provide details about where their participants live, but it is possible they may have spent at least some time in Hillbrow—as so many refugees have.[113]

At least there is one church, in nearby Braamfontein, that provides a special ministry to transgender and other queer people who may have made similar journeys across the continent.

6
A Web of Relationships

Clifford Bestall grew up in mostly white Hillbrow during the early 1980s. He returned more than two decades later and made a somber, often beautiful, documentary. *Hillbrow: Between Heaven and Hell*[1] focuses on how the neighborhood has transformed in the new century. While interviewing people from South Africa, Zimbabwe, and the DRC, he explores survival in a place that has become far more dangerous than when he was a boy.

As the subtitle implies, new arrivals who come searching for "greener pastures" end up all too often facing hellish situations. In the absence of more effective government services and better jobs, Bestall believes, survival "requires a web of relationships." In this chapter, we explore how organizations and individuals build such connections in this challenging environment.

Birthial — "I have never chased anyone away"

Tanya Zack has written a deeply poignant book about one remarkable community that developed in Hillbrow. Consisting of only eight pages of English text, with an equal number of pages in isiZulu, most of its pages are reserved for its striking photos. This is the story of Birthial, affectionately called "Gogo" (a respectful term for an older person), whose one-bedroom flat sometimes accommodates up to thirty-four or more people. It has eleven beds, with only a tiny sliver of walking space between them. People sleep fully clothed, with as many as five to a bed.[2]

Birthial tells Zack that she never rejects anyone, no matter their gender, religion, ethnicity, or state of health. She helps her subtenants find work and navigate government assistance when it is available. Among the occupants

Zack meets are an aspiring actress from KwaZulu-Natal, a former construction worker from the Transkei who has fallen on hard times, a young woman from the Eastern Cape hoping to find a nursing job, and an elderly woman abandoned by her family. Some tell her haunting stories of lives filled with tragedy.

The taps in the single bathroom do not work. The occupants use a "red fire hose that snakes into the building from the drain on the sidewalks." From it they fill kettles with water that they boil for drinking, washing, and flushing the toilet. Some of the occupants tell Zack that Birthial's apartment is far better than buildings where they have stayed nearby. One of them had stayed in the notorious Fattis Mansions, a "hijacked" building that has received considerable media attention.[3]

Gogo believes unemployment is the biggest problem facing the city. It is the foundation of all other troubles, such as the grime, poverty, and violence. Her plan, therefore, is to offer as much stability as possible as her subtenants look for work. She sets strict rules forbidding smoking, drinking, and fighting and insists that people keep their spaces clean. She consistently urges them to update their resumes, or to apply for courses, or to prepare for interviews. When people find work, they move on. Sometimes, when the work disappears, they return. There are communal prayers every evening, led by a visiting reverend who sleeps under a bridge. Zack stresses that Birthial, who seems to counsel and care for so many, is highly unusual. With great sadness, Zack reports that a week after her last visit to this extraordinary apartment, Gogo died. It is not known what has become of her numerous subtenants.[4]

George Khosi's Hillbrow Boxing Club—"It's not just about lifting weights. It's like a family"

George Khosi's Hillbrow Boxing Club is one place where relationships flourish in Hillbrow. In fact, Bestall bases much of his documentary on the connections that have developed between George and the many people—including many women—who have turned to the gym as a place to develop confidence, cope with stress, and learn self-defense. They include Busie, from Zimbabwe, who describes George as something of a father figure to her; James, from Nigeria, who coaches at the gym; and Mimie, from Zimbabwe, who says about James and some of the people she trains with: "we can talk about everything." Mimie and Busie both intend to become world boxing champions and George says that his dream is to make this possible.[5]

Nerio spoke with George in March and August 2019 and again in January

2020, each time in the gym. In his soft, gravelly voice, George explains that his family is from Zimbabwe, but he was born on the South Africa side of the border, in Musina, in 1970. He says that a "bad man," who may have been an uncle, brought him to Johannesburg when he was six years old. This man abused him until he ran away at the age of seven and ended up living as one of Hillbrow's many "street children." He befriended a group of Black and white boys — seven in total — who survived by washing cars for money, stealing, and doing odd jobs for tips. He never saw his family again until he visited Musina in 2018, when he was forty-eight.

In his early teens, the police arrested George for stealing and, for a time, he was "in and out of jail." He had no formal education, and none was provided while he was in captivity. The jails offered no services and no guidance upon release. He began to learn boxing at the age of sixteen to protect himself. He also joined a gang of men who robbed people, often violently. Out of retribution, a group of men attacked him and one of them shot him in the eye. George's accosters threw him down a steep hill and left him for dead, but he was rescued by a group of "street children" who saw him and picked him up. He sustained another injury when he fell while "train surfing," a form of daredeviling that he describes as "like Russian roulette." To this day, his left eye is clouded, and he walks with a limp.

"I could not work," he says, "and I could not box anymore. But I saw how many kids had needs. I wanted to teach them something — give them skills. I helped them by teaching them to box."

George first began teaching his boxing lessons in parks and on the streets, wherever he could find a space. After he became known in the neighborhood, Madulammoho, an NGO that provides transitional housing, began providing George with a permanent space. It is a poorly ventilated space with every inch taken by mats, free weight benches, and machines. The boxing ring is outside, under a solid covering that protects it from the rain and the sun. The equipment is extremely worn and some of it is barely functional, but visitors to the gym improvise as best they can. Dozens of photographs of those who have trained at the gym and gone on to participate in competitive boxing events adorn the walls.

George is not paid a wage or a salary, but he does receive occasional tips. He opens the gym every morning at 4:30 a.m., and all activities stop at 6:00 p.m. for a group prayer service. Attendance is free for children, and adults pay what they can.

"The kids here," he says, "they have no parents. Their life in Hillbrow — anything can happen to them. There are so much guns, so much violence.

They are living for drugs. They have no future. The kids in the ring, half of them are homeless. So it's [coming to the gym is] not just about lifting weights. It's like a family — making friendships."

Several WhatsApp groups have formed among members at the gym. In one case, a gym member lost his young son on New Year's Eve (2019) when someone dropped a bottle of beer from a balcony as the boy was walking by. The boy died instantly. The WhatsApp group immediately raised about R2,000 (about US$150) for the boy's family. Gym members assisted in the investigation by asking around to see if anyone had caught the incident on camera. They discovered that someone had indeed filmed this incident, but the police were uninterested.

"The police just think, 'This is Hillbrow,'" George says, "and they don't care."

One of the WhatsApp groups recently became dedicated to forming a running group. Others are trying to help George raise funds to buy newer equipment. George's example — of diligently making the best of a less-than-ideal setting — is also reflected in other places, such as a remarkable theater in Hillbrow.

The Hillbrow Theatre Project

The Hillbrow Theatre was[6] an extraordinary space that played a vital role in bringing young people from Hillbrow, and many parts of Johannesburg, together. It is a spacious facility in what was once the German consulate and home for elderly German South Africans. Reflecting the difficulty of raising sufficient funds, this Broadway-sized theater is in a state of advanced deterioration. The seats are frayed and some hang at precarious angles. In the vast backstage area, the floorboards creak and threaten to give way.

Though the facility might have been condemned elsewhere as a safety hazard, there is activity everywhere when Nerio visits the first time, in 2016. Children, teenagers, and adult mentors busily go over scripts and rehearse projects. Some of them gather in circular formation to listen to pep talks from their theater coaches. Amid the rough conditions of the building, the deep commitment of the young people is immensely moving. The lobby is decorated with notices for upcoming projects and posters for the plays that have just ended.

Gerard Bester[7] explains that the Hillbrow Theatre Project had become a thriving after-school program. Launched with a R20,000 (US$1,500) grant from the City of Johannesburg, it grew into a R550,000 (US$40,000)-a-year project, with funding from Rand Merchant Bank, Bread for the World, the

Ford Foundation, and the Department of Arts and Culture, and partnered with the Market Theatre Laboratory. Though headquartered in the physical building on Kapteijn Street, the project supported thirty-two facilitators who ran drama programs across the city. Second-year students from the Market Theatre worked with a total of forty schools, twenty-three of which were in the inner city. The others were as far away as Soweto or Vereeniging, a city sixty-four miles south of Hillbrow. Between 2015 and 2020, the Hillbrow Theatre Project also had an after-school and intergenerational project with Tswelopele Frail Care Centre and the Johannesburg Society for the Blind.

"When I was asked to take over the Hillbrow Theatre Project [then called the Culture Project] in 2007," Gerard says, "I was apprehensive and excited. I was very excited to run an arts project and Hillbrow seemed like the most extraordinary opportunity. I had worked in Soweto before coming to Hillbrow, but I've always felt passionately about the inner city. I was born in Hillbrow and returned when studying at the University of the Witwatersrand. I think I was sensitive when I came. I recognized that it was audacious, being a white male, coming into the space and not reflecting the communities living in Hillbrow.

"[The theatre] remains a complex and conflicted space," he continues. "I am careful about what I should impose upon the space, but I believe the work of theatre practice should provoke. When I came, I was asked to pray. I had to declare that I was not religious. But ninety-eight percent of our participants are. They pray before and after each rehearsal.

"Also when I came, I saw a whole lot of young girls crying on the stage [during their performances]," he continues. "And we had only male facilitators. I was wary of the girls being cast as victims. 'Community theatre' is a contentious term. There are so many plays about AIDS and domestic abuse — 'the misery plays,' or the 'woe is Africa' plays. I have tried to change that."

Another dynamic aspect of the theater has been its shifting language policy. The theater tries to represent a mix of languages. Most of the programs are in English, isiZulu, or isiShona, and recently they have added work in isiTsonga. It is vital for young people to engage their home languages as they explore and develop performance text. All the pieces are workshopped in collaboration with facilitators.

"We have a theme each year," he says. "The theme this year [2018] is 'African Futures' and was inspired in part by the success of *Black Panther*, which included ideas about a precolonial Africa and about the future. Last year the theme, chosen by the learners the previous year, was 'What does it mean to be a teenager?'"

Only high school youth are permitted to submit plays to the festival. The theme emerges each year from a survey of attendees, who are asked what they would like to see at the next year's event.

In addition to the festival, the theater is used for many other occasions. After-school programs use it year-round. It is also rented out to church groups on the weekends and to private interests for concerts on some evenings.

In 2013, the Lutheran Church, which still owns the facility, wanted to perform a passion play. Gerard says he was initially hesitant, but ultimately agreed on the condition that Jesus would be played by a Black woman and that there would be no crucifixion scene. Crosses were removed. In place of the death of Jesus, the performers spoke about people who had died during the apartheid struggle. The event had such an impact that the church and the theater worked together to produce several passion plays over the next three years. Some took place on the balcony of the theater and some outside on the plaza.

The relationship between the Lutheran Church and the Hillbrow Theatre is complex. Both facilities, along with three other NGOs — Mould Empower Serve (MES), the Outreach Foundation, and Madulammoho — are all located in what used to be the German consulate and home for the elderly. Though most of the German population has moved away — back to Germany or to other parts of Johannesburg — the church continues to own the theater.

"The Lutheran Church still does a service at the Friedenskirche (discussed in chapter 2) but they no longer have services at a home for German seniors," Gerard says. "But two of the white seniors from the Tswelopele Frail Care Centre in Hillbrow were in a play here last year. For the first time in many years, there was a multiracial cast on stage here."

The Hillbrow Theatre has not been without its share of tragedy. At a Saturday night concert, on August 29, 2017, a man opened fire on the crowd in retaliation for what he thought was the theft of his phone. He killed a twenty-seven-year-old man who was sitting in a chair and injured several others. The news devastated many in the community who had come to see the theater as a safe space, but Gerard was determined to keep the theater going. He succeeded, at least for a few years.

Gerard's personal connection with Hillbrow began in 1987, when he moved into a flat in Joubert Park. The queer scene in Joubert Park and Hillbrow were then in "full flower." He also points out that 1987 was the "the turning point" during which Hillbrow was becoming "truly mixed." The public spaces were integrated, even if the residential spaces remained segregated by race and class on what he calls a "building-by-building basis."

In 1991, to avoid conscription by the apartheid government, Gerard moved to London. By the time he returned, the visible queer scene was "mostly fading" from Hillbrow and the neighborhood was beginning to acquire a reputation for danger. That is when Gerard settled in nearby Yeoville.

"Yeoville kept a gay scene for a while longer than Hillbrow," he says. "But I left Yeoville in 2000. It also just became too violent. Our neighbor was shot and killed, and my partner was stabbed."

Gerard describes his partner's stab wound as "minor" and explains that he fully recovered. But the couple decided that living in Yeoville had become unmanageable. He largely stayed away from Hillbrow and Yeoville until he was asked, in 2007, to begin directing the Hillbrow Theatre Project.

When asked about the climate for queer people in Hillbrow today, Gerard says, "I like to believe that the Hillbrow Theatre contributes to tolerance here." Gender and sexuality have become topics of "consistent engagement." He points to a copy of a recent Hillbrow Theatre Festival poster, depicting three young women who take wisps of their shoulder-length hair and hold them over their mouths as if to form moustaches. He explains that this is an indication of the ways in which gender fluidity is increasingly depicted on stage.

"A young man named Sandile won the best actor award at the theatre for three years in a row by playing a woman on stage," he says. Then he chuckles as he adds that Sandile at first won for "best actress," because no one had told the judges that Sandile was a male.

One of the ways to cultivate community is by inviting speakers to engage with the aspiring performers on queer issues. Nkunzi Nkabinde was a self-identified lesbian and the author of *Black Bull, Ancestors and Me: My Life as a Lesbian Sangoma* (traditional healer). Nkabinde spoke to a large group of participants in the Hillbrow Theatre Project. Nkabinde later transitioned to male, before passing away in 2018.

When Nkabinde spoke at the Hillbrow Theatre, Gerard says, a young man spoke up and said: "This is very difficult for me, but I suppose this [your talk] has made me see you as a human being."

Albert Ibokwe Khoza is a "prominent, out gay man, a sangoma, and a solo artist" who also came to speak at the theater. "Khoza now works with the choreographer Robert Orlin in Europe. He grew up in Soweto but attended St. Enda's Secondary School, which is close to the Hillbrow Theatre, and attended the Hillbrow Theatre Project — a famous alumni!

"His mother sent him there," Gerard says, "because several inner-city schools — like St. Enda's — are considered better than township schools. When he went to school there, he used to wear a uniform which his mother believed would protect him." Khoza's mother worries that, as an adult man, his queer presentation places him in danger when he visits Hillbrow. She urges him to stay away.

The Hillbrow Theatre space is in transition. The Outreach Foundation closed the drama program in 2020 due to a shift in strategic focus.

Lesley, Sibusiso, Nhlahla—Living in and Walking through Hillbrow

Lesley[8] spent several years during his teens with the Hillbrow Theatre. He developed playwriting and directing skills and, in his newest career development, began leading walking tours through Hillbrow in 2019. Lesley works closely with Gerard and with Kathy Munro, an architectural expert and former dean of faculty at the University of the Witwatersrand. Kathy provides him with exacting historical training and tests him regularly on his knowledge. Despite his enthusiasm and dedication, the walks struggle to attract participants. Lesley attributes the suppressed demand in part to an incident that beset another organization, Dlala Nje, which also takes groups of people through Hillbrow. One of their tours was accosted by people who demanded their cellphones, perhaps leading prospective participants to hesitate before taking such tours.

Working with Kathy Munro, Lesley also led a longer tour through several Johannesburg neighborhoods. He admires Kathy's attention to historical detail. "Oh, she is so tough!" Lesley says. "I get nervous when she tests me, because I want to please her. I want to be right!"

Lesley was born in Hillbrow in the year 2000. His mother is a Sotho woman from the Free State and his father is from Zimbabwe. The couple met each other in the Free State and moved to Johannesburg, where they lived in a twenty-three-story building in Berea. When Lesley was three, the couple moved to a nearby building where the family lives now and which Lesley describes as "hijacked."

Lesley takes us into the flat where he lives with his parents. We are joined by his assistant and security guard, Sibusiso. The elevator has not worked in many years, so we climb several flights of concrete stairs. Lesley shows us the one-bedroom apartment, where he sleeps in a bed near the entrance. His parents occupy the living room and the bedroom is rented to up to eight subtenants. Two of the eight actually live on the balcony, next to the bedroom. The balcony has been sealed off from the elements. The others live on beds which have been separated by sheets hanging from the ceiling. Sometimes there are romantic couples and sometimes there is a mother and child. Lesley points out an additional space on the floor which can house yet one more subtenant whenever the family needs additional rent money. When asked what happens when a couple has sex, Lesley shrugs and says that all the subtenants are used to this.

"Whenever you want another tenant," he explains, "you can post downstairs and say that there is a bed free."

Lesley says the subtenants are always strangers when they arrive, but they have been quiet and respectful. The family and the subtenants are friendly with one another and sometimes cook and share meals together.

The apartment is scrubbed clean, but Lesley is unhappy with the overall maintenance in the building. "There is no pest control whatsoever," he says. "And the building is dirty. So we do have rats. They come into your flat. You have to chase them or kill them."

We ascend to the roof, which offers sweeping views of Berea, Hillbrow, Doornfontein, and the CBD, and Lesley offers his take on life in the area. "When we moved here," he says, "it was *the* place to be. The children would write love notes on the walls — like 'Lesley loves so and so.' It was so vibey. But then the children would get whipped for it."

Lesley continues: "The messages on the walls can say a lot. Like one day, recently, someone painted a message to the hijacker. It said they would burn her in her bed if she did not take better care of the building. And she did. She also disappeared for a while. She was scared."

About Hillbrow, he says, "It is very cheap. For R25 (about US$1.80), you can get pap [a cornmeal staple] for four people. It is only R10 (about $.75) for one person. And it is so much pap that you can't finish it! No one goes hungry or thirsty. There is always food. You can get proper fries for R5 (about US$.36), and R20 (about US$1.50) for a large. It is R3 (about US$.25) for bread and fat cakes. And you get together and everyone is talking and laughing. And you can get all kinds of food — Ghanaian, Mozambican, Angolan. I like Nigerian food the best."

From the rooftop, we can see down into Pullinger Kop, a small park once notorious for drug dealing. In more recent years, the city restored the park, installed new playground equipment, and sealed off the perimeter with a wrought iron fence. A security guard permits only children and their families to enter during certain hours, leaving the park empty most of the time. The drug dealers and their customers hang out on the other side of the fence.

Lesley and Sibusiso shake their heads in frustration when they eye a police car idling nearby. "We see them come and sit in their cars and do nothing," Lesley says of the police in general. "Or they just accept bribes. Sometimes I can stare at them, just to say, 'I see you and you are not doing your job!' But they just tell us to go away."

When asked why there seem to be fewer people around Pullinger Kop than there were previously — dozens rather than hundreds — Lesley observes, "This is because many things have been happening by the park." Addressing one of several surges of xenophobic attacks in recent years, Lesley continues, "Late last year [2018] there was a wave of xenophobic attacks, especially against Nigerians. They don't call it 'xenophobia.' Instead, the people called the attacks against Nigerians 'cleaning up Hillbrow.'

"It started with just slogans and chanting," he continues, "but then I saw that they were really beating up Nigerians. They set fire to CJ's Bar [a popular Nigerian tavern] and then they started looting Nigerian shops. After this, a lot of the dealers near Pullinger Kop moved."

Lesley and Sibo share their reflections on who is committing crime in Hillbrow. They emphatically agree that it is not, and never has been, the Malawians. "They are so religious," Sibo says. "They are like Jesus. They never commit crime. They mostly sell fruit and small things. The same with the Ethiopians. And the Nigerians do not commit crime. They do sell drugs — that is their business. They say it is below their dignity to commit crime. But it is South Africans and Zimbabweans — working together — who commit most of the crimes. The Nigerians do pay Zulus to protect them with guns. There are so many guns in Hillbrow. Everyone has a gun! The Congolese commit some crimes, but they are mostly invisible. They keep to themselves. With the Zulus and the Nigerians, at night, they fire five bullets in a row. That is how they say they are leaving for the night. They are making their mark. Zulus are there to protect — but they don't sell."

Lesley says, "The CBD is less safe than Hillbrow. The CBD is deep! Pickpocketers go to the CBD to pickpocket during the day and then they come to Hillbrow to pickpocket at night. But the criminals who commit crime in Hillbrow mostly don't live here. They would be stupid to live here because they will be caught and punished [by the community]. But, of course, some do live here."

Lesley's expression turns grave. "Just before the elections [February 2018]," he recalls, "on the next street over, the ANC closed off the street. They were Zulus in the ANC. And they said they would beat any Nigerian who came onto the street. And they would beat any Coloured person. These are the older ANC guys who tell the youth to do it. They don't pay them [the younger guys] they just give them beer. It was very scary, because it happened just as we were bringing one of our walking groups by that street. I tried to smile and charm the guys and I thought for sure they would make an exception and let us go by. They told us no! And they said that we must go away from there. They were not going to let any of these white people who were with us onto the block — and that if we tried to bring them on, they would beat them. It can get very tense here."

When asked if they ever have a chance to have fun in the neighborhood — and not just worry about crime — both young men light up. "Oh yes!" Sibo says. "We do have fun. We have a journey we have to take. We can have fun here and enjoy ourselves. But we do have to make the neighborhood better."

Asked what would make the neighborhood better, Lesley says: "We need first to clean the streets. It's embarrassing. We think it is corruption that causes the problem — that the city doesn't clean. So we need to clean it up ourselves. The second is that the schools are not good. The government schools are better, but so many people in Hillbrow go to private [profit-making] schools led by Zimbabweans. I went to one of those schools for primary school. They are very poor quality. When I went to High School at Barnato Park, I realized I didn't know anything. They were talking about photosynthesis and I had never heard of it. I had to catch up."

Lesley says, "This is why we started a book club for kids in the neighborhood. The children cannot read. We have to start with very, very simple books, even for older children. But the book club is becoming popular."

As we are leaving the building, Sibo shares his background. He was born in Alexandra township and moved to Hillbrow when he was three days old. His father died a few months after this move. His mother died in 2018, leaving him parentless at the age of nineteen. "I went to a 'fly-by-night,' school called Africombs High School," he says, "and for primary school I went to another fly-by-night school called Success School, which later changed its name to Gauteng College. The teachers were okay, but there was a very low level of education. You realize that you are behind. Some of the teachers were abusive and drunk. You get beaten a lot."

"All the teachers were abusive at those schools," Lesley adds, "But at Barnato Park School [a government-run school], they cannot hit you. At government schools, they can't touch you."

Sibo joined the Hillbrow Theatre Project in 2010, but instead of drama his participation was through music. He learned to play the drums. "Outreach [which operates the Hillbrow Theatre Project] is very important in Hillbrow. They let you become aware of things you would never know about — such as acting, music, and theater."

As we walk away from Lesley's building, we pass several apparently hijacked buildings, or buildings that appear to be in extremely bad shape — with shattered windows and piles of debris surrounding their exteriors. Among them, however, is an anomaly: a pleasant-looking, newly constructed building. Lesley and Sibo click their tongues. "Yes," they say, "it looks nice and it is new.

But only ANC members live there. When they build something like that, the ANC members always get priority. Only they can live in a place like that."

When we meet Lesley again,[9] he is joined by his handsome cousin Nhlahla, who also serves as his security guard. Nhlahla works as a model and helps manage a club. The two men generously offer to take us anywhere in Hillbrow that we would like to go. We walk first by the Eselen Clinic, which they describe as the only clinic in Hillbrow providing sex education, HIV treatment, and neonatal and postnatal care. Nhlahla, a kindly, self-confident, and cheerful young man with a broad smile, says that his ability to offer security comes not from his physical strength but from having met people throughout the neighborhood. He introduces himself wherever he goes and has become a known presence. Indeed, as we walk with him, many people call out to greet him and shake his hand. He feels confident that no one would choose to challenge or hurt him, nor confront anyone with whom he walks.

Like Lesley and Sibusiso, Nhlahla spent many years working with the Hillbrow Theatre Project. Nhlahla continues to teach drama classes.

"Theater is an escape from Hillbrow," he says. "It changes your mind. But there are so many temptations in Hillbrow."

He points to five young men huddled in the corner of a park. "I taught them drama," he says, while shaking his head. "Now they are sitting there, smoking drugs. There is a saying: When you are an orphan, you need to listen to the neighbors."

As we walk, he expresses exasperation with the police. "They are only in Hillbrow to make money," he says. "If you are arrested in Hillbrow, it means you didn't have money for bribes. You can't be arrested if you have money. You just give them R50 and they will go away. I work at a strip club and they come by and get bribes. It's like a drive-through!"

Lesley and Nhlahla point out the *malaishas*, people who carry items back to Zimbabwe, Malawi, and other countries. People all over Hillbrow and Berea bring objects to the malaishas and pay them small amounts to take them to their families. Piles of goods sit neatly stacked on several corners, waiting for the malaishas to gather them.

"People have to desperately work for everything here," Nhlahla observes. "They never stop. They are supporting many people back home. Hillbrow is cheap. It might be cheaper in Soweto, but life is here! With R50 you can eat breakfast, lunch, and dinner—and it will be a lot of food!"

Offering a somewhat different perspective from his cousin about the availability of food, Nhlahla adds, "But it can be hard to get that R50."

Mike — "Seeking greener pastures"

Despite Lesley's previous comments that anyone in Hillbrow can get food, he himself describes periods when, as a child, his family was struggling and he did not have enough food. He would visit Mike's kitchen. Mike,[10] an energetic, stocky man from Nigeria, would give him meals at no cost. When Lesley introduces us to Mike, we find him tending to several bubbling pots of food.

Mike operates a stand in a large, dimly lit hall in the basement of a Hillbrow building. Several vendors cook and serve in the same hall, which has about fifty or sixty large folding tables covered with colorful plastic tablecloths. Except for Mike's own stand, there are no clear demarcations separating one operation from another. People group together, some boiling pots of chicken and others slicing vegetables. Lesley explains that there are groups of Zimbabweans, Cameroonians, Lesothoans, and Nigerians, each preparing a wide variety of dishes for people to eat on folding chairs or to take away. Some of the vendors, whom Lesley believes are Malawians, walk about with trays piled high with oranges and other fruit. The smell of cooking is overpowering, as there is little ventilation in the hall.

Mike, whose stand is near the back of the hall, serves food to a steady stream of customers as he talks. It is cramped and tucked underneath what might be a stairway, but there is enough room for cheerful people to exchange conversation and laughter with Mike and his assistant. Mike says that he is an Igbo who came from Anambra, Nigeria, in 2011, "seeking greener pastures."

But, he says, "a lot has changed. When coming here we find no job opportunities for people without work visas. I came up with the idea of serving Nigerian food, which is delicious and healthy. But it is not easy. I sacrificed for three years, working for another cook, to raise the money. This is my first kitchen. I chose this spot because I knew the landlord and because I knew that the corner [outside] is where a lot of Zimbabweans wait for their taxis home to Zimbabwe. I knew they would need food."

Mike tells us that most of the food available in Hillbrow is highly processed and contains too much sugar, salt, and empty calories. To ensure that his dishes are nourishing and of high quality, he imports all his ingredients directly from Nigeria. His typical dishes include fruits, greens, pastas, rice, and meat. He shows us a large container that combines special Nigerian spices and traditional nutritional supplements that he adds to many dishes.

"It's delicious food!" Lesley exclaims.

Lesley says he has taken three walking tours to the hall to visit Mike and to order food. "At first it was a problem," he says. "The people did not like white people being in the hall and looking at them — and especially taking pictures. It was humiliating. But when they could see that the whites started buying food and fruits and engaging with them it became more accepted. Now, when I come in, people ask me: 'Where are the white people?' They want me to bring them more often."

The eKhaya Neighbourhood Improvement District — "We treat hijackers as neighbors"

A white woman named Josie Adler founded the eKhaya Neighbourhood Improvement District in Hillbrow in 2004. We were not able to interview her, as she was preparing for retirement in Canada by the time we arrived in Johannesburg. But during a brief phone conversation in 2016[11] she told Nerio that she had been inspired by the work of Jane Jacobs, a US urban activist.

Jacobs extolled the virtue of cities that cultivate public spaces where pedestrians interact in a natural "ballet of the streets."[12] With its urban grid, high-density housing, and many small parks and plazas, Adler believes that Hillbrow has the potential to become a safe — or safer — space for pedestrians, whose very presence makes others safer. For this reason, eKhaya pushed to improve the area and to make its sidewalks cleaner and more pleasant.

Bafikile,[13] Josie Adler's successor, has a warm but almost weary smile, as if to convey that her days managing eKhaya are rewarding but challenging. She is from KwaZulu-Natal but began making frequent visits to Johannesburg in 2004 because her husband was living in the city. "You heard stories," she recalls, "You heard you were coming to an area where you can't trust anyone. They can attack you on the streets. But when you get here, it's not as bad as that. I started living full-time in Johannesburg in 2010. I worked on several housing campaigns before I joined eKhaya in 2011."

She explains that eKhaya was founded with help from two property developers, Johannesburg Housing Company (JHC) and Trafalgar. Given the explosion of demand for housing in the inner city, their owners sensed opportunities for profits but believed that improvements to the neighborhood would be necessary before their buildings could run properly. By the mid-1990s, many landlords no longer felt safe going to their buildings to collect rent. Some relied on third parties to collect payments on their behalf, while others abandoned their properties altogether. Bafikile explains that hijackers often filled the void, taking over buildings to extract rents but generally failing to manage them properly or to pay the city for services.

"JHC bought one building on Pietersen Street [in 2002]," Bafikile says. "They bought it from the city. All other buildings on the street had been hijacked. Crime was much higher during those years and no one could go anywhere. They would take everything you had. So one building was not enough. That JHC building and another owned by Trafalgar were the only two buildings in the area occupied legally. Josie Adler came up with the idea of organizing in the neighborhood. JHC and Trafalgar took two years to say yes to her. She had been a lawyer and a community organizer. The first thing she did was to find deeds of search. She worked with the Community Policing Forum. They went door to door, to any and all buildings on the blocks around those buildings, asking who was living there. They would ask who was the owner of the building and most would say they don't know."

When Bafikile joined Josie's team in 2011, together with representatives from the South African Police, she and Josie would visit each building and ask who was in charge. "Usually, there was a caretaker of some kind, whether hired by the landlords or the hijackers," Bafikile explains. "When they were open to conversation, Josie would call meetings and people would come to share their stories. They held the meetings in the alleyways between the buildings, so that they would be public and so that the problems were visible. Most people talked about crime, grime, and service nondelivery. Some people had been living in the buildings for twenty years and didn't know their neighbors."

Echoing Jane Jacobs's sentiments, the eKhaya Neighbourhood Association believed that "breaking anonymity is the first step, because criminals take advantage of anonymity." All neighborhood meetings took place in the alleyways, which were "attractors of crime." As people came to know each other, they began to share stories with one another and to point out dangers.

"We worked to gain the trust of any building caretakers we could find," Bafikile continues. "We did so in part by assuring them that we would never attempt to enter the buildings and would leave all interior operations to the building owners and managers themselves. We wanted only to ensure that the exteriors of the buildings became safe and clean. Anyone should be able to walk along a Hillbrow sidewalk and not feel threatened." Taking an unusual stance, Bafikile explains, "We treat hijackers as neighbors."

Fourteen years after eKhaya's founding, the number of buildings in the association has grown from two to sixty-four. Most of the properties are in the southern part of Hillbrow, although an "eKhaya North" has recently formed. eKhaya works with Bad Boyz Security to patrol outside of members' buildings. Bafikile says that the presence of Bad Boyz has made the entire area much safer for walking.

Despite Bafikile's assurance, we should add that Nerio and his student were robbed by five men just around the corner from Bafikile's eKhaya office at 10:30 one morning. The men claimed they had guns, although they only showed Nerio a knife. The men took Nerio's wallet and cellphone, but mercifully permitted him to keep his notebook. Nerio's student also lost his wallet, but had been smart enough to keep credit cards and cash in his sock. The student's necklace, a gift from his grandmother, had been yanked from his neck a week before by three young men on the sidewalk.

In addition to building cleanliness and order, eKhaya attempts to make the neighborhood more livable by sponsoring social projects. They worked with the Johannesburg Development Agency (JDA) to restore and maintain eKhaya Park.

"Until eKhaya took responsibility for it, it was an open space where people sold clothes, drugs, and anything they could find," Bafikile says. "There were several killings. But it was right in the middle of the eKhaya Improvement District and was therefore a threat to tenants. The property owners were interested in stabilizing the space. They searched to find the owners of the land — it was not a city park yet — and found them overseas. The former owner told us that they had given the land to the city and that the city had simply left it in a state of neglect. However, someone from the city was collecting rent from all of the sellers in the park. A corrupt city official had taken the files and hidden them. Now eKhaya manages the park and it has become the model for a successful park in the inner city. We have twenty-four-hour security, but the park is only open from 6:00 a.m. to 6:00 p.m. It's reserved for positive activities only. We have a Pensioners Day and we have a Kids Day once a year with three hundred kids. We have soccer tournaments, with thirty teams, all in the neighborhood. The tournaments happen four times a year."

The park is indeed green and beautiful, with a stone passageway, attractive spaces to sit, and brightly colored swings and monkey bars. It is also surrounded by a solid, wrought-iron fence that rises well over seven feet. The building owners who contribute to eKhaya derive the benefit of a clean and safe park nearby. Other buildings derive the same benefit but refuse to contribute.

Bafikile compares eKhaya to other neighborhood improvement strategies. The highly successful Maboneng development, in a nearby area that had once been marked by blight and poverty, offers an obvious comparison. Though it has become one of inner-city Johannesburg's top destinations for suburbanites and tourists, it has also been criticized for gentrifying the neighborhood — building and expanding at the expense of the poorest residents who once called the area home.

"Our approach is different," Bafikile insists. "We start at the bottom going up. We are open to all. We say, 'If you forget the people behind you, they will create problems.' We bring everyone along together. We are working now with the High Commissioner of Canada, who has praised us for our inclusiveness and we work with MES. In contrast, other improvement districts say: 'It's just money that works. Chase everyone [else] away. We want this place clean.'"

When asked about the affordability of the buildings that are part of the eKhaya Association, Bafikile responds: "Jozi Housing and Trafalgar are called affordable, but for most renters they're not. It does become a question of who is being served. Most can't afford [to live in] a restored building."

Megan—"The need in the neighborhood far outpaces what we can provide"

Bafikile spends her workweek managing eKhaya and her weekends volunteering for the St. Ann's, a church group, at the Cathedral of Christ the King on the border of Hillbrow and Doornfontein. On Sunday mornings, she volunteers at a soup kitchen that operates on property owned but not run by the church. She introduces us to Megan.

Megan[14] is an energetic white woman of eighty, with a no-nonsense manner and a head of white hair. For two decades, she has been managing the soup kitchen at Christ the King, an imposing edifice with stunning stained-glass windows that serves as the cathedral for the Johannesburg diocese. Her family is of Norwegian and Scottish background, and she was born and grew up in the town of Springs, about thirty-one miles east of Johannesburg. The family moved to Johannesburg in 1962, when Megan's mother became ill and needed better medical treatment than Springs could offer.

From 1962 to 1972, Megan lived with her brother in a Hillbrow flat so that they could be close to their mother. She moved into a rent-controlled building across from Christ the King in 1972, where she continues to live. She recalls with fond amazement that, under rent control, her monthly payments were only R46 (about US$3.35). As noted in chapter 3, rent control ended in the 1980s.

"It was an all-Jewish building then, except for my flat and one other, because it was so close to the Wolmarans Shul [also called the Great Synagogue]," she says. "But all the Jews left long ago. Now I am only one of two white people living in the building."

Megan says she feels safe because people in the neighborhood know her and someone always walks her to and from the church, across the street. She has a friend who will pick her up and drive her in a car when she needs to go somewhere.

On June 3, 2005, an intruder stabbed and killed a male tenant, a friend of hers, from down the hall. Other than that incident, there have been no problems in the building. Megan insists she "quite likes it there" and has no intention of moving. "My friends have suggested that I go to a retirement home, since I am going to be eighty-one, but I am not ready to go." She shrugs: "I know that I will have to go eventually."

When asked about her memories of Hillbrow from her earlier years in the building, she says: "Oh, Hillbrow was wonderful! I used to go to the movies on Kotze Street and walk home at midnight. Hillbrow was *the* place. Life was there!"

It was in the late 1980s that she started to become wary. "There were a lot of angry young men who were starting to move into the area," she explains. "And there was so much political turmoil in the country."

When Megan began attending Christ the King in the 1970s, it had an all-white congregation. She explains that this was due to the geography of apartheid, in which all the neighborhoods around the church were zoned for whites only, and not due to church policy. Now the church has transformed. She estimates that she is one of only about six white members. Most attendees are Nigerians, but there are dedicated masses at certain points during the month for Zimbabweans, Ugandans, Malawians, Congolese, and Sotho speakers. The church holds up to 2,500 people and often reaches capacity during mass.

Megan has managed the soup kitchen as a volunteer since 1998. The kitchen provides basic meals to about one hundred people per day and about two hundred people on a Sunday. Seven to ten people volunteer every night to prepare the food for morning distribution, during which another seven or so volunteers hand out coffee or tea along with soup, pap, peanut butter and/or jelly sandwiches, and, on rare occasions, chicken and rice. On some days, they also hand out necessities such as toothpaste and deodorant and on other days they provide donated items such as shoes and blankets. On many occasions, other groups join in and help Megan and other volunteers.

"The need in the neighborhood far outpaces what we can provide," Megan says. "And most of the people who queue for food here are on a circuit. They start at 8:00 a.m. at the Afrikaans church down the street, but that church does not provide food unless the recipients attend the services, so not everyone likes to go there. Then they come here, to Christ the King. Later, they go to a church in Yeoville that distributes food, and at night they go to a food distribution center at the Oriental Plaza [a shopping mall in nearby Fordsburg]."

The soup kitchen has a strict policy of serving homeless people only. It frustrates Megan that sometimes the "flat ladies" (people who live in nearby apartments) occasionally queue at the church for "free meals." When she sees repeat offenders, she will "chase them away." One of the volunteers overhears her say this and responds that she does not agree with this policy. People in the flats can be hungry, too. Then she quickly adds that she defers to Megan, who has more experience at the soup kitchen.

Supplies are so limited, Megan explains, that it is not possible to feed the housed as well as people who are homeless. Just that morning, they had nearly run out of food and when that happens it can set off a small panic among people who are waiting for their soup or sandwiches.

The church underwent a massive renovation in 2012, after which the soup kitchen moved into a refurbished building opposite the main cathedral. Before the refurbishment, Megan says, the kitchen operated from a "run-down building" on the other side of the complex. The kitchen is now in a spacious area with somewhat more modern equipment. The same building also houses a local branch of the St. Vincent de Paul organization, whose volunteer members visit people in their homes and in hospitals and prisons. The Missionary Sisters of St. Charles Borromeo (commonly called the Sisters of Scalabrini), a South American organization that works with refugees around the world, also maintains a small office in the building. They meet with refugees at Christ the King, but house people elsewhere.

When Nerio meets Megan[15] on another Sunday at the soup kitchen, she is just about to turn eighty-one. She performs a quick, impromptu dance when she announces her age, as if to say that she will never slow down. She gives directions to her volunteers with great confidence and does not hesitate to reprimand people lining up outside the gate for getting too close to the building before the food distribution is about to start. She says that she was able to travel to many parts of the world when she was young but is now interested only in serving as a volunteer manager every day in the kitchen.

Megan has a crew of three teenage girls, perhaps fifteen to seventeen, and a boy of about sixteen, helping her this morning. As we boil three massive pots of water for instant coffee, Megan tells the volunteers that Nerio is there to study and write a book about Hillbrow. One of the girls pours an entire five-pound bag into the pot and the boy shakes his head and says, with a mournful tone, "Hillbrow." There is no peanut butter on this day, so we open giant cans of jam (the term used for jelly in South Africa) and spread their contents onto white bread. As Nerio slathers the gelatinous goo onto the slices, he thinks about the 150 to 200 people outside who will receive meals composed entirely of starch and sugar.

Megan introduces Nerio to Petrus, whom he had met briefly the previous year. At that time, Petrus was the only paid member of the kitchen staff and serves mostly to keep order when needed. People are hungry and, in their eagerness to eat, occasionally try to push others out of their way. Megan tells Nerio, when Petrus is out of earshot, that he came to her when he was twenty-two after suffering a stroke.

"He could barely move his hands," she recalls. "All these years later, he is able to help carry massive pots of boiling coffee from one room to the next. It is very important to Petrus that he feels strong. He likes to do as much heavy lifting as he can."

A few minutes later, Megan admonishes Petrus for telling some of the people near the gate "that the ATM is now open."

He was referring to Megan, who is apparently known to hand out R10 notes (about 70 cents) every so often. It costs about R15 to stay in a shelter, so people are eager to receive those notes whenever possible. But Megan has no cash on this day and does not want the people gathered outside of the gate to become too eager.

Megan explains that the church provides the space for the soup kitchen but absolutely no funding. There is a single donor—a woman who lives in a northern suburb—who gives Megan R14,000 a month (about US$1,000) to run the kitchen. Other small donors give a few hundred rand at a time. Their building has no water, as it is R1 million in arrears, so they bring water in large jugs from elsewhere to use in the coffee and tea and for cleaning up. The church does not permit them to use its faucets. On the first Sunday of every month, a group of Portuguese volunteers comes from another suburb to work in the kitchen. Once every other month a group of Indians comes from Lenasia Township. On such days, the church is able to serve plates of chicken and rice alongside the soup.

Nigel—"Hillbrow is the wound of South Africa and the center of white fears"

When Nigel,[16] a large, curly-haired white man, met Nerio he was wearing a green T-shirt that reads: "Jesus was an African immigrant." Almost two decades after most whites had left Hillbrow, Nigel made the choice to move in the opposite direction. It was a winding path taken with careful deliberation.

Nigel was born in Bulawayo, Zimbabwe (when the country was still called Rhodesia). His parents were of Dutch and French backgrounds and his great-grandfather made his living traveling through Rhodesia by wagon, selling various items. His father grew up in a Zambian orphanage from age eleven, after his mother committed suicide. The boy's father, Nigel's grandfather, died a year later, in a car accident.

"There has been so much brokenness in my family," Nigel says, accounting for why he has committed to finding ways to heal some of the suffering in the world.

Nigel's family moved to South Africa in 1972, when he was just a few years old. Until 2013, he says, he was living a "very comfortable life" in the Midrand, a sprawling network of prosperous suburbs between Johannesburg and Pretoria. He describes the Midrand as a "bubble of naked excess."

"I began questioning my Christianity and wrestling with a view of salvation," he says. "Surely, Christianity is more than life after death. It must have something to say about this arena, about life on earth — economic inequality, injustice, racism."

Nigel and his wife, who is also a Christian, read the National Planning Commission's Report and were dismayed to learn about the extent of inequality in the country. In 1994, South Africa had a Gini coefficient of .55, which went down very slightly to .54 during Nelson Mandela's years in office. The Gini coefficient is a statistical measure of a country's inequality and can range from a low of 0 (which would mean everyone in a country has exactly the same income) to a high of 1 (which would mean one person in a country earns all of the income and the rest of the population earns nothing). Under Mandela's successor, Thabo Mbeki, the Gini shot up to .69 and then to .77. At .77, South Africa became the most unequal society on earth. More than half of all workers were paid less than R3,500 per month (less than US$300), while the two richest South Africans had as much wealth as the bottom 50 percent.

"We read this report ten years ago and realized we are part of the problem," Nigel recalls. "We were living in privilege. We had a six-bedroom home, a swimming pool, a large yard, and two cars. We tried to do our bit, but we didn't really tackle the issue. We kept asking ourselves: 'What world do we want our kids to be part of?'"

The couple began a dialogue with one another. They concluded that four "worldviews" control how the world operates: greed/consumerism; materialism; racism; and patriarchy. Together, these worldviews were driving the country to unsustainable extremes. As a family, they contemplated such questions as: "How would Christ live?" Their conversations also led them to adopt a Marxist analysis. Their central question, Nigel says, was how to create a counternarrative in opposition to the dominant worldviews.

"We thought we were living by the ethic of 'confront greed — live generously,'" he says, "but we realized that is not sufficient. Generosity comes from your excess. Sharing, not generosity, is the proper response."

Nigel was a social worker. He estimates that, as a consultant to the United States Agency for International Development (USAID) in the late 1990s and early 2000s, he was earning ten times the average wage. He and his wife felt this was not a Christian way of life in a society where one-third of the population lacked sufficient money for food.

"So, we began a downwardly mobile path. If you keep climbing, it doesn't work," he told me. "We realized we were living in a bubble of excess, backed up by violence. So we decided to commit class suicide. We pared down, then moved to Hillbrow in solidarity with those who had been given a tough deal in life."

Nigel says that he and his wife simultaneously decided that Hillbrow would be their new home. "That is because Hillbrow is the wound of South Africa," he explains, "and the center of white fears. Of course, we were scared but we had no more rights, we were no more deserving than others."

The couple has six children, and they involved the children in their conversations. Nigel describes them as "very informed," and the children were each invited to weigh in on the decision.

They moved permanently into an apartment building near the Hillbrow Theatre. He acknowledges that "at first, there was a bit of a white savior complex."

But that "complex" evolved. He was held up five times during the family's first year in Hillbrow. These incidents led him to reflect on Matthew 5, which says: "Give to anyone who asks, love your enemies. To the man who asked for my cellphone. I said: 'Here you go, my brother.'"

He says he was not frightened during the moment of the first holdup, but afterward felt deeply shaken. "I experienced a bit of a breakdown and I wept. I asked myself: 'What have I exposed my family to?'"

As part of his path toward healing, Nigel began by speaking to the street vendors. When he told them what had happened, the vendors walked with him to the place where the mugging had happened. They gathered and prayed as a group and asked for God's forgiveness and to help Nigel keep a soft heart. A few days later, Nigel brought twenty friends from the Midrand to Hillbrow. They walked together to the fish and chip shop and ordered everything on the menu and handed out food.

"We tried to sow love."

After the incident, Nigel attended a trauma debriefing and decided to buy apples from the street vendors. He gave out apples and talked to people as he did so.

"I decided not to talk to community leaders," he insists. "Rather, I wanted to talk only to the poorest of the poor. The mission was to become a good neighbor—not a leader, not a consultant, not an authority."

He re-registered as a social worker and thought his prior occupation would prove useful in the neighborhood, but he decided that was too professional—and too distant. He has come to object to a field that uses the term "client." Instead, he uses "friend." When he speaks to "friends," he uses language such as "we are going to fight this world together."

Both he and his wife provide therapy, guidance, and job training. They receive donations from Christian churches. His business card lists only "neighbor" as his occupation.

"We are calling out from Hillbrow to the northern suburbs, those exploitative places of whiteness and capitalism," he says.

"What is the message for white South Africans?" he asks. "It must be class suicide. We must give up our prosperity and our belongings until we have broken poverty. There is enough for everyone. The real corruption is white South Africans. You can say it is [former President Jacob] Zuma, but it is whites who don't share."

Providing Support for Targets and Victims of Xenophobia

Liebe[17] is a social work supervisor at Sophiatown Community Psychological Services in Bertrams, a neighborhood just east of Hillbrow and Berea. She explains that the organization's founder established the center following the xenophobic attacks of 2008.

"Fire destroyed many, many homes in Bertrams and Jeppestown [during those attacks]," Liebe explains. "Before the fires, the counselors used to meet clients in the park in Bertrams. For a while the Jeppestown Police Station became a refuge."

Liebe stresses that xenophobia takes many forms and has multiple impacts.

"There is also a psychological state of xenophobia," she explains. She elaborates that a story was widely circulated among migrants as the 2010 World Cup approached that, as soon as the cup was over, migrants would be chased and killed. There was another wave of both psychological and physical xenophobia in 2015, followed by the attacks in 2019.

"Economic need is at the roots," Liebe says. "The neediest South Africans are pitted against the people coming in. It is two vulnerable groups [low income or unemployed South Africans and migrants] and it suits those in power to have two vulnerable groups fighting each other. The New Refugees Act is horrendous.[18] No one may campaign or lobby against their own country without the permission of the South African government. This is despite the fact that those countries welcomed the South African freedom fighters in exile. When questioned, the government says: 'But we were not refugees, we were freedom fighters.'"

Liebe's mention of freedom fighters in exile refers to a period from 1960, when the ANC was banned in South Africa, to 1990, when the ban was lifted. After the ban, most of the ANC's leadership, and many of its rank-and-file members, went into exile in places such as Tanzania, Zambia, Botswana, the

UK, and, following their independence, Angola, Mozambique, and Zimbabwe. From roughly 1963, when most of the leadership remaining in South Africa was arrested, to the Soweto Uprising of 1976, so many ANC members were living in exile that the organization almost went "extinct" within South Africa.[19] Because so many other countries provided shelter for ANC exiles, many voices — such as Liebe's — now criticize the ANC government's harsh stance toward immigrants.

Most clients and visitors to the Sophiatown center's Bertrams location are from the DRC, because Bertrams has a large Congolese population. But there are also clients from Zimbabwe, Mozambique, and Angola. The center has three full-time counselors and two-part time counselors. The full-timers provide counseling to clients at all age levels (children, teenagers, and adults) while the part-timers work only with children.

The center itself is located behind a brightly painted security fence, but on the other side of the fence are four cheerfully painted small buildings that house offices, playrooms, and counseling facilities. The center provides walk-in services for visitors with urgent issues. Walk-ins and others who make appointments can be screened for their needs. Clients who commit to counseling are eligible for longer-term services.

But Liebe stresses that 80 percent of undocumented children in the country were born in South Africa and moved from rural areas. If their parents or grandparents were never able to obtain their own documents, their children are unable to obtain them for themselves. New, stringent rules require birth and, where applicable, death certificates of parents, and many people have no idea where they would get such records. This leaves such children in precarious situations. They are South African citizens but are treated as if they are stateless.

Another phenomenon which Liebe discusses is that of child-headed households. In some cases, up to eight children live in such households, which can be found both in townships and in cities. Children of sixteen or seventeen years old are looking after their siblings. They, too, are usually unable to obtain documents and therefore are unable to access state services.

In 2012, Liebe points out, the government did away with the Crown Mines Home Affairs Office, which had enabled asylum seekers to visit the Home Affairs Office in Johannesburg. Now they must travel to Pretoria (as mentioned in the previous chapter). This is part of a general tightening up of provisions for asylum seekers.

The counseling center operates largely with funding from Germany and Canada. In addition to one-on-one counseling, the center offers a women's group "which is a space to share traumas and the challenges of everyday life" with one another. There is a "suitcase group" for children whose parents recently came to the country. Liebe notes that children often pick up on the stresses of their parents. When they are very young, they may know little more than the name of the country they have come from without remembering the details of how they arrived in South Africa. A teens' group prepares teenagers for assimilating and fitting in.

The Saturday Study Buddies group is for high school students, and often the tutors at this group are students at local universities who were once children in the counseling center. The Tuesday night "Loving Learning" group is for young children. The Community Project in the Park enables counselors to meet with children in fun, outdoor spaces where children can play while also discussing emotional and other challenges.

Debbie has been a volunteer counselor at Sophiatown Community Psychological Services Centre "on and off" for several years. She describes herself as a "remedial therapist," with duties that include "assessing children for literacy and numeracy, but mostly just creating a space for children to breathe and play and be children."

Debbie was born into an Afrikaner family that, she says, "anglicized early and wanted nothing to do with Afrikaner culture." They lived in Rivonia, a northern suburb that was still fairly rural at the time. In 1984, when she was eighteen, Debbie moved to Yeoville, where she could live with her boyfriend and study at the University of the Witwatersrand. "Yeoville," she says, "was so cosmopolitan, and liberated, and also Jewish. It was like a village within a city. It was safe, quaint, and exciting — a fantastic place to live in your early twenties. There was a lot of activism, but it was still white. It was all white people who were trying to prove they were groovy and not racist — like, 'look how clever we are.' But as soon as 1994 hit, the whites were gone. For all their activism, they left. Some even left the country. Almost everyone I went to high school with has left the country."

But Debbie bought a flat in Yeoville one week before the 1994 elections and has remained there to the present day. "I was so excited," she recalls, "but everyone else [in her circle of white friends] was horrified. They said: 'You can't be serious!' Whites had stockpiled food and candles — but I only wanted to live in Yeoville, nowhere else. I had always worked in Black education. I was an English as a second language (ESL) teacher and became the vice principal of an all-girls school for a while. I started teaching at Joburg Girls School [in Berea] for one year — after it integrated."

At the age of twenty-four, Debbie became the deputy principal of a small private school in Yeoville whose proprietor had absconded with all the school's money. She and another woman took over the school and managed to salvage it (it is still running today). The school had several girls from Mozambique, who were funded by the Catholic Church. Many had experienced trauma during the civil war and some of them had been raped. Debbie began to teach them speech therapy and became so interested in that job that she decided it would become her primary occupation.

"I believe that the most qualified should be with the most needy," she says. "The migrants' stories here are about incredible strength. It is very, very humbling."

Most of the young people she has met at the center are from the DRC, although some are from Mozambique and Angola. She worries that many children are unable to go to school.

"We have a centralized school placement system," she explains, "which is hell. You need internet access and many families don't have it. Children go on waitlists if they cannot get placed. There are no truant officers and the population comes and goes so quickly that there is no way to trace which children are or are not in school. Education is compulsory to grade nine, but it is not free. Parents have to pay according to their income quintile — with the lowest quintile paying R250 to R350 (about US$18 to US$25) a month, which can be a fortune."

7

Hillbrow's Credoscapes—Spaces of Hope and Connection

Tanja Winkler documents that 70 percent of Hillbrow's residents are affiliated with religious organizations, which she calls "credoscapes"—or "spaces of hope." The number and type of faith affiliations, she writes, has "increased phenomenally" since the mid-1990s, to include roughly seventy-five kinds of religious practices and groups. Some involve *sangomas* (traditional healers) and *inyangas* (traditional healers who specialize in herbalism) and about 15 percent combine traditional healing with Christian practices. These syncretic groups are often informal, in the sense that they rent spaces or meet in their leaders' apartments or in parks. Others have longer and more established histories, such as the numerous African independent churches, Zionist churches, or Apostolic churches, but lack the financial resources to own their own houses of worship. The Hillbrow Recreation Centre rents to at least ten such organizations, and the Jewish community leases the Great Synagogue to an African independent church. Pentecostal churches, which typically own their own facilities, have also grown rapidly and claim about 45 percent of Hillbrow's residents as members. Only 10 percent of the people who live in Hillbrow attend "mainline" Protestant churches, such as the Anglican (Episcopalian), Lutheran, Methodist, or Presbyterian denominations, or Catholic and Greek Orthodox churches.[1]

The churches in this last category—mainline, Catholic, and Orthodox—generally have access to the largest national and international networks and are therefore able to sponsor numerous local development programs. The formal organizations often provide the kinds of programs that "have been abandoned by the state," such as food pantries, shelters for people who are homeless, and legal and financial help for newcomers. Some provide daycare centers, tutoring for children in schools, HIV/AIDS hospices, and programs that attempt to mitigate xenophobia.[2]

Most of the religious organizations in Hillbrow operate in isolation and some, such as the rapidly growing Pentecostal movement, proffer exclusionary identities. Nonetheless, they create space where values, beliefs, and a sense of belonging are shared. "Credoscapes," Winkler writes, "are creating nodes of hope, order and stability amid perceived chaos and decay."[3]

Alex Wafer, who has also examined religion in Hillbrow, writes that in a city often unwelcoming or hostile to immigrants, a spiritual life may provide a sense of belonging and protection. He spent time observing a Bible study group that doubles as a soup kitchen at a church on Honey Street. Attendees number between ten and thirty people on any given day, "their thin bodies wrapped in layers of dirty, ill-fitting clothes." The small crowd is as diverse as Hillbrow, with people from Ghana, the DRC, Rwanda, and Zimbabwe, as well as a couple of white men who are homeless. Some surreptitiously sniff glue as they wait for the church gates to open. The pastor is a Zimbabwean man who easily shifts between English and isiZulu. Conversations start with Bible passages, Wafer observes, but usually "digress into discussions about the difficulty of life on the streets, about temptation and human weakness, about sharing hardships as a group."[4]

We cannot hope to capture the full range of "credoscapes" in Hillbrow, but we explore a small sampling of them in this chapter.

Berea Christian Tabernacle—"Eventually you have to pack your bags and leave"

Bongani[5] is a tall, trim man in his late twenties with a large network of friends across Hillbrow and Berea. Although he has now converted to Islam, he grew up as a member of the Berea Christian Tabernacle. He credits the tabernacle for the success he has enjoyed in his life. During his early teens, he was briefly a member of a gang and occasionally participated in acts of theft. He describes his stepfather as a vengeful man whose violent outbursts made his home life feel menacing. But his mother insisted that he attend the church with her and his two sisters and join the tabernacle's youth group. "It played a big role," he recalls. "It kept me from the streets. I was always engaged, with lots to do. I don't want to think about what might have happened to me without it." Bongani has become a personal trainer and part owner of a small record company.

Bongani introduces us to Niri,[6] whom he calls "Sister Niri." A charismatic Indian woman with flowing, dark curls, Niri serves as the church's executive secretary. She grew up in the Indian township of Tongat, close to Durban, and moved to Pretoria to attend university. She arrived in Johannesburg in 1990 and began working for the church. The tabernacle, she explains, is part of the Apostolic Faith Mission (AFM), the largest Pentecostal denomination in South Africa. The AFM started early in the twentieth century as an inter-racial church but split into a "white" branch and a "Black" branch during apartheid — when it was impossible for people of different racial classifications to attend the same church together.

The Berea church had been an all-white congregation until Niri began her job there. The first minister Niri worked for, Pastor Willett, had earlier begun the process of integration as part of what became a national process of rejoining Black and white churches within the AFM. Pastor Willett met some resistance but was also praised for his efforts at the Berea Tabernacle.

Unfortunately, one night in the mid-1990s he was awakened by a noise in his apartment on the second floor of the church. An intruder pointed a gun at him and took his watch and wallet. Niri explains that the terrified pastor immediately fled. He left the congregation and moved to Port Elizabeth.

The church now has a mostly pan-African congregation.[7] There are mul-tiple services on Sundays in English and several African languages, each of which is attended by about 200 to 250 people. Niri estimates that about 50 to 60 percent of the congregants are Zimbabweans, as the AFM is very popular in Zimbabwe. The remainder are from the DRC, Tanzania, Malawi, Nigeria, and South Africa in roughly that order. The membership is always revolving, as many of the congregants do not stay in the inner city for long.

Pastors no longer live in the church, but the congregation owns a six-story building next door where some of its members and staff live. Niri resides in the building with her twenty-eight-year-old son. She feels safe in the building, which has a security gate and neighbors who look out for each other. "We have only ever had one incident," she recalls. "That was the day that [Robert] Mugabe was removed [as president of Zimbabwe, on November 19, 2017]. Masses of Zimbabweans came out to celebrate! At night, some men broke into the back of the building and stole our clothes off the line. But that was a special occasion."

Niri says, "I came to Johannesburg because I like the independent living of the city — and the diversity." In terms of security, Niri claims that "Durban is just as unsafe [as Johannesburg]. Indian women cannot walk around without people trying to steal their chains." But she feels that Berea, and especially Hillbrow, are becoming more difficult places to live. "The biggest problem is overcrowding," she explains. "It is getting tighter [here] all the time. It is so, so dense. You can barely move on Pretoria Street. And Hillbrow is rotting. It is getting worse. My son and I ask each other all the time, 'Why is Hillbrow like that and why is Berea so clean?' It must be deliberate. There are plenty of cops, but the cops are benefiting from drugs and crime. They do make arrests, but then they let people go. The cops are connected to the [drug] trade."

The city has been making upgrades to Berea, she notes, but she believes those upgrades are counterproductive. "They have widened the pavements, for instance," she says. "That is good for a first-world city, but bad for this area. Wide sidewalks invite street hawkers. The park across the street has been upgraded by City Parks and is now a 'first-class, five-star park.' But it is very dangerous. The city used to close the park at night but now they don't, so criminals stay in the park all night. Young men — fifteen-year-olds — are hanging around in the park, robbing passersby. This is new since September, when crime has spiked.

"The pastor and I called the chief of Visible Policing,"[8] she continues. "He came and sat right here. We talked. He said, 'We will be happy to engage here.' But then nothing happened. Crime is getting much worse. We ask for more public housing, but nothing helps. We are getting mugged left, right, and center in broad daylight. My son was held up in his car at gunpoint a couple of days ago. I was chased by a gang of kids who wanted my watch. I screamed at them: 'Don't you dare! I don't have anything that is yours!'"

Children, Niri believes, are still safe to play in the park. Thieves generally will not bother young children unless they are carrying cellphones.

Niri explains that the church used to be more active in the community but has had to cut back because of the crime. They have cancelled their Sunday evening services and stopped their door-to-door and sidewalk-level evangelizing. "It was part of our service to do evangelizing," she says. "But we don't do it anymore. It's not safe . . . One of our members was stabbed for her cellphone and left in a pool of blood — but she survived. A father and son were assassinated a few days ago by Ponte . . . Eventually, you have to pack your bags and leave. The people are unemployed and idle. Until they get jobs, this will happen." Making a statement that aligns with more conservative South Africans, she adds, "We need to control the borders. We need investment. We need entrepreneurship."

Then she shrugs and says: "My son went to Kenya and Malawi earlier this year. He told me that I should feel lucky. Johannesburg at least has water and electricity. It is not reliable in Kenya and Malawi. Sometimes there's no water at all."

Pastor Thomas

Pastor Thomas[9] grew up and lived his first three decades in Lubumbashi, the second-largest city in the DRC. He left permanently in 2000, two years into the Second Congo War, which ultimately killed over five million and left millions more displaced. "I went to Johannesburg," he says. "I took a massive drive in the back of a truck, through Zambia and Zimbabwe, until I was dropped off in Hillbrow. I was in search of greener pastures."

Energetic and self-assured, Pastor Thomas recalls his first impressions. "I was in shock," he says while shaking his head. "South Africa looked nothing like what I expected. Hillbrow was terrifying and crime was massive! Much worse than it is now. I was afraid to go anywhere, and I had to rent a flat with seventeen other people."

The other people in the flat — all men — were also from the Congo and he came to feel safe in their company. He quickly found work in a store and then as a security guard. One day, he met the woman who would become his wife when they were both waiting in line at a gas station. She had a similar religious devotion, in the apostolic tradition, and she helped him establish and grow a church. He moved out of Hillbrow and they built their congregation in the prosperous northern suburb of Rivonia. A glossy photo of the couple, not unlike those found in evangelical megachurches in the US, hangs on the wall.

But Pastor Thomas returns each first Saturday of the month to a small, concrete park near the base of the Ponte City tower to pass out food and offer fellowship. One Saturday, Nerio joined Pastor Thomas and a dozen or so members of his congregation, who spent the previous day cooking pap (cornmeal), stews, vegetable curries, and bread. The group pours sodas and dishes out heaping plates to roughly one hundred people. Many of the needy they feed sleep on soot-stained mattresses or piles of blankets under the highway overpass near the tower, while others live in nearby apartment buildings. They are mostly in their late teens and twenties, although some are in their thirties and forties. A few appear stunned as they shuffle over to Pastor Thomas's group, while others seem healthier or more robust.

As the people line up, some have their heads down. While Nerio hands out the sodas, they point listlessly toward the sugary drinks, perhaps ashamed to accept charity. Others in line seem more energized and request orange, or grape, or another flavor with a half smile and a thank-you. Most in line are remarkably gentle although a few are more assertive, grabbing the cup and insisting that its contents be topped off.

Pastor Thomas has an easy way with the people in line, addressing many of them by name and offering gentle or sometimes playful words of encouragement. He huddles with groups of two or three for short prayers. He pulls one young man aside and gently chastises him. Pastor Thomas explains later that he had been working with this young man for some time to help him stop using drugs and find work. He is disappointed to see the glassy look in the young man's eyes. The young man smiles sheepishly at the interrogation. It is clear to everyone listening that the pastor's words, though stern, are infused with love.

"They sometimes say to me, 'We cannot survive without these drugs,'" he explains, with considerable sympathy but not without exasperation. "Sometimes they show me the drugs in their hands. They tell me the police sell them drugs. I encourage them to go to drug treatment programs. We try to help them find jobs. But they backslide. We just keep working with them."

We note that "backsliding" is a term whose effect may be to blame the victim. It is not clear how young people who live under a highway overpass might find work in a city with a staggering unemployment rate. While dedicated and well intended, the congregation seems to view those in line through a conservative lens. A girl of about ten, who is ladling soup, tells Nerio that she believes some of the people are "not poor" because she has seen them with cellphones. She seems to think that people who are not completely destitute should not line up for food. One of the adult women begins speaking of prayer and admonishing the people near her to remember that everything comes from God. "Jobs don't come from people," she says. "They come from God. Therefore, you must reflect on your lives and pray."

After two hours, and when half of the food is distributed, Pastor Thomas and his companions pile into their cars and head to Yeoville. We spend two more hours there, handing out food near the Piccadilly Centre, a large open-air market where dozens of people can be found sleeping along the sides of the building. Here, the people who queue for food skew older than those in the first location—they are in their thirties and forties—and seem more desperate. There are fewer joyful interactions between Pastor Thomas and the people here than there were by Ponte. People quietly and urgently take their cups and their plates and shuffle away. Some of the passersby commend Pastor Thomas and the church members for their kindness.

"Once every other month," Pastor Thomas says, "we hold a braai [a barbecue] at this location. It allows us more time to interact with the folks here. People loosen up. They are more reachable."

Pieter—"Work, give, become involved, assist"

Pieter[10] spends every day in Hillbrow. Though retired, he seems to have boundless energy which he pours into volunteering at one of MES's three emergency shelters. He also runs one of the organization's two soup kitchens. Our conversation takes place at one of the kitchens.

Pieter is a tall, slender white man who grew up, he says, accepting apartheid as a given. He was born in the Free State, which he describes as an "ultra-Afrikaner area" and his family attended the Dutch Reformed Church (NGK) every Sunday. During his adolescence he became interested in theology, but by the time he completed his divinity degree he had become "turned off" by the politics and culture of the NGK. Though a licensed minister, he never had a congregation.

"Our family did not discuss apartheid," he says. "We thought it was okay. Even in theology school, we never talked about it. I studied in Bloemfontein and Stellenbosch — two Afrikaner strongholds — and no one mentioned apartheid. The church was very strict. Everyone had to conform — in dress, in thought, in manner. But I came to feel I did not belong."

He finished his degree in the mid-1980s, but instead of religious work he pursued audiovisual work in the film industry. "I wanted something totally secular," he says. "I did that for a year, but I could not fully run away from the NGK spiritually. Someone told me about MES in Hillbrow, which had started in 1987 as a Dutch Reform organization. But that [religious focus] had started to change by 1990. I came to Hillbrow in 1990. I looked around and I thought: 'Hillbrow is freedom.' It was perfect for me. I became exposed. It was a change of mind that took place over years."

MES's Johannesburg branch office is managed by Pastor Nicodemus Setshedi, an NGK minister who grew up in Soweto. "Nicodemus and I have talked about this," Pieter says, his voice softening at the gravity of his words. "While he was in Soweto throwing stones [in political protests], I was living a comfortable and oblivious life. He had terrible things happen to him. He had horrible experiences. I just didn't know what was going on."

Pieter says it is difficult to know how many homeless people live in Hillbrow. Various attempts to count the number of people living on the streets have arrived at numbers between two thousand and five thousand, but because people move around so much it is impossible to be certain.

He and other volunteers regularly drive or walk around the neighborhood. "If they are not in the shelter," he says, "they are on the streets. We go out and speak to them. We tell them about the shelter and about the kitchen. We provide them with pamphlets. I do not ask where they are from or what brought them, but they sometimes tell me. They have very, very sad stories. And the only difference between me and them is birth. It's only birth. Why should I have all these advantages that they did not have? When I can at least feed them, I feel a little better."

He pauses and says, firmly, "This is all caused by apartheid. We [Afrikaners] must do something. I am not saying we have to go around saying, 'sorry, sorry, sorry.' But we must live it out: work, give, become involved, assist. Offer compassion and community. They [people who are homeless] need to experience that."

Pieter volunteers at the eKhaya Shelter (not related to the eKhaya Neighbourhood Improvement District), which has 120 beds. People usually make their way to the shelter by first visiting the assessment center, which determines degree of need. The fee for a night in the shelter is R15 (about US$1), but the assessment center can provide free vouchers to the very neediest. One of the two soup kitchens opens at 10:00 a.m. to serve breakfast and the other — directly across the street — opens at noon. A meal at either kitchen costs R5 (about thirty US cents), but people are not turned away if they are unable to afford this sum.

Pieter estimates that 30 percent to 40 percent of the 120 people in the eKhaya Home, the shelter he helps manage, are non–South Africans. Reflecting on their paths to Johannesburg, he says: "They said to themselves, 'Here I will meet my dreams. This is Madiba's country.' Then they arrive and they are stuck. Many don't want to stay here, but they have no way to go home — or they just cannot go home. We work with them to give them a better life, but sometimes selling one's body is just easier and faster. HIV/AIDS is affecting more and more people. As many as 45 percent of the people in Hillbrow are infected and it is escalating.[11] Treatment is readily available. The drugs [to treat HIV/AIDS] are available to [everyone]. One of the reasons we supply food is that it is essential to eat while taking the drugs.

"When people become very sick," he continues, "health workers will pick them up and take them to a hospital for treatment. But then they release them back onto the streets. There is no other option. Sometimes they come back to the shelter — but they won't talk about it. AIDS is still highly stigmatized. The very ill go off to a couple of spaces in Hillbrow [to die]. Even there, there is some community."

Temple Israel and *Tikkun Olam*

Temple Israel is the "mother synagogue" of Progressive (Reform) Judaism in South Africa and the only shul operating in Hillbrow. It is a beautiful, if weathered, art deco building with a large assembly hall, a smaller room for weekend services, and a school building where seders and holiday celebrations are still held. Built in 1936, it once held seats for over five hundred people and regularly reached capacity. By the late 1990s, its regular attendance had dropped to fifteen or so, a number that rises to between sixty and eighty on major holidays. It has not been able to afford a full-time rabbi since 1994, so it relies on lay readers for services.

The congregation is a remarkable mix of older whites who live in the area or have historic ties to the temple, and Black people from Nigeria, Congo, and South Africa. In recent years, its spiritual leaders have included Lael Bethlehem, a lesbian who is an expert in urban development, and David Bilchitz, a gay legal scholar. Bill Hoffman, a white man who turned ninety years old in 2019, has led Friday night services since the late 1990s. Previously the choir mistress, Ruth is a white woman possibly in her late eighties. She used to drive herself to the temple until she experienced a serious car accident. But she remained determined to keep attending Temple Israel, so a relative has insisted on driving her to Hillbrow since then.

Marion,[12] whose parents were married in the synagogue in 1942, recalls crowds so large that congregants had to park blocks away and walk to Friday evening and Saturday morning Shabbat services. "But by the late 1980s," she says, "it wasn't fun to go there [Hillbrow] anymore on Friday nights. People would accost you, wanting money. One time another car forced my car onto the pavement [sidewalk]. It became a real challenge as the neighborhood became dangerous and dirty."

Those challenges have not stopped Marion from attending every Saturday. Serving on the board since 1994, she works tirelessly to prepare the synagogue's hall for holidays such as Rosh Hashanah, Passover, and Tu BiShvat. Nerio has attended several such events and has been deeply impressed by Marion's attention to every decorative detail, such as making certain that everyone receives a small gift during Purim. The meals, prepared by a kosher caterer at cost, bring together old and young, Black and white, and create a genuine sense of community. Nerio had the privilege of attending a Passover seder in 2018. The banquet room was simply but beautifully decorated and every table was filled, with a crowd of about fifty altogether. Black and white people sat together at each table and there were several Black and white children present. Everyone seemed delighted to be enjoying the company of their neighbors.

Marion explains that, even as the neighborhood acquired a reputation for danger, the temple continued to draw substantial crowds into the early 1990s. "Rabbi Steinfeld (now in the UK) was there then," she says, "and he was absolutely dynamic. His services were well attended. But Hillbrow had lost most of its Jewish population by then. Eventually, he wanted to sell and merge with Beit Emanuel [a synagogue in nearby Parktown]."

That is when Reeva Forman, now the temple's committee chair, became involved. Reeva was once one of South Africa's top models, a "businesswoman of the year" (in 1983), and is now proprietor of Reeva Beauty and Health. She could not bear to see the "mother synagogue" of Progressive Judaism close. She put together a committee to raise funds, preserve the temple, and conduct outreach. In 2014, she and her committee succeeded in having Temple Israel declared a Heritage Site. In 2016, with the launch of the Temple Israel Heritage Centre, they installed a visual history of the temple, and of Reform

Judaism in South Africa, in the lobby, and they invite community members and organizations to visit. The little income Temple Israel receives comes from renting part of the hall to a neighborhood prekindergarten program.

"We are committed to the Jewish mission of *tikkun olam* [to repair the world]," Reeva says.[13] "Many people are scared of coming to Hillbrow and Temple Israel. They won't come. But then we manage to do something that raises interest. Last year, we had a Refugee Seder for Pesach. We also had a gala evening for the Progressive Movement. Chief Justice Mogoeng Mogoeng was the speaker and he came to speak about the future of South Africa. Two hundred fifty people came!

"At the Freedom Seder for Refugees, about forty refugees came," Reeva continues. "We partnered with the Outreach Foundation and David Benjamin came from Israel. Another wave of xenophobic attacks had happened in Hillbrow in April of this year [2015]. It was huge. People were afraid to leave their flats. We could not have the service at night because people were scared, so we had it during the daytime. Marion set up the hall beautifully. People came and shared their thoughts on what it is like to be a migrant in Johannesburg. Then we took ten Hillbrow homeless people to Kensington to have them talk to homeless migrants. With the Outreach Foundation, we undertook blanket distribution. Every university in the world and all the professors are discussing the migrant crisis, but nothing [concrete] is happening! What we must change is attitudes. This was a step in that direction."

"You must understand that social justice is in the very bricks of Temple Israel," Reeva[14] says on another occasion. "It was a temple built on activism. This peculiar thread of social justice began in 1936, when the shul opened — even before it opened. Rabbi Weiler came here from what was then Palestine and was immediately concerned about the plight of Black South Africans. He sent the women from Temple Israel to build a school in Alexandra Township. He was in opposition to Bantu Education. When the government was tearing down Black education, Temple Israel was committed to raising it up. The dream is to fulfill the prophetic mission in the new era. Bricks have a DNA, an energy that has carried over into the present. We must maintain a Jewish presence in Hillbrow. Hillbrow is the real South Africa. It is a more exciting neighborhood than any other because it is filled with the kinds of people who represent the New South Africa. It is where immigrants have always been absorbed."

Regular attendees include Melvin,[15] a stocky white man who has lived in Hillbrow for forty-five years. He says that 95 percent of the tenants who live in his apartment building are migrants, mostly from Zimbabwe. He says he feels safe in Hillbrow and has only experienced one mugging during all of those forty-five years. Jennifer,[16] a white woman somewhere in her fifties, has lived in Hillbrow most of her life and walks to the temple alone on Friday nights and Saturday mornings. After a Saturday morning service, Jennifer takes Nerio on a walk through Hillbrow toward her apartment building near Constitution Hill. "Nothing has ever happened to me in all of the years I have lived here," she says. She makes a sweeping gesture with her hands, motioning to the traffic and the crowds on Claim Street. "Does any of this scare you? It is absolutely fine!"

Patricia is a middle-aged white woman who moved from Britain to South Africa in 1973, when, she says, "Hillbrow was a paradise." She now finds herself lonely and isolated, living in a Hillbrow apartment building occupied by migrants who come and go, rarely staying long in the building. She is not Jewish but says she regularly attends Temple Israel "because I need to come here — there is food and it lifts my spirits."[17] Mark is a young Black man from Soweto who studied music at the University of Cape Town and now runs his own music production company that hosts inner-city concerts. Several years ago, he was walking by Temple Israel and heard the music of the choir. He walked in, felt himself welcomed, and decided to undergo conversion classes. He almost never misses a Shabbat service on Saturday.[18]

Michael is a fifty-six-year-old Black, Jewish man from Nigeria who moved to South Africa in 1997. "I came right to Hillbrow," he says, "and life was tough! There was shooting and killing, all the time. When I came here, I heard it was a beautiful area. I was not expecting crime. Temple Israel helped me survive. They provided some financial help and then they hired me as a security guard."[19]

Samuel, who identifies as an Igbo, is another Black Jewish man from Nigeria. He attends every Saturday service with his five-year-old daughter, who has memorized many parts of the Shabbat service in Hebrew. She has a beautiful voice that sometimes outshines that of the cantor.

Arnold[20] is a Black paramedic who rides with a crew in an ambulance through Hillbrow five nights a week. A dedicated member of the community, Arnold goes directly from his Friday night shift to attend services at 10:00 a.m. on Saturday mornings. Solo[21] is a Black Nigerian Jewish man who met his wife, Regina, in Hillbrow. Together, they have been attending Temple Israel since 2013. They took eighteen months of conversion courses together at the synagogue. "In 2018, my conversion was complete," Solo says. "It was the happiest day of life."

Jacob,[22] who serves on the Temple's executive committee, has been a member of the congregation since 1983. But when he experienced a major life change a decade ago, he began attending more regularly. "They have been there for me," he says. "The rabbi was really there for me. It is the only shul I have ever really known. Our Shabbat attendance is down to about twenty. The only hope we really have [of maintaining a congregation] is Black people from Congo and Nigeria. Now, there are five them."

Jacob notes that the congregation's resources have diminished. The structure is very large and over eighty years old, but there are almost no funds to pay for critical maintenance. "The building is absolutely crumbling—truly crumbling," Jacob says. "We have a beautiful library upstairs but there are leaks. The books are getting damaged."

Rabbi Sa'ar Shaked,[23] of Beit Emanuel, a progressive shul in nearby Parktown, reflects on the role of Hillbrow in Johannesburg's Jewish history. "Hillbrow is the point of origin and the final frontier for Jews in Joburg," he says. "If Temple Israel were to close it would be the loss of a Jewish presence in an authentic African space. That would be a tremendous loss. Johannesburg is like New York and Hillbrow is like Ellis Island. People from all over—Somalia, Sudan, Malawi. So being in Hillbrow is like having an agency—there should be a Jewish presence there. It is the melting pot. It is a heartless place. It is one of the harshest places in the world, objectively speaking. As long as Reeva is there, it [the Temple] is in hand."

In 2016, when Reeva was out of the country, she received news that there had been a break-in at the temple. The burglars stole several pieces of office equipment, which fortunately were insured. But they also stole the ancient gold and silver breastplates and adornments of the synagogue's historic Torah scrolls, which Reeva estimates were worth millions of rand—although they left the precious scrolls themselves.

"I was devastated," Reeva says, "but I decided there would be no public announcement. Had we gone public, we might have gotten help from other shuls—but I did not want to confirm Hillbrow's reputation and contribute to more stereotyping. We kept it quiet."

We find it fitting to conclude this exploration of Hillbrow's credoscapes with Reeva's recounting of a small miracle. As so often happens in Hillbrow stories, slivers of hope come despite profound difficulty. "As we were assessing the damage," she says, "we walked into the temple library—which was no longer being used. We discovered that behind a wall was a huge collection of historic scrolls from Europe and other parts of the world—along with many photographs and documents dating back to the 1930s and even earlier. They must have been collected over the decades, especially by Rabbi Weiler. When examined by experts, it was revealed that they were a major treasure." This finding contributed to the opening exhibition and the launch of the Heritage Centre in 2016.

Conclusion

Since the 1890s, people have journeyed from many parts of the world to restart their lives in Hillbrow. Some traveled across continents. Others arrived from nearby townships or from the countryside. But given South Africa's legacy of racial separation, even a move of twelve miles can make a transformative difference.

Many of Hillbrow's earliest residents were Jewish Lithuanians who had fled deadly riots that destroyed entire villages. They took wagons or trains overland and piled into ships to reach South Africa. Those who moved to Johannesburg found themselves in a teeming city that had in its first decade of existence become the largest in southern Africa. Its growing fortunes depended on a gold rush and the exploited labor of Black African people.

The work of materialist scholars such as Immanuel Wallerstein provides a lens through which to understand why so many people have taken what could be difficult and dangerous paths that led to Hillbrow. Hillbrow was founded as a neighborhood in 1894, a decade after several European powers met in Berlin to carve up the entire African continent among themselves. Nearly all parts of the globe were now tied in a system of either outright colonization or dependency on Europe or North America. Johannesburg's gold mines drew people from across many parts of the world system, many of whom were fortune seekers from Europe. But most labor on the mines was performed by Black people who were forced to work in conditions of subordination to white people and to live in "locations" separate from whites.

During its first decades, Hillbrow was a privileged respite for whites, a place with horses and stables. Jewish Eastern Europeans whose fortunes had risen left poorer neighborhoods such as Ferreirasdorp and Doornfontein and moved to Hillbrow and nearby Berea and Yeoville. They were joined by other Europeans or the descendants of Europeans, including Jewish and Protestant Germans. The city and the country around Hillbrow were building an increasingly brutal system of racial stratification. If Hillbrow was clean and quiet, the majority of South Africans were facing violence, trauma, racial exploitation, and hegemonic masculinity.

In the 1920s and 1930s, Hillbrow was roiled by fascist organizing. The German Club, which had been started by Jewish Germans, was taken over by Nazi-sympathizing "Greyshirts." Though the Greyshirts, and other groups like them, attempted to intimidate the Jewish population, the Jewish community flourished. Less than a mile away from the German Club, Hermann Kallenbach, a close friend of Mohandas Gandhi, designed and helped build Temple Israel, the "mother synagogue" of Progressive Judaism in South Africa.

As Hillbrow developed into a neighborhood of high-rise buildings and urban density, it became home to both reactionaries and rebels. Some of our participants spoke of restaurants that celebrated Adolf Hitler's birthday well into the 1950s. But Hillbrow's density also provided spaces for the defiance of authority. John Kani told us about writing plays with members of the anti-apartheid Market Theatre and then visiting the jazz clubs and eating halls that provided something like a "postcard" from what he hoped would become South Africa's postracist future. The doctor and activist Paul Davis told us about patients of his who found spaces in Hillbrow where they could evade the apartheid police and the death squads.

Despite harsh, and deeply racist and sexist, "morality laws," Hillbrow became one of Johannesburg's most significant places of queer expression. Its high-rise apartment buildings, cabarets, and nightclubs attracted young people and a budding queer community. One building in the 1950s was home to so many queer people that it became known as "Radclyffe Hall," after the author of a groundbreaking lesbian-themed novel from the 1920s. The 1970s brought a further "pinking" of Hillbrow, as it developed more and more queer spaces. Such bars and clubs began as all-white establishments, but they gradually transformed into places of greater diversity. Black and white men were, for instance, arrested together in 1978 during a New Year's Eve raid some have called "South Africa's Stonewall."

During the waning, but extremely violent, final years of apartheid, Black, Coloured, and Indian South Africans made their way to Hillbrow to live, to work, and to socialize. Sam, a biracial Indian and Coloured woman, told of the profound, but incomplete, freedom she felt upon discovering the neighborhood in the late 1980s. Philip moved from Limpopo to work in Ponte City and found himself living in one of its "locations in the sky" and subjected to pass laws until 1986.

With its landscape of high-rise apartment buildings and commercial and entertainment spaces in the 1990s, Hillbrow beckoned to more and more people. Even as it became more dangerous for many, and as its buildings were overcrowded and beginning to deteriorate, tens of thousands of people would make their way there. Many of our participants chose it because "all transportation routes go to it and through it." Some told us they found Hillbrow to be one of the few places where they could rent an apartment without documentation.

As it has always been, Hillbrow remains a place for migrants and immigrants. Our participants told us about their moves from South Africa's Eastern Cape, from the Limpopo Province, and from Soweto. They held high aspirations and were thrilled the first time they saw Johannesburg's skyline at night. Some now describe Hillbrow as "hell," and look for an opportunity that will enable them to leave. Others have found a network of friends who facilitate a feeling of safety. They delight in Hillbrow's many entertainment spaces and find succor in its many faith communities.

Other participants took longer journeys, in planes from Nigeria, in trucks from the DRC or the Republic of Congo, or in vans from Zimbabwe. What Adekeye Adebayo calls "the curse of Berlin" — the colonization of Africa — continues to leave economic difficulty, political tumult, or civil war in its wake, decades after formal colonization ended.[1] The people we spoke to looked to Johannesburg for safety, for employment, and for stability. They have not always found such promises fulfilled in Hillbrow, but they struggle to build lives for themselves.

A film from the 2010s called Hillbrow a "Gangster's Paradise." We did not find a gangster's paradise as we traveled through Hillbrow. But we did meet members of a "gang" who were kind enough to share their stories with us. They told us of their journeys from Zimbabwe and from Limpopo to a city where they could not find work and where they subsist in informal housing. "We live in an evil place," one of them told us, as he described the brutality and corruption of the police.

The members of that group have formed friendships with a circle of amateur artists and musicians, many of whom were once members of the "gang" themselves. Most of those artists among them live together, write music, perform songs, and draw. They plan for a better future.

What we observed in Hillbrow was the human capacity to build life and human connections in some of the most difficult conditions imaginable. Many of our respondents seek not only better futures for themselves, but to bring better lives and conditions to others, through justice work, through queer outspokenness, through a refusal to be silenced. Some who have seen their economic conditions improve have left the neighborhood but return for the Nigerian, or Congolese, or Malawian restaurants that remind them of home. Others, like Pastor Thomas, come to pass out food in a neighborhood where he once lived, in a flat with seventeen people, when he arrived from the DRC.

In economic terms, apartheid has not ended, nor has the "curse of Berlin." South Africa remains one of the most unequal societies on earth. People continue to take roads that lead them to Hillbrow, but the state is largely unresponsive to their needs. They survive by building a web of relationships.

Epilogue
The COVID-19 Crisis in Hillbrow

When the authors made their final trip to Johannesburg in January 2020, they were unaware that a deadly novel coronavirus was spreading across the world. It would soon cause national shutdowns, economic implosions, and a staggering global death toll. Doctors reported the first known cases in Wuhan, China, on December 31, 2019. The virus had spread to the West Coast of the United States by January 20, 2020, and New York City recorded its first infections in late February. South Africa registered its first case when one of its citizens, who had traveled to Italy, returned home to KwaZulu-Natal and tested positive on March 5, 2020.[1]

In the days following that first case, South Africa experienced a rapid increase in the infection rate, and within weeks the virus had spread to all nine provinces. Though the first outbreaks were in the Western Cape and in KwaZulu-Natal, Johannesburg had the highest number of cases of any city on the continent by the middle of July 2020.[2]

The virus affected every aspect of life in Hillbrow. South Africa's government received praise for acting quickly to declare a state of emergency on March 15, just ten days after the first reported incident, and for instituting a national economic lockdown on March 27. Its decision to deploy thousands of community workers to carry out an extensive health education campaign paid off initially, as the infection rate peaked and then declined. But these measures could not prevent the trauma and economic dislocation caused by the pandemic.

The South African photographer Jerome Delay, who has had extensive experience covering Ebola outbreaks in other parts of Africa, documented pictorially the impact of COVID-19 in Johannesburg's central city. He noted that, while people in the wealthier suburbs were able to maintain safe distances, the same was not possible in neighborhoods like Hillbrow. One of his most striking photographs is taken from a Hillbrow sidewalk and shows hundreds of people in a high-rise building, standing on their balconies and peering at the street below. They had no choice but to remain indefinitely in their overcrowded tower.[3]

For several weeks, tenants in Hillbrow's flats were not permitted outside for anything other than buying essential items such as food or medicine. The sidewalks emptied of the normally flourishing fruit and vegetable stands, whose workers lost their incomes. Likewise, the thousands of people who would normally commute each day to work in the restaurants and shops in the northern suburbs faced mass unemployment and uncertain futures.

As necessary as the lockdown may have been, the police and military — who were also called in to enforce lockdown — were often overzealous and, in many cases, brutal in enforcing it. Rather than providing information and issuing warnings, officers sometimes used tear gas, rubber bullets, and water cannons to disperse crowds.[4] One of the government's prevention measures was to ban all sales and consumption of alcohol, given that alcohol-related illness is one of the leading causes of hospitalization in the country. But police officers took the alcohol ban as license to arrest, terrify, and brutalize anyone caught consuming it. In Alexandra Township, for instance, police officers killed a man named Collins Khosa by first strangling him, slamming him against a wall, and then butting him with a machine gun because they suspected he had cups of alcohol in his yard.[5] In Hillbrow, police officers were seen driving up and down the street, getting out of a vehicle, and using *sjamboks* (heavy leather whips) on pedestrians.[6]

At least one sergeant in Hillbrow told reporters that he saw no choice, given that some people refused to comply with quarantine orders. He insisted that he and his fellow officers were trying to save lives, because a single infection in such a densely populated community could quickly turn into an unthinkable disaster.[7]

It appeared at first as if a health disaster on that level would not materialize in Johannesburg's inner city. The nation's top virologist, Shabir Madhi, noted that South Africa's death rate was, for a time, far lower than expected.[8] But by July 2020, the country was recording numbers of "excess" deaths 60 percent higher than normal, suggesting that COVID-19 deaths were underreported. Soweto and Johannesburg's CBD (next to Hillbrow) were hit particularly hard.[9]

The five-week economic lockdown during South Africa's first COVID-19 wave (March through April 2020) led to a 30 percent drop in both employment and income. In response, the government announced a R502 billion (US$26 billion) stimulus package — among the highest in the world when measured as a portion of GDP. The funding was used for additional health support, unemployment insurance, and social grants for adults and children. Haroon Bhorat's analysis finds the program to be remarkably pro-poor and praises it for providing relief to about 63 percent of the population.[10]

Nonetheless, hardships caused by the pandemic were and remain severe for Hillbrow's residents and their families, many of whom live in other parts of Africa. Asylum seekers and undocumented migrants were ineligible to receive COVID-19 stimulus aid or food parcels provided to citizens and formal refugees. South Africa's borders closed for more than six months, preventing many would-be migrants from reaching Johannesburg and preventing those who were already in South Africa from leaving. Zimbabwe, on the northeastern border, had already been facing severe food shortages. Patrol guards were posted along the border fence to prevent entry and, once the border reopened in September 2020, were directed to apprehend anyone attempting an illegal entry. Hundreds were arrested for trying to smuggle groceries from South Africa to Zimbabwe.[11]

Many international migrants who leave their countries to live in Johannesburg do so to send money to families back home for food, housing, school fees, and medical costs. Such remittances are vital for the survival of hundreds of thousands of people. The World Bank projected that the COVID-19 pandemic would lead to the sharpest drop in remittances in recent history, with the biggest drop — of 23.1 percent — occurring in sub-Saharan Africa.[12] With COVID-19 tests costing anywhere from US$15 to US$45 in Zimbabwe, remittances to family members may have been more important than ever. As of late August 2020, only 1.6 percent of Zimbabweans had been tested.[13]

Notably, however, the World Bank's projections were off. Instead of a massive decline in remittances from South Africa to Zimbabwe, for instance, Zimbabweans living in South Africa sent more money home than ever. During the period from June to September 2020, remittances to Zimbabwean families (from all countries) increased by 45 percent over the same period the previous year.[14] For all of 2020, remittances were up 42 percent.[15] As Mwaona Nyirongo has shown, transnational migrants in South Africa often prioritize the financial needs of family members in their home countries and will sacrifice in any way possible to support them.[16] Many who lost work during the COVID quarantine were unable to send remittances, but others redoubled their efforts.

In October 2020, the authors convened a virtual panel on the impact of COVID-19 on asylum seekers, refugees, and other migrants in Johannesburg at New York's Fordham University. Most of the speakers, including Simon Kikouta of Mould Empower Serve (MES), Ethel Munyai of the Migrant Support Centre at the Outreach Foundation, Richa Kamina Tshimbinda of Migrant Woman's Voice, and Bafikile Mkhize of the eKhaya Neighbourhood Improvement District and the soup kitchen at the Cathedral of Christ the King, were from Hillbrow. Their consensus was that the pandemic had led to severe disruptions and increased hardships in the neighborhood.[17]

Munyai noted that her work with migrants in Hillbrow has gotten noticeably more difficult because the government mandated that asylum seekers and unauthorized border crossers would not be eligible for any emergency COVID-19 aid. The government also accelerated its drive to deport unauthorized migrants. In light of these challenges, a Christian organization known as Bread for the World has assisted Outreach's Migrant Support Centre with food aid and with other funding to enable migrants who have lost their jobs to launch income-generating businesses.

When most economic activity ceased from late March through August 2020, many international migrants saw no choice but to return home. Without government aid, and with both formal and informal economic activities curtailed, income for many migrants had dropped to zero. Xenophobia, Munyai added, had also intensified and many hospital workers were refusing to assist migrants.

"Police visibility was very high at the borders," she continued, making it hard for everyone to get in or out of the country. "Our funders agreed that the Support Centre could assist people who were trying to go back home. But not everyone wanted to go home. Some think that home is worse."

That comment from Munyai, that home countries might be even worse places to be during the crisis, drew affirmative responses from other members of the panel. International migrants in Johannesburg have families depending on them in countries whose economies had experienced even more severe disruptions.

"People feel really bad about remittances," Simon Kikouta said. "They have very huge responsibilities, and they are going through terrible stress knowing that they cannot send money home — where people are counting on them."

Mwaona Nyirongo, a graduate student at Rhodes University in South Africa, joined the panel from Malawi. He noted that "many families might not understand why remittances stopped. They may think their family members have been lazy or simply careless. Returning home could be a source of great humiliation."

In 2018, 83 percent of Malawi's remittances came from South Africa, Nyirongo noted. "There was never a war in Malawi, so most Malawian migrants enter South Africa illegally because the government refuses to grant refugee status," he explained. "The government has [also] refused to acknowledge that Malawians do experience hunger, even though there have been many periods of hunger in the country. So, without refugee status, most Malawians who go to South Africa work illegally. . . . But now [with the decline in remittances] Malawi is badly affected. It is running out of foreign exchange. People cannot send money home [to Malawi]."

Richa Kamina Tshimbinda is from the DRC and recently helped form Migrant Woman's Voice along with other women from Kenya, Angola, and Ghana. "We believe migrant women can become the key to development," she noted. "[So] there was so much frustration during the crisis. No one could go to work. There was also much fighting at home because people were cooped up inside. We are losing hope."

The loss of income led to a wave of evictions. The government ordered a moratorium on evictions of formal tenants, but many subtenants with informal arrangements had no such protections. "With COVID-19," Bafikile Mkhize reported, "we have been hit so hard. Most people in Hillbrow were working in the restaurant industry and lost their jobs. Many were allowed to go without paying rent, but even so there was the expense of food. At the Cathedral, we are a 'Sub-Saharan African Cathedral,' and we were hit so hard. The [soup] kitchen was closed for weeks, but it is now open."

Simon Kikouta added that most of the buildings that are properly managed have complied with the eviction moratorium. "The people have not been kicked out," he said. "The evictions are [happening in] buildings that are not properly run."

Mkhize agreed. "We have different kinds of buildings in Hillbrow," she noted. "In the hijacked buildings, all they want is money. As soon as someone cannot pay, they are kicked out. When people are 'sub-sub-subtenants,' they often find themselves kicked out."

Kikouta, whose organization, MES, operates several shelters, noted that those facilities experienced a sharp increase in demand. "During this period," he said, "a huge number of new people were coming to the shelters. You cannot go to the police over evictions [despite the moratorium], so you end up in the shelters. . . . We could not always accommodate extra people because the shelters were full. But we were ready to respond. Many of our shelters took more migrants and citizens alike. Some of the shelters do offer a plate of food every day, and some do not."

Despite the hardships, Richa said many migrant women do not want to go home. "We are the fruits of our irresponsible leaders," she proclaimed. "Although we experience xenophobia, we still see in South Africa freedom. It is the only place where women have rights. Congolese women are raped every day. We are raising our voice, looking for help. Congolese women would prefer to die in South Africa. They would never want to go back."[18]

The pandemic led the International Organization for Migration (IOM), a United Nations–related organization, to support the voluntary return of migrants from South Africa to Malawi, Zimbabwe, Zambia, and Mozambique. By mid-September 2020, IOM had helped four hundred nationals leave South Africa with funding provided by the European Union. The returnees are nationals who "decide they would be better off returning home." For instance, in late August and in mid-September, IOM sponsored two chartered flights to carry 111 migrants back to Malawi. One of the returnees was a forty-five-year-old man who had been living in South Africa for three years. He told IOM that he had been earning an income that was small, but enough to "live decently" and to permit him to send money home. He lost that job and decided to "go back home and figure things out with the people I have missed all this time."[19]

Another group of Malawians was arrested in October 2020 at the Ressano Garcia checkpoint on the South African border, as they attempted to go back home by crossing through Mozambique. At least some of them had been living in Johannesburg and found it no longer possible to remain there. Funding from the European Union's Southern Africa Migration Management provided for their flights to Lilongwe and onward transportation to their hometowns.[20] Even as economic activity resumes in South Africa, it is impossible to estimate whether or when migration to Johannesburg will return to previous levels. In fact, many still are returning home. IOM found that 200,000 migrants living in South Africa, Malawi, and Botswana had returned to Zimbabwe by the first quarter of 2021. The main reasons for leaving host countries included "hunger and loss of accommodation, lack of access to medical assistance, mental health support, identity document issues and the risk of assault in the country where they were working."[21]

As the crisis proceeded, the authors received updates from some of our interviewees in Hillbrow. Johan, formerly of the Outreach Foundation's Counselling Centre and now a job training specialist with the foundation, informed us that the asylum seekers he and his former colleague Sizwe introduced to us were all "doing fine." Koko, from the DRC, lost his job giving piano lessons for a few months when the foundation had to lay off all members of its "enrichment staff." Over time, he was able to return to work. Thokozile, from Malawi, and Doreen, from Zimbabwe, both went to nail and beauty school and were working in salons.

Bongani, who had introduced us to numerous people from Berea and Hillbrow, lost his primary source of income as a personal trainer for many months when all gyms in the country were ordered to close. The impact was so dire that his landlord threatened eviction. He avoided eviction with aid from the Islamic Society of South Africa until he was able to return to personal training again in October 2020. What he was most excited about was that he was able to resume the production of music videos, although he lost one of his most talented recording artists when the artist's family was evicted and had to move away from Johannesburg.[22]

Through Bongani, the authors met several talented musicians and musical technicians. Some of them were living together in a small apartment in Doornfontein, just south of Hillbrow. During the pandemic, they lost the apartment because the leaseholder—they were subtenants—wanted to reclaim it. Lacking sufficient funds to stay within the central city, they saw no other alternative but to move to a home owned by one of their family members. That home is in Tembisa, a township of nearly 500,000 people in the far north of Johannesburg's outer rings, approaching Pretoria. At twenty-five miles away from Hillbrow, the distance will make regular artistic collaboration with others in the city more difficult.

Bafikile told us that Megan, the eighty-one-year-old director of the soup kitchen at the Cathedral of Christ the King, was forced to stay confined to her apartment. When the soup kitchen closed, other volunteers prepared food in their own homes, packaged it, and brought it to the cathedral grounds where they provided it on a to-go basis to people who were homeless. By September 2020, the facility was allowed to formally reopen and, without Megan present, various teams rotated to manage the kitchen on a week-to-week basis. By late October, Megan had returned to help the volunteers at the kitchen but, for her safety, was no longer present every day.[23]

Simon[24] explained that, like many other NGOs in the area, MES had responded to the crisis by widely distributing daily food parcels. They included nonperishable food items and other critical supplies such as toothpaste, soup, and deodorant. Recipients of the MES parcels were mostly parents of children who had been attending MES-run crèches (prekindergartens), all of whom the agency contacted to ask if they needed help. Most NGOs operated the same way, by contacting people they were already helping. A result is that those who had been working but lost their jobs were not likely to receive food parcels because they were not already on existing lists. Likewise, asylum seekers and unauthorized migrants were missing from most NGO lists because the government does not permit tax-supported agencies to distribute aid to migrants (with the exception of formally recognized refugees).

One of the consistent themes of this book has been the transformation of Hillbrow into a visible queer space from the 1950s through the early 1990s. Though it remained home to many LGBTQ+ people after the 1990s, it experienced yet another transformation as most — but not all — of the overtly queer spaces closed. Though the authors were not able to interview any queer Hillbrow residents for this epilogue, it is clear that the pandemic has exerted a severe toll on the queer population throughout the sub-Saharan region.

In June, The Other Foundation, a Johannesburg-based African trust that advocates for freedom and equality, hosted a panel on COVID-19's impact on queer sub-Saharan Africans. Panelists represented organizations in Zambia, Namibia, Zimbabwe, Kenya, and South Africa. Though none addressed Hillbrow specifically, the experiences they described are applicable. Sebenzile Nkambule, the executive officer of the foundation, noted that queer people were already, often, on the fringes of many societies and COVID-19 had made their lives even more challenging. The lockdown forced many queer organizations to shut down, at least temporarily, and to halt vital services such as health care. Jholerina Timbo, from Namibia, noted that, while police often harass LGBTQ+ people, the extra police presence during the shutdown has led to increases in such abuse. In Zimbabwe, even water has become scarce as most households do not have indoor plumbing but are not permitted to leave their homes to get water. Queer people have had to end relationships and move back home with families because of a loss of income, but their families may already have ostracized them or may continue to humiliate them. For queer people across the region who depended on sex work as a source of support, the COVID-19 lockdowns have drastically if not totally disrupted the trade.[25]

By June 2021, South Africa was experiencing its third wave of COVID-19 infections. The World Health Organization (WHO) reported the presence of the more infectious Delta variant in South Africa and in all of its neighboring countries. As of June 4, 2021, Africa had recorded 131,734 deaths, nearly 50 percent of which occurred in southern Africa. With South Africa being the most affected country on the continent — and with nearly 57,000 deaths as of June 11, 2021 — the government imposed another strict lockdown. Intensive care units were at full capacity.[26] At the same time, the vaccination rate was a dismal 2.8 percent of the population, leaving South Africa significantly behind several other African countries — including Zimbabwe.[27]

Ethel Munyai,[28] of the Outreach Foundation's Migrant Support Centre, reports that as of May 2021 documented and undocumented transnational migrants continue to encounter severe hardships. The informal sector, she says, "has been extremely impacted" as there is far less foot traffic and almost no customers. Despite the moratorium on evictions, many continue to lose their homes, and government-supported shelters are not accepting undocumented migrants or asylum seekers.

Ethel and her colleagues now travel regularly to Musina (at the Zimbabwe border) and Harare (Zimbabwe's capital) to hold workshops with would-be migrants. They advise people at the border — some of whom are Zimbabwean and some of whom are Congolese — to stay in Zimbabwe because trying to relocate in Johannesburg at this time "will only lead to trauma, especially if there are children." She holds skills-training workshops in Zimbabwe to help people start local businesses in carpentry, hair and nail treatments, sewing, and food preparation as an alternative to migrating to Johannesburg. But people continue to cross the borders into South Africa. "Mozambicans," she says, "don't want to go back home. They say their suffering is worse at home. We don't know what will happen. And the elections are coming. Politicians exploit the migrant issue, promising voters to send migrants home. It is the only thing all parties agree on."

Richa[29] started Migrant Woman's Voice in 2019 with women from Ethiopia, Somalia, Rwanda, Ghana, and the DRC. "We are coming as one African woman," she says, explaining the organization's name, "and all these women have come together to speak with one voice." The goal was to create an organization in Johannesburg that would empower women to become entrepreneurs and to offer a resource that would help people understand their rights and their options. The organization's 167 members are women who run small businesses ranging from cooking and selling food, vending fruits and vegetables on the pavements, and selling secondhand clothing.

Business has dropped dramatically during the pandemic and now Migrant Woman's Voice is raising money for people who want to return to their home countries. "Many migrants have lost their places to stay," Richa says, "and many have gone deep into debt to landlords. And every month there is an increase in rent. People are trying to pay their arrears. People have moved into smaller apartments. They are existing on food parcels from churches and shelters. I have been in this country for eighteen years. I came to Johannesburg with lots of ambition. I did the course on entrepreneurship. I have learned a lot. But maybe, some day, I could go home [to the DRC] and start something there."

COVID-19 has led to a "terrible homelessness crisis," says Simon, from MES.[30] The MES shelters are at capacity and cannot accommodate more people. Since January 2021, Simon has volunteered to receive after-hours calls every day after MES closes for business. "People are calling, begging, pleading," he says. "I get calls from all races. They just want a place for the night. Hospitals call and want to discharge patients, but they have nowhere to go. We don't have room for them. Many young kids are sleeping around the corners of Highpoint. The government shelter at Constitution Hill is absolutely packed."

People are sleeping on the street, he says, but the state has opened many new shelters and partnered with NGOs to fast-track new shelters. Asylum seekers and undocumented migrants cannot use government shelters, but MES does not check for documents. "Migrants in Hillbrow are telling their families not to come [to South Africa]," he says. "They are advising them 'we can't take care of you right now.'"

Nonetheless, more and more migrants are moving from other locations to Hillbrow. "Xenophobia is a touchy subject right now," Simon says, "when so many people have lost work. Neighbors in the townships see migrants with bags of food. Violence can happen at any time. So it is much safer to be in Hillbrow or Berea. People are selling their homes in the townships to live in Hillbrow. In a township, you could pay less but you could be gambling with your life." Simon reminds us of the ongoing importance of Hillbrow in so many people's lives: "It is hard to let go of Hillbrow. It is still the cheapest and safest option."

Acknowledgments

Many more people were involved and helpful in the completion of this book than we can possibly acknowledge. We are, first and foremost, grateful to the people of Hillbrow, Berea, and Yeoville for the openness with which so many greeted us. Several are mentioned in this book, but we learned from countless others whom we passed along the way on sidewalks and street corners, in shops and houses of worship, at fruit and vegetable stands, and in places of entertainment.

Glenn Speer provided indispensable editorial help and feedback. Derek Steele drew the map included in this volume. Hayley Augustyne, Damaris Calderon, Christina Cosares, Greg Fazio, and Angelica Lisiewski of the College of Staten Island of the City University of New York (CUNY); Duygu Altuntas of the Graduate Center, CUNY; and Leo Barnabei, Rylie Stolze, and Veer Shetty of Fordham University also provided insight and valuable research assistance for this book.

Several people were especially instrumental in helping us make important connections throughout Hillbrow and its surrounds, thereby making it possible for us to meet and spend time with people deeply knowledgeable about the rhythms and daily life of this extraordinary neighborhood. We are indebted to Adele Gluckman for introducing us to numerous members of the Jewish community in Hillbrow, past and present, as well as to teachers, social workers, and volunteers. One of those social workers was Radha Pillay, who became our first regular contact in Hillbrow and who spent countless hours over the years talking to us about her experiences running two crèches at Mould, Empower, Serve (MES). Simon Kikouta, Radha's friend and co-worker, was likewise endlessly generous with his time and insights.

Bongani Nduvana invited us into his home, introduced us to his family members, and walked with us around Hillbrow more times than we can count. Each time we met with Bongani, he introduced us to yet more people willing to share their time and their perspectives. Bongani also spent countless days over two years taking most of the photographs in this book. We thank TJ Nerio for help with resizing the images.

Temple Israel, in Hillbrow, permitted us to attend multiple services and always made us feel at home among their congregation. Reeva Foreman, its executive director, gave her time selflessly to us and introduced us to members of the broader Jewish community in Johannesburg. We are deeply grateful to the members of Temple Israel, especially to Lael Bethlehem, Solo, Samuel, Marion, Jacob, and Jennifer for the many conversations we had with them.

The directors and staff at Mould, Empower, Serve (MES), the Outreach Foundation, and Madulammoho contributed greatly to our familiarity with the community. We would especially like to thank Nicodemus Setshedi, Alan Childs, Gerard Bester, Robert Michel, and Leona Pienaar. Johan, Sizwe, and Ethel, of the Outreach Migrant Support Centre, met with us and introduced us to members of the asylum-seekers community.

Nic Barnes and Lethu Khanyile of Jozi Housing and Nosihle Tshabalala of the Hillbrow Community Improvement District also gave us several hours of their time to discuss housing issues in Hillbrow and Berea. Bafikile Mkhize, of the eKhaya Neighbourhood Improvement District, also opened her office to us many times over the years and introduced us to members of the Hillbrow St. Ann's volunteer organization, congregants at the Cathedral of Christ the King, and members of a soup kitchen on the grounds of the cathedral — especially Megan and Liz.

Kathy Munro, former Dean of Faculty of Commerce, Law, and Management at the University of the Witwatersrand and now of the Johannesburg Heritage Portal, and Tanya Zack, who has written several papers and short books related to Johannesburg neighborhoods, welcomed us into their homes and spent many hours discussing the history, development, and current environment of Hillbrow. Kathy also provided invaluable corrections to many parts of our text. We still have much to learn from her!

We are grateful to Kathy for introducing us to Lesley and Nhlahla, who walked us through Hillbrow and proved invaluable sources of information about life in the neighborhood. Marc Latilla, whose well-researched blog on Johannesburg (*Johannesburg 1912*) is an excellent resource in itself, provided historical context. We thank John Kani for giving his time to us and Paul Davis for his willingness to meet with us many times.

We would like to thank our dear friend Dickie King for his wonderful hospitality. He opened his home to us and permitted not only the authors but their family members a place to stay. Likewise, we thank Mike and Kathleen Parker for their kindness and support throughout this project.

Notes

Prologue 1: Return to Hillbrow

1. What are called "sidewalks" in the United States are typically called "pavements" in South Africa.

2. The term "lesbian and gay" was more common in 1990, but we generally use the more inclusive term "queer." However, when appropriate to the era we occasionally use the terms "gay," "lesbian," or "gay and lesbian" except when quoting or referring to usage by others.

3. Anna Hartford, "Ponte City," *n+1*, June 14, 2013, https://nplusonemag.com/online-only/online-only/ponte-city/.

4. Phaswane Mpe, *Welcome to Our Hillbrow* (Scottsville: University of KwaZulu-Natal Press, 2001), 3.

5. Clifford Bestall, *Hillbrow: Between Heaven and Hell*, *Al Jazeera Witness*, February 28, 2012, https://www.aljazeera.com/program/witness/2012/2/28/hillbrow-between-heaven-and-hell.

6. Bestall.

7. Most of this prologue was written in 2013, when Ron Nerio returned to South Africa for the first time in twenty-three years.

8. *Epilogue to Hillbrow, RIP*, author unknown, listed on YouTube as "angrysouthafrican2," April 22, 2008, http://www.youtube.com/watch?v=kEOFt5F-gpk.

9. *The Death of Johannesburg*, author unknown, listed on YouTube as "Vinscient," April 2, 2010, http://www.youtube.com/watch?v=LW6lOdxqSUE.

10. Yusuf Omar, *Hillbrow: Home of the Homeless*, May 2, 2012, https://www.youtube.com/watch?v=FvQfLlENdYA.

11. *Hillbrow: The Danger Zone Some Call Home, Mail & Guardian* (South Africa), April 1, 2011, https://www.youtube.com/watch?v=zRaJka_1l28.

12. Guy Ailion and Dana Fayman, *Receive Me Hillbrow*, March 4, 2008, https://www.youtube.com/watch?v=-UEAcmpj8qs.

13. Bestall, *Hillbrow.*

14. While Di's Bistro still exists, it is no longer a queer-oriented establishment.

15. Mendel Kaplan and Marian Robertson, *Founders and Followers: Johannesburg Jewry, 1887–1915* (Johannesburg: Vlaeberg, 1991).

16. John Hunt, *The Boy Who Could Keep a Swan in His Head* (Cape Town: Umuzi, 2018).

17. Because "racial" categories were created by colonization and apartheid, there is considerable debate in South Africa as to how, and whether, to continue using the racial labels formerly created by the state. We will discuss these debates in subsequent chapters. Here, we use the terminology adopted by the democratic government's most recent (2011) census and used by South African government bureaucracies and colloquially by most South Africans: "Black African," "Asian/ Indian," "Coloured," and white. More than 99 percent of respondents selected one of these terms to self-identify their race (Statistics South Africa, "Census 2011" [Pretoria, 2011], 17).

18. John Kani, interview with Nerio, August 20, 2016. We found that almost every participant to whom we spoke was comfortable with allowing us to use their full, real names; nonetheless, to protect their identities we use first names only. The exception is when the person is a well-known, public figure (and has granted us permission to use both their first and last name; we do change some first names).

19. Matthew Krouse, interview with Nerio, August 31, 2018.

20. Leswin Laubscher, "Afrikaner Identity and the Music of Johannes Kerkorrel," *South African Journal of Psychology* 35, no. 2 (June 1, 2005): 308–30, https://doi.org /10.1177/008124630503500209.

21. "Bomb Explodes at Johannesburg Synagogue," *South African History Online*, March 16, 2011, https://www.sahistory.org.za/dated-event/bomb-explodes -johannesburg-synagogue.

22. Janet Smith, "The Forgotten Story behind Hillbrow Café Bombing," *The Star*, November 16, 2016.

23. Bestall, *Hillbrow.*

24. Mpe, *Welcome to Our Hillbrow.*

25. Sue Nyathi, *The Gold-Diggers* (Johannesburg: Pan Macmillan South Africa, 2018).

Prologue 2: Being White and the Politics of Not Seeing

1. Linda Gordon, *The Second Coming of the KKK: The Ku Klux Klan of the 1920s and the American Political Tradition* (New York: Liveright, 2017).

2. Kathleen Belew, *Bring the War Home: The White Power Movement and Paramilitary America* (Cambridge, MA: Harvard University Press, 2018), 80.

3. Belew, 15, 23, 26–27.

1. South Africa: A History of Land Dispossession and Migration

1. World Economic Forum, *Migration and Its Impact on Cities* (Geneva: World Economic Forum, 2017), 10, http://www3.weforum.org/docs/Migration_Impact _Cities_report_2017_low.pdf.

2. Aurelia Segatti, "Migration to South Africa: Regional Challenges versus National Instruments and Interests," in *Contemporary Migration to South Africa: A Regional Development Issue*, ed. Aurelia Segatti and Loren B. Landau (Washington, DC: World Bank, 2011), 9–28, esp. 9; and Jonathan Crush, "Southern Hub: The Globalization of Migration to South Africa," in *International Handbook on Migration and Economic Development*, ed. Robert E. B. Lucas (Cheltenham, UK: Edward Elgar, 2015), 230–40.

3. International Organization for Migration (IOM), *World Migration Report 2020* (Geneva: IOM, 2020), esp. 49 and 80.

4. World Bank Group, *Mixed Migration, Forced Displacement and Job Outcomes in South Africa* (Washington, DC: World Bank, 2018).

5. Letlhogonolo Gaborone, foreword to *Still Searching for Security: The Reality of Farm Dweller Evictions in South Africa*, by Marc Wegerif, Bev Russell, and Irma Grundling (Polokwane, SA, and Johannesburg: Nkuzi Development Association and Social Surveys, 2005), vi.

6. Loren B. Landau and Jean Pierre Misago, "Who to Blame and What's to Gain? Reflections on Space, State, and Violence in Kenya and South Africa," *Africa Spectrum* 44, no. 1 (2009): 102.

7. Ogujiuba Kanayo, Patience Anjofui, and Nancy Stiegler, "Push and Pull Factors of International Migration: Evidence from Migrants in South Africa," *Journal of African Union Studies* 8, no. 2 (August 2019): 220.

8. Loren B. Landau, "Transplants and Transients: Idioms of Belonging and Dislocation in Inner-City Johannesburg," *African Studies Review* 49, no. 2 (2006): 123–45, esp. 130.

9. Hayley Gewer and Margot Rubin, "Hillbrow," in *Resilient Densification: Four Studies from Johannesburg*, ed. Alison Todes, Philip Harrison, and Dylan Weakley (Johannesburg: University of the Witwatersrand, 2015), 71–105, esp. 77 and 97; and Alex Wafer, "Precarity and Intimacy in Super-Diverse Hillbrow," in *Diversities Old and New: Migration and Socio-spatial Patterns in New York, Singapore and Johannesburg*, ed. Steven Vertovec (London: Palgrave Macmillan, 2015).

10. Tanja Winkler, "Why Won't Downtown Johannesburg 'Regenerate'?: Reassessing Hillbrow as a Case Example," *Urban Forum* 24, no. 3 (2013): 309–24, esp. 317.

11. In South Africa, "suburb" is a term used to connote a neighborhood.

12. Tanja Winkler, "Reimagining Inner-City Rejuvenation in Hillbrow, Johannesburg: Identifying a Role for Faith-Based Community Development," in *Dialogues in Urban and Regional Planning*, vol. 3, ed. Thomas L. Harper, Anthony Gar-On Yeh, and Heloisa Costa (New York: Routledge, 2008), 133–49, esp. 134.

13. Gewer and Rubin, "Hillbrow," 77 and 97.

14. "Key Migration Terms," International Organization for Migration, accessed May 17, 2021, https://www.iom.int/key-migration-terms.

15. Reece Jones, *Violent Borders: Refugees and the Right to Move* (London: Verso, 2017), 28, 73, 87.

16. Gail Nattrass, *A Short History of South Africa* (Johannesburg: Jonathan Ball, 2017), esp. 92.

17. Keith Beavon, *Johannesburg: The Making and Shaping of the City* (Pretoria: University of South Africa Press, 2004), esp. 20–22.

18. Beavon, 20–22.

19. Nattrass, *Short History of South Africa*, 91–92.

20. Beavon, *Johannesburg*, esp. 23–27.

21. Charles van Onselen, *New Babylon, New Nineveh: Everyday Life on the Witwatersrand, 1886–1914* (Johannesburg: Jonathan Ball, 1982), 1.

22. Ivan Turok, "South Africa's Tortured Urbanisation and the Complications of Reconstruction," in *Urban Growth in Emerging Economies: Lessons from the BRICS*, ed. Gordon McGranahan and George Martine (Oxfordshire, UK: Routledge, 2014), 3.

23. Beavon, *Johannesburg*, esp. 34.

24. Beavon, 36.

25. Philip Harrison and Tanya Zack, "The Power of Mining: The Fall of Gold and Rise of Johannesburg," *Journal of Contemporary African Studies* 30, no. 4 (October 2012): 554–55.

26. Andries Bezuidenhout and Sakhela Buhlungu, "From Compounded to Fragmented Labour: Mineworkers and the Demise of Compounds in South Africa," *Antipode* 43, no. 2 (2011): 244.

27. Charles van Onselen, *The Night Trains: Moving Mozambican Miners to and from the Witwatersrand Mines, 1902–1995* (Johannesburg: Jonathan Ball, 2019), 5–7.

28. Bezuidenhout and Buhlungu, "From Compounded to Fragmented Labour," 244.

29. Bezuidenhout and Buhlungu, 244.

30. Bezuidenhout and Buhlungu, 244–46; Turok, "South Africa's Tortured Urbanisation," 4–6.

31. The original borders of the city were on a patch of unused, unfarmable land called Randjeslaagte. The northern apex of Randjeslaagte would become Hillbrow.

32. Jonathan Stadler and Charles Dugmore, "'Honey, Milk and Bile': A Social History of Hillbrow, 1894–2016," *BMC Public Health* 17, article 444 (2017), https://doi.org/10.1186/s12889-017-4345-1.

33. Paddi Clay and Glynn Griffiths, *Hillbrow* (Cape Town: Don Nelson, 1982), 25; and Marc Latilla, "History of Hillbrow Part 1," Johannesburg—Suburb by Suburb Research, January 7, 2016, https://johannesburg1912.com/2016/01/07/history-of-hillbrow-pt-1/.

34. Beavon, *Johannesburg*, 75.

35. Alan Morris, *Bleakness and Light: Inner-City Transition in Hillbrow, Johannesburg* (Johannesburg: Witwatersrand University Press, 1999).

36. Winkler, "Why Won't Downtown Johannesburg 'Regenerate'?," 309–24, esp. 317.

37. Marc Latilla, *Johannesburg: Then and Now* (Johannesburg: Struit Nature, 2018), 102.

38. Nechama Brodie, ed., *The Joburg Book*, rev. ed. (Johannesburg: Sharp Sharp Media, 2014), 168.

39. Sonia Shah, *The Next Great Migration: The Beauty and Terror of Life on the Move* (New York: Bloomsbury, 2019), 67–75.

40. Adam Hochschild, *King Leopold's Ghost: A Story of Greed, Terror, and Heroism in Colonial Africa* (New York: Houghton Mifflin, 1999).

41. Chinua Achebe, *There Was a Country: A Personal History of Biafra* (New York: Penguin Books, 2012), 1.

42. Hochschild, *King Leopold's Ghost*, 121.

43. Akil Kokayi Khalfani and Tukufu Zuberi, "Racial Classification and the Modern Census in South Africa, 1911–1996," *Race and Society* 4, no. 2 (2001): 161–76, esp. 164, 167.

44. Keith Breckenridge, "The Book of Life: The South African Population Register and the Invention of Racial Descent, 1950–1980," *Kronos* 40, special issue (November 2014): 227, 231.

45. Breckenridge, "Book of Life," 231, 234.

46. Benjamin Pogrund, *Robert Sobukwe: How Can Man Die Better?* (Johannesburg: Jonathan Ball, 2012), ebook location 1655 of 8765.

47. Khalfani and Zuberi, "Racial Classification and the Modern Census," esp. 164, 167.

48. Richard van der Ross, *In Our Own Skins: A Political History of the Coloured People* (Johannesburg: Jonathan Ball, 2015), 74–75.

49. Rodney Davenport and Christopher Saunders, *South Africa: A Modern History*, 5th ed. (London: Palgrave Macmillan, 2000), 21–26.

50. Davenport and Saunders, 25–34.

51. Davenport and Saunders, 25–34.

52. Pumla Dineo Gqola, *Rape: A South African Nightmare* (Johannesburg: MF Books Joburg, 2015), 42–48.

53. Van der Ross, *In Our Own Skins*, 29.

54. Davenport and Saunders, *South Africa*, 25–34.

55. Martin Meredith, *Diamonds, Gold, and War: The British, the Boers, and the Making of South Africa* (New York: Public Affairs, 2007).

56. Van der Ross, *In Our Own Skins*, 36.

57. Gqola, *Rape: A South African Nightmare*, 48–50.

58. Davenport and Saunders, *South Africa*, 79–81.

59. Davenport and Saunders, 86–91.

60. Meredith, *Diamonds, Gold, and War*, 7–10 and 64.

61. Meredith, 43.
62. Meredith, 43.
63. Meredith, 64.
64. Davenport and Saunders, *South Africa*, 215–17.
65. Davenport and Saunders, 228.
66. Harrison and Zack, "Power of Mining," 555.
67. Beavon, *Johannesburg*, 67–71.
68. Beavon, 67, 82.
69. Harrison and Zack, "Power of Mining," 558.
70. Susan Parnell, "Race, Power, and Urban Control: Johannesburg's Inner City Slum-Yards, 1910–1923," *Journal of Southern African Studies* 29, no. 3 (2003): 615–37.
71. Van Onselen, *New Babylon, New Nineveh*, 40–42.
72. Beavon, *Johannesburg*, 77–78.
73. Susan Parnell, "Sanitation, Segregation and the Natives (Urban Areas) Act: African Exclusion from Johannesburg's Malay Location, 1897–1925," *Journal of Historical Geography* 17, no. 3 (1991): 273–75.
74. Davenport and Saunders, *South Africa*, 234–40.
75. Van der Ross, *In Our Own Skins*, 42.
76. Turok, "South Africa's Tortured Urbanisation," 28.
77. Beavon, *Johannesburg*, 105.
78. Stadler and Dugmore, "'Honey, Milk and Bile.'"
79. Clive M. Chipkin, *Johannesburg Transition: Architecture and Society, 1950–2000* (Johannesburg: Real African, 2008), 29, 51, 401.
80. Harrison and Zack, "Power of Mining," 558.
81. Beavon, *Johannesburg*, 120–22.
82. Beavon, 120–27.
83. Beavon, 125.
84. "The Big Debate on Racism," *Big Debate South Africa*, 2014, https://www.youtube.com/watch?v=jpLFdtSNwpU.
85. Gqola, *Rape: A South African Nightmare*.
86. One colony remains on the continent: Western Sahara is a colony of Morocco.
87. Rajohane Matshedisho and Alex Wafer, "Hillbrow, Johannesburg," in *Diversities Old and New: Migration and Socio-spatial Patterns in New York, Singapore and Johannesburg*, ed. Steven Vertovec (London: Palgrave Macmillan, 2015).
88. Wafer, "Precarity and Intimacy."
89. Caroline Wanjiku Kihato, *Migrant Women of Johannesburg: Everyday Life in an In-Between City* (London: Palgrave Macmillan, 2013).
90. Njabulo Ndebele, foreword to *The Next Twenty-Five Years: Affirmative Action in Higher Education in the United States and South Africa*, ed. David L. Featherman, Martin Hall, and Marvin Krislov (Ann Arbor: University of Michigan Press, 2009).

2. Hillbrow and Apartheid

1. Richard Mendelsohn and Milton Shain, *The Jews of South Africa: An Illustrated History* (Johannesburg: Jonathan Ball, 2009), 34.

2. Margot Rubin, "The Jewish Community of Johannesburg, 1886–1936: Landscapes of Reality and Imagination" (master's thesis, University of Pretoria, 2006).

3. Gideon Shimoni, *Community and Conscience: The Jews in Apartheid South Africa* (Hanover, NH: University Press of New England for Brandeis University Press, 2003), esp. 3.

4. Mendelsohn and Shain, *The Jews of South Africa*, 106.

5. Katrin Zürn-Steffens, "The Confessing Church in Johannesburg: Pastor Johannes Herrmann and the Friedenskirche Congregation in Hillbrow," in *Contested Relations: Protestantism between Southern Africa and Germany from the 1930s to the Apartheid Era*, ed. Hanns Lessing, Tilman Dedering, Jürgen Kampmann, and Dirkie Smit (Wiesbaden, Germany: Harrassowitz, 2017), 122–39, esp. 127; and Marc Latilla, "History of Hillbrow Pt. 1," *Johannesburg—Suburb by Suburb Research* (blog), January 7, 2016, https://johannesburg1912.com/2016/01/07/history-of-hillbrow-pt-1/.

6. Zürn-Steffens, "Confessing Church in Johannesburg," 122–39.

7. Darryl Egnal and Irwan Manoim, "Capturing the Beginnings," in *Temple Israel 80, 1936–2016* (a publication of Temple Israel on the occasion of its eightieth anniversary, Johannesburg, 2016), 12–15.

8. Egnal and Manoim, 12–15.

9. Shimoni, *Community and Conscience*, esp. 3.

10. Egnal and Manoim, "Capturing the Beginnings," 12–15.

11. Mendelsohn and Shain, *The Jews of South Africa*, 145.

12. Egnal and Manoim, "Capturing the Beginnings," 12–15.

13. Mendelsohn and Shain, *The Jews of South Africa*, 135.

14. Shimoni, *Community and Conscience*, 13–14.

15. Pierre L. van den Berghe, "Apartheid, Fascism and the Golden Age," *Cahiers d'études africaines* 2, no. 8 (1962): 598–608, esp. 599.

16. Bill, interview with Ron Nerio, March 25, 2019. Note: Our convention is to use first names for interviewees (with their permission) or a pseudonym when they choose. We use first and last names when referring to authors. In the case of well-known public figures, we use both first and last names (again, with their permission) when they have been interviewed.

17. Barry and Eve, interview with Nerio, June 26, 2014.

18. Clive M. Chipkin, interview with Nerio, March 28, 2019.

19. Federico Freschi, Brenda Schmahmann, and Lize van Robbroeck, *Troubling Images: Visual Culture and the Politics of Afrikaner Nationalism* (New York: New York University Press, 2020), Google Book without pagination.

20. Clive M. Chipkin, *Johannesburg Transition: Architecture and Society, 1950–2000* (Johannesburg: Real African, 2008), 96.

21. Chipkin, *Johannesburg Transition*, 401.

22. Lael Bethlehem, interview with Nerio, March 27, 2018.

23. Martin J. Murray, *City of Extremes: The Spatial Politics of Johannesburg* (Durham, NC: Duke University Press, 2011), 140.

24. Mark Gevisser and Edwin Cameron, "Defiant Desire," in *Defiant Desire: Gay and Lesbian Lives in South Africa*, ed. Mark Gevisser and Edwin Cameron (New York: Routledge, 1995), ebook, esp. loc. 612 of 9574.

25. Mark Gevisser and Edwin Cameron here conjoined the two neighborhoods into a singular amalgam, "Joubert Park/Hillbrow," as the two neighborhoods are so close to one another.

26. Gevisser and Cameron, "Defiant Desire," esp. loc. 612 of 9574.

27. Marc Latilla, "Theatres and Bioscopes in Early Johannesburg," *Johannesburg 1912 — Suburb by Suburb Research* (blog), July 29, 2013, https://johannesburg1912 .wordpress.com/2013/07/29/theatres-in-early-johannesburg/.

28. Gevisser and Cameron, "Defiant Desire," esp. loc. 791 of 9574.

29. Isak Niehaus, "Renegotiating Masculinity in the South African Lowveld: Narratives of Male-Male Sex in Labour Compounds and in Prisons," *African Studies* 61, no. 1 (2002): 77–97, esp. 77–79.

30. Niehaus, esp. 78.

31. Gugu Hlongwane, "'Reader, Be Assured This Narrative Is No Fiction': The City and Its Discontents in Phaswane Mpe's *Welcome to Our Hillbrow*," *ARIEL: A Review of International English Literature* 37, no. 4 (2006): esp. 70.

32. "Apartheid Legislation, 1850s–1970s," *South African History Online*, March 21, 2011, https://www.sahistory.org.za/article/apartheid-legislation-1850s-1970s.

33. Loren Kruger, *Imagining the Edgy City: Writing, Performing, and Building Johannesburg* (New York: Oxford University Press, 2013), esp. 58.

34. Census of South Africa, 2011, https://census2011.adrianfrith.com/place /798015093; South African Press Association, "Sophiatown Lives Again," *Independent Online*, February 13, 2006, https://www.iol.co.za/news/south-africa/sophiatown-lives -again-266248.

35. "Apartheid Legislation, 1850s–1970s."

36. *The Man Who Drove with Mandela* (documentary), directed by Greta Schiller, written by Mark Gevisser, produced by Greta Schiller and Mark Gevisser (New York: Jezebel Productions/Beulah Films, 2008), DVD; and "Sophie Thoko Mgcina (1938–)," South African Government, accessed February 9, 2022, https:// www.gov.za/about-government/sophie-thoko-mgcina-1938.

37. *Man Who Drove with Mandela*.

38. *Man Who Drove with Mandela*.

39. *Man Who Drove with Mandela*.

40. Yein Pyo, "South Africans Successfully Boycott Buses in Johannesburg, 1957," Global Nonviolent Action Database, September 30, 2012, https://nvdatabase

.swarthmore.edu/content/south-africans-successfully-boycott-buses-johannesburg
-1957.

41. Mary-Louise Hooper, "The Johannesburg Bus Boycott," *Africa Today* 4, no. 6 (November–December 1957): 13–16, esp. 13.

42. Hooper, 13–16.

43. "Sharpeville Massacre, 21 March 1960," South African History Online, accessed May 23, 2020, https://www.sahistory.org.za/article/sharpeville-massacre-21 -march-1960.

44. Nicolas van de Walle, "Sharpeville: A Massacre and Its Consequences," *Foreign Affairs* 90, no. 6 (2011): 196–97.

45. Chipkin, *Johannesburg Transition*, 404.

46. Chipkin, 404.

47. Gerald Shaw, "Wolfie Kodesh" (obituary), *The Guardian*, November 12, 2002.

48. Murray, *City of Extremes*.

49. Alan Morris, "Physical Decline in an Inner-City Neighborhood: A Case Study of Hillbrow, Johannesburg," *Urban Forum* 8, no. 2 (1997): 153–57.

50. Jonathan Stadler and Charles Dugmore, "'Honey, Milk and Bile': A Social History of Hillbrow, 1894–2016," *BMC Public Health* 17, article 444 (2017), https://doi .org/10.1186/s12889-017-4345-1.

51. Alan Morris, *Bleakness and Light: Inner-City Transition in Hillbrow, Johannesburg* (Johannesburg: Witwatersrand University Press, 1999), esp. 7.

52. Gevisser and Cameron, "Defiant Desire," esp. loc. 866 of 9574.

53. Gevisser and Cameron, esp. loc. 879, 890, and 1169 of 9574.

54. Morris, "Physical Decline," 153–57.

55. David, interview with Nerio, July 30, 2019.

56. "Grinker, Leopold," Artefacts (website), accessed May 23, 2020, https://www .artefacts.co.za/main/Buildings/archframes.php?archid=662.

57. Paul Davis, interview with Nerio, July 29, 2019.

58. Gevisser and Cameron, "Defiant Desire," esp. loc. 1200 of 9574.

59. Gabriel Hoosain Khan, "A Hillbrow Mixtape: The History of Skyline, SA's Longest Running Gay Bar," *News24*, June 24, 2018, https://www.news24.com /news24/travel/a-hilbrow-mixtape-the-history-of-skyline-sas-longest-running-gay-bar -20180624.

60. Gevisser and Cameron, "Defiant Desire," esp. loc. 1347 of 9574.

61. Gary, interview with Nerio, August 24, 2018.

62. "Fontana," Fontana Holdings, accessed May 20, 2020, https://www .fontanaholdings.co.za/history.

63. Melinda Silverman, "Changing the Skyline: Hillbrow, Berea and the Building of Ponte," Book 3 in *Ponte City*, ed. Mikhael Subotzky and Patrick Waterhouse (Göttingen, Germany: Steidl, 2014), 4–5.

64. Silverman, esp. 3.

65. Silverman, esp. 7.

66. Silverman, esp. 14.

67. Denis Hirson, "Perec/Ponte," Book 9 in *Ponte City*, ed. Mikhael Subotzky and Patrick Waterhouse (Göttingen, Germany: Steidl, 2014), esp. 9.

3. Uprising and Change, 1976–93

1. Sifiso Mxolisi Ndlovu, "The Soweto Uprising," in *The Road to Democracy in South Africa*, vol. 2, 1970–1980, ed. South African Democracy Education Trust (Johannesburg: Unisa, 2007), 317–68.

2. Ndlovu, "Soweto Uprising"; "The June 16 Soweto Youth Uprising," South African History Online, May 21, 2013, https://www.sahistory.org.za/article/june-16 -soweto-youth-uprising.

3. Clive M. Chipkin, *Johannesburg Transition: Architecture and Society, 1950– 2000* (Johannesburg: Real African, 2008), 76.

4. Paddi Clay and Glynn Griffiths, *Hillbrow* (Cape Town: Don Nelson, 1982), 28.

5. Ta-Nehisi Coates, "The Case for Reparations," *The Atlantic*, June 2014, https:// www.theatlantic.com/magazine/archive/2014/06/the-case-for-reparations/361631/.

6. In South African real estate terminology, a "bachelor flat" is similar to a "studio" or "efficiency" apartment in the US lexicon: a one-room unit with a small kitchen and bathroom.

7. Clay and Griffiths, *Hillbrow*.

8. Daniel Conway, "Queering Apartheid: The National Party's 1987 'Gay Rights' Election Campaign in Hillbrow," *Journal of Southern African Studies* 35, no. 4 (November 2009): 849–63, esp. 853.

9. Richard Mendelsohn and Milton Shain, *The Jews of South Africa: An Illustrated History* (Johannesburg: Jonathan Ball, 2009).

10. Alan Morris, *Bleakness and Light: Inner-City Transition in Hillbrow, Johannesburg* (Johannesburg: Witwatersrand University Press, 1999).

11. Morris, 20–33.

12. Morris, esp. 53–55.

13. Melinda Silverman, "Changing the Skyline: Hillbrow, Berea and the Building of Ponte," Book 3 in *Ponte City*, ed. Mikhael Subotzky and Patrick Waterhouse (Göttingen, Germany: Steidl, 2014).

14. David Beresford, "'Great Crocodile' of Apartheid Dies at 90," *The Guardian*, October 31, 2006.

15. Beresford.

16. John Kani, interview with Ron Nerio, August 20, 2016.

17. "John Kani: South African Theatre Great," Gauteng Pages, accessed May 20, 2020, http://www.gauteng.net/pages/page/john_kani.

18. "Bonisile John Kani," South African History Online, accessed February 7, 2022, https://www.sahistory.org.za/people/bonisile-john-kani.

19. Theodore Reunert, whose family moved into the Windybrow in 1896, was not in fact a "Randlord." Rather, he was a scientist and founder of an engineering firm, a major advocate for education who campaigned for a liberal university in

Johannesburg, and a supporter of the Johannesburg Observatory. See Kathy Munro, "Windybrow in Context — From Theodore Reunert Home to Windybrow Arts Center," The Heritage Portal, July 26, 2017, http://www.theheritageportal.co.za/article/windybrow-context-theodore-reunert-home-windybrow-arts-centre.

20. Mark Gevisser and Edwin Cameron, "Defiant Desire," in *Defiant Desire: Gay and Lesbian Lives in South Africa*, ed. Mark Gevisser and Edwin Cameron (New York: Routledge, 1995), ebook.

21. Gevisser and Cameron, esp. loc. 1004 of 9574.

22. Luiz DeBarros, *Metamorphosis: The Remarkable Journey of Granny Lee*, directed by Luiz DeBarros (Johannesburg: Underdog Entertainment, 2012), DVD.

23. Gevisser and Cameron, "Defiant Desire," esp. loc. 1219 of 9574.

24. Gevisser and Cameron.

25. Gevisser and Cameron.

26. Bev Ditsie, *Simon and I*, directed by Bev Ditsie and Nicky Newman (Cape Town: Day Zero Film and Video, 2001), DVD.

27. Simon Nkoli, "Coming Out as a Black Gay Activist in South Africa," in *Defiant Desire: Gay and Lesbian Lives in South Africa*, ed. Mark Gevisser and Edwin Cameron (New York: Routledge, 1995), ebook, esp. loc. 6041 through 6214 of 9574.

28. Daniel Herwitz, "The Future of the Past in South Africa: On the Legacy of the TRC," *Social Research: An International Quarterly* 72, no. 3 (2005): 531–48, esp. 532.

29. Ditsie, *Simon and I*.

30. Nkoli, "Coming Out," loc. 6041 through 6214 of 9574; Ditsie, *Simon and I*.

31. Gevisser and Cameron, "Defiant Desire."

32. Ditsie, *Simon and I*.

33. Ditsie.

34. Mark Gevisser, "Simon Nkoli: South Africa's First True Renaissance Man," *POZ*, July 1, 1999.

35. Ditsie, *Simon and I*.

36. DeBarros, *Metamorphosis*.

37. Gevisser and Cameron, "Defiant Desire."

38. "Gay" was the word used by the media and activists at the time.

39. Daniel Conway, "Queering Apartheid," *Journal of Southern African Studies* 35, no. 4 (2009): 855.

40. Conway, 849–63, esp. 860.

41. Paul Davis, interviews with Nerio, March 25, 2019, and July 29, 2019.

42. Philip, interview with Nerio, March 31, 2018.

43. Wendy, interview with Nerio, July 28, 2019.

44. Olusola Olufemi, "Street Homelessness in Johannesburg Inner-City: A Preliminary Survey," *Environment and Urbanization* 10, no. 2 (1998): 223–34, esp. 225 and 233.

45. The Editors, "Joubert Park over the Years," *City Press*, October 19, 2014, https://www.news24.com/Archives/City-Press/Joubert-Park-over-the-years-20150430.

46. Noluvuyo Mjoli, "Joubert Park," YouTube, accessed May 20, 2020, https://www.youtube.com/watch?v=wWM5DaNzAuA.

47. Hugeaux South Africa, "Chess in Joubert Park," Hugeaux Photography, April 27, 2012, https://www.youtube.com/watch?v=7BMqfMAJjOs.

48. Wendy provided the spelling for the name of this dish, but the authors were unable to verify it.

49. Racine Edwardes, "Lorna Court: Fire-Ravaged Historical Building Built in 1931," *Rosebank Killarney Gazette*, April 1, 2016, https://rosebankkillarneygazette.co.za/287613/lorna-court-fire-ravaged-historical-building/.

50. Greg Nicolson, "In Search of Joburg's Condemned Buildings," *Daily Maverick*, April 12, 2012, https://www.dailymaverick.co.za/article/2012-04-12-in-search-of-joburgs-condemned-buildings/#.Vvz8rT5JlYc.

51. Edwardes, "Lorna Court."

52. Nicolson, "In Search of Joburg's Condemned Buildings."

53. Sam, interview with Nerio, March 26, 2019.

54. Nadine Gordimer, "Apartheid and Censorship," *Index on Censorship* 23, no. 3 (1994): 151–52 (first written in 1972).

55. Dickie, interview with Nerio, March 26, 2019.

56. Goren, interview with Nerio, August 17, 2018.

57. Claudine, interview with Nerio, August 24, 2018.

58. Marc Latilla, "History of Fordsburg," *Johannesburg 1912 — Suburb by Suburb Research* (blog), November 21, 2019, https://johannesburg1912.wordpress.com/2019/11/21/history-of-fordsburg/.

59. 2015 Honors in Journalism Class, "Mayfair and Fordsburg, Johannesburg," University of the Witwatersrand (website), accessed May 20, 2020, https://mayfair.joburg/.

60. Statistics South Africa, "Athlone," Statistics Department of the Republic of South Africa (website), accessed May 20, 2020, http://www.statssa.gov.za/?page_id=4286&id=319.

61. Paul Davis, interview with Nerio, July 29, 2019.

62. Rodney Davenport and Christopher Saunders, *South Africa: A Modern History* (London: Palgrave Macmillan, 2000), 562.

63. Davenport and Saunders, 565–66.

64. Binyavanga Wainaina, *One Day I Will Write about This Place* (Minneapolis, MN: Greywolf, 2012).

65. Wainaina, esp. 90.

66. Wainaina, 101, 98.

67. Wainaina, 101–2, 107; and Staff Reporter, "Down and Out in Brenda Fassie's Hillbrow," *Mail and Guardian* (South Africa), July 14, 1995.

68. Wainaina, *One Day I Will Write*, esp. 106.

69. Wainaina, esp. 106.

70. Wainaina, esp. 114.

71. Wainaina, 114, 117.

72. Wainaina, 172.

4. Hillbrow in a New Country, 1994–99

1. "Preamble to the Constitution of the Republic of South Africa," South African Government (official webpage), accessed May 20, 2020, https://www.gov.za/documents/constitution-republic-south-africa-1996-preamble.

2. Alec Russell, *After Mandela: The Battle for the Soul of South Africa* (London: Windmill Books, 2009), esp. 61 and 87.

3. Richard Tomlinson, Robert A. Beauregard, Lindsay Bremner, and Xolela Mangcu, "The Postapartheid Struggle for an Integrated Johannesburg," in *Emerging Johannesburg: Perspectives on the Postapartheid City*, ed. Richard Tomlinson, Robert A. Beauregard, Lindsay Bremner, and Xolela Mangcu (London: Routledge, 2003), 2–20, esp. 15.

4. Claire Bénit-Gbaffou, "Who Control the Streets? Crime, 'Communities' and the State in Post-apartheid Johannesburg," in *African Cities: Competing Claims on Urban Spaces*, ed. Francesca Locatelli and Paul Nugent (Leiden: Brill, 2009), 56–79.

5. Pali Lehohla, "Numbers and Geo-Space," *Independent Online*, February 21, 2017, https://www.iol.co.za/business-report/opinion/numbers-and-geo-space-7857207.

6. Carrol Clarkson, "Locating Identity in Phaswane Mpe's *Welcome to Our Hillbrow*," *Third World Quarterly* 26, no. 3 (2005): 451–59.

7. UN Development Programme, *Human Development Report 1992*, Oxford University Press, 1992, accessed May 20, 2020, http://hdr.undp.org/sites/default/files/reports/221/hdr_1992_en_complete_nostats.pdf.

8. Charles van Onselen, *The Night Trains: Moving Mozambican Miners to and from the Witwatersrand Mines, 1902–1955* (Johannesburg: Jonathan Ball, 2019).

9. Sally Peberdy, *Synthesis Report: Setting the Scene: Migration and Urbanisation in South Africa* (New York: Atlantic Philanthropies, 2010).

10. Jonny Steinberg, *A Mixed Reception: Mozambican and Congolese Refugees in South Africa* (Pretoria: Institute for Security Studies, Monograph Number 117, 2005).

11. Ricardo Soares de Oliveira, *Magnificent and Beggar Land: Angola since the Civil War* (London: Hurst, 2015), 39.

12. Mines Advisory Group, "Angola," MAG (website), accessed May 20, 2020, https://www.maginternational.org/what-we-do/where-we-work/angola/.

13. Sarah Crowe, "New Agreement Paves Way for Angolans to Return from South Africa," UNHCR, the UN Refugee Agency (website), December 15, 2003, https://www.unhcr.org/en-us/news/latest/2003/12/3fdde4384/new-agreement-paves-way-angolans-return-south-africa.html.

14. Jonathan Crush, Abel Chikanda, and Godfrey Tawodzera, "The Third Wave: Mixed Migration from Zimbabwe to South Africa," *Canadian Journal of African Studies* 49, no. 2 (2015): 363–82, https://doi.org/10.1080/00083968.2015.1057856.

15. Gareth Newham, "Promoting Police Integrity at Station Level: The Case of the Hillbrow Police Station," *Urban Forum* 13, no. 3 (July 2002): 20–52.

16. Keith Beavon, *Johannesburg: The Making and Shaping of the City* (Pretoria: University of South Africa Press, 2004), 197–234.

17. Antjie Krog, *Country of My Skull* (New York: Three Rivers, 2000), 38–39, 59, 65.

18. Jill Swart, *Malunde: The Street Children of Hillbrow* (Johannesburg: Witwatersrand University Press, 1990), 59.

19. Jonny Steinberg, *Midlands* (Cape Town: Jonathan Ball, 2008).

20. Lindsay Bremner, *Writing the City into Being: Essays on Johannesburg, 1998–2008* (Johannesburg: Fourthwall Books, 2010), esp. 2, 74.

21. Bremner, 22.

22. Martin J. Murray, *City of Extremes: The Spatial Politics of Johannesburg* (Durham, NC: Duke University Press, 2011), esp. xi.

23. Prishani Naidoo, "The Making of 'The Poor' in Post-apartheid South Africa: A Case Study of the City of Johannesburg and Orange Farm" (PhD thesis, University of KwaZulu-Natal, 2010), esp. 238–42.

24. Murray, *City of Extremes*, esp. xvii.

25. Murray, 26.

26. Murray, 150–57; quotations are from 157 and 150, respectively.

27. Murray, esp. 169, 155, 170.

28. John Kani, interview with Ron Nerio, August 19, 2016.

29. Chris McMichael, "The Re-militarisation of South Africa's Borders," openDemocracy, July 20, 2012, https://www.opendemocracy.net/en/re-militarisation -of-south-africas-borders/.

30. Tania Monteiro, "'Hundreds Killed' by South Africa's Border Fence," *New Scientist*, January 27, 1990, https://www.newscientist.com/article/mg12517011-000 -hundreds-killed-by-south-africas-border-fence/.

31. "Mozambique Border Fence," Global Security, accessed May 23, 2020, https:// www.globalsecurity.org/military/world/rsa/fence-mozambique.htm.

32. Jonathan Crush and David A. McDonald, "Evaluating South African Immigration Policy after Apartheid," *Africa Today* 48, no. 3 (2001): 1–13, esp. 4.

33. Tom Head, "Migrants Pour into SA from Zimbabwe through Broken Border Fence," *South African*, January 3, 2020, https://www.thesouthafrican.com/news /zimbabwe-migrants-enter-south-africa-beitbridge-border-video/.

34. Teresa Dirsuweit, "Johannesburg: Fearful City?," *Urban Forum* 13, no. 3 (July 2002): 3–19.

35. Crush and McDonald, "Evaluating South African Immigration Policy," 13.

36. Crush and McDonald, 13.

37. Alan Morris, *Bleakness and Light: Inner-City Transition in Hillbrow, Johannesburg* (Johannesburg: Witwatersrand University Press, 1999).

38. Richard Bourne, *Nigeria: A New History of a Turbulent Century* (London: Zed Books, 2015).

39. Morris, *Bleakness and Light*, 309–11.

40. Morris, 309–11.

41. Mike Dick, interview with Nerio, March 31, 2018.

42. The Hillbrow Police Station, though located within the boundaries of Hillbrow, covers an area far larger than Hillbrow itself. It is responsible for policing Hillbrow, Berea, Joubert Park, Killarney, Parktown, and Braamfontein (a territory covering about six and a half square miles). The 1997 crime statistics quoted here are for Hillbrow alone, and not for the entire territory.

43. Morris, *Bleakness and Light*, 196–97.

44. Morris, 196–97.

45. Robert McCrum, "Johannesburg, the Most Dangerous City on Earth?," *The Guardian*, May 30, 1999, https://www.theguardian.com/world/1999/may/30/southafrica1.

46. Dirsuweit, "Johannesburg: Fearful City?," 3–19.

47. Dirsuweit, 3–19, esp. 6.

48. Bremner, *Writing the City into Being*, 98, 218.

49. Bremner, 98, 218.

50. Clifford Bestall, *Hillbrow: Between Heaven and Hell*, from *Witness*, Al Jazeera, February 28, 2012, https://www.aljazeera.com/program/witness/2012/2/28/hillbrow-between-heaven-and-hell.

51. Ivan Vladislavic, *Portrait with Keys* (New York: W. W. Norton, 2009), 73.

52. Jonny Steinberg, ed., *Crime Wave: The South African Underworld and Its Foes* (Johannesburg: Witwatersrand University Press, 2000), 1.

53. Steinberg, 6.

54. Steinberg, 6.

55. Pumla Dineo Gqola, *Rape: A South African Nightmare* (Johannesburg: MF Books Joburg, 2015).

56. Russell, *After Mandela*, esp. 115.

57. Morris, *Bleakness and Light*, 321.

58. Steinberg, *Crime Wave*, 9.

59. Newham, "Promoting Police Integrity," 20–46, esp. 52.

60. Newham, 20–52, esp. 34.

61. Newham, 20–52, esp. 26.

62. Steinberg, *Midlands*, 46.

63. Steinberg, 132, 136.

64. Steinberg, 68.

65. Marc Latilla, interview with Nerio, July 31, 2019.

66. Necklacing is a form of extrajudicial execution that involves placing a tire filled with petrol (gasoline) over a person's head and setting it alight.

67. This building was "reclaimed" in 2021.

68. Kagiso Patrick (Pat) Mautloa, interview with Nerio, August 15, 2018.

69. Melinda Silverman, "Changing the Skyline: Hillbrow, Berea and the Building of Ponte," Book 3 in *Ponte City*, ed. Mikhael Subotzky and Patrick Waterhouse (Göttingen, Germany: Steidl, 2014).

70. Richard Mendelsohn and Milton Shain, *The Jews of South Africa: An Illustrated History* (Johannesburg: Jonathan Ball, 2009).

71. Mendelsohn and Shain, 27.

72. Adele, interview with Nerio, August 22, 2018.

73. Margot Rubin, "Johannesburg's Bad Buildings Programme: The World Class City Hegemony at Work?," in *Urban Governance in Post-apartheid Cities: Modes of Engagement in South Africa's Metropoles*, ed. Christoph Haferburg and Marie Huchzermeyer (Pietermaritzburg: University of KwaZulu-Natal Press, 2015), 211–31, esp. 215.

74. Nic Barnes, interview with Nerio and Halley, January 22, 2020.

75. Although the character Kunene believes it is Karl Marx who described all private property as theft, it was actually the French anarchist Pierre-Joseph Proudhon.

76. Kamau Mutunga, "*Jerusalema*: A Gangster's Life under Apartheid," *East African*, January 23, 2010.

77. Jono Wood, interview with Nerio, March 29, 2019.

78. Matthew Wilhelm-Solomon, "Decoding Dispossession: Eviction and Urban Regeneration in Johannesburg's Dark Buildings," *Singapore Journal of Tropical Geography* 37, no. 3 (2016): 378–95, esp. 385; Matthew Wilhelm-Solomon, "The Ruinous Vitalism of the Urban Form: Ontological Orientations in Inner-City Johannesburg," *Critical African Studies* 9, no. 2 (2017): 174–91.

79. Wilhelm-Solomon, "Decoding Dispossession," 378–95, esp. 385.

80. Affordable Housing and Retail Spaces in Johannesburg (Ahfco), accessed April 24, 2021, https://www.afhco.co.za/.

81. Rubin, "Johannesburg's Bad Buildings Programme," 211–31.

82. Morris, *Bleakness and Light*, esp. 313.

83. Alan Morris, "'Our Fellow Africans Make Our Lives Hell': The Lives of Congolese and Nigerians Living in Johannesburg," *Ethnic and Racial Studies* 21, no. 6 (1998): 1116–36, esp. 1130.

84. Phaswane Mpe, *Welcome to Our Hillbrow* (Pietermaritzburg: University of KwaZulu-Natal Press, 2001), 23.

85. Barbara, interview with Nerio, March 27, 2019.

86. Soweto is an agglomeration of thirty-two townships with a population of roughly 1.27 million.

5. Hillbrow in the Twenty-First Century

1. Mould Empower Serve (MES) is a nonprofit organization headquartered in Hillbrow. When interviewed by Ron Nerio in 2018, Alan Childs was the chief executive officer. He has since left the organization.

2. As a reminder, we use first and last names only for well-known public figures we interview (such as Alan Childs, Matthew Krouse, and Sanza Sandile). With all others, we use only first names.

3. Tanja Winkler, "Kwere Kwere Journeys into Strangeness: Reimagining Inner-City Regeneration in Hillbrow, Johannesburg" (PhD diss., University of British Columbia, Vancouver, 2006), 15, 39.

4. Tanja Winkler, "On 'Spaces of Hope': Exploring Hillbrow's Discursive Credoscapes," in *Changing Space, Changing City: Johannesburg after Apartheid*, ed. Philip Harrison, Graeme Gotz, Alison Todes, and Chris Wray (Johannesburg: Witwatersrand University Press, 2014), 487–93.

5. Loren B. Landau, "Transplants and Transients: Idioms of Belonging and Dislocation in Inner-City Johannesburg," *African Studies Review* 49, no. 2 (2006): 125–45, esp. 130, 127.

6. Landau, 125–45, esp. 130, 127.

7. Matthew Wilhelm-Solomon, "Introduction," in *Routes and Rites to the City: Mobility, Diversity and Religious Space in Johannesburg*, ed. Matthew Wilhelm-Solomon, Lorena Núñez, Peter Kankonde Bukasa, and Bettina Malcomess (New York: Palgrave Macmillan, 2017), 1–30, esp. 8.

8. "Neighbors in Need: Zimbabweans Seeking Refuge in South Africa," Human Rights Watch, June 19, 2008, https://www.hrw.org/report/2008/06/19/neighbors-need/zimbabweans-seeking-refuge-south-africa.

9. Sarah Chiumbu and Muchaparara Musemwa, "Introduction: Perspectives of the Zimbabwean Crises," in *Crisis! What Crisis?: The Multiple Dimensions of the Zimbabwean Crisis*, ed. Sarah Chiumbu and Muchaparara Musemwa (Cape Town: HSRC Press, 2012), esp. x.

10. Chiumbu and Musemwa, esp. xvi.

11. Nic Barnes, interview with Ron Nerio, August 27, 2018.

12. AfrAsia Bank and New World Wealth, "Africa Wealth Report 2019," September 2019, https://e.issuu.com/embed.html?u=newworldwealth&d=africa_2019.

13. Staff Writer, "Here's How Many Super Wealthy South Africans Have Left the Country," BusinessTech, April 15, 2019, https://businesstech.co.za/news/wealth/311376/heres-how-many-super-wealthy-south-africans-have-left-the-country/.

14. Lynsey Chutel, "Post-apartheid South Africa Is Failing the Very People It Liberated," Quartz Africa, August 25, 2017, https://qz.com/africa/1061461/post-apartheid-south-africa-is-failing-the-very-people-it-liberated/.

15. Carl-Ulrik Schierup, "Under the Rainbow: Migration, Precarity and People Power in Post-apartheid South Africa," *Critical Sociology* 42, no. 7/8 (November 2016): 1051–68, esp. 1054 and 1061.

16. "Fact Check: South Africa's Official Poverty Numbers," Africa Check, February 15, 2018, https://africacheck.org/factsheets/factsheet-south-africas-official-poverty-numbers/.

17. Mike Davis, *City of Quartz* (New York: Vintage, 1990), esp. 228–58.

18. David P. Thomas, "The Gautrain Project in South Africa: A Cautionary Tale," *Journal of Contemporary African Studies* 31, no. 1 (2013): 77–94.

19. Ivan Turok, "South Africa's Tortured Urbanisation and the Complications of Reconstruction," in *Urban Growth in Emerging Economies: Lessons from the BRICS*,

ed. Gordon McGranahan and George Martine (Oxfordshire, UK: Routledge, 2014), 1–33, esp. 13 and 33.

20. Stuart Wilson, Jackie Dugard, and Michael Clark, "Conflict Management in an Era of Urbanisation: 20 Years of Housing Rights in the South African Constitutional Court," *South African Journal on Human Rights* 31, no. 3 (2015): 472–503, esp. 473 and 502.

21. Jean du Plessis and Stuart Wilson, *Any Room for the Poor? Forced Evictions in Johannesburg, South Africa* (Johannesburg: Centre on Housing Rights and Evictions, 2004); online at Humanitarian Library, March 8, 2005, https://www .humanitarianlibrary.org/resource/any-room-poor-forced-evictions-johannesburg -south-africa-0.

22. Du Plessis and Wilson.

23. Du Plessis and Wilson.

24. "Nowhere Else to Go," Doctors Without Borders, March 2011, https://www .msf.org/sites/msf.org/files/nowhereelsetogo.pdf.

25. Jonathan Torgovnik, quoted by Olivier Laurent, "The 'Hijacked' Life of Migrants in Johannesburg," *Time*, January 11, 2016. Photos by Jonathan Torgovnik can be viewed at https://www.torgovnik.com/STORIES/Hijacked-life-in -Johannesburg/thumbs.

26. Hayley Gewer and Margot Rubin, "Hillbrow," in *Resilient Densification: Four Studies from Johannesburg*, ed. Alison Todes, Philip Harrison, and Dylan Weakley (Johannesburg: University of the Witwatersrand, 2015), 71–105, esp. 77 and 97.

27. Robert Michel, interview with Nerio, January 27, 2020.

28. United Nations High Commissioner for Refugees, "Global Trends, Forced Displacement in 2015," UNHCR, the UN Refugee Agency (website), https://www .unhcr.org/uk/statistics/unhcrstats/576408cd7/unhcr-global-trends-2015.html.

29. "Is South Africa Home to More Than a Million Asylum Seekers? The Numbers Don't Add Up," AfricaCheck, August 15, 2016, https://africacheck.org/fact -checks/reports/south-africa-home-more-million-asylum-seekers-numbers-dont-add.

30. Nyasha Chingono, "Zimbabwe on Verge of 'Manmade Starvation,' Warns UN Envoy," *The Guardian*, November 29, 2019, https://www.theguardian.com/global -development/2019/nov/29/zimbabwe-on-verge-of-manmade-starvation-warns-un -envoy.

31. Nic Barnes, interview with Ron Nerio and Jean Halley, January 22, 2020.

32. Tawanda Karombo, "62% Rise in African Migrants," *Business Report*, Independent Online, January 28, 2019, https://www.iol.co.za/business-report /economy/62-rise-in-african-migrants-19004740.

33. Oscar Hemer, *Fiction and Truth in Transition: Writing the Present Past in South Africa and Argentina* (Munster, Germany: LIT Verlag, 2012).

34. Zethu Matebeni, "Tracks: Researching Sexualities Walking abOUT the City of Johannesburg," in *African Sexualities: A Reader*, ed. Sylvia Tamale (Nairobi: Pambazuka, 2011), 50–56, esp. 52; *Jo'Burg Tracks: Sexuality in the City*, GALA exhibition at the Women's Prison [Museum], Constitution Hill, Johannesburg, viewed by Nerio, July 27, 2013.

35. BBC News Reality Check Team, "South Africa Crime: Can the Country Be Compared to a 'War Zone'?," BBC Online, September 18, 2018, https://www.bbc.com/news/world-africa-45547975.

36. Buhle Lindwa, "Crime Statistics: Here Are the Most Dangerous Places in South Africa," *South African*, September 12, 2019.

37. "New York City Crime Map," The City of New York, accessed March 13, 2020, https://maps.nyc.gov/crime/.

38. "Statistics," CrimeStats, accessed March 13, 2020, https://www.crimestatssa.com.

39. Rajohane Matshedisho and Alex Wafer, "Hillbrow, Johannesburg," in *Diversities Old and New: Migration and Socio-Spatial Patterns in New York, Singapore and Johannesburg*, ed. Steven Vertovec (London: Palgrave Macmillan, 2015), esp. 82–83.

40. Christopher McMichael, "Urban Pacification and 'Blitzes' in Contemporary Johannesburg," *Antipode* 47, no. 5 (2015): 1269.

41. McMichael, 1271, 1265, 1267.

42. McMichael, 1271.

43. Claire Bénit-Gbaffou, "Who Control the Streets? Crime, 'Communities' and the State in Post-apartheid Johannesburg," in *African Cities: Competing Claims on Urban Spaces*, ed. Francesca Locatelli and Paul Nugent (Leiden: Brill, 2009), 78.

44. Aphiwe, interview with Nerio and Halley, January 17, 2020. This first name has been changed.

45. Aphiwe, second interview with Nerio and Halley, January 20, 2020.

46. Carol, interview with Nerio, August 17, 2018.

47. Lindiwe, interview with Nerio, August 17, 2017.

48. Kevin, interview with Nerio, March 23, 2014.

49. Kevin, second interview with Nerio, May 24, 2015.

50. Kevin, third interview with Nerio, August 14, 2018.

51. Solo, interview with Nerio, April 1, 2018.

52. Anna Hartford, "Ponte City," *n+1*, June 14, 2013, https://www.nplusonemag.com/online-only/online-only/ponte-city/.

53. Perfect Hlongwane, *Jozi* (Pietermaritzburg: University of KwaZulu-Natal Press, 2013), 1.

54. Hlongwane, 9.

55. Hlongwane, 75.

56. Hlongwane, 1.

57. Kingsley, interview with Nerio, February 16, 2017.

58. Sizwe, interview with Nerio, January 27, 2020.

59. Koko, interview with Nerio, January 27, 2020.

60. Thokozile, interview with Nerio, January 27, 2020.

61. Rebecca Walker, "Selling Sex, Mothering and 'Keeping Well' in the City: Reflecting on the Everyday Experiences of Cross-Border Migrant Women Who Sell Sex in Johannesburg," *Urban Forum* 28, no. 1 (2017): 59–73, esp. 69.

62. Walker, 59–73, esp. 63.

63. Elsa Oliveira, "'I Am More Than Just a Sex Worker but You Have to Know

That I Sell Sex and It's Okay': Lived Experiences of Migrant Sex Workers in Inner-City Johannesburg, South Africa," *Urban Forum* 28, no. 1 (2017): 43–57.

64. Oliveira, 43–57.

65. Oliveira, 43–57.

66. Greta Schuler, "'At Your Own Risk': Narratives of Migrant Sex Workers in Johannesburg," *Urban Forum* 28, no. 1 (2017): 27–42.

67. Schuler, 27–42.

68. Schuler, 27–42, esp. 34.

69. Schuler, 27–42, esp. 36.

70. Walker, "Selling Sex, Mothering and 'Keeping Well,'" 59–73, esp. 61.

71. Walker, 59–73, esp. 67.

72. Walker, 59–73, esp. 69.

73. Walker, 59–73, esp. 65–66.

74. Hlongwane, *Jozi*, 2.

75. Hlongwane, 2.

76. Lindsay Bremner, *Writing the City into Being: Essays on Johannesburg, 1998–2008* (Johannesburg: Fourthwall Books, 2010).

77. Nele Dechmann, Fabian Jaggi, Katrin Murbach, and Nicola Ruffo, *Up Up: Stories of Johannesburg's Highrises* (Johannesburg: Fourthwall Books, 2016), esp. 63.

78. Wendy, interview with Nerio, July 28, 2019.

79. Johan and Sizwe, interview with Nerio, January 27, 2020.

80. Simon, interview with Nerio, January 26, 2020.

81. Jan Bornman, "Mashaba's Xenophobic Legacy," *Daily Maverick*, November 7, 2019, https://mg.co.za/article/2019-11-07-00-mashabas-xenophobic-legacy/.

82. "Ebola Virus Disease Distribution Map: Cases of Ebola Virus Disease in Africa since 1976," CDC, Centers for Disease Control and Prevention, accessed May 20, 2020, https://www.cdc.gov/vhf/ebola/history/distribution-map.html.

83. South African Broadcasting Corporation, "Law Enforcement Officials Raid Hillbrow," YouTube video, accessed May 29, 2020, https://www.youtube.com/watch?v=809aSovaN9Q.

84. "Nowhere Else to Go."

85. "Hillbrow Hooligans," interview with Nerio, August 18, 2018. We are keeping the location vague to protect the men's identity. Their names have been changed.

86. "Hooligans," second interview with Nerio and Halley, January 21, 2020.

87. For more information, see https://minorityrights.org/minorities/ndebele/.

88. Sandile, interview with Nerio, August 17, 2018.

89. Mono, interview with Nerio, March 16, 2019.

90. Marius Pieterse, "Perverts, Outlaws and Dissidents: (Homo)Sexual Citizenship and Urban Space in Johannesburg," *Urban Forum* 26, no. 2 (2015): 97–112, esp. 105.

91. Pieterse, 97–112, esp. 106, 107.

92. Hugo Canham, "Mapping the Black Queer Geography of Johannesburg's Lesbian Women through Narrative," *Psychology in Society*, no. 55 (2017): 84–107, esp. 99.

93. Canham, 84–107, esp. 100.

94. Pieterse, "Perverts, Outlaws and Dissidents," 97–112, esp. 108.

95. Pieterse, 97–112, esp. 108.

96. Pride of Africa, "Pride has No Borders," Johannesburg Pride, accessed May 20, 2020, https://www.prideofafrica.org/who-we-are.

97. Matthew Krouse, interview with Nerio, August 31, 2018.

98. Marian Nell and Janet Shapiro, "Out of the Box: Queer Youth in South Africa Today," a report commissioned by the Atlantic Philanthropies, July 2011, https://www.atlanticphilanthropies.org/news/out-box-queer-youth-south-africa-today.

99. Mbulelo, interview with Nerio, July 28, 2019.

100. According to South Africa's most recent census (2011), people who speak isiZulu as their first language constitute a plurality of Hillbrow's residents at 37 percent. The second-largest group, isiNdebele speakers, constitute 16 percent of the population. The remaining language groups in Hillbrow include English (10 percent), Sepedi (7 percent), isiXhosa (6 percent), and numerous other categories each constituting 4 percent or less of the population (South African Census, 2011).

101. Keval Harie, interview with Nerio, January 23, 2020.

102. GALA's queer history tours resumed in 2021, in partnership with Dlala Nje (https://dlalanje.org/tours/pride-walk/56).

103. Bill Corcoran and Jennifer Dorsey, "LGBTQIA+ Ministry," Holy Trinity Catholic Church, accessed May 26, 2020, https://trinity.org/lgbtqia-ministry/#.

104. Ndileka Lujabe, "Love Thy Neighbour?," News 24, April 2, 2017, https://www.news24.com/news24/southafrica/news/love-thy-neighbour-20170402-4.

105. GALZ, An Association of LGBTI People in Zimbabwe, "Frequently Asked Questions," GALZ (website), accessed May 26, 2020, https://galz.org/get-in-touch/faq.

106. Jeffrey Moyo, "Worse Than Dogs and Pigs: Life as a Gay Man in Zimbabwe," Reuters, September 3, 2017, https://www.reuters.com/article/us-zimbabwe-rights-lgbt/worse-than-dogs-and-pigs-life-as-a-gay-man-in-zimbabwe-idUSKCN1BF03Z.

107. Lujabe, "Love Thy Neighbour?"

108. B Camminga, *Transgender Refugees and the Imagined South Africa: Bodies over Borders and Borders over Bodies* (Cham, Switzerland: Palgrave Macmillan, 2019), esp. 13.

109. Camminga, esp. 12, 165.

110. Camminga, esp. 166, 205.

111. Camminga, esp. 178.

112. Camminga, esp. 205.

113. Camminga, esp. 254.

6. A Web of Relationships

1. Clifford Bestall, *Hillbrow: Between Heaven and Hell*, from *Witness*, *Al Jazeera*, February 28, 2012, https://www.aljazeera.com/program/witness/2012/2/28/hillbrow-between-heaven-and-hell.

2. Tanya Zack, *Bed Room* (Johannesburg: Fourthwall Books, 2016).

3. Zack, 8–9.

4. Zack, 27.

5. Bestall, *Hillbrow: Between Heaven and Hell*.

6. Though the theater was still functioning when the authors visited, the organization was disbanded in 2020.

7. Gerard Bester, interview with Nerio, August 20, 2018.

8. Lesley, interview with Nerio, July 29, 2019.

9. Lesley and Nhlahla, interview with Nerio and Halley, January 19, 2020.

10. Mike, interview with Nerio, July 29, 2019, and with Nerio and Halley, January 19, 2020.

11. Josie Adler, phone conversation with Nerio, May 23, 2016.

12. Jane Jacobs, *The Death and Life of Great American Cities* (New York: Vintage, 1992).

13. Bafikile, interviews with Nerio, March 23, 2018, and August 16, 2018.

14. Megan, interview with Nerio, August 26, 2018.

15. Megan, second interview with Nerio, March 24, 2019.

16. Nigel, interview with Nerio, August 30, 2017.

17. Liebe, interview with Nerio, January 27, 2020.

18. Liebe is referring to the 2019 amendments to the 1998 Refugees Act. The amendments provide for the stripping of refugee status from anyone who engaged in political activities related to their home countries. For instance, those who wish to organize or participate in protest against a state that they fled are prohibited from doing so. The amendments have drawn criticism for violating the United Nations 1951 Refugee Convention, which recognizes the rights of asylum seekers and refugees to participate in lobbying or otherwise participate in the political affairs of their countries. See Nation Nkoya, "Amended Refugee Act Restricts Fundamental Rights," *Mail and Guardian*, January 20, 2020, https://mg.co.za/article/2020-01-20 -amended-refugee-act-restricts-fundamental-rights/.

19. Stephen Ellis, "The ANC in Exile," *Foreign Affairs* 90, no. 360 (1991): 439–47, esp. 439.

7. Hillbrow's Credoscapes — Spaces of Hope and Connection

1. Tanja Winkler, "On 'Spaces of Hope': Exploring Hillbrow's Discursive Credoscapes," in *Changing Space, Changing City: Johannesburg after Apartheid*, ed. Philip Harrison, Graeme Gotz, Alison Todes, and Chris Wray (Johannesburg: Witwatersrand University Press, 2014), 487–93.

2. Winkler, esp. 491.

3. Winkler, esp. 492.

4. Alex Wafer, "The Spirit of Hillbrow: Religion and the Ordering of Social Space in Inner-City Johannesburg," in *Routes and Rites to the City: Mobility, Diversity and Religious Space in Johannesburg*, ed. Matthew Wilhelm-Solomon, Lorena Núñez,

Peter Kankonde Bukasa, and Bettina Malcomess (New York: Palgrave Macmillan, 2017), esp. 126.

5. Bongani, interview with Nerio, March 27, 2018.

6. Niri, interview with Nerio, March 27, 2018.

7. As discussed in chapter 2, we use the term "African" in the way that it is typically used in South Africa to denote people who are the descendants of indigenous African groups. Niri includes herself as part of this classification but, as a woman of Indian descent, may not be seen this way by everyone in the congregation.

8. The Visible Policing Division is one of six divisions of the South African Police Service.

9. Pastor Thomas, interview with Nerio, February 4, 2017.

10. Pieter, interview with Nerio, January 23, 2020.

11. The authors were unable to confirm this claim.

12. Marion, interview with Nerio, September 2, 2017.

13. Reeva Forman, interview with Nerio, July 27, 2019.

14. Reeva Forman, interview with Nerio, August 18, 2018.

15. Melvin, interview with Nerio, September 2, 2017.

16. Jennifer, interview with Nerio, May 9, 2015.

17. Patricia, interview with Nerio, August 13, 2016.

18. Mark, interview with Nerio, February 1, 2017.

19. Michael, interview with Nerio, May 9, 2015.

20. Arnold, interview with Nerio, March 24, 2018.

21. Solo, interview with Nerio, March 28, 2018.

22. Jacob, interview with Nerio, August 25, 2018.

23. Rabbi Sa'ar Shaked, interview with Nerio, March 28, 2019.

Conclusion

1. Adekeye Adebajo, *The Curse of Berlin: Africa after the Cold War* (New York: Oxford University Press, 2013).

Epilogue: The COVID-19 Crisis in Hillbrow

1. Anita Powell, "South Africa Confirms 1st Coronavirus Case," *Voice of America News*, March 5, 2020, https://www.voanews.com/a/science-health_coronavirus -outbreak_south-africa-confirms-1st-coronavirus-case/6185311.html.

2. Joseph Cotterill, "Johannesburg Covid-19 Crisis: 'The Storm Is upon Us,'" *Financial Times* (SA), July 14, 2020, https://www.ft.com/content/99d6c1e3-f326 -417c-8833-2dfd591d0a7b.

3. Peter Beaumont, "Photographing Poverty's Pandemic: 'It's a Different Beast in South Africa,'" *The Guardian*, April 13, 2020, https://www.theguardian.com/global -development/2020/apr/13/photographing-povertys-pandemic-its-a-different-beast-in -south-africa.

4. Edwin Ntshidi, "Police Use Teargas to Disperse Large Groups in Hillbrow," *Eyewitness News* (SA), March 27, 2020, https://ewn.co.za/2020/03/27/police-use-teargas-to-disperse-large-groups-of-people-in-hillbrow; Katie Trippe, "Pandemic Policing: South Africa's most vulnerable face a sharp increase in police-related brutality," *AfricaSource* (blog), Atlantic Council, June 24, 2020, https://www.atlanticcouncil.org/blogs/africasource/pandemic-policing-south-africas-most-vulnerable-face-a-sharp-increase-in-police-related-brutality/.

5. Trippe, "Pandemic Policing."

6. David Gilbert, "Video Shows Police Whipping People for Violating Coronavirus Lockdown in South Africa," Vice News, March 31, 2020, https://www.vice.com/en/article/jge9nk/video-shows-police-whipping-people-for-violating-coronavirus-lockdown-in-south-africa.

7. Graeme Hosken and Alaister Russell, "Police Threaten Hillbrow's Homeless with Sjamboks to Enforce National Lockdown," Times Live (SA), March 28, 2020, https://www.timeslive.co.za/news/south-africa/2020-03-28-police-threaten-hillbrows-homeless-with-sjamboks-to-enforce-national-lockdown/.

8. Andrew Harding, "Coronavirus in South Africa: Scientists Explore Surprise Theory for Low Death Rate," BBC News, September 3, 2020, https://www.bbc.com/news/world-africa-53998374.

9. Jason Burke, "South Africa Records 60% Rise in Excess Deaths, Suggesting High COVID-19 Toll," *The Guardian*, July 23, 2020, https://www.theguardian.com/world/2020/jul/23/south-africa-sees-60-spike-in-excess-deaths-suggesting-high-covid-19-toll.

10. Haroon Bhorat, Morné Oosthuizen, and Ben Stanwix, "Social Assistance amidst the COVID-19 Epidemic in South Africa: A Policy Assessment," *South African Journal of Economics* 89, no. 1 (March 2021): 66, 79.

11. Jerry Fisayo-Bambi, "Illegal Crossings at Zimbabwe-South Africa Border," Africa News, October 2, 2020, https://www.africanews.com/2020/10/02/illegal-crossings-at-zimbabwe-south-africa-border//.

12. "World Bank Predicts Sharpest Decline of Remittances in Recent History," April 22, 2020 (Press Release), The World Bank, https://www.worldbank.org/en/news/press-release/2020/04/22/world-bank-predicts-sharpest-decline-of-remittances-in-recent-history.

13. John Cassim, "Amid COVID-19, Fears of a Mental Health Crisis in Zimbabwe," Anadolu Agency, August 29, 2020, https://www.aa.com.tr/en/africa/amid-covid-19-fears-of-a-mental-health-crisis-in-zimbabwe/1957341.

14. Reuters Staff, "Zimbabwe Jan-Sept Diaspora Remittances up 45% Year-to-Year Due to Lockdowns," Reuters, November 19, 2020, https://www.reuters.com/article/ozabs-uk-zimbabwe-remittances-idAFKBN27Z1TJ-OZABS.

15. Valentine Muhamba, "Remittances to Zimbabwe Increased by Over 42% in 2020," TechZim, January 26, 2021, https://www.techzim.co.zw/2021/01/remittances-to-zimbabwe-increased-by-over-42-in-2020/.

16. Mwaona Nyirongo, *Staying Rooted: Value Transfer and Integration of Malawian Migrants* (Medford, MA: Tufts University Refugees in Towns Project, 2019), online at Tufts University, Feinstein International Center, accessed June 12, 2021, https://fic.tufts.edu/publication-item/malawian-migrants-south-africa-refugees/.

17. Ron Nerio, "The Impact of COVID-19 on Migrants in Johannesburg, South Africa (2020)," YouTube video, 1:40, November 1, 2020, https://www.youtube.com/watch?v=NFv6WqsasNg&t=21s.

18. Nerio.

19. "Stranded Malawian Migrants Return Home from South Africa," IOM News, September 11, 2020, https://www.iom.int/news/stranded-malawian-migrants-return-home-south-africa.

20. "Stranded Malawian Migrants."

21. "More Than 200,000 People Return to Zimbabwe as COVID-19 Impacts Regional Economies," IOM News, April 20, 2021, https://www.iom.int/news/more-200000-people-return-zimbabwe-covid-19-impacts-regional-economies.

22. Bongani Nduvana, phone interview with Nerio, November 15, 2020.

23. Bafikile Mkhize, phone interview with Nerio, December 1, 2020.

24. Simon Kikouta, phone interview with Nerio, January 13, 2021.

25. "LGBTQI+ Communities and COVID-19: A Southern Perspective," a virtual panel hosted by The Other Foundation, Johannesburg, June 30, 2020.

26. Tatenda Mazarura and Mark Heywood, "Red Alert: Southern Africa in the Crosswinds of a Third Wave of Rising Infections and World-Beating Mortality," *Daily Maverick*, June 10, 2021.

27. Josh Holder, "Tracking Coronavirus Vaccinations around the World," *New York Times*, June 11, 2021.

28. Ethel Munyai, virtual interview with Nerio, May 17, 2021.

29. Richa Kamina Tshimbinda, virtual interview with Nerio, June 10, 2021.

30. Simon Kikouta, virtual interview with Nerio, June 12, 2021.

Index

Accone, Darryl, 87
Achebe, Chinua, 20
acting, 64–66, 104, 198
Adebayo, Adekeye, 227
Adler, Josie, 51, 200–1
Affordable Housing and Retail Spaces (Afhco), 121–22
Afghanistan, 127
Afhco. *See* Affordable Housing and Retail Spaces
AFM. *See* Apostolic Faith Mission (AFM)
African National Congress (ANC), 5, 49, 59–61, 72–73, 93–94, 97, 101, 107, 113, 197–98, 209
African World War, 100
Afrikaner nationalism, 40, 43
Afrikaner Weerstandsbeweging (AWB), 5
Afrikaners, 22, 29, 30, 31, 38–40, 55, 57, 73, 78, 93, 211, 218–19
AIDS, 69, 122, 167–68, 191, 198, 214, 220
Alexandra, 49–50, 102, 116
Algeria, 20
Aliens Control Act, 106
All Under Heaven: The Story of a Chinese Family in South Africa (Accone), 87
ANC. *See* African National Congress (ANC)
Anglo-Boer War, 39
Angola, 34, 61, 72, 97, 99, 152, 168, 210, 212, 233
anti-Semitism, 4, 38–41, 222
apartheid, 2, 5, 9–10; accommodationist stance toward, 66; Botha and, 63; Con-gress of the People and, 48–49; end of, 78, 97–98, 102–3, 110–11; Indians and, 61; Informations Act and, 83; nonviolence and, 49; police and, 112; political economy of, 110; religion and, 219; rise of, 46–47
Apostolic Faith Mission (AFM), 214
architecture, 42–44, 53
AWB. *See* Afrikaner Weerstandsbeweging (AWB)

Bad Buildings Programme, 122
Ban Ki-Moon, 13
"Bantu," 21
Bantu Authorities Act, 46
Bantu Education Act, 46
Bantu Homelands Citizen Act, 59
Barnato, Barney, 15
Barnes, Nic, 119, 129, 135–36
Basothos, 26
Basutoland, 20
bauxite, 99
Beauregard, Robert A., 98
Beavon, Keith, 28, 100
Bechuanaland, 49
Berea, 2, 37–38, 51, 103, 117
Bestall, Clifford, 2, 110, 187
Bester, Gerard, 190, 192–93
Bethlehem, Lael, 43–44, 220–21
Better Buildings Programme, 132
Bezuidenhout, Andries, 18
"Black African," 5, 20–22, 28, 31, 46–47, 51–52, 60–62, 74–76, 104, 118, 131, 244n17

Blumenbach, Johan, 20–23
Boers, 24, 27, 29–30. *See also* Afrikaners
bookstores, 54
Bophuthatswana, 63
Botha, P. W., 63
Botswana, 18, 24, 34, 49, 76, 168, 209, 234
boxing club, 188–90
Braamfontein, 105
Brazil, 43, 130
Bremner, Lindsay, 98, 102, 110, 159
British, 24–30, 34, 40, 50, 62, 152
Buhlungu, Sakhela, 18
Burma, 133
Burundi, 27, 100, 136
bus boycott, 49–50
Buthelezi, Mangosutho, 122

Cameron, Edwin, 44, 52, 57, 66–67, 74
Cameroon, 133, 199
Canada, 135, 200, 202, 210
Canham, Hugo, 175–76
capitalism, 16, 20, 117, 209
categorization, racial, 21–23, 244n17
Cele, Bheki, 113, 136–37
Censorship Act, 84
Chamber of Mines, 17–18
Chevrah Kadisha, 117
Childs, Alan, 125, 127
China, 34, 99, 229
Chinese South Africans, 23, 28, 85–87
Chipkin, Clive M., 40–44, 48, 51, 60
Chiumbu, Sarah, 128
Ciskei, 63
Clark, Michael, 131
Clarkson, Carrol, 99
classification, racial, 21–23, 244n17
Clay, Paddi, 19, 60
Cold War, 34, 96, 99
colonialism, 13–18, 20, 24, 34, 58, 80, 88, 105,
    111, 129–30, 181, 225, 244n17, 248n86
"colour bar," 23–32
Colour, Confusion, and Concessions (Yap
    and Man), 86–87
"Coloured," 22–25, 27, 29–30, 46–47, 53,
    61–63, 83, 85, 92–93, 226
Communist Party, 48–49, 71, 94
Congo War, 100
Congress of the People (COPE), 48–49
conscription, military, 61, 72, 192
Conservative Party (CP), 62, 73
"Coolie Location," 29–30

COVID-19 pandemic, 229–38
CP. *See* Conservative Party (CP)
credoscapes, 213–24
crime, 2–3, 60–61, 109–12, 115, 118–22, 127,
    136–37, 140–42, 144, 174. *See also* violence
Criminal Law Amendment Act, 46
Criminal Procedure Act, 47
Crush, Jonathan, 106
Cuba, 99, 116

Davenport, Rodney, 93
Davis, Paul, 54–57, 74–76, 93–94
de Beer, Leon, 73–74
De Beers Corporation, 27
Dechmann, Nele, 159
DEIC. *See* Dutch East India Company
    (DEIC)
Delay, Jerome, 229–30
Delmas Treason Trial, 68
democracy, 6, 20, 35, 97–100, 102, 111, 149,
    180, 182
Democratic Republic of the Congo (DRC),
    3, 14, 16, 34, 100, 108, 135, 151, 227
diamonds, 15, 26–27, 99
Dick, Mike, 108–9
Diepsloot, 103
Dingane, 25
Dirsuweit, Teresa, 106, 109–10
Disraeli, Benjamin, 27
Ditsie, Beverley, 68–69
Dlala Nje, 194
Doornfontein, 2, 37–39, 53, 121, 225–26
DRC. *See* Democratic Republic of the
    Congo (DRC)
Dugard, Jackie, 131
Dutch East India Company (DEIC), 23–25
Dutch Reformed Church, 66–67
Dying Screams of the Moon, The (Mda), 64

East Africa, 23, 27, 184
education, 46, 59, 66, 92, 95, 105, 163, 171–72,
    198, 211
Edwardes, Racine, 82
eKhaya, 2–3
eKhaya Neighborhood Improvement Dis-
    trict, 200–3
eKhaya Shelter, 219–20
Emergency Services Group, 75
Emile, Kaze, 136
Eskom, 129
Ethiopia, 20, 100, 159

"European or white," 21
evictions, 62, 121, 131–32, 233, 235, 237

Famous Dead Men (movie), 71–72
Fassie, Brenda, 95–96
Ferreirasdorp, 37, 225–26
Fiction and Truth in Transition (Hemer), 136
Force Publique, 20
Forman, Reeva, 221–22
Freedom Charter, 48–49
"freehold townships," 31
Freschi, Federico, 43

Gaborone, Letlhogonolo, 13
GALA. *See* Gay and Lesbian Memory in
    Action (GALA)
GALZ. *See* Gays and Lesbians of Zimbabwe
    (GALZ)
Gandhi, Mohandas, 39
Gangster's Paradise: Jerusalema (film), 118,
    227
GASA. *See* Gay Association of South Africa
    (GASA)
Gay and Lesbian Memory in Action
    (GALA), 176, 181–82
Gay and Lesbian Organization of the Witwa-
    tersrand (GLOW), 68–69
Gay Association of South Africa (GASA),
    67–68
gay men, 44–45, 48, 52, 53, 56–57, 63, 66,
    67, 69, 70–74, 80, 81, 85–89, 118, 136, 175,
    179–80, 184, 186, 193, 221. *See also* lesbians;
    queer community
gays. *See* queer community
Gays and Lesbians of Zimbabwe (GALZ),
    183–84
Gentile National Socialist Movement, 38
German Club, 226
Germans, 38–39, 54
German School, 38
German West Africa, 27
Germany, 27–28, 192, 210
Gevisser, Mark, 44, 52, 57, 66–67, 74
Gewer, Hayley, 133–34
Glenhazel, 117
GLOW. *See* Gay and Lesbian Organization
    of the Witwatersrand (GLOW)
gold, 15–17, 20, 26, 32, 46, 225
Gold Diggers, The (Nyathi), 6
Goldreich, Samuel, 19
Goldstone, Richard, 62

Gordimer, Nadine, 84, 111
Gqola, Pumla Dineo, 24–25, 111
Granny Lee, 71
Greyshirts, 38, 226
"grey zones," 1
Griffiths, Glynn, 19, 60
Grinker, Leopold, 53
Griqua, 26
Griqualand East, 26
Griqualand West, 26
Group Areas Act (GAA), 46, 51, 62, 83, 86, 98

Hani, Chris, 94
Harie, Keval, 181, 183
Harrison, George, 16, 26
Harrison, Philip, 28–29
Hartford, Anna, 1
healers, 213
Hemer, Oscar, 136
herbalists, 213
hijacking, 115, 118–22, 140–41, 200–3
"Hillbrow" (Kerkorrel), 5
Hillbrow: Between Heaven and Hell (docu-
    mentary), 2–3, 187
Hillbrow Boxing Club, 188–90
Hillbrow: Home of the Homeless (documen-
    tary), 2
Hillbrow Hooligans, 164–67
Hillbrow Theatre Project, 190–94, 198
Hillbrow: The Danger Zone Some Call Home
    (documentary), 2
Hillbrow Vernacular, 42–43
Hirson, Denis, 58
Hitler Youth, 38
HIV/AIDS, 69, 122, 167–68, 191, 198, 214, 220
Hlongwane, Gugu, 45–46
Hlongwane, Perfect, 149, 158
Ho, Ufrieda, 87
homosexuality. *See* queer community
Homosexual Law Reform Fund, 52
Hooper, Mary-Louise, 50
housing: costs, 61, 132; inner city, 131–34;
    rights, 131–32; segregation, 46, 62, 100–1
hyperghetto, 103

IDP. *See* Independent Doctors Panel (IDP)
IFP. *See* Inkatha Freedom Party (IFP)
IMF. *See* International Monetary Fund
    (IMF)
Immorality Act, 46
Independent Doctors Panel (IDP), 75

Indians, 5, 21–23, 29–30, 46, 53, 61–63, 65, 75, 81, 83, 85, 89, 91–92, 100, 115, 147, 181, 214–15
Informations Act, 84
Inkatha Freedom Party (IFP), 61, 93–94, 101, 113
International Monetary Fund (IMF), 95, 139–40
International Organization for Migration (IOM), 234
inyangas, 213
IOM. *See* International Organization for Migration (IOM)

Jabavu, 33
Jacobs, Jane, 200
Jewish people, 35, 37–44, 61, 116–18, 203, 213, 220–24
Johannesburg Art Gallery, 79–80
Johannesburg Development Agency (JDA), 202
Johannesburg Housing Company (JHC), 200–1
Johannesburg Pride, 176–77
Johannesburg Town Council, 28, 100
Jones, Reece, 15–16
Joubert Park, 2, 32, 44, 48, 52, 63, 79, 80–84, 90, 149, 159, 162
Jozi (Hlongwane), 149
Jozi, Vuka, 108

"Kaffir Location," 30
Kallenbach, Hermann, 39, 226
Kani, John, 5, 64–66, 71, 104–7, 226
Kaplan, Mendel, 4
Kapnek, James, 39
Kathlehong, 102
Kenya, 94–96, 134, 216
Kerkorrel, Johannes, 5
Khalfani, Akil Kokayi, 20–21
Khoikhoi, 24, 26
Khosa, Collins, 230
Khosi, George, 188–90
Khoza, Albert Ibokwe, 193
Kihato, Caroline Wanjiku, 36
Kikouta, Simon, 232–33, 235–36
Klipspruit, 29–31
Krog, Antjie, 101
Krouse, Matthew, 5, 69–73, 126, 177, 179
Ku Klux Klan (KKK), 9, 11
KwaZulu-Natal, 25, 114, 172

Landau, Loren, 127–28
Latilla, Marc, 91, 114–15
Le Corbusier, 42–43, 53
Lekota, Terror, 68
Lenasia, 61, 63, 83–85, 206
Leopold of Belgium, 20
lesbians, 44–45, 52–53, 57, 66, 68–70, 74, 95, 175–77, 180, 184, 193, 221, 226. *See also* queer community
Lesotho, 20, 136
Lithuania, 37, 39, 225
Loomba, Ania, 25
Lorna Court, 80, 82–83
Lujabe, Ndileka, 183

Machile, Lebo, 36
Malan, D. F., 38, 40
Malawi, 14, 18, 99, 136, 233
Man, Dianne Leong, 86–87
Mandela, Nelson, 49, 51, 93, 97, 104–6, 112, 207
Mandela, Winnie, 49
Mangcu, Xolela, 98
Manim, Mannie, 66
Man Who Drove with Mandela, The (documentary), 47–48
Marshalltown, 37
Martindale, 31
Mashaba, Herman, 164
Mashile, Lebogang, 33
Matshedisho, Rajohane, 137
Matter of Honor, A: Being Chinese in South Africa (Park), 87
Mautloa, Kagiso Patrick (Pat), 116
Mbeki, Thabo, 105, 207
McDonald, David A., 106
McGregor, Chris, 51
McMichael, Christopher, 137–38
Mda, Zakes, 64
medical care, 74–76
Mendelsohn, Richard, 38–39
Meredith, Martin, 25, 27
Mgabadeli, Siki, 33
Mgcina, Sophie, 47
Michel, Robert, 134–36
middle class, 4, 19, 39–40, 63, 98, 103, 109, 115, 119
Migrant Woman's Voice, 237–38
migration, 13, 15, 37, 104–8, 128–29, 133, 148–55, 234, 237
military conscription, 61, 72, 192

mining, 16–18, 26–27, 32, 99
"Mixed and Coloured other than Bantu," 21
Mkhize, Bafikile, 232–33, 235
Montagu, Lilly, 39
Morocco, 248n86
Morris, Alan, 61, 107–9, 111–12, 122
Mozambique, 6, 14, 18, 34, 61, 99, 106, 122, 136, 210
Mpe, Phaswane, 1–2, 6, 122–23
Mugabe, Robert, 140
Munro, Kathy, 194
Munyai, Ethel, 232, 237
Murray, Martin J., 44, 51, 102–3
Murray, Simba, 72
Musemwa, Muchaparara, 128
music, 64, 72, 95, 153, 165, 170–75, 197, 235

Namibia, 18, 34, 152, 236
Natalia, 25
Natal Province, 25
National Front, 62
nationalism, Afrikaner, 40, 43
National Party, 40, 48, 62, 73–74, 97, 112
Native Laws Amendment Act, 46, 76
Natives (Urban Areas) Act of 1923, 31–32
Natives Land Act of 1913, 31
Natives Resettlement Act, 46–47
Natives Taxation and Development Act, 47
Nazis, 38, 226
Ndebele, 121, 123, 166, 168
Ndebele, Njabulo, 36
Ndebele Kingdom, 26
Nell, Marian, 177–78
Newclare, 31
Newham, Gareth, 112–13, 145
New Year's Eve, 67, 78–79, 89–90
Niehaus, Isak, 45
Nigeria, 14, 99–100, 122, 159, 227
Nine Point Programme, 40
Nkabinde, Nkunzi, 193
Nkoli, Simon, 67–69, 177
Nkosi, Lewis, 64
nonviolence, 42, 49–50
Norwood, 117
Nyathi, Sue, 6
Nyirongo, Mwaona, 232–33

Observatory, 105
Official Secrets Act, 84
oil, 60, 99
Oliveira, Elsa, 156

One Day I Will Write about This Place (Wainaina), 94–96
Orange Farm, 102–3, 168
Orange Free State, 26
Orlando East, 33

PAC. See Pan Africanist Congress (PAC)
Pan Africanist Congress (PAC), 50, 61, 101
pandemic, 229–38
Paper Sons and Daughters (Ho), 87
Park, Yoon Jung, 87
Parktown, 19, 39, 54, 56
Parnell, Susan, 29
Pedi, 27
Pevsner, Nikolaus, 43
Phalhane, Khamotso, 113
Phiyega, Riah, 113
Pieterse, Marius, 175
PNP. See Purified National Party (PNP)
Pogrund, Benjamin, 22
Poland, 37
police, 45–52, 56, 59–61, 67, 72, 83–84, 112–14, 122–23, 137–39, 144, 156, 161–64, 198, 227
Pondoland, 28
Ponte City, 58, 62–63, 77, 121, 147, 217
Population Registration Act of 1950, 21
Portugal, 18, 41, 51, 88, 99
Portuguese East Africa, 18
"post-race," 102–4
poverty, 129–30, 133–36
Progressive Federal Party, 73
Progressive Judaism, 39
Public Safety Act, 46
Purified National Party (PNP), 38

queer clubs, 69–73
queer community, 1, 3, 44–47, 52–53, 192–93, 226, 236
queer politics, 66–69
queer space, 175–86
queer vote, 73–74

race, 20–23, 244n17; housing and, 46, 51–52; sexuality and, 46. See also apartheid
racial categorization, 21–23, 244n17
racism, 10–12, 39–40, 108, 159
rail system, 130–31
Randjeslaagte, 246n31
rape, 24–25, 109–10, 112, 156, 175–76, 178, 212, 254

Receive Me Hillbrow, 3
refugees, 135, 153–54, 185, 222
religious organizations, 35, 156, 213–24
Republic of Congo, 3, 34, 100, 227
revolution, urban, 18–19
Rhodes, Cecil, 27
Rhodesia, 10
Robertson, Marian, 4
Rubin, Margot, 37, 118, 121–22, 133–34
Rwanda, 27, 100, 133

Sandile, Sanza, 125
sangomas, 213
SAPS. *See* South African Police Service
    (SAPS)
SAR. *See* South African Republic (SAR)
Saro-Wiwa, Ken, 107
Saturday Group, 67–68
Saunders, Christopher, 93
Schierup, Carl-Ulrik, 130
Schmahmann, Brenda, 43
Schuler, Greta, 156
Second Congo War, 217
segregation, 46, 51–52, 62, 100–1
Selebi, Jackie, 113
Setshedi, Nicodemus, 219
sexual violence, 12, 24, 138–39, 176–77
Sexwale, Kay, 33
sex work and sex workers, 1, 51, 57, 113,
    155–59
Shain, Milton, 38–39
Shapiro, Janet, 177–78
Sharpeville massacre, 49–51, 60
Shimoni, Gideon, 39
Silverman, Melinda, 58, 117
Simon, Barney, 66
Sisonke Sex Worker Movement, 156
Sisulu, Walter, 49
Slovo, Joe, 49
slums, 30
Slums Act of 1934, 31–32
Sobukwe, Stephen, 50
Social Democratic Party, 107
Somalia, 100, 135
Sophiatown, 31, 46–47, 51, 64, 209
Sorkin, Michael, 103
South African Police Service (SAPS), 112
South African Republic (SAR), 17, 26–27
Southey, Richard, 27
Southwest Africa, 27
Soviet Union, 99

Soweto, 29, 60, 100, 102, 227
Soweto Pride, 182
Soweto Uprising, 4–5, 59–62, 113, 115
Soyinka, Wole, 65
state violence, 101
Steinberg, Jonny, 101, 111, 113–14
Structural Adjustment Programme, 139–40
Suppression of Communism Act, 46
Swart, Jill, 101
Swazi, 27
Sydenham, 117

Tanzania, 27, 100
taxation, 17, 19, 33, 47
Tembisa, 102
Temple Israel, 5, 39–41, 118, 220–24
Terre'blanche, Eugene, 94
theatre, 190–94
Themba, Can, 64
Tokhoza, 102
Tomlinson, Richard, 98
Torgovnik, Jonathan, 133–34
townships, 19, 47, 49–61, 63–64, 67, 83, 85,
    116, 123, 126, 143, 168, 193, 197, 206, 214, 222,
    230, 235, 238
transgender people, 185–86. *See also* queer
    community
Transvaal, 26, 28, 30. *See also* South African
    Republic (SAR)
Truth and Reconciliation Commission, 101
Tshimbinda, Richa Kamina, 232–33, 237
Tswana, 26–27
Turok, Ivan, 131

Uganda, 92, 94–95, 134, 204
Ukraine, 37
Umkhonto we Sizwe, 5
unemployment, 29, 101–2, 110–11, 114, 126–28,
    134–36, 150, 187–88, 209, 230–31
Union of South Africa, 30–31
United Party, 38, 40
uranium, 99
urban revolution, 18–19

vaccine, COVID-19, 236–37
van den Berghe, Pierre, 40
van der Ross, Richard, 25
van Onselen, Charles, 16–17
van Robbroeck, Lize, 43
Vendas, 27, 63
Verwoerd, Hendrik, 52, 72

Vietnam, 34
violence, 162–63; in 21st century, 136–37; sexual, 12, 138–39, 176–77; state, 101. *See also* crime
Vladislavic, Ivan, 110–11

Wafer, Alex, 137, 214
Wainaina, Binyavanga, 94–96
Walker, Rebecca, 155, 157–58
Weiler, Moses Cyrus, 39
Welcome to Our Hillbrow (Mpe), 1–2, 6, 122–23
Western Sahara, 248n86
While You Weren't Looking (movie), 72
white supremacy, 10–12, 17, 29, 33–36, 66, 97, 112
Wilhelm-Solomon, Matthew, 121
Williams, Cecil, 48–49
Winkler, Tanja, 14, 127, 213
Witwatersrand, 16–18, 27, 29
Witwatersrand Native Labour Association (WNLA), 18
WNLA. *See* Witwatersrand Native Labour Association (WNLA)
Wood, Jono, 120

World Trade Organization (WTO), 98
World War II, 4, 32, 39–42, 44, 48
WTO. *See* World Trade Organization (WTO)

xenophobia, 122–24, 160–64, 209–12, 238
Xenopolous, Taki, 57
Xhosas, 25–27

Yap, Melanie, 86–87
Yeoville, 2, 37–38, 103, 105, 117

Zack, Tanya, 28–29, 187–88
Zambesia, 27
Zambia, 3, 18, 27, 34, 100, 122, 134, 148–49
Zimbabwe, 3, 14, 18, 27, 34, 99–100, 106, 122, 128–29, 133–34, 136, 140, 156, 183–84, 210, 222, 231, 236
Zimbabwe African National Union (ZANU), 128–29
Zuberi, Tukufu, 20–21
Zululand, 28
Zulus, 26–27
Zürn-Steffens, Katrin, 38

Ron Nerio is a research programs director at the Central Office of the City University of New York and an adjunct lecturer of sociology at Fordham University.

Jean Halley is a professor of sociology at the Graduate Center and the College of Staten Island CUNY. She is the author of five books, including the recently published *Horse Crazy: Girls and the Lives of Horses*.

POLIS: Fordham Series in Urban Studies
Edited by Daniel J. Monti, Saint Louis University

Tom Hare, *Zonas Peligrosas: The Challenge of Creating Safe Neighborhoods in Central America*
Maria Francesca Piazzoni, *The Real Fake: Authenticity and the Production of Space*
David Faflik, *Urban Formalism: The Work of City Reading*
Ron Nerio and Jean Halley, *The Roads to Hillbrow: Making Life in South Africa's Community of Migrants*

www.ingramcontent.com/pod-product-compliance
Lightning Source LLC
Chambersburg PA
CBHW040930030426
42334CB00007B/106